Relics, dreams, voyages

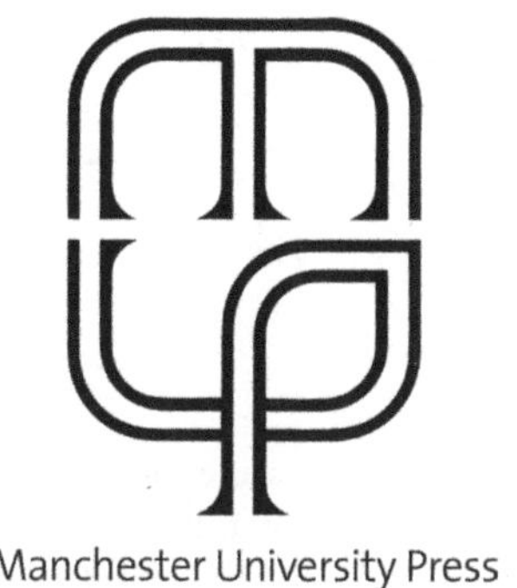

Manchester University Press

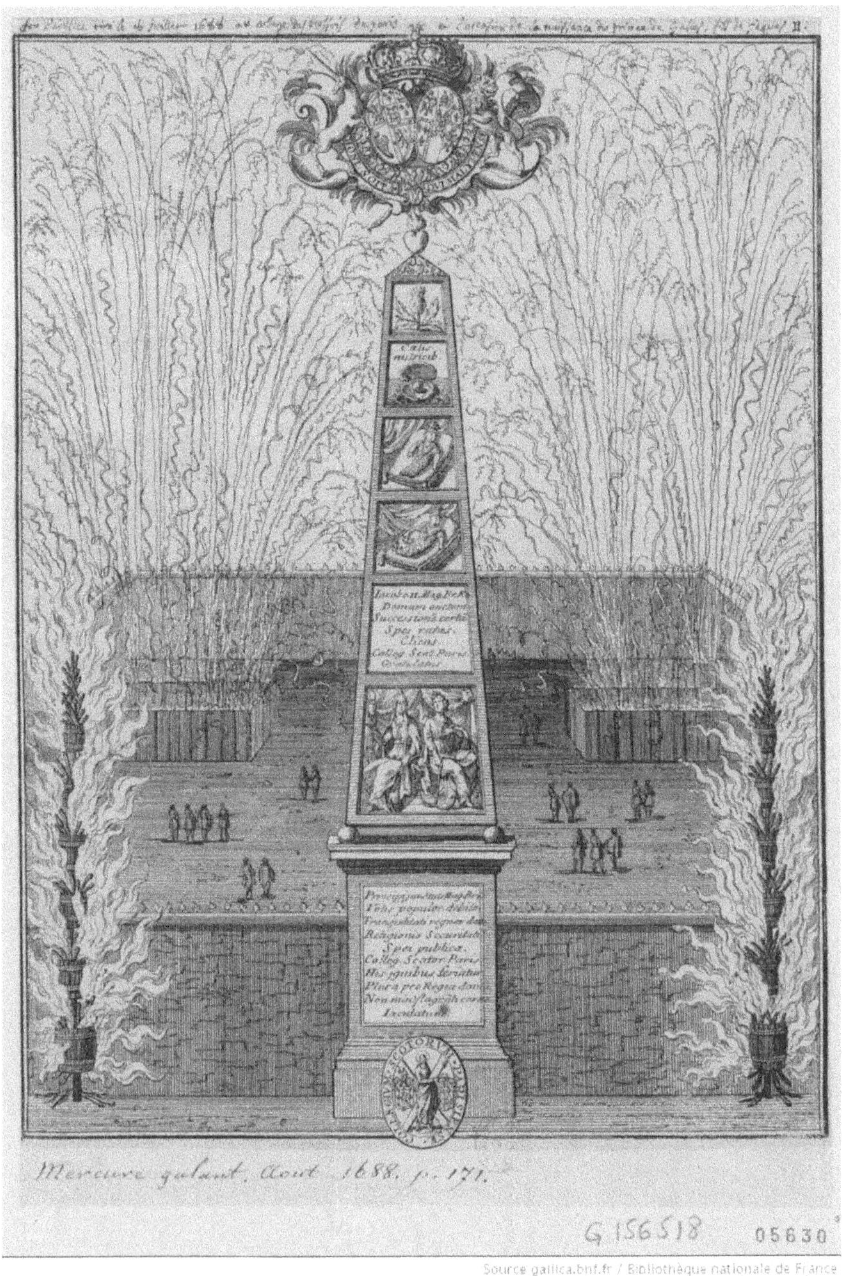

Frontispiece Firework display celebrating the birth of James Francis Edward Stuart, mounted at the Scots College in Paris on 8 July 1688. Anonymous engraving from *Le Mercure Galant*, August 1688.

Relics, dreams, voyages

World baroque

Peter Davidson

MANCHESTER UNIVERSITY PRESS

Published by Manchester University Press
Oxford Road, Manchester, M13 9PL

www.manchesteruniversitypress.co.uk

British Library Cataloguing-in-Publication Data
A catalogue record for this book is available from the British Library

ISBN 978 1 5261 6934 1 hardback
ISBN 978 1 5261 9554 8 paperback

First published 2024
Paperback published 2026

EU authorised representative for GPSR:
Easy Access System Europe – Mustamäe tee 50,
10621 Tallinn, Estonia
gpsr.requests@easproject.com

Typeset by Newgen Publishing UK

For Paulina Kewes

Contents

Part III: Designs of the imagination

Illustrations

Acknowledgements

I am grateful to all members of Campion Hall, past and present: Jesuit community, Senior Common Room, and students. I am especially grateful to the past and present Masters, James Hanvey SJ and Nick Austin SJ, for many things, not least exceptional *cura personalis*. I am continually indebted to conversations with John Barton, Frank Turner SJ, Diarmaid Macculloch, and Brian MacCuarta SJ. I am much in the debt of my kind friends Stephen Withnell (*de eodem in comitatu Lancastrensis*), Mark Aloysius SJ, Joseph Simmons SJ, Matthew Dunch SJ, Philip Moller SJ, and, especially, Vijay D'Souza SJ, who has taught me so much about Goa, as well as reciting and singing the *Kristapurāna*.

At Jesus College, there is not only the most happy debt to the colleague and friend which the dedication acknowledges, but to all the undergraduates who I've taught over the last few years, and to those kind, learned, and astonishingly generous colleagues from whom I have learned so much: Marion Turner, Ayoush Lazikani, Amy Lidster, Will Ghosh.

In Oxford I have been fortunate to have the advice and encouragement of many good and most learned friends: Fiona Stafford, Mark Williams, Nandini Das, Kathryn Murphy, Noel Malcolm, Jane Cooper, Kate Bennett, Deborah and Henry Woudhuysen, Katie McKeogh Woudhuysen and George Woudhuyen, Andrew Bowyer, Melanie Marshall, and Mark Edwards.

Debts extend back over many years to all of those who have helped with access, information, hospitality, and good advice: Dr Jill Bepler (Wolfenbüttel), the late Mgr Michael Williams, Dr Javier Burrieza Sánchez (Valladolid), former and present archivists of the British Province of the Society of Jesus, Fr T. M. McCoog SJ and Rebecca Somerset, Mgr Denis Carlin (Royal Scots College, Salamanca), John Bruce (NRS), Dr Barbara Paca, Dr Stephen Holmes, Dr David Walker *filius*; Professor Richard Fawcett, Dr Anne Dillon, Dr Gabriele Cingolani (Recanati), Ann Buchanan (Loreto School) and Hugh Buchanan, Naomi Johnson (Oscott), Fr. Micheàl MacCraith (Galway), Geraint Evans (Swansea), Dr Deborah Clarke

(Holyroodhouse), Mr Gerard Boylan (Oscott), Joe Reed (Stonyhurst), John Seward, Ian McLellan, Duncan Michie.

I must here thank once more my pandemic-years correspondents in Leuven, Dr Werner Thomas and Dr Johan Verberckmoes, who helped me most generously with advice about Antwerp and the Americas.

The information about textile history which underpins the section on the Fetternear vestments is all due to the generosity of Prue King at Blairs Museum, to whom I would like to extend particular thanks and acknowledgment.

I am constantly grateful that my health is in the expert hands of Nick Wooding and Matt Queralt.

I would like to thank those of my friends who have been continual sources of sustenance through the considerable time which it has taken to draw this collection together: Fr. Robert Hendrie, James Stourton, Alison Shell, Janet Graffius, Andrew Biswell, Anny Jones, Mary Pryor, Laura Tosi, Robert Macfarlane, Maurice Whitehead, Colin Barr, Juliette Paton, Susan Bassnett, Alan Powers, Earle Havens, Eddy Coulson.

This book would not exist at all without the brilliant (I use the word advisedly) group of research assistants and friends who have given it its final form: Daniel Maccannell, Raphaela Rohrhofer, Leah Veronese Clucas, Christopher Archibald, Johnny Aslet, Simon Whittle, Altair Brandon-Salmon.

My greatest and most profound thanks are to Harry Gilonis and to Jane Stevenson, who have both contributed unstintingly, with immense kindness, to the final form of this book.

Abbreviations

ABSI	Archivium Britannicum Societatis Jesu (Jesuit archives, Mount Street, London)
ARSI	Archivium Romanum Societatis Jesu (Jesuit Archives, Borgo Santo Spirito, Rome)
BNE	Biblioteca Nacional de España, Madrid
NLS	National Library of Scotland
NRS	National Records of Scotland (formerly Scottish National Archives)
RCIN	Royal Collection Inventory Number
SCA	Scottish Catholic Archives (the historic archive is located in Aberdeen University Library)
TT	James Fraser, *Triennial Travels*, Aberdeen University Library, MS 2538
VEC	archive of the Venerable English College, Rome

Prologue: The gestures of the skeletons: reticulations of the baroque world

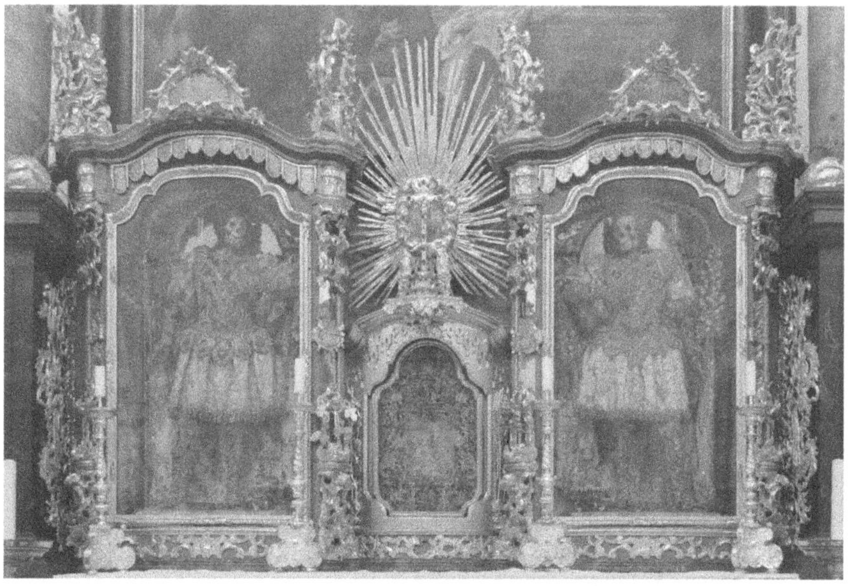

Figure 0.1 Anon., eighteenth century, *Katakombheiligen* ('skeleton reliquaries') in the Basilica, Waldsassen, Germany.

Irrecoverable baroques: petals, gestures, snow. Virus-maculate, flaked, striped flowers.[1] Hands moving through air so long ago, in the pulpit, on the stage. *Mute eloquence which is fecund silence.*[2] The snow statues in the streets of Antwerp, three centuries ago: the transient Hercules of 1718,[3] the Hercules who vanished with the thaw of 1772.[4] Memory as fragile as paper-quill reliquaries, and gone as easily to dust and nothing. Tastes evoked and half conjectured – the Grand Duke of Tuscany's chocolate scented with jasmine,[5] evoked in Latin verse by the Jesuit savant Tomasso Strozzi.[6] Sir Kenelm Digby's *Cordial Liquor of Sack with Clove-gillyflowers.*[7] The marzipan academy of 1636, which Archbishop Laud contrived for Charles I:

The ladies watered ('bout the mouth) to see,
And tast so sweet an University.[8]

Hands moving through the air, so long ago, in the pulpit, on the stage of the *accademia*.

Haver in seno, stringer alcuna cosa al seno, mani in seno, spiegar il seno, aprir il seno, guarder nel'altrui seno, squarciarsi il seno.[9]

On the stage of the Court Opera, of the Jesuit College: the right hand is pointing upwards, the left is lowered, unfurling: decorum, devotion, revelation.[10] And from this comes a moment of extraordinary connection, which is that the gestures of the standing skeletons in the reliquaries of the Abbey Church at Waldsassen exactly mirror those of the Jesuit stage and the Court Opera: golden heroic dress clothes the bones from the catacombs (see Figure 0.1).[11] These skeleton reliquaries, the figures articulated and adorned with clothing so close to opera costume – jewelled, draped, framed in cases of old glass as by a sacred proscenium – are caught out of time. Their gestures are the transient hieroglyphics of the stage made perpetual. The postures and dress of these *Katakombheiligen* are ghosts of the operas of three hundred years ago.

But they are in themselves insistent works of art, albeit, for many anglophone viewers, strange and disquieting ones. In pose and clothing, they share much with the gestural language of baroque sculpture and baroque oratory, or, in the case of the recumbent figures, with the languages of funerary sculpture and ritual, the discourses of the effigy and the *chapelle ardente*. They constitute an unexpected stream of evidence for the coherence of baroque gesture across genres, between the living and the dead. Those catacomb skeletons, which shimmer in gold and silver armour, overlap in turn with the spectacles of state, the military parades, the *carrousels*.[12] Some manifestations of reliquary art defy classification, such as the rococo cabinets with masked and crowned skulls on richly embroidered cushions in the church of St Nicholas at Hall in Tirol near Innsbruck.[13] Or are their crowns aureoles, tongues of flame, *flamma aurea*, supernal fire? Considered purely in visual terms, this cabinet in the Waldauf Chapel at Hall is a sumptuous and beguiling work. It offers testimony of a strain of sacred collecting, the accumulation of relics as much as of *Kunstkammer* objects, which is characteristic of many of the Habsburg territories. The crux with (or the objection to) the appreciation of this work, and of *Katakombheiligen* in general, is, for many viewers, the presence of human bones within the installation. An opinion lingers, perhaps especially in the anglophone countries, that this is extravagant and inappropriate adornment for human remains, and that the adornment as much as the display of the bones is barbaric.

It is perhaps worth trying to comprehend the intentions of those baroque congregations and religious who fostered the cults of the adorned *Katakombheligen*, for surely the intention of adornment is as much theological as aesthetic. The adorned skeletons enact the blessed condition of the souls who once inhabited them. (The image of the child-soul imprisoned within the rib-bars of a skeleton ornamented one of the most popular emblem books of the whole baroque age, Herman Hugo SJ's *Pia Desideria*.)[14] So all the adornments of the relics (golden armour, cloth of silver, filigree of golden wire) enact their present condition among the blessed in heaven; the dress of the heroic theatre, golden armour and golden palms testify to their condition as victors, saints, rewarded heroes and heroines. The glimmering gauze, the precious stones in the eye sockets, the jewelled carapaces are enactments of the glory and worth of those whose souls now inhabit a celestial city, a city visualised as composed of lucent precious stones. The jewels are the jewels of the bride, the City of God, who reflects the light of the Bridegroom, God, in an eternity where there is no need of any other light.[15]

This is but one frontier of the baroque little explored in English; there are other manifestations of sacred art which experiment with the portrayal of intense facsimiles of the human with little interposing stylisation. Perhaps the very Spanish word for applying the gesso and paint to the polychrome statue – *encarnación*: 'incarnation', 'making flesh' – is emblematic of the difficulties which viewers and art historians feel with that hyper-real art which is the corollary of baroque meditation by visualisation.[16] It was notable that the London National Gallery exhibition 'The Sacred Made Real' in 2009 did include highly realist polychrome sculpture, and did include one photograph of a statue dressed in velvet robes and with metal flame-halo in the catalogue, but included no dressed or jewelled statues in the exhibition itself. The dressed statue represented in the photograph, the *Jesús del Gran Poder* from Seville, the work of Juan de Mesa, is a work much replicated in those statue paintings which are a constant of baroque art in the Iberian world, Europe and South America alike. These works, which truly blur representational boundaries, seem to be rarely discussed and not always recognised for what they are, as with the seventeenth-century Sevillano representation of the statue by Juan de Mesa, *Jesús del Gran Poder*, which forms the altarpiece of Magdalen College Oxford. And, beyond the dressed and jewelled statues, there are territories of verisimilitude – mixed media, wax, glass, hair – barely explored.

One of the most remarkable crossings of frontiers of medium and genre, live and inert, comes in the former Jesuit Church of S. Charles Borromeo (*olim* S. Ignatius) at Antwerp. It had machinery by which the four *pala d'altare* paintings above the high altar might be exchanged, a tour de force yet more virtuosic than the moveable painting on the altar of S. Ignatius in the Gesú in Rome. Beyond this,

> [o]n very special occasions, all four paintings were stored and a small stage allowed the creation of a *tableau vivant*. [As background to this] the summary fresco painting representing greenery and Trinitarian delta with the eye of God surrounded by light (the latter painted on canvas, nailed and glued on the wall) still survive.[17]

This is a remarkable crossing of a frontier, using human bodies as statues in a little stage built into the reredos above the altar. This again complicates generic boundaries in a fascinating way: the spectacles of state of Antwerp, including the entry of Archdukes Albert and Isabella in 1599, had made extensive use of *tableaux vivants*, which were a strong local tradition of the Low Countries *rederijkerskamers* or literary societies, from the late Middle Ages.[18] This stage for the *tableau vivant* as temporary altarpiece brings together local traditions: the influential dramatic practice of the Jesuit colleges, the spectacle of state and the baroque sensibility of the most eminent parishioner of the Church of S. Ignatius, Peter Paul Rubens (1577–1640), who was intimately involved with the decoration of the church, including designs for sculpture and the marble work that framed the actors.[19]

It is on Rubens that I would like to focus, and on a dressed statue, the focus of a syncretic and remarkable cult, far away from Antwerp in what is now Bolivia: what I hope to do is to offer a thought experiment positing a connection between them, or speculating whether there might have been a connection. These speculations *pars pro toto* are to introduce a major strand in this series of reflections on baroque: the idea of many parallel baroque networks (connected Habsburg territories, Jesuit networks of travel and reporting, to name the two most obvious ones) circulating objects and ideas in multiple directions. Energies and influences travel both ways to and from Europe (and also, vitally, between Asia and the Americas). This is what I would like to explore in this speculation on Rubens and the Virgin of the Andes.[20]

There is a further object in Antwerp which embodies a narrative about the Americas and Europe more certainly, more explicitly, and more mysteriously: the carved marble altar rails in what was then the Jesuit church which Rubens attended. Although these carved altar rails are hard to date absolutely, the statements which they implicitly make about American religious experience seem intensely Jesuit and are in themselves testimony to Jesuit policies of dialogue and accommodation.[21]

The Virgin of the Andes is possibly present in shadowy form amidst the formal, learned, humanist decorum of the spectacles and arches devised for the 1635 entry of the Cardinal-Infante into Antwerp, a spectacle of state magnificently designed by Rubens. The Antwerp spectacle offers complex ideas about religion, assimilation, and hybridity, displayed most clearly by the last arch of triumph, designed by Rubens for a site near the city's mint, which is, interestingly, an addition or supplement to the usual triumphal route. It depicts general aspects of America as well as a specific depiction of the ore-rich mountain of Potosí.

The source of much of its imagery is the Jesuit José de Acosta's work on America, *Historia Natural y Moral de las Indias* (which was published in Seville in 1590). Acosta worked as a missionary and educator in the Peruvian cities of Lima and Cuzco, and resided at the Jesuit college at Julí near Lake Titicaca. He was also instrumental in founding a college at Potosí.[22] I note this connection, as the possible Andean source for Rubens's arch (to which I will return later) relates to Potosí (see Figure 0.2).

Due to ongoing war with the United Provinces, the Antwerp of the 1630s was a ghost of what it had been as a mercantile city (something about which the whole 1635 spectacle is in denial), but it retained its cultural importance, as a centre of printing and engraving and as a cultural entrepot for the dissemination of texts from the whole of the Catholic world. It had also at various times been a centre for the dissemination of Catholic propaganda against England. The surviving attendants of Mary Queen of Scots lived there, and joined forces with the vitriolically anti-English journalist Richard Verstegan to publish an illustrated book, the *Theatrum Crudelitatem Haereticorum* of 1592, which culminates in a graphic account of the execution of the Scottish queen.[23] It was also the final residence of the northern Scottish Jesuit John Hay of Delgaty, and the place where he published his anthology of global Jesuit observations, a Latin recension of reports from the Jesuit missions in Japan, India, and Peru in 1605.[24]

The *Pompa Introitus Ferdinandi* – the account of the spectacle of state of 17 April 1635 – was engraved and published after the event, one of the most sumptuous illustrated books of baroque Europe. The last triumphal arch displayed was the arch of the Mint, perhaps both an innovation and an afterthought; although there is a description of this arch in the published account of the festival, no other contemporary documentation for it appears to survive.[25]

It was devised by the Flemish humanist Jan Caspar Gevaerts (1593–1666), who had been educated by the Jesuits and at the University of Leuven. He had held civic posts in Antwerp from 1621 onwards, and was secretary to the Jesuit devotional society for educated laymen, one of several branches of the Antwerp Sodality of our Lady, which had its own building, adjacent to the Jesuit church – then St Ignatius, but, since the 1773 suppression of the Jesuits, rededicated to St Charles Borromeo. The sodality building dates from 1621 and had an altarpiece by Rubens in the downstairs sodality

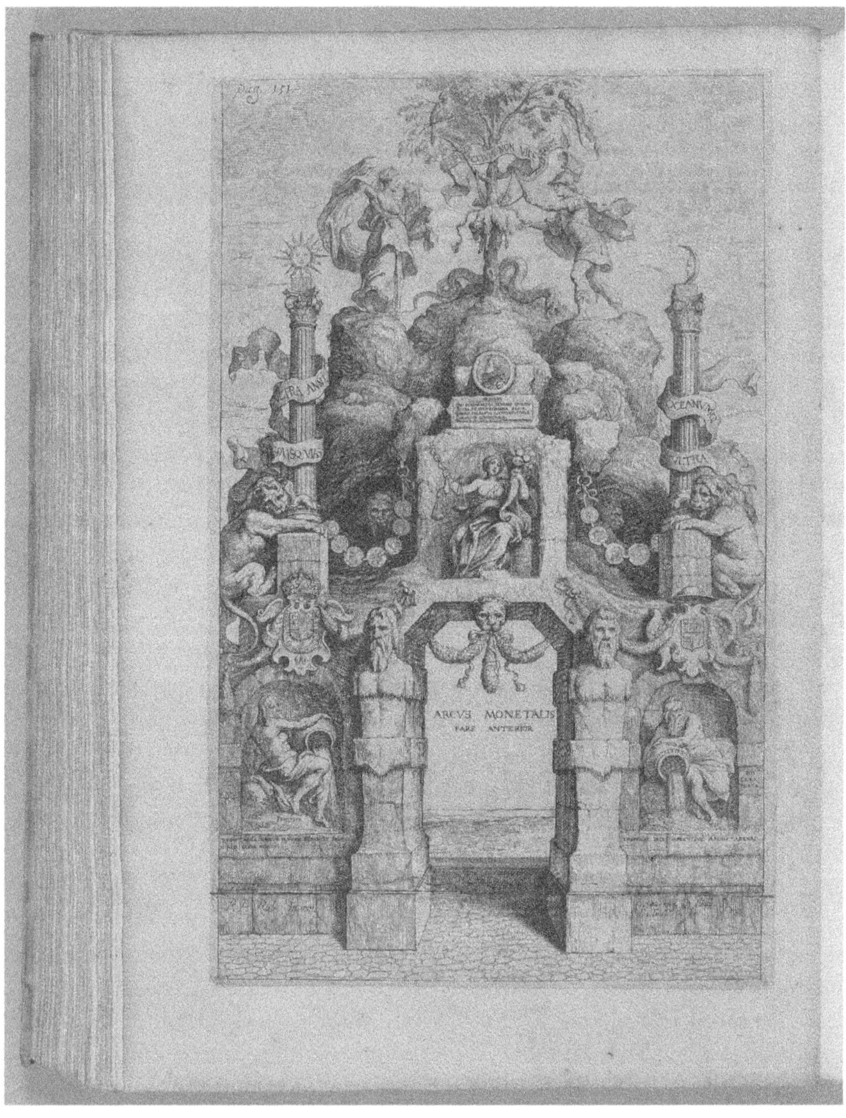

Figure 0.2 Theodore van Thulden, engraving after Peter Paul Rubens, 'The Arch of the Mint', from Jan Caspar Gevaerts, *Pompa Introitus Honori … Ferdinandi Austriaci* (Antwerp, 1641).

chapel. Rubens himself was also a member of the Sodality, and a parishioner of the Jesuit church, with whose design and construction he assisted, from 1613 to 1637. Rubens was very much in the orbit of the Jesuits, locally and internationally: among many other activities, he designed engravings to illustrate the life of St Ignatius, the founder of the Jesuits. Here Rubens belonged to an intellectual nodal point of intellectual life in Antwerp which, because of Jesuit internationalism and global communications, also had access to a remarkable body of information from all over the globe.

Some of this information was used by Gevaerts and Rubens in this innovative arch. As befits a structure close to the town mint, the subject is gold and silver, mining and the making of coin. Broadly, it celebrates the gold-bearing nature of the Iberian Peninsula, as well as the mineral wealth of the Americas. The rear face of the arch, as first sketched, offers various aspects of the idea of Spain as golden Hesperides: it depicts Jason and the Golden Fleece, thus echoing the Habsburg chivalric Order of the Golden Fleece. It also links this idea to the revenue flowing to Spain and the Empire from the richest metal-bearing mountain in the Spanish American territories of what is now Bolivia, the mountain of Potosí. The whole structure which surmounts the arch is in the form of a mountain, a particular Andean mountain, with realistic miners derived from Acosta's first-hand description. The herms at the bottom are the personifications of the Andean rivers Pern and Condorillo.

It is the front face which is of precise concern: it represents the revenue accruing to the Spanish Crown from the metal-bearing mountain of Potosí. What is important here is that this design was considerably changed in the process of execution between the *modello* or sketch in oil paint and the engraved representation of the arch as actually exhibited on 17 April 1635. The first ideas, Hercules and a personification of Hispania, were removed to the rear face and were replaced by Jason, the Golden Fleece, and Felicitas, personification of prosperous or fortunate voyages. In addition, between the *modello* and the final work the proportions of the mountain were considerably changed, growing larger and broader.[26] The personification of minting coins, Moneta, and the South American river gods are still there.

I am haunted by the way in which, in the engraving, the sun and moon have replaced the globes on those columns, which represent the Pillars of Hercules, those rocks at the mouth of the Mediterranean, which appear, then and now, on the arms of Spain. Both depictions break with heraldic tradition, which usually terminates them in crowns, or leaves the tops vacant. Gevaerts says, in his published commentary, that he associates the sun and moon here with gold and silver and with the transmutations of the Alchemists.[27] The visual message is different: gold and silver, sun and moon are associated here with the Pillars of Hercules, the mouth of the Mediterranean at the Straits of Gibraltar, the Atlantic gate to the metals of the Americas.

This alteration, and the change which it works on the whole aspect of the depicted mountain, leads to a wild, but beguiling, speculation. In this final version of the front face of Rubens's arch, the position of the sun and moon in relation to the mountain could call to mind a striking and syncretic picture from the Andes, painted in a studio and workshop staffed by First Nations Andean painters. This complex, intensely hybrid image is known as *The Virgin of the Cerro Rico of Potosí*, or *Our Lady of the Cerro Rico of Potosí* (see Figure 0.3).

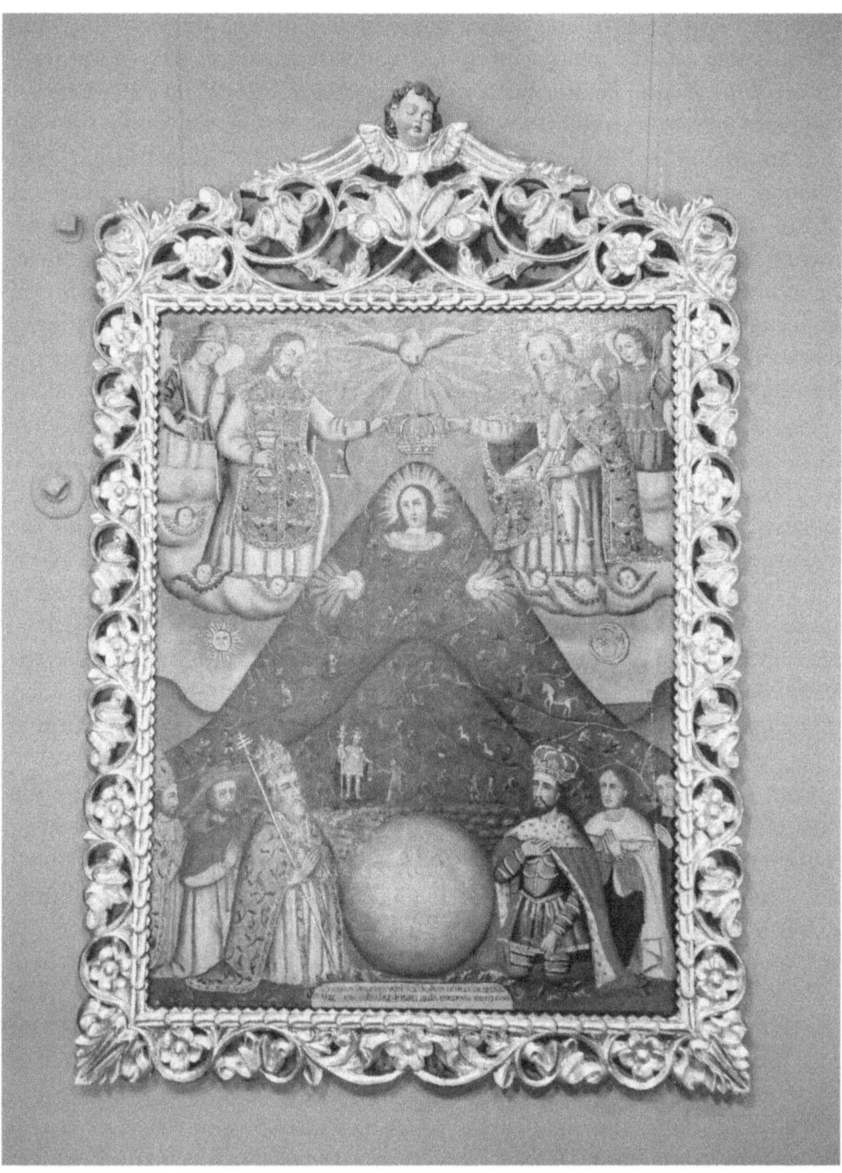

Figure 0.3 Anon. Bolivian artist, eighteenth century, after a sixteenth-century archetype, *Virgen del Cerro Rico de Potosí*, oil on canvas, Casa Nacional de la Moneda, Potosí, Bolivia.

It fuses the appearance of a Spanish draped statue of the Virgin with the representation of the mountain of Potosí, which had long been venerated, before the arrival of the Spaniards, as a manifestation of the universal mother, widely known in the Americas as Pachamama. It is an extraordinary image, a hybrid of two cultures, an expression of a permeable baroque Catholicism which can express itself in any number of local languages and dialects worldwide. The essence of this Andean iconography is expressed in Alonso Ramos Garcilán's *Historia del Celebre Sanctuario de Nuestra Señora de Copacabana*, published in 1621, who writes of the possible theology of the Blessed Virgin as mountain: '[A]s the sun rays fall on the earth, so God sent Mary. Mary was the mountain whence was hewn the rock without hands or feet, Christ.'[28] The reference here is to Christ as the 'stone that the builders rejected',[29] and by this ingenious conflation of metaphor the specifically Andean image of the Virgin as mountain has been assimilated to the global tissue of baroque Christianity. This kind of assimilation and syncretism is most closely associated with the policies of cultural accommodation practised in the mission field by the Society of Jesus.

At the foot of the statue-mountain are venerating figures: Charles V, Pope Paul III, a cardinal bishop, and a First Nations American, who has been ennobled in the order of Alcantara. These figures are presented in a posture of homage, with the globe placed in the middle of them; there is an apparent assertion here of a new universality, of the Catholic world coming to venerate an explicitly Andean expression of the sacred. The figures date the image: Paul III, the pope painted by Titian, died in1549; Charles V died in 1558, suggesting that the origin of this complex image is the middle of the sixteenth century. The continuous production of replicas, sometimes over centuries, was very much part of the way in which the Andean, specifically Cuzco, studios producing religious art worked. There are several surviving examples of this picture type, all of which appear to date from the early eighteenth century or later, but earlier examples clearly existed. Since we know that these images were painted in multiple copies, I advance the speculation that Rubens might have seen one of them in Antwerp, most likely in the orbit of the Antwerp Jesuits, or possibly during his visit to Spain or Italy.

These speculations are grounded in possibility: Rubens was intensely involved with the Antwerp Jesuits, through the Confraternity, and as designer and illustrator of numerous Jesuit publications, most notably work for the sumptuous anniversary volume *Imago Primi Saeculi/Afbeldinghe van d'eerste eeuwe der Societyt IESU*, published by Plantin at Antwerp in 1640, the year of Rubens's death.[30] He also contributed many paintings and designs to the Antwerp Jesuit church, collaborating in design with Fr Peter Huyssens SJ (1577–1657), and painting the panels for the aisle ceilings, destroyed in a fire in the eighteenth century, and also painting the altarpieces.[31] From 1629 he was secretary of the Jesuit Latin Sodality there.[32] There were a number of Jesuits from the Spanish Netherlands who travelled to Ibero-America, as the *Imago Primi Saeculi* testifies in the Emblem, whose picture shows a personification of Divine Love with globes of two hemispheres, whose motto asserts that one world is not enough – *unus non sufficit orbis* – and whose verse asserts that the Flemish Jesuits have travelled as far as, and further than, Hercules and Alexander.[33] Five Flemish Jesuits are documented as setting forth for South America in the years 1616 and 1617, five in the years 1627 and 1628, and also eight in the year of Rubens's death, 1640.[34] In addition, there were other occasions in Rubens's life when he might well have seen one of multiple copies of an Andean painting brought back to a Jesuit house or to the Spanish court. In 1605 Rubens worked for the Jesuits in Mantua, and in 1603 and from 1628 to 1630 he was at the Spanish court, first in Valladolid and then in Madrid.[35]

Even with all these possible conjectures of connection, it is difficult to advance any certainties about the resemblance between the Andean image of the *Virgin of the Cerro Rico of Potosí* and Rubens's final design for the arch of the Mint. But the possibility is most seriously worthy of consideration, as are all possibilities of multiple and multidirectional currents of circulation within the baroque world. Nobody can prove if sight of the Andean painting of *Our Lady of the Cerro Rico of Potosí* influenced Gevaerts and Rubens in the radical, last-minute changes which they made to the iconography and appearance of the arch of the Mint for the 1635 entry. But we ought at least to admit of the possibility, in the certainty that people in Antwerp, especially in the spiritual and cultural circles associated with the Jesuit church, had a nuanced and detailed knowledge of the Americas.

Unequivocal testimony of this is found in the marble altar rails of the church (shown in Figure 0.4). Here, certainty is possible: the iconography incontrovertibly treats of the Eucharist and the Americas. There are roundels of Jesuit saints on the piers, while the Lamb of the Book of Revelation is in the centre. The wreaths and scrolls which form the panels of the rails are of wheat ears and wine. So far, this is conventional, as are the paradisal roses; but other grain crops, realistically rendered, are also present: maize and amaranth, as well as a plant which may well be quinoa. The cultural and ecclesial implications of the presence of such New World plants in a sacred context are extraordinary, as is the juxtaposition of American grain plants with medallions of Jesuit saints. It is hard to read these altar rails as anything but a Jesuit meditation on possible ways of thinking about the Eucharist outside Europe, and endorsement of the validity of American experience and devotion.

It seems clear from these altar rails that the Antwerp community contained, or was in correspondence with, an individual or individuals who

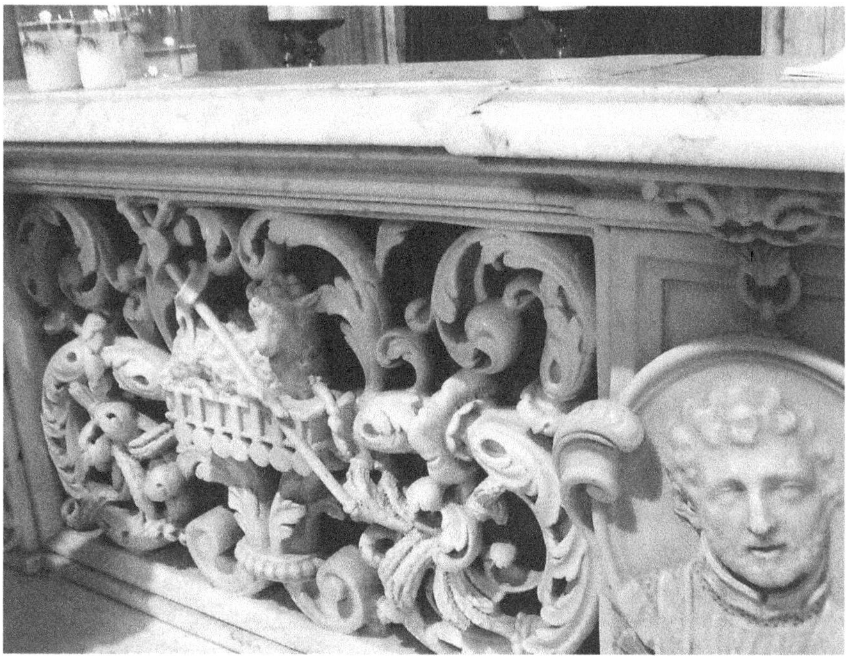

Figure 0.4 Anon., mid-seventeenth century, carved marble altar rails in the Church of St Karl Borromaeus (formerly St Ignatius), Antwerp.

had been in the Americas, and had practised the cultural accommodation typical of the Society. These carvings make a statement about Catholic and Jesuit universality, explicitly inclusive of the first peoples of South America, consistent with the Jesuit advocacy for, and protection of, the Americans. The inclusion of amaranth is particularly worthy of note, as its cultivation had been banned in Mexico because of the vital part which it played in the ritual (a ritual with echoes of the Christian Eucharist) of the enactment of the death and resurrection of the Aztec solar and war god Huitzilopochtli, in which, at the feast of Panquetzaliztli, an image of the god made out of amaranth seeds and honey was divided into small pieces and eaten by his votaries.[36] This, the presence of amaranth on these altar rails, is not only testimony to a process of accommodation and cultural understanding but also an endorsement of Mexican religious practice as a version of Eucharistic truth, consistent with the ideas current in seventeenth-century Mexico, especially in the circle of the savant Carlos Sigüenza y Góngora, that the religion of the Aztecs contained traces of memory of a remote Christian evangelisation by the Apostle Thomas. This belief of a half-buried religious truth and its restoration in the syncretic Catholicism of the Mexico of the Viceroys is brilliantly expressed in the *loa*, or prologue, which Sor Juana Iñez de la Cruz wrote for the comedy *El Divino Narciso*, with its assertion of a profound continuity between Aztec ritual and Christian belief.

> ¡Vamos, que ya mi agonía
> quiere ver cómo es el Dios
> que me han de dar en comida,
> (*Cantan la América y el Occidente y el Celo:*)
> diciendo que ya
> conocen las Indias
> al que es Verdadero
> Dios de las Semillas!
> Y en lágrimas tiernas
> que el gozo destila,
> repitan alegres con voces festivas:
> ¡Dichoso el día
> que conocí al gran Dios de las Semillas![37]

Indeed, this syncretic perception of continuity in religion gave rise to other phenomena of accommodation in early modern Mexico, such as Christian sculptures, especially processional crucifixes, made of corn pith, *pasta de Caña*. The origins of these sculptures, and the processions in which they were carried, were most probably syncretic, as was the inclusion of leaves of pre-Hispanic codices within the inner layers of their paste.[38] So the altar rails in Antwerp allude to, and epitomise, this whole tradition of accommodation, while also affirming, in tangible imagery, the universality of the church. This was not the only church in the Low Countries to have this American iconography incorporated into the altar rails: seventeenth-century rails carved with a festoon of finely carved maize are now found (*ex situ*) in St James's, Piccadilly, London. They form part of a composite memorial to the artist Francis Ernest Jackson (1872–1945) incorporating other elements of earlier works of art.[39]

Huitzilopochtli had a considerable afterlife in Europe, in both popular and high art:

> This view of the Aztec gods as devils was to have considerable duration, transmitted in sixteenth- and seventeenth-century accounts of the New World. 'Vitzliputzli', a corruption of Huitzilopochtli, even entered German folklore at least by the first half of the eighteenth century as one of the devils in the puppet play of Dr. Faustus on which Goethe based his great work; there, Vitzliputzli joined Astarot, Haribax, and other ancient foreign deities to compose the group of evil spirits from which Mephistopheles was chosen.[40]

It was also under the name of Fitzli-Putzli that Huitzilopochtli found a place in one of the strangest sculptural ensembles of the European baroque. Graf Frantz Anton von Spork (1662–1738) adorned his estate on the headwaters of the Elbe, at Kuks in eastern Bohemia (which contained a spa and a vast charitable hospital, as well as the count's own house), with moralised walks branching right and left from the hospital chapel, adorned by over-life-size statues of the Virtues and Vices, all carved by the studio of the virtuosic Tyrolean-Bohemian sculptor Matthias Braun (1684–1738). There is also a (surviving) *bosco sacro* with a Nativity and three-times-life-size figures of penitents carved out of the living rock.[41]

It is a satirical statue that particularly concerns us: embroiled in lawsuits, in 1720 Spork commissioned Braun to carve a bearded giant in a suit of armour adorned with dragons. This statue, which they called Herkomannus, bore a bitter inscription against lawyers. Shortly afterwards Spork erected a statue by Braun and his studio of 'the Notary of Herkomannus', which depicted an enthroned demon, attended by serpents and a lesser devil, with horns branching like corals, goats' legs, and bearing a book inscribed *Per fas et nefas*. The statue was named Fitzli-Putzli:

> For a long time it was believed that the name Fitzli-Putzli was just a fantasy (Spork wrote to his friend Gross in 1725 that he had invented the name Fitzli Butzli for the statue). It is not an invention, it is a confused version of the name of the Aztec god Huitzilopochtli, who in contemporary engravings mostly has horns on the head, and goats' legs, and two snakes as attributes.[42]

The most plausible visual source for Braun's Fitzli-Putzli is a plate in Antonio de Solis's *Histoire de la conquête de Mexique, ou de la Nouvelle Espagne* (Paris: Jean Boudot, 1691), which represents the deity naked, seated on a throne with serpents' legs, with a horn in one hand and snake in the other. It was perhaps part of Spork's intention, in commissioning a statue of this devilish notary, to imply that he consumed or destroyed human victims, as, in the engraving which I have tentatively identified as source, a victim is sacrificed in front of the statue.[43] The engraved sources do not supply all the elements of Braun's baroque monster; they would appear to have hybridised in his imagination with the demon masks and the winter *Krampus*-devils of his native Tyrol.[44] The statue certainly gave grave offence, and was destroyed by order of the local ecclesiastical authorities.

There were very many lines of transmission in the reticulation which composed the baroque world, and every line carried objects and ideas in both directions. If the American grain plants represented in Antwerp are indicative of complex and flourishing relations with South America, the feathers of the bird of paradise indicate equally strong lines of association with Asia.

It has been often remarked that the black Magus in Rubens's *Adoration of the Magi* (1609–10) in the Prado wears a turban adorned with a bird of paradise (see Figure 0.5).[45] This extraordinary aigrette draws the eye of the viewer to the centre of the composition, to the two columnar figures of the

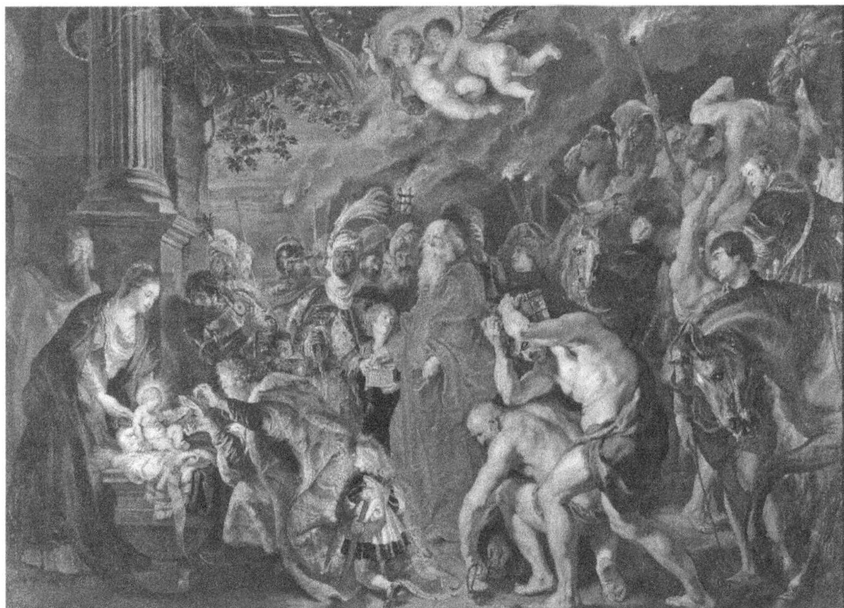

Figure 0.5 Peter Paul Rubens, *The Adoration of the Magi*, 1609 and 1628–29, oil on canvas, Museo Nacional del Prado, Madrid.

standing Magi: this flame-like panache echoes the wind-stirred flames of the torches carried by their retinue in this haunting night painting. Originally this work was intended to remain in Antwerp, but it made its way to Madrid, having been given to the Antwerp-born noble Rodrigo Calderón, who took it to Spain.[46] Bird of paradise skins and feathers (another appears adorning a hat in Robert Peake's portrait of the young Charles I, now in the Scottish National Portrait Gallery) come from south-east Asia and have been known in Europe at least since the early sixteenth century.

As well as documenting trade with Asia there is a poetic or speculative element to the presence of the bird of paradise, signalled by the degree to which its diagonal sets the strong series of wind-blown diagonals which dominate the picture's sky and form the background for the hovering angels. These birds were perceived as mysterious, God's sparrows, themselves angelic inhabitants of an otherworld, as Marcaida observes:

> Writing in the 1520s, the apothecary Tomé Pires notes: 'Those which are prized more than any others come from the islands called Aru, birds which they bring over dead, called birds of paradise ('pasaros de Deus'), and they say they come from heaven, and that they do not know how they are bred … Similarly, António Galvão – governor of the Moluccas from 1536 to 1540 – refers to the birds as 'passaros myrrados'.[47]

They were documented, in repeated texts,[48] throughout the sixteenth and seventeenth centuries, all of which iterated the mystery of their habitat and their distant origins. The same mystery and distance attends the Magi who appear in the second chapter of the Gospel of Matthew, perceive and affirm the truth of the Incarnation, reverence the Christ Child, and then return by back roads to their own countries – *per aliam viam reversi sunt in regionem suam.*

Birds of paradise are also found in the *constkamer* paintings for which Antwerp was famous. This genre of painting, characteristic of Antwerp the world city, had begun to develop around 1610. One especially global example, complete with birds of paradise, is by Hieronymous Francken II and Jan Breughel the Elder and shows *The Archdukes Albert and Isabella Visiting a Collector's Cabinet.*[49] The birds' plumage is on a velvet-covered table, with shells, corals, and gems; there is also a celestial globe and mathematical instruments. The richly dressed man standing by has his hand on an open book of what seem to be sea-marks: bays and mountain horizons seen from the water, the fine-grained knowledge from far travel.

This sense of global navigation and collecting, with Antwerp as a major nodal point in the reticulation, is captured also in Rubens's haunting drawing of a *Man in Korean Costume*, dating from around 1617.[50] The costume, *cheollik* with a *dapho* overgarment, is authentically Korean, although the face is generic, for all the lively sideways glance of the eyes, and it may be that Rubens to some degree invented the figure, as part of his preparation for his *Miracles of St Francis Xavier*, 1617–18, originally in the church of St Ignatius in Antwerp, in which a version of the same figure forms part of the central group in the painting.[51] What is especially haunting in the black chalk drawing is the faint indication of a galleon sailing away on the figure's left. This indication – a few finely judged lines – of the vessel which connects distant parts of the globe almost hints at a narrative, another baroque ghost. The beautiful monograph on the drawing, edited by Stephanie Shrader, has found traces of perhaps two Koreans who could have been in Europe and who could possibly have met Rubens.[52]

What is more certain is that Rubens did make drawings of European Jesuits in Oriental dress,[53] and that the Antwerp Jesuits did own a considerable range of clothing from the Far East, and that in their festival for the canonisation of the first two Jesuit Saints, Ignatius of Loyola and Francis Xavier, in July 1622,

> [s]tudents of the Jesuit college, acting as catachumens, walked six by six in procession, wearing costumes native to Tamil Nadu, Paravar, Malacca, Japan, Malaysia, and China.[54]

The multiple uses of this collection of clothes include festivals and college drama, clothing figures in the works of painters associated with the Antwerp

Jesuits, and with their church and confraternities. Did they also appear on the little stage for living pictures which was revealed when Rubens's canvases sank out of sight behind the high altar?

Orazio Grassi's libretto for Kapsberger's 1622 opera for the canonisation of the first two Jesuit saints, *Apotheosis sive Consecratio SS Ignatii et Francisci Xaverii*,[55] articulates a polity encompassing the whole world, but its perception of the territories outside Europe is emphatically spiritual rather than mercantile, even if it is expressed in emblems drawn from material things.[56] Asian birds (more in the form of a hornbill than of a bird of paradise) adorn the heads of the dancers representing India in this global triumph, with emissaries coming to pay homage to the first two Jesuit saints.[57] It offers a baroque vision of a harmonious world, albeit a world where Christians are martyred, full of symbolic objects with spiritual significance: Arabian incense (the gift of the second Magus), Indian pearls (emblems of purity and of the virgin birth), and Japanese 'green palm trees' (emblems of constancy, perseverance, and martyrdom.) It is a classicising work from an age of empires, but the polity which it celebrates is, like the bird of paradise, not of this world and its empires in any simple sense.[58]

In one of the leather-bound collections of Latin play-scripts from the English Jesuit College at Saint-Omer (then in the Spanish Netherlands), two long feathers from an exotic bird have been placed deep in the binding gutter between two gatherings of pages (the feathers are found before f. 142, the beginning of the play *Monacella*).[59] The play thus marked dates from 1714, and concerns the sixth-century Welsh hermit-saint and abbess Melangell, Latinised as Monacella. The play dramatizes the episode in which the prince of Powys ('Utherus' in the play) goes hunting in deep woodland, and the hunted hare takes refuge with the hermit-saint. The placing is clearly deliberate, a message to the future, much stranger and more haunting than any skeleton leaf or pressed flower, and as hard (harder) to interpret. This play celebrated the arrival of relics of the saint at Saint-Omer, and was acted with considerable elaboration, with brocades and jewels as well as feathers being supplied from Paris to the Rector, Fr. Sabran. The feathers cost 36 livres.[60]

This feather at Stonyhurst is one of the baroque ghosts, a whisper of connection when all precise traces are lost: the lone, scarcely explicable object which has travelled an immense distance – as in this astonishing sentence of John Aubrey's:

> When the Queen mother came to Oxon to the King, she either brought (as I thinke) or somebody gave her, an entire Mummie from Egypt a greate raritie, which her Majestie gave to Mr Bushell. But I believe long ere this time the dampnesse of the place has spoyled it with mouldinesse.[61]

The timing is as strange as the object: deep in wartime, moving south from York in July 1643, Henrietta Maria was travelling at the head of reinforcements to join the king and Parliament at Oxford, after two years spent in Holland. The recipient is strange – the mining engineer and hermeticist, Thomas Bushell: extravagant penitent, quasi-religious solitary, at his baroque grotto-hermitage at Enstone in Oxfordshire.[62] The place where the mummy perished was strange too: an underground room formed around a natural rock face, which had been worn into fantastical shapes, and adorned with petrifications, by the dripping water from springs rising around it. The whole was made into a fantastical, disquieting cave of illusions, rendered stranger by the whole baroque repertory of mirrors and concealed windows.

> This Rocke, being naturall, is very rare and admirable … for indeed, many strange formes of Beasts, Fishes and Fowles doth appeare; and with the pretty murmuring of the Springs; the gentle running, falling and playing of the waters; the beating of a Drum; the chirping of a Nightingale, and other strange, rare and audible sounds and noyses doth highly worke vpon any Mans Fancy; the couzning windowes about it, makes you thinke that another such strange Rocke appeares on the other Side, where at first view I began to suspect my owne Posture.[63]

This is a withdrawn and idiosyncratic environment, infinitely smaller in scale, but of the same order as Count von Spork's fantastical estate, with its grottos for the stone penitents, in Bohemia. We will never know how Henrietta Maria obtained the mummy, although a provenance in Holland is just possible. With both a brother and a husband who were important collectors, and a court of men and women who also collected across the range of baroque art and *virtú*, she lived in a milieu in which not to collect would be the exception rather than the rule. Gerard van Honthorst's painting of Charles and Henrietta Maria as Apollo and Diana, receiving the seven liberal arts, embodies a crucial aspiration of the Caroline court.[64]

But Egyptian mummies were extremely rare, especially in northern Europe, so the example which seems to have accompanied the fugitive queen in her journey through wartime England becomes a riddle without a solution – one of those baroque ghost-objects that cannot be conjured to speak. It is possible to gain some sense of the rarity of the object from Athanasius Kircher's *Oedipus Aegyptaicus*, one of the most sumptuous as well as one of the strangest of the publications of the mid-seventeenth century.[65] In this work, Kircher recognised the Coptic affinities of the language which hieroglyphics represented, but he failed to see them as anything but pictograms or emblems, a failing about which posterity has been perhaps disproportionately spiteful. Regardless of this, his Egyptian treatise is a compendious, all-encompassing account of the baroque world of learning's knowledge of matters Egyptian (Kircher wrote also on the subterranean world and on other matters which might have been of considerable interest to Bushell the 'Projector and Hermetist'). Later reports of the grotto at Enstone even claimed that there had been two mummies, but to imagine one mummy to have eluded Kircher and his correspondents is problematic enough; to imagine that two remained unknown to learned Europe, at a time when even fragmentary mummies were still objects of intense interest, is all but incredible.

Oedipus Aegyptaicus does not mention England at all: at the beginning of the section on mummies, Kircher cites informants and correspondents in Tuscany, Amsterdam, France, Germany, and the Spanish Netherlands. He describes two complete mummies in the collection of Petrus à Valle (Pietro della Valle, 1586–1652) the Italian traveller in Egypt and author of the *Itinerarium*, which constituted early modern Europe's chief source of information on the contemporary state of Egypt.[66] (Kircher also records and illustrates a mummy in the collection of the Medici grand dukes of Tuscany, and discusses the hieroglyphics on the cases of the Tuscan mummies in some detail, speculating on their relation to the inscriptions on the obelisks of Rome.)[67] Kircher describes and illustrates only one other complete example, with an inner and outer case, in the collection of the Amsterdam merchant Hieronimus van Waerle.[68]

These mummies are the only examples which Kircher illustrates and describes. The mummy which Henrietta Maria would appear to have carried through warring England, until it found its last resting place in the grotto at Enstone, cannot have been one from van Waerle's collection, which was reported as intact in the 1650s. A mystery remains as to why such a precious mark of royal favour should have been bestowed on Bushell. Bushell and Henrietta Maria had indirect contact with Kircher and his circle through the virtuoso Sir Kenelm Digby (1603–65), but this contact comes too late to shed any light on the mummy.[69] Digby was Henrietta Maria's chancellor for most of his life, and it has been suggested that Kircher may have sounded Digby out as to whether Henrietta Maria might be a patron and dedicatee for the final part, the third volume, of his *Oedipus* – that part which in fact contains the section on mummies. One of Digby's two more or less unhappy and fruitless visits to Rome in 1645 and 1647 must have been the occasion of this contact.

The mystery resists solution, but an Egyptian object (however fugitive, however incredible) seems a fitting gift for a hermeticist: Egypt remained the third, silent term of antiquity for the early modern world, known little, and that mostly from rumours of Horapollo and Hermes Trismegistus, and in reports of variable accuracy. Thus it became the place and culture in antiquity onto which hopes and aspirations for the present could be projected, as in the 1680 Mexican triumphal entry which Carlos de Sigüenza y Góngora devised for the viceroy, in which the Egyptians were claimed as the ancestors of the Mexicans.[70]

There are more scrutable instances of people and ideas travelling great distances. The English Jesuit Thomas Stephens (1547–1619), born in Wiltshire and educated at Oxford, travelled as a missionary to India.[71] His epic in the Marathi language, the *Kristapurāna*, embodies an extraordinary moment of cultural bilinguality. Two world-traditions find a point of confluence in a poem which re-imagines the Biblical narratives within Hindu intellectual and imaginative conventions.[72] As Stephens's editor and translator phrases it,

> What takes place in the Kristapurāna is the communication of the whole of the Christian Biblical story in another language (Marathi) and in another tradition, namely, the Hindu Vaişṇavaite. What is more, it is not just an encounter between the two but a mutual fecundation ... [T]his text shows an encounter between two major worlds: one world is the Vaişṇava world and the other is the world of Tridentine theology.[73]

In the prologue to the epic (*Kristapurāna*, I, 122–23), Stephens sings of the beauty of his adopted language, and of his love for it:

> As amongst the gravel, a lustrous gem
> Or among the jewels, the blue carbuncle;
> So among languages, the excellent
>   Language is Marathi.
> As among the flowers is the
> Jasmine flower or among the
> Scented perfumes, Musk, so among
> The languages is the gracefully neat,
>   Marathi language.[74]

But the assimilation goes beyond language: the Nativity is imagined entirely in Asian terms – the lullaby of the angels ('jō jō jō jēju bāḷakā'/ 'lully, lully, Jesus the child') and the adoration of the shepherds (who have become cowherds):

> Making garlands of small shells we would,
> Have put them around your neck for adornment.
> We would have decorated your ears with
>   Bunches of Gunja.
> Weaving garlands of wild flowers,
> We would have adorned your neck
> And chest. And also wreaths
> Around the forehead and head.[75]

Yet the world of the European baroque has not departed entirely from Stephens's mind, but it has been transmuted by India. The flight into Egypt, magnificently imagined as a crossing of immense Asian mountains, contains a moment when the Christ Child pities his parents and weeps, and the Virgin weeps with him:

> The eyes of the Virgin
>   Were full of tears.
> The drops of tears fell down
> Showered on the body of Jesus;
> As if on a statue of crystal,
>   Pearls fell.[76]

This catching of the foreshadowing moment, this prescient image, is shared by a Christian epic from the other side of the world, another poem that draws worlds and environments together. The Jesuit Diego José Abad y Garcia was born in Mexico in 1727 and died in European exile in 1779, after the suppression of the Old Society of Jesus. This moment comes from the second part of his Latin epic *De Deo heroica carmina*, first published at Cádiz in 1769.[77] The shepherds bring flowers to the Christ Child, among them the 'flos Mexiceus', the Mexican passion flower. The Mexican poet, like any painter of the Cuzco school in Peru, visualises sacred places in terms of the locality in which he had grown up, confidently rooting sacred history in American place. The Mexican passion flower echoes across to the Goan garlands of white shells. Languages and ideas travel as readily as plants and seeds in the baroque world:

> Pastores huc o celeres plenisque canistris
> (Quandoquidem ridet, fert et nunc omnia tellus)
> Ferte citi flores et circumfundite florem
> *Mexiceum* florum regem, Florum decus ingens;
> Nam gestat secum nostra argumenta salutis,
> Tergeminos alto capitatatos vertice clavos,
> Cupside obarmatos imo, et ferrugine tinctos
> Tristi: surgentem in medio arrectamque columnam
> Marmoream: et quasi vibratum, intortumque flagellum
> Et spisse circumtextam, implexamque coronam:
> Quinaque sanguineis magnis extantia guttis
> Vulnera. Flos equidem Puero gratissimus hic est.[78]

[The shepherds come quickly hither, with baskets full of flowers, quickly bring and spread around the Mexican flower, the most beautiful king of flowers, carrying within it the proof of our salvation: the three nails borne at the top their sharp ends stained with sad rust colour, a column of marble rising in the middle, shaking filaments like whips, and five drops like blood. This indeed is the flower most pleasing to the Boy.]

These lines embody something of the same thinking as the amaranth and maize in the Antwerp altar rails: the passion flower is a divine communication displayed in a plant which did not grow in Europe. Signs from God are spread lavishly and equally about the globe. The linking here of the Nativity and the Passion, in the image of the Mexican flower, is reminiscent of the way in which St Ignatius's meditation on the Nativity in his *Spiritual Exercise* imagines the road from Nazareth to Bethlehem, and contemplates the new-born Child, then moves, almost at once, to anticipation of the Passion. Calvary is foreshadowed in the stable. After meditation on the place and persons present, he invites meditation on

> the things which are being done there, as of the journey, the labours, and the causes on account of which the highest Lord of all was born in the greatest need; about to bear also, together with perpetual poverty, labours, hunger, thirst, heat, cold, reproaches, blows; and about to undergo at last the cross, and that for my sake.[79]

All of this is implicit in the moment of the choice of the passion flower. This Ignatian apprehension of the Nativity is the whole matter of the audacious and beautiful Neapolitan Christmas song *Ninna Nanna al Bambino Giesù.*[80] Many works of baroque art express a hybridity between cultures from different places: this song is a hybrid of high and popular Italian musical traditions, the popular Christmas lullaby to the Christ Child, deepened and refined by Counter-Reformation meditation. (The syllables 'Ninna nanna' are syllables without meaning, non-lexical vocables, exactly like the 'jō jō jō' of the shepherds in the *Kristapurāna.*) *Jō jō jō jēju bāḷakā* coincides, from half a world away, with the opening words of the Neapolitan lullaby – *Ninna nanna, dormi figlio*. In both works a kind of vernacular innocence and sweetness is called forth by the circumstances and the season. Here is the gentle opening:

> Ninna nanna, ninna nanna,
> Dormi figli, dormi amore.[81]
> [Lully lully/ Sleep my son, sleep my love.]

Then the shock of grief and magnificence which comes with the fourth line:

> Con quel pianto e quella voce
> Brami, Ohimé, brami la croce.
> [With your tears and your voice/ You long, alas, you long for the cross.]

Then the return to a lullaby, immeasurably deepened, truth telling:

> Or ch'è tempo di dormire
> Dormi figlio e non vagire
> Verrà il tempo del dolore
> Dormi amore ...
> [Sleep and do not weep/ The time of sorrow will come/ Sleep my love]

Then the exposition of the meaning of the child's tears, cast in simple words, but grave with the authority of prophetic knowledge:

Altri pecca e tu ne piange,
E la vita in morte cangi,
E ne godi del dolore
Per dar vita al peccatore.
Complirai questo desio,

[Others sin and you weep for it/ And change life into death/ And rejoice in the pain/ To give life to sinners. You will fulfil this desire,]

The rhyme word 'desio' is arresting. You hear the inevitable answering rhyme before it is uttered, think it perhaps too audacious to be uttered; then it is pronounced, and the lullaby grows vast, unbearable, solemn:

Dormi, o Dio.

[Sleep, o God.]

And you give way in admiration and astonishment. What a vital baroque response this is: to be overwhelmed, to surrender. *Seduxisti me Domine et seductus sum; fortior me fuisti et invaluisti factus sum.*[82] The right hand to the heart, lowered eyelids, head inclined. *Mute eloquence which is fecund silence; the lost baroque continually reborn.*

Notes

1 Anne Goldgar, *Tulipmania: Money Honor and Knowledge in the Dutch Golden Age* (Chicago: University of Chicago Press, 2007); Sam Segal, *Flowers and Nature: Netherlandish Flower Painting of Four Centuries* (Amstelveen: Hijnk International, 1990).

2 Giovanni Bonifaccio, *L'arte de' cenni: con la quale formandosi fauella visibile, si tratta della muta eloquenza, che non e' altro che vn facondo silentio: diuisa in due parti* (Vicenza: Francesco Grossi, 1616).

3 Herman Pleij, *De sneeuwpoppen van 1511* (Amsterdam: Prometheus, 1998), p. 19.

4 See https://janlampo.com/2012/11/05/literatuurkunstgeschiedenis-de-antwerpse-sneeuwpoppen-van-1772 (retrieved 13 May 2023).

5 See https://recipes.hypotheses.org/5454 (retrieved 13 May 2023).

6 Yasmin Haskell, *Loyola's Bees: Ideology and Industry in Jesuit Didactic Latin Poetry* (Oxford: Oxford University Press for the British Academy, 2003), p. 84.

7 Sir Kenelm Digby, *The Closet Opened*, ed. Jane Stevenson and Peter Davidson (London: Prospect Books, 2010), p. 66.

8 Edmund Gayton, *Epulae Oxonienses* (Oxford: no publisher, 1636), f. 1r.

9 *L'arte de'cenni*, sig.b7. 'To hold in the breast, to press something to the breast, hands on the breast, to disclose the breast, to open the breast, to look into another's breast, to tear at one's breast.'

10 Franciscus Lang SJ, *Dissertatio di Acione Scenica cum figuris eandam explicantibus* (Munich: Riedin, 1727), fig. III, p. 28. 'De Brachiis, Cubitis etc. Manibus.'

11 For the Waldsassen Catacomb saints, see Paul Koudounaris, *Heavenly Bodies: Cult Treasures and Spectacular Saints from the Catacombs* (London: Thames & Hudson, 2013), p. 64; and, more generally, see Carol Alkabes, *Martyrs: Les reliques oubliées* (Lausanne: Favre, 2018); Trevor Johnson, 'Holy Fabrications: The Catacomb Saints and the Counter-Reformation in Bavaria', *The Journal of Ecclesiastical History*, 47.2 (1996), pp. 274–97; Noria Litaker, 'Lost in Translation? Constructing Ancient Roman Martyrs in Baroque Bavaria', *Church History*, 89.4 (2020), pp. 801–28.

12 Koudounaris, *Heavenly Bodies*, p. 92.

13 *Ibid.*, p. 26.

14 *Pia desideria emblematis, elegiis & affectibus SS. Patrvm illustrat* (Antwerp: Boetius a Boelswart, 1624).

15 Rev 21:2, 19–23.

16 See www.nga.gov/features/slideshows/spanish-polychrome-sculpture.html#slide_15 (retrieved 17 May 2023); Xavier Bray, *The Sacred Made Real* (London: Yale University Press for the National Gallery, 2009), esp. pp. 59–71.

17 Léon Lock, 'Rubens and the Sculpture and Marble Decoration', in Piet Lombaerde (ed.), *Innovation and Experience in the Early Baroque in the Southern Netherland: The Case of the Jesuit Church in Antwerp* (Turnhout: Brepols, 2008), pp. 155–74, at p. 170.

18 See https://historiek.net/rederijkers-rederijkerskamer-middeleeuwen/79496 (retrieved 17 May 2023).

19 Ria Fabri and Piet Lombaerde (eds.), *The Jesuit Church of Antwerp* (Corpus Rubenianum XXII, 3) (London: Harvey Miller, 2018).

20 This thought experiment was the subject of a number of conversations with Gauvin Alexander Bailey about a decade ago.

21 The 1621 account of the chancel of the church – given in Fabri and Lombaerde, *The Jesuit Church of Antwerp*, p. 225 – does not discuss details 'lest by too close and excessive display of individual parts I will detract from the majesty of the work as a whole'. I am indebted (personal communication) to Léon Lock of the Low Countries Sculpture Society for confirming the complexity of this dating, since so many items in the church were repositioned after the disastrous fire of 1718.

22 *Historia natural y moral de las Indias en que se tratan las cosas notables del cielo, y elementos, metales, plantas y animales dellas y los ritos y ceremonias, leyes y govierno y guerras de los indios* (Seville: Juan de Leon, 1590). Cf. David Brading, *The First America* (Cambridge: Cambridge University Press, 1993)

23 See Chapter 8, pp. 144–157.

24 *De rebus Japonicis, Indicis et Peruanis epistolae recentiores* (Antwerp: Martinus Nutius, 1605).

25 Reference is consistently to John Rupert Martin, *The Decorations for the Pompa Introitus Ferdinandi* (Corpus Rubenianum XVI) (London: Phaidon, 1972).

26 Modello in *Ibid.*, p. 101; engraving by T. van Thulden of finished arch, p. 192; discussion of arch, pp. 189–93.

27 *Ibid.*, p. 191.

28 Alonso Ramos Garcilán, *Historia del Celebre Sanctuario de Nuestra Senora de Copacapana* (Lima: Geronymo de Contreras, 1621).

29 Psalm 118:15–27.

30 J. Richard Judson and Carl van de Velde, *Book Illustrations and Title Pages* (Corpus Rubenianum XXI) (London: Harvey Miller, 1978).

31 The extent of this involvement is documented in Fabri and Lombaerde, *The Jesuit Church of Antwerp*.

32 *Ibid.*, p. 16.

33 *Imago Primi Saeculi* (Antwerp: Plantin, 1640), p. 326.

34 John Everaert, 'De verovering van de Indiaanse Ziel: missionarissen uit de Lage Landen in Spaans-Amerika (1493–1767)', in *Amerika bruid van de Zon* [exhibition catalogue] (Antwerp: Koninklijk Museum voor Schoene Kunsten Antwerpen, 1992), pp. 59–68. I must here thank once more my pandemic-years correspondents in Leuven, Dr Werner Thomas and Dr Johan Verberckmoes, who were infinitely helpful with suggestions and advice on the subject of the Spanish Netherlands and Ibero-America.

35 Martin Warnke, *Rubens: Leben und Werke* (Cologne: DuMont, 2011).

36 Cf. Edward M. Test, 'Seeds of Sacrifice: Amaranth, the Gardens of Tenochtitlan and Spenser's *Faerie Queene*', in J. G. Singh (ed.), *A Companion to the Global Renaissance: English Literature and Culture in the Era of Expansion* (Oxford: Wiley-Blackwell, 2007), pp. 242–61; also Jaime Lara, 'Sacred Blood: The Liturgy of Human Sacrifice (in a Christian Context)', https://ism.yale.edu/sites/default/files/files/Sacred%20Blood.pdf (retrieved 4 July 2023). The overview is the magnificent article by Elizabeth H. Boone, 'Incarnations of the Aztec Supernatural: The Image of Huitzilopochtli in Mexico and Europe', *Transactions of the American Philosophical Society*, 79.2 (1989), pp. 1–107.

37 See https://portalacademico.cch.unam.mx/sites/default/files/publicaciones-digitales/2021–10/divinonarciso_interiores_final.pdf (retrieved 5 July 2023); English translation: 'Let us begin, for my longing aches to see what the God is like who will be served to me as food (AMERICA, OCCIDENT, and ZEAL all sing) saying that only now do the Indies perceive who the true God of Seeds really is! And so we say that with tender tears distilled by our great joy, let all gaily repeat and raise rejoicing voices: Oh let us bless the day when we came to know the great true God of Seeds!' (https://olli.gmu.edu/docstore/400docs/1801–406-sj%20loa%20to%20the%20divine%20narcissus%20eg%20trans.pdf (retrieved 5 July 2023)).

38 See https://smarthistory.org/corn-pith-sculptures (retrieved 5 July 2023).

39 My thanks to the Rev. Dr Ayla Lepine for drawing this memorial to my attention.

40 Boone, 'Incarnations of the Aztec Supernatural', p. 68.

41 D. Z. Bor, *František Antonín hrabě Špork: významný mecenáš barokní kultury v Čechách* (Prague: Trigon, 1999), pp. 29–33.

42 *Ibid.*, pp. 40–2.

43 Boone, 'Incarnations of the Aztec Supernatural', p. 64.
44 See www.maskmuseum.org/krampuslauf-blog (retrieved 6 July 2023).
45 A full discussion of the painting of birds of paradise in European art is found in José Ramón Marcaida, 'Rubens and the Bird of Paradise: Painting Natural Knowledge in the Early Seventeenth Century', *Renaissance Studies*, 28:1 (2014), pp. 112–27.
46 *Ibid.*, p. 114.
47 *Ibid.*, p. 115.
48 *Ibid.*, p. 116.
49 Baltimore, Walters Art Museum, 37.2010.
50 Los Angeles, J. Paul Getty Museum, 83.GB.384.
51 Now Vienna, Kunsthistorisches Museum, Gemäldegalerie, 519.
52 Stephanie Schrader, with contributions by Burglind Jungmann, Kim Young-Jae, and Christine Göttler, *Looking East: Rubens's Encounter with Asia* (Los Angeles: J. Paul Getty Museum, 2013).
53 *Ibid.*, pp. 39–51.
54 *Ibid.*, p. 51.
55 See https://imslp.org/wiki/Apotheosis_sive_Consecratio_SS_Ignatii_et_Francisci_Xaverii_(Kapsperger%2C_Giovanni_Girolamo) (retrieved 16 July 2023).
56 Cf. Ralph P. Locke, 'Exotic Elements in Kapsberger's Jesuit Opera (Rome, 1622) Honoring Saints Ignatius and Francis Xavier', at https://gupea.ub.gu.se/handle/2077/54931 (retrieved 16 March 2023).
57 *Ibid.*, p. 16.
58 A virtuosic meditation on feathers in the baroque world can be found in Jelena Todorović, *The Concept of Fluidity in the Baroque Age* (Newcastle upon Tyne: Cambridge Scholars Publishing, 2023), pp. 6–9.
59 Stonyhurst College, MS C V 32, before f. 142. Costumes for Saint-Omers plays are discussed at length by Dr Janet Graffius in her doctoral dissertation, "Bullworks against the Furie of Heresie': Relics, Material Culture and the Spiritual and Cultural Formation of the Sodality of St Omers English Jesuit College, 1593–1650' (PhD diss., University of Aberdeen, 2020), pp. 243–7.
60 *The Letter Book of Lewis Sabran SJ*, ed. Geoffrey Holt SJ (London: Catholic Record Society, 1971), pp. 36–7, 53, 64–5.
61 John Aubrey, *Brief Lives*, ed. Kate Bennett, 2 vols (Oxford: Oxford University Press, 2015), I, pp. 314–15.
62 *Ibid.*, I, pp. 311–15.
63 Nathaniel Hammond, ed. L. G. Wickham Legge, *Relation of a Short Survey of the Western Counties ... in 1635* (London: Royal Historical Society, 1936; Camden Miscellany XVI) p. 82. The workings of Bushell's various hydraulic contrivances are investigated in Robert Plot, *The Natural History of Oxford-Shire* (Oxford: Lichfield, Brome, Nicholson, 1705), pp. 241–4.
64 See www.rct.uk/collection/405746/apollo-and-diana (retrieved 14 July 2023).
65 Athanasius Kircher, *Oedipus Aegyptaicus*, 3 vols (Rome: Mascardi, 1652–54).
66 *Ibid.*, III, pp. 406–7.
67 *Ibid.*, III, pp. 412–13.

68 *Ibid.*, III, p. 428; the folding plate is at page 429.

69 See https://doi-org.ezproxy-prd.bodleian.ox.ac.uk/10.1093/ref:odnb/7629 (retrieved 10 July 2023).

70 Carlos de Sigüenza y Góngora, *Teatro de virtudes políticas que constituyen a un príncipe: advertidas en los monarcas antiguos del Mexicano Imperio, con cuyas efigies se hermoseó el Arco triunfal que la … Ciudad de México erigió para … recibimiento del … Virrey Conde de Paredes, Marqués de La Laguna …* (Alicante: Biblioteca Virtual Miguel de Cervantes, 2005) [www.cervantesvirtual.com/nd/ark:/59851/bmcs4718 (retrieved 10 July, 2023)].

71 Brijraj Singh, 'The First Englishman in India: Thomas Stephens (1547–1619)', *Journal of South Asian Literature*, 30.1/2 (1995), pp. 146–61.

72 Thomas Stephens SJ, *Kristapurāna*, ed. and trans. Nelson Falcao SDB (Bangaluru: Kristu Jyoti Publications, 2012), p. lxii.

73 *Ibid.*, pp. lxii–lxiii.

74 *Ibid.*, p. 18.

75 *Ibid.*, p. 693 (8: 88–89).

76 *Ibid.*, p. 743 (12: 51–52).

77 *Musa americana, seu de Deo carmina: ad usum scholarum Congregationis S. Philippi Neri municipii S. Michaelis in Nova Hispania* (Cadiz: apud D. Emmanuelem Espinosa, 1769). The quotation is from Book XXIII, ll. 98–109; for recent commentary on Abad, see Manuel Fabri, 'Los Jesuitas y a construction de la Nación Mexicana', *Artes de México*, 104 (December 2011), pp. 48–9.

78 Diego José Abad, *De deo deoque homine* (Casena: apud haeredes Blasinios, 1693), p. 168.

79 St Ignatius of Loyola, *Spiritual Exercises*, 'Second Day of Second Week' [www.sacred-texts.com/chr/seil/seil18.htm (retrieved 10 July 2023)].

80 Rome, Biblioteca Castanense, Cod. 2490; edited and recorded by Philippe Jaroussky and L'Arpeggiata, under the direction of Cristina Pluhar, *Via Crucis*, Warner Classics, 2010.

81 Lully lully/ sleep my son, sleep my love/ With your tears and your voice/ Alas, you long for the cross/ Sleep and do not weep/ The time of sorrow will come/ Sleep my love … Others sin and you weep for it/ And change life into death/ And rejoice in the pain/ To give life to sinners/ You will fulfil this desire, sleep, O God.

82 Jeremiah, 20:7.

Part I

Centres and peripheries

1

James Fraser: experiencing the arts of Italy in the mid-seventeenth century

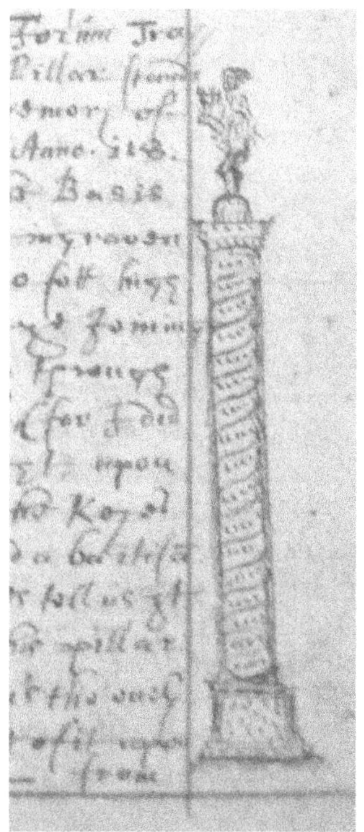

Figure 1.1 A page from James Fraser's manuscript *Triennial Travels*, volume II, with his drawing of Trajan's column, manuscript fair copy, 1670s, Aberdeen University Library, MS 2538 (f. 72r).

Occasionally a figure from the far margins makes a journey to the acknowledged cultural centres of the baroque world: one of the most comprehensive records of such travel is found in the three volumes of the unpublished journal of James Fraser (1634–1709), Episcopalian minister of Kirkhill near

Inverness, a fair copy of the diaries which he had kept during an extensive tour of Britain and western Europe in the years 1657 to 1660 (see Figure 1.1).[1] His own descriptive title for these three volumes of closely written, crow-quill pen manuscript was *Triennial Travels, containing a succinct and breefe narration of the journay and voyage of Master James Fraser through Scotland, England, all France, part of Spain, and over the Savoyan Alps to Italy, 1 June 1657 – April 1660.* Fraser remains a fascinating figure, a test case of baroque connectedness: a Gaelic-speaking Highland sage with one foot in the Celtic realm of clans and second sight, and the other in the Latinate, diasporic commonwealth of cosmopolitan, highly educated Scots, and thence in the international republic of learning. He was a friend and correspondent of the pioneering archaeologist James Garden, Professor of Divinity at King's College, Aberdeen, and supplied Garden (and thus Garden's correspondent, John Aubrey) with accounts of Highland beliefs about second sight, which were printed in Aubrey's *Miscellanies* of 1696.[2] He could compose a bardic praise poem with the same ease with which he could write a philological letter to the Celtic linguist Edward Lhuyd for publication in learned circles in London.

He was the son of William Fraser of Phopachy, Inverness-shire, born in 1634. He graduated MA at King's College, Aberdeen, in 1655, a geographically remote but cosmopolitan institution which furnished him with all the languages and knowledge he needed to enter the republic of letters. A Stuart Loyalist and Episcopalian, bilingual in English and Gaelic and with a good knowledge of Latin, Greek, and Hebrew, he was moved to travel as temporary respite from Cromwellian Britain between June 1657 and April 1660. He returned to the Scottish Highlands in 1660, and was appointed to the parish of Kirkhill and Wardlaw in 1661, where he remained until his death in 1709.

It is possible to derive some idea of his intellectual scope from the other works of his which survive: his *Homilies and Exercises Spiritual and Moral* are in Aberdeen.[3] His only work in print, apart from the letters reproduced by Aubrey, is William Mackay's edition of his Chronicles of the Frasers, entitled *Polichronicon seu Policratica Temporum, or, the true genealogy of the Frasers, 916–1674*, which was issued by the Scottish History Society in 1905, as *The Wardlaw Manuscript.* Many of his other works have disappeared, including a Gaelic dictionary and pioneering works on popular beliefs and traditions of the north of Scotland – a parallel to Aubrey's *Remaines of Gentilesme and Judaisme.*[4] Like so many remotely located early modern savants, he focused his activity chiefly on expounding the community in which he lived to the learned world. The corollary – to bring the learned world into the remote community – is accomplished not only by Fraser's university education but also by this journal and by the documentary material incorporated into its pages.

Fraser's *Triennial Travels* have never been transcribed in full, nor studied at any length. Even allowing for the fact that Fraser borrowed substantially from contemporary printed works for his factual descriptions of places, his journal is still one of the most substantial texts about travel from early modern Britain to remain unpublished. At his best, Fraser is an observant recorder of the minutiae of daily life, of half-forgotten events, as in the London of 1657, where he notes the statue of Charles I at the Royal Exchange subjected to *damnatio memoriae*:

> But as the Treacherous Rebells used himselfe so did they his picture for August 10 1650 by order of there parlement it was defaced and broken down to pieces, and this inscription set behind the head of it in golden letters. *Exit Tyrannus Regum Ultimus, Anno Libertatis, Angliae Restitutae primo anno Dom. 1648. Jan 30* – O with what a bleeding heart and blubering eyes did I read it.[5]

He also saw the captured banners of Scottish Royalist regiments from the defeat at Worcester in 1651 in Westminster Hall:

> Those Ensigns & standards are all hanging here yet on both sids of the Hall from the one end to the other set up 6 yeares agoe. it truly galled my Spirit & dashed my very soul to behold them.[6]

He was in Rome in 1658 'about the close of October' to observe the general rejoicing which celebrated the report of Cromwell's death on 3 September, intelligence which seems to have arrived in letters to the rectors of the Scots and English colleges. (Fraser appears to have seen the letter to the Scottish Rector.)[7]

> [A] set day of ioy and Solemnity keept all Rome over, wth boonfires and other demonstrations of joy so great that it passes beleef in the general acclamation. But the greatest show of all was in the Spanish piazo of the stages set up a fire ship withall and an Artificiall fight, with flying firy squibs and a fountain running wine all day: besids the ravishing musick of various instruments.[8]

He also had the chance to see the most advanced contemporary stage machinery in the theatres of Rome:

> What finer than the Roman balls stage playes Comedies Tragedies done with such admirable art cunning and set forth with wonderfull changes of scene that nothing can be more surpriseing … [T]he finest passages of Sacred and Profane story acted most lively upon stages, Rivers running, Boats roweing, ships landing upon stages, serpents & creeping beasts crawlinge upon the stage, men flying, armyes feighting, whole townes wt men in streets markets exchanges lively personated and presented. Dark night with the Clowd, moone & starres, the sunn riseing and chaseing away darknesse confitts like haile and snow falling upon heads, ribbons and laces fancies flying in your faces. I saw the Ascention acted with such life that nothing exceeded it.[9]

Despite many such lively records and evocations, the text remains unpublished. The visit to London in 1657 is the subject of a short article, which makes use of only a dozen pages of volume I,[10] and there is an overview of the *Travels* in David Worthington's pioneering study of Fraser in his Highland context,[11] but otherwise the *Triennial Travels* remain in manuscript.

Perhaps the most significant historical witness offered by Fraser's travels is their consistent documentation of the sheer extent of the networks of expatriate Scots in Europe. Almost every city visited by Fraser has a colony of Scottish merchants, or of Scottish soldiers in foreign service, a Scots Catholic college or religious house or, at the very least, one Jesuit or Benedictine of Scottish birth. In this respect, Fraser's northern origins and education were a distinct advantage: the Catholics of Scotland, and the expatriate mercenaries and merchants from the Catholic community, were almost all of north-eastern or Highland origin, and thus they shared a milieu, an education, and even kinship networks with Fraser. His own royalist and socially conservative attitudes were unlikely to offend any of them and, in Catholic countries, he was willing to pass for a Catholic, although his temporary membership of the Papal Guard did trouble him. As a royalist Episcopalian, he was also wholly acceptable to Protestant political exiles. Moving in and through these circles and institutions, it is remarkable how much hospitality and charity he received in the course of his travels.

His attitudes to continental Europe are also distinctly Scottish: he engaged openly with the communities through which he moved, and communicated confidently in his excellent Latin (and once, memorably, in the synagogue in Rome, in Hebrew),[12] while also trying to pick up elements of whichever language he heard around him. The evidence of the journal would suggest that his extended stay in Rome furnished him with a reasonable command of Italian. He seems to have had few of the anxieties about boundaries, confessional compromise, and potential loss of identity which troubled many early modern English travellers on the Continent. North-eastern Scots especially, coming from the confessionally mixed and generally mutually tolerant communities in and around Aberdeen, were on the whole untroubled about religion. As Fraser phrased it to himself, when he was clearly passing as a Catholic in Rome, '[B]e free of your hatt, but reserve your heart.'[13] He continued to seek out compatriots, wherever he found himself, confident that he would find them and that he would receive companionship and help, as he did when the Scottish physician Dr Thomas Forbes, whose brother was a lecturer at Marischall College Aberdeen, treated a sprained ankle, gave him dinner, and guided him round Pisa.[14] To take another example, from his stay in Rome:

I mett here with a Franciscan Scotts man Father Henderson, a kind soule as ever I converst w^t, he gave me an Ivorie mort head that hung to his cord in girdle; and entertained us to purpose wt good fare and afterwardes bought us out to see the found of a College or seminarie intended by Monsegnior G. Conn a little before his death, and told us there were revenues lost to furnisse and finish it.[15]

In Rome, Fraser gravitated inevitably to his fellow countrymen, to the Scots College in the Via Quattro Fontane. He was grievously disappointed there on St Andrew's Day 1658, when the college failed to keep open hospitality. Scots who attended the Solemn High Mass wore a St Andrew's Cross in their hats for recognition: 'This day being Our Saints Day … as the usual manner was we expected to be highly treated at the Scots College but non of us was called.' His indignation was shared by a fellow Scot, Patrick Conn from Aberdeenshire, a nephew of the celebrated George Conn, who had been nuncio to Henrietta Maria, who was employed by Cardinal Francis Barberini as an agent for buying books and intelligencer.[16]

Signiour Patrick Con inquired of Mr Burnet and myselfe what treat and fare we got in our own Seminary: This we told him yt not a bit nor were we bidden, what said he, the base Churlish pack have discredit our Nation. pray let it not be heard; and so the gentleman gave us a Hungere [Hungary] Pistol in gold go Dine together upon my cost then and Drink my health. His Commands were forth with obeyed and sexteen of us wt two or 3 Irish commerads as many English went to the new Tavern qr we fared sumptuously: on S. And: his day.[17]

Towards the end of his continental travels, at Middelburg in Zeeland, he offers us a haunting glimpse of an eminent fellow Scot, Sir Thomas Urquhart (writer, translator, defeated royalist commander, fellow Aberdeen alumnus) in exile among the Scottish community of merchants there:

Sr Thomas Vrqhart of Cromarty was here all this summer & is now going for Antwerpe … we lodged in one Alexander Wilson's house. Clerk recorder to the Scottish company of Marchants, a pretty man. Here Sir Thomas Urqhart had his Chamer.[18]

And, indeed, the last record of Urquhart, in the last year of his life, is Fraser's recollection of him on the ferry from Zeeland to the coast of Brabant – one of his finest records of a conversation.

The Gale and sea favouring we shipped from Flushing to Antwerp 4 October at about 7 in the morning having 12 leagues long to sail, but they seemed to me but a stride in company w^t Sr Thomas Vrquahart, a most smart Scollar, cheerfull and facetious fellow who entertained us wt Philosophy, history peotery [*sic*] yt I wuld hardly take the leasure to lay by my pen, but still writing the fine observes that dropt from him.[19]

Having caught a glimpse of Charles II at Brussels, Fraser returned to a London where the regime of Richard Cromwell was failing in the days leading up to the Stuart Restoration. Having repeated at gloating length all the rumours about Cromwell's deathbed, Fraser summed up the Interregnum in a little beast-fable of his own devising:

> The vultur dies, and out of his Ashes rose a Titmouse, who wt the Frog in the Fable being swollen up with flatteries & fond advice of his Councellors durst vie his greatness wt the Royal right till the turnd buble burst and vanished into nothing.

And, with that, he turned for home to take his remote, far-northern place in the new society of Restoration Britain, and to spend the rest of his life as an active, if geographically peripheral, citizen of the international republic of letters.

The texture of the volumes themselves is humbly eloquent: they are illustrated with pasted-in prints, rubbings of coins, careful amateur drawings, painstaking pen facsimiles of passports and letters of recommendation. An engraving of Alexander VII is tipped into f. 110v of the second volume, and at f. 112r there are careful drawings of the money current in Rome in the 1650s. This is only one aspect of Fraser's fascination with everyday life, with passing time and place, with the object on the table in front of him as he writes, and is evidence of his desire never to forget his travels, using these visual evidences to preserve memory, as much as the words of his journal. In this, they are a modest whisper or echo of the paper museums of the period: drawings and documentation carried back to the Highlands to preserve the memory of Europe for a lifetime; a small, distant reflection of the *museo cartaceo* of Cassiano del Pozzo.

Fraser and the arts of Italy

What sets Fraser's continental tour apart from contemporary travel journals, such as John Evelyn's connoisseur's descriptions of cities, architecture, and works of art, is that Fraser was a pilgrim, dependent on pilgrim hostels and monastic hospitality, as well as on members of the Scots diaspora. He was, despite this, curious about, and intensely responsive to, architecture and works of art, especially those from antiquity, devoting much space in his journal to recording them. His delight on setting forth to see Florence on a spring morning is unmistakable: 'Next morrow we sturr betimes (Florence being a fitt garden to be seene on a May day).'[20] Fraser experienced continental cities, especially Rome, at a slow, self-guided pace and visited galleries and monuments on those days when they were open to the general public.

His visits to collections were not constrained by the hospitality elicited by letters of introduction. Fraser is, therefore, a rare source of information on how sights and collections were experienced either with a public guide or self-guided by books and pamphlets bought for that purpose. A selective comparison between Fraser's experience of particular places and that of John Evelyn, that exemplary elite traveller, is set forth below.[21]

It is possible to conjecture something of the knowledge of visual art which Fraser might have acquired before he set out on his travels. In his years at King's College, Aberdeen, he would have dined in the common hall of the college, which was, in the seventeenth century, residential like an Oxford or Cambridge college. Many of the works of art there with which he would have been familiar survive to this day, among them a fine Flemish Renaissance portrait of the founder of the university, Bishop William Elphinstone, dating from the first years of the sixteenth century. The common hall also contained a set of Sibyls, painted by George Jamesone in a broadly Netherlandic style; it may be conjectured that it also contained some of the Jamesone portraits still in the university collection. A gallery or chapel, painted with the mysteries of the Rosary, in the Aberdeen town house known as Provost Skene's House, dating from the 1620s and conjectured to remain in use until the mid-1640s, is the modest work of local painters, but its sources give an indication of those continental prints which were circulating in the city: Golzius, de Vos, Marcantonio Raimondi, and Dürer.[22] Thus, although Aberdeen was a comparatively visual society by the austere standards of post-Reformation Scotland (Kings College Chapel would still have had the Flemish Elphinstone monument, and it can be conjectured that many of the fittings of the cathedral had only recently been removed),[23] all the most important aspects of Fraser's formation, in his native Gaelic culture, as well as in the humanist curriculum of his university days, were historical, verbal, and literary rather than visual. He is a sharer in many, but not all, baroque preoccupations: he is intensely responsive to the magnificent and to the marvellous; he is *curious*; but he knows very little of visual art, and typically responds to the subject rather than the execution of any work of art – an essentially literary response; and he is invariably struck by *Kunstkammer* objects, by the intensely worked, the rare and far-fetched, the *meraviglia*.

All of these characteristics can be seen in his response to the Treasury of the Basilica of Loreto in the Marche. He responds to sheer splendour, to the 12 lamps hanging before the cult Statue of the Virgin ('twelve lampes of pure gold, each as big as a foot ball'),[24] the exotic and wondrous object, the Mexican feather-work picture; and he responds to language and narrative, to the multilingual inscriptions expounding the miracle of the Holy House, some of which are still in the Basilica to this day:[25]

> In another cupboard I saw the picture of the blessed Virgin wrought in Indian feathers most curiouslie, and by the varieties of the naturall glance and Lusture it chaunges Colloures. Upon the great Pillars of this Church, is ingravd in 14 or 15 languages the History of the holy house for the informatione of strangers.[26]

Similarly, the objects to which he responds most intensely in the Treasury of the Basilica are two ex-votos with contemporary historical and political significance, one with specific Scottish relevance:

> The first thing they shewed us was the Crowne and sceptre of Q. Christina of Sweden late prosolet [to] the Roman faith anno 1655. Next we saw a heart of Gold as bigg as both youre fists ioyned; sent hither by the late Q. mother of England Hen: Maria. It is without of blew enambling and on the one side IHS and on the other side MARIA and it opens in two, and within on one side is the Picture of the B. Virgen with the Babe in her arms and other the picture of the fors[ai]d Q. Mother all in natural Colloures of pretious stone.[27]

Queen Christina's abdication and conversion were among the most celebrated events of the mid-century. To a Scottish Royalist, Henrietta Maria's ex-voto would have been of particular significance: as R. W. Lightbown has recorded,[28] this locket of blue enamelled gold, with the Holy Names in diamonds, with the internal enamel figures executed by Jean Petitot, was presented to the shrine at Loreto by Henrietta Maria in 1639, the year of the first risings against the king in Britain, when Charles I led an army to the Scottish Border. Some of the first skirmishes had taken place in Aberdeen and Aberdeenshire, well within the living memory of Fraser's community.

The way in which ordinary travellers, or pilgrims, were shown ecclesiastical or princely treasuries seems consistent throughout Fraser's account: one or two priests or attendants would act as guides, opening cupboards or presses one by one, and offering a degree of commentary on the objects which were thus revealed. This appears to have been how Fraser, with three companions, saw the Medici collections in Florence: they viewed the collections at leisure, in the presence of a keeper, whose intervention in the visit intensifies when the party progresses to the cabinets or treasure rooms. Fraser's responses to the works which he sees remain essentially literary and historical:

> Betwixt this Pallace and the river stands the Famous Gallerie of Florence, which is properlie the Dukes treasurie: & it being such a rich and rare thing I shall here describe it. Yow goe up a large stare which leads in to the old pallace on the left hand, and in to the Gallerie on the Right, and first yow enter into a vast long Roome, all a lamp of light having 28 Large Glass windowes, towards the streets, and the reflex of the Light on the siluering above dasles

the eyes of a beholder: qh is curiouslie guilded wt the historie of Christ from birth to death: over and under these windowes are sett Close rowes of lively pictures representing the most famous persones ancient & modern for armes and artes about sex score in number, among qh I noticed Scipio Africanus in brass representing old Roman habit, the statue of Seneca and Cicero in marble, that of Diana, Leda, Hercules, Bachus; &c and over against the windowes on ye other side of the Gallerie, are sett thie pictures of all the Dukes of Florence wt their famelies, done to the life among other Pictures.[29]

It is clear that he barely distinguishes between paintings and bas-reliefs; subject is everything to him, and he reads any collection of pictures essentially as a Parnassus, gathered for the eminent examples offered by the subjects – a sort of visual Plutarch. A minor point is that he finds the representation of a figure from antiquity in antique costume a novelty, underlining that his own background, well beyond the northernmost *limes* of the empire, precluded his having seen excavated antique sculpture. Fraser's response to Michelangelo's *Brutus*, the bust now in the Bargello, which the art historian Johannes Wilde thought was unfinished,[30] is characteristic of Fraser's own Royalist preoccupations.

I tooke speciall notice of the head of Brutus one of Caesars murderers: It was done by Michael Angelo that famous painter and Limner of Italie begun but not finished & the reson is given in a distich underneath

:M: Dum Bruti effigiem Sculptor de marmore ducit – A
:B: In mentem sceleris venit et Abstinuit – F

[While the Sculptor was drawing the image of Brutus from the marble, [the latter's] crime came into his mind, and he ceased.]

These four letters first and last are for four words and signifie this – that Michael Angelo Bonarota fecit.[31]

The bronze plaque with the distich is still attached to the socle of the bust: it serves to sanitise the image of a regicide, and remove any possible republican connotations which it might carry or have carried, thus fitting it for a grand-ducal collection, and commending the inscription to the Royalist traveller. Again, Fraser responds to the verbal, the anecdotal, the historical. Hence his somewhat credulous response to the collection of *uomini illustri*, his belief that all these images are likenesses:

Close by this are ye head of Michaell Angelo Bonarota in pure brasse done by his owne hand.[32] Here also I saw the statue of Hanniball ... of Alexander Farnese, of whm it is said he never Lost a pitcht field; the statue of Machiavell, the Florentin Politician, Petrarch, Guicardin [the historian and diplomat Francesco Guicciardini], Columbus Americus, and manie more ... [W]e spent a prettie time viewing the faces of those famous worthies and Heroes, qh

> cannot chuse but ravish the beholder, to consider the livelie lookes of these statues and transport him wt thoughts of those they represent: at the farr end of the gallerie, yow see two statues of brasse vively done sett upon pedestalls of marble, the old Images and Gods of the ancient Romans; the keeper told us that the Duke valued these at a high rate.[33]

By this time a keeper has clearly appeared to conduct them into the smaller rooms, with their precious and more portable contents. All the contents of these rooms fall within the baroque aesthetic of the marvellous, the *meraviglia*, but they are otherwise fluid combinations of Treasury, armoury, and *Kunstkammer*.

> [F]rom this Gallerie we are led into the roomes and Chambers, and the first he led us to ws ye Armory where we saw the armes and habits of the Ianesaries made of reed velvet set thick wt nailes of Gold, the habits of the Indian Kings, sewed curiouslie together of Parrot feathers, the habit of ye King of China; here we saw Hannibals helmet, and Charles the fift his helmet, the reall sword of famous Scanderbey the sword of Hen: 4 of France …[34]

It sounds here as if Fraser is rehearsing what the keeper has told him: some of the claims seem surely extravagant, as with the bizarre armaments and magnetic wonders which follow in the armoury room:

> Stepping to another Room, we see a long Gun the barrell of gold massive and thick, as heavie as a man can Levell with, valued at 1500 pistolls; other pistells of Gold, sett in iron frames, another raritie, five pistoll barrells ioind together to be putt in yur hat qh is discharged at once as yow salute your enemy & bid him farewell … another pistoll wt eighteen barrells in it to be shot desperatly and scatter through a room as yow enter … In the side of the Chamber, is the statue of Philip the 4 King of Spain of pure brass on horsback: over your head a Loadstone holding up 60 pound weight of Iron, and sex keyes the one to ye other.[35]

The next cabinets, with their *pietra dura*, amber, turned ivory and distorting mirror, are more closely allied to the *Kunstkammer* of the period; the mirror is reminiscent of Athanasius Kircher's contemporary museum at the Collegio Romano:[36]

> From this Room we were led into a cabinet, where hanges a Curious hearse or Candlestick, wt its seven spreadeing branches all of yallow amber, wt transparent whit spottes in it an excellent master piece. This was a gift of the Duke of Saxony to Prince Mathias brother to Ferdinand 2, Duke of Florence: In this Cabinet also I sawe a square table of polished precious stones of various birds, floures, trees: Inlayed in a Casket also the head of Tiberious Caesar in a turkey stone as bigg as an egge: of incredible value, In this Cabinet also yow see two casements of Ivory Cups, a rare sight, here I saw also 3 brasen Idolls, qh the Barbarians usd of old.

> In the next Cabinet as ye enter is sett an ovall table of polished stones representing the Prague in Boheme, wt the Pictures of men, horses, birds, trees in naturall Colloures; In this Room hang two Globs, being made within the Chamber, and so big that they can never be brought out or caried into it by the door: also here are the statues of 4 of the Grand Dukes in Porphiry, two in each side. Over to the door stand a large mirrour of glass which being sett over the picture of any man, by a Curious reflexion yow see in it the picture of his wife if he hath one & yt most lively.[37]

The next room has an ebony cabinet, more *pietra dura*, and an ivory casket, which the keeper, wholly implausibly, attributes to Michelangelo:

> In the 3 Cabinet or Chamber, I saw a great Cabinet of Ebony besett wt precious stones on the outside and wt in the history off the holy Scriptures curiously expressed in small Cutts. In ye midle of this Room is a pure square table of polished stones re- presenting the toune and haven of Lighorn, most accuratlie done here is also hanging a Casket of Ivory, wt ye passion of our Saviour wt the picture of our Saviour and the twelve Apostles all of amber and Ivorie curiouslie cutt, by the hand of Michaell Angelo.[38]

When he finally comes to the *Tribuna* of the Uffizi, he barely registers the presence of the paintings, save by subject, and his focus is almost entirely on *Kunstkammer* objects, on the two robust objects (gold nugget, narwhal tusk) which the keeper allows him to handle, and on the alleged value of the finest items.

> In the 4 Cabinet which is the richest of al, and called *Il Tribuno* we see the top like a vault painted wt a deep reed sett full wt the shells of mother of pearle, the walls of the roome is hung wt green silk and full of prime pictures, the Picture of Leo 10 Pope of Rome, and two Cardinalls Julius Medicis, and Rossi Medici one on each hand of the Pope lively done: also the Picture off our Lady wt the babe in her armes rarely done in Miniatur or vermilion Limning, here they give you in your hand a massive Lump of Gold not stamped into Coine as yet, verie heavie and ponderous and I could have wished to have it els or in some other form – wt in the wall of this Room is a Cupboard full of Cups of Cristal, amber, agget, Lazuli stone, and such curious britle mater of most rare frames & shapes. This Cupboard is valued at a hundered thousand Crounes; In the midle of this room stand a pillar of Orientall Alabaster 3 yards high, transparent & glistering, a rare piece; and the Vnicorns horn, qh yow take in your hand to mesure, yet short of that which I saw att S. Denis in France at the furthest end of this Chamber stands a great Cabinet of Ebonie full of ancient medalls of Gold silver and brass of ye ancient Consules and Emperours of Rome; this Cabinet is sett wt precious stones of great bigness & value such as Rubie Saphyra, emerauld, Diamonds, & pearles as bigg as a haslenutt, such in deed I never saw. This Cabinet wt qt is in it is estimate at 400 thousand Crounes, it is indeed a rare thing. The onelie raretie in this

room is the ovall table, admirablie made of Inlaid pretious stones, purlie polished and cutt into birds, floures and other fancies that one can hardlie gett his fill of it, and would forget to fill his hungrie stomach & rather feed his eyes wt ye sight. There is in this table 10 sorts of precious stones: onix, Saphir amethist, Carbuncle, Cornelian, emerauld, rubie, pearle, agate and Cristall of the rock, and these so artifically cutt and sett that I never saw a more lively peece, nay the honnisuckle was so naturallie represented in its vive colloures that till I had laid my hand on it [I] concluded it to be the naturall flour. This is so rare a peece of art that the Duke values it to 3d his Dukedome as the keeper told us.[39]

As a pendant to his visit to the Uffizi, Fraser does, however, offer a clear glimpse of the mid-seventeenth-century state of the never completed altar for the Chapel of the Princes in San Lorenzo:

The 5 and last Cabinet is in the furthest end of the Gallerie southwards in which stands the famous alter that was made for S Laurence his Chappell; which wt the Tabernacle being now finished is to be sett up there. This same master peece of art and worth cannot be sufficientlie described nor aboundentlie admired: It is fixd on a Pedestill or basis of black marble fetcht from Greece, the sex pillares curously wrought are of Rock Cristall and each above a yard Long, thier Chapiters of pure Gold; the antepend is of saphire, onix, Cornelian and carbuncle; full of pictures of precious inlaid stones, the Glob upon the Top wt our saviours Statue on it & the Cross in his right hand is a wonder ... [T]he keeper assured us that it was ten yeares a makeing and I could truely beleeve it.[40]

Michelangelo's name comes up repeatedly in Fraser's account, suggesting that the keeper attributed most of the outstanding treasures to him. Evelyn, by contrast, a decade earlier, was aware of other artists represented in the collection – Raphael, Andrea del Sarto, Perugino, and Coreggio – implying growing personal knowledge or, at the least, a more knowledgeable guide.[41] Both men were shown the same rooms, but Evelyn saw 'a pearl as big as a hazel nut', which suggests that at least one cabinet in the Tribuna was actually *opened* for him, and, in the *pietra dura* room, the nail – half iron, half gold – allegedly converted by the German alchemist Leonhard Thurneysser, again suggesting a more leisurely tour with a higher level of access to objects.[42] The difference in the two descriptions suggests that Evelyn was given a personally conducted tour by someone able to open cabinets and display small and valuable items, whereas Fraser and his friends wandered in the first gallery and then were given a rather shorter guided tour; Fraser's text appears to record the cursory and wonder-focused commentary offered to his group. Although Fraser took note of the names of famous painters honoured in the Parnassus at the Accademia della Crusca, when his group visited there later in the day, at no point in his six days in Florence does painting seem to be a subject of genuine interest to him.[43]

In Florence, Evelyn had a recommendation to the house of Sig. Baritiere in the Piazza dal Spirito Santo, where he lodged.[44] Fraser, by contrast, in his pilgrim's dress, encountered a guard at the gate of Florence, who took minute details of their appearance and origins but, once satisfied, gave them a ticket to the pilgrim hospital, which accommodated them handsomely for one night.[45] After what must have been a strenuous morning, when Fraser and his companions came to Santa Croce around noon, they were lucky enough to find some Irish Franciscans, who asked them to dine with them (did they speak in English, Latin, or Irish?) and invited them to return there to sleep – an offer which was gratefully accepted. For his last two nights in Florence, Fraser and his travelling companion Mr Waite managed to persuade an Englishwoman to take them in:

> [W]e lodged the two last nights here in one Mistress Anna Farme an English womans house who keept a tabling: a very discreet courteous Charitable woman, where neither bed, board, washing or mending cost us nothing. She put our linnings into a good dresse, and I am sure mine had need of such handling & thankt the good woman.[46]

This kindness may have been charity extended to those assumed to be fellow Catholics, but Fraser's account also suggests that there was an almost automatic tendency for English, Irish, and Scots settled on the Continent to give travellers from the three kingdoms a helping hand, perhaps particularly in the 1650s, when it was a reasonable assumption that they were staying out of the way of the Cromwellian régime. Both travellers subsequently made their way to Rome: Fraser via Assisi, Macerata, and Loreto; Evelyn down the Via Francigena via Siena.

Their experience in Rome was also radically divergent. Evelyn and his party, on horseback, were caught in a thunderstorm and arrived, via the Vatican Gate, and were directed to a hotel kept by a Frenchman, M. Petit, near the Piazza di Spagna.[47] Fourteen years later Fraser entered by the Flaminian Gate, and, since it was 29 June, St Peter's Day, hastened to St Peter's to see the pope conducting Solemn High Mass.[48] Subsequently he repaired to the pilgrim hospice, Ospedale Trinità dei Pellegrini, where he found numbers of Scots and English, who advised that it was unwise to travel in the heat of summer, so he decided to break his journey and stay in Rome until the following spring. With dwindling resources, he decided to maintain himself by joining a regiment of the Papal Guard, though even the normally relaxed Fraser had misgivings here about religious compromise: he particularly mentions an oath which he had to swear on joining. His diary falls into the patterned vowels of Gaelic verse (as it does at many moments of heightened emotion) as he debates how to maintain his identity when so much immersed in Roman company:

> My onlie Course was to enter into the Regiment of guard; vulgarly called the Papal foot-guard and one day walkeing in the streetes I meet the Leutenant, and his Scrivener wt him who asked me if I would take othe; It was no time now to deliberate, and the offer was too good to refuse; and so I gaue him my name. and My Name inrolled he tristes me the next morrow to come to Caball de Casa the street qr the Regiment quartered. which I heartily did and receved my Muskat: July 7. 1658: I looke upon my selve now as a privileged Roman, I am one of their number, none of their nature, I love their Reson not their Religion, I must converse wt them, not be converted by them; I fancie their fare, their aire, their education, I must be warr of their infection; the way to shun their evill is to be Civill; be free of your hatt, but reserve your heart; but I forgett my errand. Being now fixt in the Regiment, and consequently in Rome, so that now I may be of her acquaintance ... now being at rest and having some respit I have time and Leasure, to looke about me.[49]

A decade earlier, Evelyn had been equally determined to look about him. On his first morning in Rome he began to move directly into circles of élite expatriated English Catholics:

> I got acquainted with several persons who had long lived at Rome. I was especially recommended to Father John, a Benedictine monke and Superior of his Order for the English College of Douay, a person of singular learning, religion and humanity; also to Mr Patrick Cary, an Abbot, brother to our learned Lord Falkland, a witty young priest who afterwards came over to our church; Dr Bacon and Dr Gibbes, physicians who had dependence on Cardinal Caponi, the latter being an excellent poet;[50] Father Courtnee, the Chiefe of the Jesuites in the English College; My Lord of Somerset, brother to the Marquiss of Worchester; and some others, from whom I received instructions how to behave in towne, with directions to masters and books to take in search of the antiquities, churches, collections, &c. Accordingly the next day, Nov. 6, I began to be very pragmatical.[51]

Clearly Evelyn, an Anglican, has no qualms about presenting himself to the English Catholic community in Rome, being 'pragmatical', and asking for their help, any more than Fraser worried about turning to English, Irish, and Scottish religious at various points in his travels, although the oath which he swore on joining the Papal Guard does seem to have troubled him.

Thus advised, Evelyn's next move was to recruit a 'Sights-man' (the term the men themselves preferred was 'antiquary') to guide him. Fraser in the 1650s explains that being an antiquary was a distinct profession, and that one could be found who commanded any language which might be required.

> Thus, if you please to bestow mony; there are Antiquaries of everie nation and Language, if you imploy one of these he will in 7 dayes guid yow out and in through the Cittie, and give both right and exact account of all the Antiquities of Rome ... and the perfect historie of the same, and call you everie morning at your Chamber, conduct you everie dayes Journay till the Close and will ordinarilie [agree] with you for 5 Crownes, if your generosity will bestow more, he will not cast it at his foot. Another usuall way is to buy a little booke in Italiane called Guida Romana Rome's Guide, if ye understand the Language this booke will describe the Citty, with every dayes taske and it hath in it in talladuce the Cutts or pictures of the most remarkable things ancient and modern within and without the Cittie, so that yow find with little help will make in a short time aquantit with Rome and a Roman to the good.[52]

Fraser also advises that it is possible to attach oneself to groups of foreigners being guided around the city by a local antiquary, and concludes,

> So that I made a pennilesse Journay through Rome ... so that I got the sight and the knowledg of the rarities of Rome and cost me nothing but my travail to walke and viu them gradually as they fell in my way.[53]

It seems likely that Fraser's guidebook would have been the 1653 edition of *Roma Antica e Moderna*; one in a long series of illustrated guides stretching back into the sixteenth century, which is when most of its illustrations were engraved.[54]

By the close of his first day, as Evelyn explored the ruins of ancient Rome, it became clear that he had recruited another assistant. Admiring 'fower basso relievos, viz. the triumph and sacrifice of Marcus Aurelius', he set 'my painter Carlo Neapolitano' to copy one of them.[55]

On his third day in Rome Evelyn's Italian contact procured him an introduction to the famous Jesuit virtuoso, Athanasius Kircher: 'Father Kircher (professor of Mathematics and the Oriental tongues) shew'd us many singular courtesies', taking him round the Collegio Romano, and finally, 'into his own study, where, with Dutch patience, he shew'd us his perpetual motions, catoptrics, magnetical experiments [etc.]'.[56] Although Evelyn and his nameless antiquary spent much of their time exploring publicly accessible monuments both classical and Christian, he continued to have privileged access to private collections: he writes that, on 21 November, 'I was carried to see a great virtuoso Cavaliero Pozzo, who shew'd us a rare collection of all kinds of antiquities, and a choice library, over which are the effigies of most of our late men of polite literature'. He also had a collection of curiosities and albums of drawings of antique bas-reliefs: the celebrated 'paper museum',[57] of which Fraser's diary with its pasted-in additions forms a very distant, very modest echo.

A decade later Fraser, when on duty, stood sentry before the palace of Queen Christina of Sweden, among other tasks, and, when he was free, went around Rome with his guidebook, making simple sketches of notable antiquities such as the pyramid of Caius Cestius. Both travellers were entertained by the Venerable English College on the feast of St Thomas Becket on 29 December. In 1644 Evelyn had been invited by the English Jesuits to dinner, as an honoured guest, writing that 'we din'd in their common refectory, and afterwards saw an Italian comedy acted by their alumni before the cardinals';[58] in 1658 Fraser joined the crowd of citizens of the three kingdoms:

> This day was kept very splendid and solem by the English nor was there an English or Scot in the City but was invited and well treated by the English colledge they were more civill to us then our own Country men.[59]

There are some notable passages in Fraser's descriptions of Rome: the sense of inhabiting the fragments of antiquity as he entered the court of the Palazzo dei Conservatori, to find the scattered fragments of the colossus of Constantine:

> Into the 2. Palace on the south west side of the court called ye Conservatorie where usually the Senators meet called the Senatores Camerae Almae Urbis. All bills, passes, Licenses Rightes are Deated from this. As ye enter into the court there lies about you on the pavement scattered the marble head, hands, Legs of the great Collosus that stood in the Amphitheater. Nearer the wall stands a rare statue in marble of a Lyon tareing a horse, then in another corner the brazen head of the Emperor Commodus and partlie in the wall of the court the famous old Tomb of the Emperour Alexander Severus and his mother Mammea Alba and an old brazen idol set up on this tomb.[60]

Perhaps the most felt episode of his whole sojourn in Rome is his sight of a first-millennium Scoto-Irish manuscript from the scriptorium of Iona in the Vatican Library: his whole visit to the library is alive with an awareness and engagement which he rarely feels for architecture or the visual arts:

> [T]he Vatican Liborarie … the onely Place I longed most to see in all the whole world. now by the permission and Manduction of Father John Curtney an English Jesuit and one of its keepers we got accesse to it … There are too the orderlie cupbords and Presses where the Manuscripts and printed books are kept most neatly and Closelie from mice and moistness. In the summer they are aired by the Windowe and in the Winter by Charckcole fires … they will be so bold to tell yow that the Gospell is written by the Apostles hands and preserved here the Acts of the Apostles written in Greeke by S. Lukes owne hand. Bookes on barkes of trees and China wood. The Septuagint translation in Greeke and Latin it was written a thousand yeare agoe. A ms of the old Egiptian Characters called Hierogliphics, the old roman Historians and Poets some of them written in their owne hand. They would needs point me out here

> (being a Scotsman) books of our old Monasteries and Liberaries in Scotland ... and the old Registers of the Scottish Cloisters; and also an old peece written by a Monck of S. Columcill 800 yeares agoe, his name was Daniel Odrad monachus Cellae Columbi and I thought this was no less than a Monument. It was the substance of the Canon Law, and al[so] the Occurences of our Nation time and date, and truly I coveted not a booke in the Vatican but this one manuscript.[61]

It seems both touching and indicative that, at this mid-point of his continental travels, Fraser should have felt so deeply for a manuscript from the Western Isles of Scotland, from the same Gaelic Scoto-Irish culture into which he was born.

To conclude: Evelyn, well instructed by his conversations with virtuosi (he learned Italian, as well as the common language of Latin) and with his antiquary, acquired a good working knowledge of Italian art. He had a great admiration for Bernini, his contemporary. By contrast, Fraser, who was in Rome at precisely the time when Bernini was transforming the city at the behest of Alexander VII, never mentions him, and had no eyes for any artist other than Michelangelo. He wrote with engaging wonder about the fountains in the piazza in front of St Peter's but seems not to have known the name of the architect of the great projected colonnades:

> A vast fountain running and throws up such a torrent and streame of water that it casts a fume & fogg about it so that none can come neare it, the impetuous flux of water is so strong. There is a vast worke intended round about this Piazza by this Pope. All ys begun this Summer. It is to be an Ovall Court or Portico and all the building is to stand upon 4 rowes of great stone pillars; some of which I sawe lying here ready of a houge bigness.[62]

Although Fraser took great satisfaction in having seen things for himself, he did so at a level of understanding dictated by his own limited visual education; he was, on the other hand, highly sensitive to the word, especially to the inscription, and the emblem. No coincidence that, amid celebrated statues in the streets and squares of Florence, his eye rested most gladly on a simple *impresa*: joined hands and the motto 'CONCORDIA'.[63] He was drawn to this simple verbal and visual artefact, such as might have been found in northern Scotland on a painted ceiling in a burgess house, or on one of the carved fireplaces of Huntly Castle: the emblem was always the form of visual culture with which early modern Scotland was most at ease. Fraser was inward with more vernacular aspects of Italian culture, however: he had a fluent command of the language as spoken in the streets, and he ate, lived, and worked with Italians, frequented the popular theatre,[64] queued for free dinners on festal days,[65] and even had his fortune told in a tavern.[66] This very Scottish pattern of assimilation to the local community gave him a stratum of knowledge which few, if any, élite travellers would have cared to acquire.

A last contrast: Evelyn naturally acquired paintings, copies after the antique, and objects of *virtú* as a prime objective of travel in Italy, not the least of his acquisitions being the celebrated *pietra dura* cabinet now in the Victoria and Albert Museum.[67] Fraser acquired only what he could carry on the long walk home: his own sketches and diary entries, a handful of coins, a few printed pages, the ivory mort-head which Fr Henderson had given him. These, carried by foot all the way back to the north-westernmost frontiers of the republic of learning, were the raw materials for the three volumes of his *Triennial Travels*.

Notes

1 These three volumes of manuscript journals form Aberdeen University Library, MS 2538 (henceforth TT).

2 Cosmo A. Gordon, ed., 'Professor James Garden's Letters to John Aubrey', in *The Miscellany of the Third Spalding Club* (Aberdeen: Spalding Club, 1960), pp. 42–50; John Aubrey, *Three Prose Works*, ed. John Buchanan-Brown (Fontwell: Centaur Press, 1972), pp. 117–20.

3 Aberdeen University Library, MS 630.

4 Edited by John Buchanan-Brown in *Three Prose Works*.

5 TT I, f. 18v.

6 *Ibid.*, f. 31r.

7 TT II, f. 173r: '[The Spaniards] will debat upon the mater wt the English and question the certainty of the Relation. Father Manners Rector of the Scots College told them plainely, he was no forger of newes, nor was it the custome to coin such Relations, yett upon that head he would beat a hundered Spanish Pistoles that Oliver Cromwell died September 3 at Whythall and his corps privatly removed from thence to Somerset House: and his Funeralls ordered to be celebrated at a vaster charge than hath formerly beene used for the best of Kings in the richest times: which were the words of the Letter.'

8 *Ibid.*

9 *Ibid.*, f. 185v.

10 Joad Raymond, 'An Eye-Witness to King Cromwell', *History Today*, July 1997, pp. 35–41.

11 David Worthington, *Rev. James Fraser, 1634–1709: A New Perspective on the Scottish Highlands Before Culloden* (Edinburgh: Edinburgh University Press, 2023).

12 TT II, f. 80r.

13 *Ibid.*, f. 56r.

14 *Ibid.*, f. 14r.

15 *Ibid.*, f. 99v.

16 The cardinal was assembling a collection that would form the *Biblioteca Barberini*, which remained in the family's possession until purchased by the Vatican in 1902. It was then incorporated into the *Biblioteca Apostolica Vaticana*.
17 TT II, f. 175r.
18 TT III, f. 103v.
19 *Ibid.*, f. 120r.
20 TT II, f. 22v.
21 Reference hereafter is to Evelyn's *Diary*, edited by William Bray as *The Memoirs of John Evelyn Esq. F.R.S.* (London: Henry Colburn, 1827).
22 Fern Insh, 'Recusants and the Rosary: A Seventeenth-Century Chapel in Aberdeen', *British Catholic History*, 31.2 (2012), pp. 195–218.
23 William Orem, *A Description of the Chanonry, Cathedral, and King's College of Old Aberdeen, in the Years 1724–5* (Aberdeen: John Rettie, 1830), pp. 68–73.
24 TT II, f. 46v; the seventeenth-century Aberdeenshire ballad *the Young Laird of Craigston*, more familiar as *The Trees They Do Grow High*, has the painfully young husband sent to 'the College', where he 'plays at the ball', and there are other traces of a very early form of football (in the modern sense) being played at King's College Aberdeen. Once more Fraser is seeing Italy in the visual language of his early formation.
25 Cf. Chapter 2.
26 TT II, f. 47v.
27 *Ibid.*, f. 47r.
28 R. W. Lightbown, 'Ex-votos in Gold and Silver: A Forgotten Art', *The Burlington Magazine*, 121.915 (June 1979), pp. 353–9.
29 TT II, f. 23r.
30 Johannes Wilde, *Michelangelo: Six Lectures* (Oxford: Oxford University Press, 1978), p. 9.
31 TT II, f. 23v.
32 Most likely the 1564 bust by Daniele da Volterra, now in the Galleria dell'Accademia in Florence.
33 TT II, f. 53v.
34 *Ibid.*, f. 23v.
35 *Ibid.*, ff. 23v–24r.
36 Athanasius Kircher, ed. and trans. Jane Stevenson, Anastasi Callinicos, and Daniel Höhr, *The Celebrated Museum of the Roman College of the Society of Jesus: A Facsimile of the 1678 Amsterdam Edition of Giorgio de Sepi's Description of Athanasius Kircher's Museum* (Philadelphia: St Joseph's University Press, 2015).
37 TT II, f. 24r.
38 *Ibid.*
39 *Ibid.*
40 *Ibid.*, f. 25r.This altar was never installed, and elements of it were reused in the eighteenth century. The seventeenth-century altar and ciborium for the Chapel of the Princes in San Lorenzo, a remarkable ensemble which was never to be completed, was kept in a room of the Uffizi Gallery, then dismantled in 1779, and its countless elements in semi-precious stones were reused in the creation

of three new altars: that of the Palatine Chapel; that of the Basilica of San Lorenzo; and that of the chapel of the villa of Poggio Imperiale, which was dismantled in 1820 [www.uffizi.it/en/artworks/paltine-chapel-altar (retrieved 2 August 2023)].

41 Evelyn, *Diary*, I, p. 144.

42 This was a Medici showpiece; see David Howarth, *Lord Arundel and his Circle* (New Haven, CT: Yale University Press, 1985) pp. 21, 226 fn 31.

43 Fraser's list of painters is garbled: almost all the names are new to him, and he creates at least one notable chimera. 'For Painters & Sculptores their picturs and statues some in Alabaster others on Colloures are here sett up and had in high esteeme by all the beholders. They are verie manie, such as, Michaell Angelo, Andrea del Sarto and Raphaell Urbin; the 3 non such of their age in Europ for painting are set up in one size be themselves: rarely done & wt great Life. Laurentius Cion, Franciscus Bartolomeo, Al. Alori, Andrea Varruchio; Titianus Vinci; Hans Holbain, Baccio Bandinell; Jacomo Pontero Joannes De Bologna all Singular Painters, whose names for my oune Satisfaction I have sett doune.' TT II, f. 30v.

44 Evelyn, *Diary*, I, p. 139.

45 TT II, f. 21v.

46 *Ibid.*, f. 34v.

47 Evelyn, *Diary*, I, p. 155.

48 TT II, f. 55v.

49 *Ibid.*, f. 55r.

50 This was James Alban Gibbs, a neo-Latin poet of real distinction.

51 Evelyn, *Diary*, I, p. 156.

52 TT II, f. 56r.

53 *Ibid.*

54 Cf. Maarten Delebke and Anne-Françoise Morel, 'Roma Antica, Sacra, Moderna: The Analogous Romes of the Travel Guide', *Library Trends*, 61.2 (2012) ['Information and Space: Analogies and Metaphors', Wouter Van Acker and Pieter Uyttenhove (eds.)], pp. 397–417.

55 Evelyn, *Diary*, I, p. 162.

56 *Ibid.*, p. 166.

57 *Ibid.*, p. 200.

58 *Ibid.*, p. 212.

59 TT II, f. 176r.

60 *Ibid.*, f. 76r.

61 *Ibid.*, f .62v. No early modern Scot seems able to spell 'library' consistently; I conjecture that the word 'biblioteck' would have been the more usual term.

62 *Ibid.*, f. 57v.

63 *Ibid.*, f. 23r.

64 *Ibid.*, f. 185v.

65 *Ibid.*, ff. 156–57.

66 *Ibid.*, f. 178v.

67 See https://collections.vam.ac.uk/item/O9058/the-john-evelyn-cabinet-cabinet-on-stand-benotti-domenico (retrieved 3 August 2023).

2

The Jesuits and the languages of Britain: the case of Robert Corbie SJ

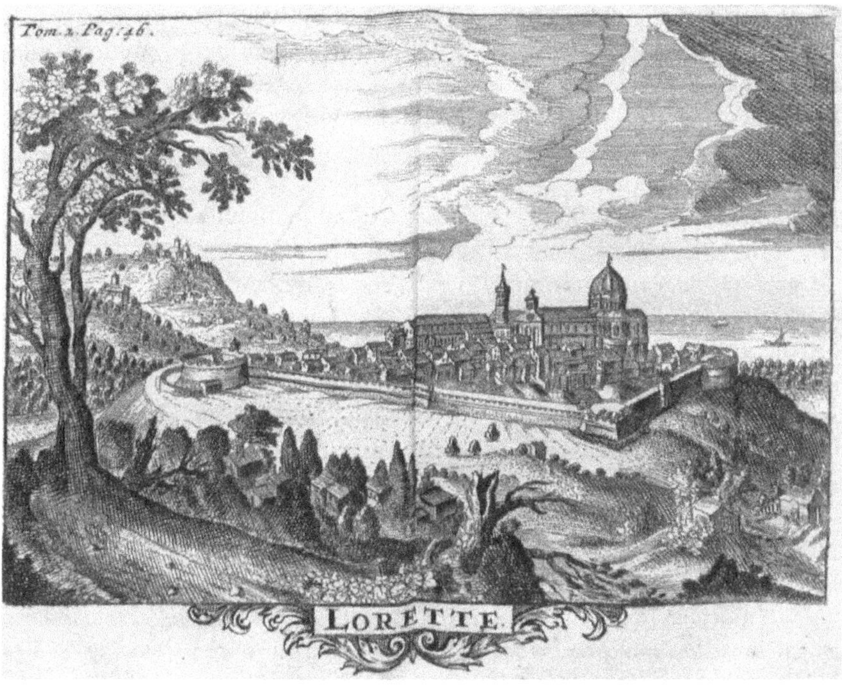

Figure 2.1 A view of Loreto, from Alexandre de Rogissart, *Les Delices de l'Italie*, volume II (Leiden: Pieter van der Aa, 1709).

To understand the perceptions of Britain and Ireland among Catholics exiled from the three kingdoms, it has to be realised that the Protestant regime in England was engaged, from the time of the Henrician schism onwards, in the enterprise of rewriting history. England had to be recast as independent of the Continent, and as naturally superior within the archipelago. Generalisations on English centrality and superiority are found in

Spenser, Camden, and John Speed, as well as in the infinitely less subtle and reputable works of propagandists such as John Bale, who was early in the articulation of the thesis of the natural supremacy of the English over the Irish.[1] This chapter is about the cultural response, especially the linguistic response, in the exiled Catholic communities on the Continent to this kind of rewriting of religious and cultural history.

I have written at length elsewhere of the Catholic responses to the new histories emerging from Protestant England and of the forms which these took in the cultural life of the exiled English colleges and religious houses on the Continent.[2] In early modern Europe, it was usual to argue merit from antiquity, and so these confessional arguments are to a considerable extent a war over possession of the past. This contention found expression in allegorical historical drama,[3] and in the devising of emblems and iconographies. The battle for the past was also extended into the realm of the visual arts, not only through the publication of engraved depictions of martyrdoms but also, as we shall see in Chapter 6, in imaginary depictions of ancestors and monarchs.[4]

Another form of direct response to the national mythmaking of Protestant England is a Jesuit college play which adapts and changes aspects of Camden's historical narrative to expound Catholic perceptions of antiquity and continuity: Joseph Simons's *Mercia or piety crowned*, first performed at Saint-Omer in February 1624.[5] This play opposes the evil deceits of the pagan priests of ancient Mercia to the benign figure of the seventh-century Catholic hermit-bishop St Chad. The saint is depicted as a force of pristine virtue, the agent who reveals truth, truly at home in the deep oak woods of England. This figure of benign Catholicism is a powerful counterweight to Milton's (subsequent, perhaps responsive) imagination of malign Catholicism infiltrating the deep forests on the Welsh frontiers of England, the enchanter Comus.[6] In Milton's masque, the dangerous, quasi-Catholic, outland magician exists at the edge of English civilisation (and English language) in an entertainment devised for the English élite governing 1630s Wales from the frontier castle at Ludlow.

But now I turn to the main focus of this chapter: the ways in which the exiled Catholic community, especially members of the Society of Jesus, perceived a diverse Britain and Ireland, made up of a diversity of peoples and languages. In every part of the seventeenth-century world, the Jesuit enterprise extended to language and the learning of languages, as well as to drama, controversy, and poetry, and this very much applies to Jesuit perceptions of Britain and Ireland.

Four inscriptions surviving in the nave of the Basilica at Loreto (Marche, Italy), by Robert Corbie (or Corbington) SJ (1596–1637), are the point of departure for this preliminary investigation: they describe the miracles of the Holy House of Loreto in Irish, Scots, Welsh, and English – descriptions written by an Englishmen who had learned the other languages of the archipelago (see Figure 2.1).[7] Corbie was himself a graduate of the English College at Valladolid, the linguistic policies of which are discussed below.

These inscriptions provide an example of the complete inversion of an expected pattern of language use, whereby a speaker of a 'minority' language would learn English or communicate (as was frequently the case) with educated English speakers in spoken or written Latin. These inscriptions are logically part of a global Jesuit cultural policy, however, which applies to the diverse cultures of Britain as much as to the cultures of the Americas or of the Far East. The Jesuit policy of cultural accommodation as applied here to the three kingdoms and four peoples, the learning of the languages of those who have no access either to Latin or to Standard English, could not offer a starker contrast to Tudor supremacism. When the Aberdonian wandering scholar James Fraser arrived in Loreto in the 1650s, he fell in with two friendly expatriated countrymen, who gave him a copy of Corbie's text, the broadside printed in Scots (he could presumably have equally well understood the Irish):

> I saw ther Father William Monteth and Father Allexr Sharp Scotts Jesuites whom I found exceeding Civill and kind. Evrie pilgrim that comes here getts a printed paper given him containing the narration of the flitting and transport of the holy house of Loretta and Father Monteith gave me one the verie expres words without altering one sillable I have sett doune here. In the old plaine Scottish Language as followeth …[8]

I would like to consider the career of the Jesuit linguist who wrote the multilingual inscriptions still to be seen in the Basilica of the Holy House at Loreto. Robert Corbie SJ (his alias surnames were 'Corbington' and 'Flower') was born at Dublin in about 1596, his Catholic parents having fled to Ireland from religious persecution in their native north of England. (His two brothers were also Jesuits: B. Ralph Corbie SJ was martyred at Tyburn in 1644; Ambrose Corbie/Corbington SJ, 1604–1649, was a professor at the Collegio Romano.) Robert Corbie was partially brought up thereafter in the north of England and educated on the Continent, initially at the Jesuit seminary at Watten. Importantly, he was at the English College in Valladolid in 1615, and among his fellow students in that year is recorded one 'Nicholaus Pritchardus, Cambrobrittanus'.[9] In 1624 he was on the English mission in Durham.[10] He appears to have taken his final vows as a Jesuit in 1626; thereafter he was in Rome,[11] and subsequently at Loreto (1634–35), acting in both places as confessor to Irish and British pilgrims.[12] He was sent to London in 1636,[13] and died in England, once more in Durham, on 17 April

1637. The assessment of his character preserved by the meticulous reports of the Jesuits is that he was well educated in 'humane letters', albeit mediocre as a practitioner of them, but a skilled theologian. He was described as in good health, but 'choleric' in temperament.[14]

Although we can assume that he learned Irish in his childhood, and Welsh from his fellow students, how he learned Scots is less certain; it is wholly possible that he had contact with Scottish Jesuits in Rome, or that he had heard Scots spoken frequently in the north of England. Certainly, the Scots language in his inscription is convincing and wholehearted, as this example demonstrates:

> The Kirk of Laureto was a caumber of the house of the Blest Virgin neir Ierusalem in the toune of Nazaret, in whilk she was borne and teende up, and greeted by the Angel, and thairin also conceaved and nourisht har sonne IESVS whill he was he was twalle zear avvd. This caumber, efter the Ascensione of our B. Saviour was by the Apostles hallowed as a *Kirk* in honur of our B. Ledy, and S. *Luke* framed a pictur to har vary lyknes thair zit to be seine.[15]

It is a remarkable artefact: one of the few surviving examples of early modern Scots as a learned language.[16] It challenges many preconceptions about hierarchy of language in the early modern world, but it is, in fact, in accord with the universal Jesuit policy of the use of every vernacular which can be learned.

Hints of how the global linguistic policy of the Jesuits on minority languages was applied to the languages of Scotland can be recovered from manuscript material in their Roman archives. There is scattered evidence in these documents that the Jesuits were well aware of the linguistic disposition of Scotland, of the possibility of an Irish Gaelic speaker serving the Gaelic-speaking Scottish Highlanders, of the difference between Scots and English in the Lowlands, and of the difficulties and questionable usefulness of sending an Englishman on the Scottish mission.

This can be traced in a series of letters and memoranda of various administrators of the small but valiant Jesuit mission to seventeenth-century Scotland – all variations on the essential perception of the distinction of Highland and Lowland, and the parallel perception that the Scots and the English are antipathetic, being divided by custom, law, and language, and that their antipathy is to be compared to that of the Castilian and the Portuguese, the diversity of language to Dutch and German.[17] An early seventeenth-century memorandum on the state of Scotland also emphasises that only Scots are of service on the Scottish mission, except for the Gaelic Highlands, which may be served from Ireland. Indeed, there was one Irish Jesuit definitely on the mission in the Highlands in the later part of the century.[18] The memorandum goes further in asserting that Scots and English are barely mutually intelligible as spoken languages, and that it is extremely difficult for an English speaker to adapt his dialect to one acceptable to the Scots.[19] As late as 1713 the Scottish Jesuit returns are still distinguishing between those who know Scots or English as opposed to 'Erse'.[20]

This awareness was also shown in 1592, when the English College at Valladolid received the king of Spain, Philip II. As part of the ceremonial which welcomed the monarch, he was offered a series of orations in the various languages known to students and staff of the college, among which were Welsh and Scots.[21] It is possible that this inclusion of Welsh and Scots (and, indeed, on a subsequent occasion – August 1600 – Cornish)[22] was part of a deliberate policy of linguistic inclusiveness: a revised representation of British diversity, formulated in exile.

What is said about the Scots language in the 1592 Valladolid record is in itself interesting (although, unfortunately, the oration's own text has not survived):[23]

> Subio luego el sexto, que dixo en lengua Escocesa: la qual come se usa ordinariamente in la Corte, y mejores partes de Escocia, no es muy differente se nostra lengua Inglesa, como V.M. sabe (aunque en las partes de las montañas de aquel Reyno, y en las Islas circunuezinas de Orcades, y Hebrides, su lengua es Irlandesa) y esta es la causa que algunos de nuestra nacion, que nacieron hazia las partes del Norte de Inglaterra, o han tenido al guntrato en aquel Reyno, hablan aquella lengua, y el deste dia la hablò con harta propiedad …
>
> [Then followed the sixth, which was in the Scottish language. That which is used ordinarily in the Court and in the greater part of Scotland, as Your Majesty knows, it is not much different from our English language (however, in the mountainous parts of that kingdom and in the offshore Islands, as the Orcades and Hebrides, their language is Irish) and that is the reason that some of our nation born in the Northern parts of England speak that language, through contact with that nation, and it was spoken on that day with the fullest accuracy …]

Again, this suggests that the boundaries between the languages are permeable and that this part of exiled England is perfectly respectful of Scots as a language in its own right.

A further example of Jesuit openness to the languages of Britain is found in a manuscript recording the *chapelle ardente* constructed in the Venerable English College in Rome to mark the funeral of Cardinal Odoardo Farnese, who died on 21 February 1626. The cardinal was distantly related to the house of Lancaster, and had at one time nursed not wholly realistic ambitions of inheriting the English throne. He had acted as Cardinal Protector of England, and as protector of the English colleges in Douai, Valladolid, and Rome.[24] For all these reasons, it was particularly fitting that he should be commemorated by the English College. The *chapelle ardente*, adorned with emblems exploring symbolic aspects of the heraldic lilies of the Farnese, and with verses, including verses in English, Irish, and Welsh, was erected in the chapel, and then commemorated in the Farnese funeral manuscript. By this time Robert Corbie was in Rome, and it is not impossible that he could have played some part in confecting or adapting these verses, just possibly as author of the Welsh lines, and involved, if only as scribe, with the Irish verse.

Fr Micheàl MacCraith of the University of Galway has most generously communicated his expert findings on the Irish 12-line 'sonnet', namely that it recycles verses composed in the Spanish Netherlands by Bonabhentura Ó hEodhasa and published in a pamphlet annexed to his *Teagasg Críosdaidhe* ('Christian Doctrine') published at Antwerp in 1611. The Irish Franciscan scholar Anthony Hickey, who had spent seven years in Louvain before coming to Rome, is a very probable candidate for the person to have transmitted the verses. In this case, it is possible that Corbie may have been involved in this Irish verse only as scribe.[25]

His involvement with the Welsh verse, which is on the adjacent page in the Farnese manuscript, is perhaps more complex. On the evidence of the Loreto inscription, and of the fact that Corbie's duties at Loreto would have potentially included hearing confessions in Welsh, it is safe to conclude that he had a reasonable command of the language. There are inconsistencies in the Welsh verse which might be those of a learner attempting composition in a language only partly mastered,[26] although it has some sense of Welsh poetic idiom. The verse begins:

> Crwylaist pen welaist a Chalon dolorus

And might be translated:

> Thou looked closely when thou sawest, with grieved heart,
> My wretched tears and my face in misery,
> being the mark of the death of some dear kinsman:
> 'Tell me, Welshman, why dost thou lament?'
> 'It is neither a friend who preserved me, nor a brother who has caused me this pain;
> Nor is it a father who has brought about this grief of mine;
> But rather it is a common father, the whole company of Wales in one,
> And the patron-dignitary of the lands.
> The finest fragrant herb in the garden,
> It was as fair, as lovely, and as blessed to see him
> as to look upon fresh snow –
> alas, that he has died so soon!'[27]

Content here to raise only the possibility of Corbie's involvement with these verses in Welsh and Irish, there can be no doubt that the Farnese Funeral Manuscript is typical of the multilingual apprehension of the archipelago which prevailed in the exiled British and Irish colleges.

What can we conclude from this very preliminary survey of the three kingdoms seen from the perspective of Catholic exile? Their perception of the three kingdoms and their languages was more complex than was that allowed by the Anglocentric focus of the propagandist antiquaries of Henry VIII and Elizabeth of England, and this complexity was closely related to Jesuit perceptions of linguistic realities on the ground, as well as to Jesuit cultural policies of acculturation. There is a vast quantity of work still to be done on those aspects of the high cultures of Wales, Scotland, and Ireland which are preserved in the surviving archives and libraries of the British and Irish Catholic colleges now or formerly on the Continent.

Appendix

A Roman cantata associated with the Corbie family

Robert Corbie's brother, B. Ralph Corbie (1598–1644), was a Jesuit missionary in the north of England, arrested while saying Mass at Hamsterley Hall on 8 July 1644, detained in Newgate Prison in London and tried on 4 September the same year, and executed in London three days later. There is the text of a cantata, employing an effective, if not unprecedented, variation on the image of the martyr as the athlete of God, whereby Corbie in his martyrdom is figured as *pugil Dei*, 'God's fighter', even 'God's boxer'. It is tempting to associate this text with the third Corbie brother, Ambrose, professor of rhetoric in the Collegio Romano and author of a hagiographical account of three Jesuits martyred on the English mission (including his brother), *Certamen Triplex*, published at Antwerp in 1646.[28]

Cantus de R P. Rodulpho Corbaeo, dum post Examinationem Londini, in carcerem Noua Porta nomen est, ob Religone[m] Catholica[m] coniiceretur

Chorus

Angusta nouae limina portae
Succede Pugil Noua porta tibi
Aurea pandet limina caeli.

[Voce sola recitatiua]
Ingredere nigri carceris umbras:
Perfer amate crucis aerumnas
Auferet umbras aeterna dies

Merces Crucis est aeterna quies.
O illa dies! O illa quies!
Pretio quouis mereanda dies!
Mille catenis crucibus mille.
Nece millena redimenda quies!

Chorus
Hanc suspiret, corpere vincto,
Mente soluta pectoris ardor.
Optet, anhelet generosus amor.

[Voce sola recitatiua]
Eia caducas exue curas.
Laeta propinquat, fausta propinquat
Instat amanti, venit optanti.
O illa breuis mora tormenti.
Illa o felix hora coronae!
Laetare pugil. momenta tibi
Fragilis vitae pauca supersunt:
Spatia ad meta[m] pauca supersunt
Citat ad pugna[m], citat ad palma[m].
Amor ille tuus, vita, salusq[ue],
Dux tuus, et lux dulcis Iesus.
Pretiosa sacro laurea capiti
Im[m]inet horto sata caelesti
Cingetq[ue], coma[m] fronde perenim

Chorus
Auspice Iesu, Iesuque Duce,
Gaudente polo, mirante solo,
Spectante Deo vince, triumpha.

Canticle on the reverent Father Ralph Corbie, when after interrogation in London, in the prison called Newgate, he was confined for the Catholic Religion

Chorus

O fighter, step over the strait thresholds of Newgate; the golden thresholds of heaven lie open to you.

Solo voice recitative

Endure entering the shadows of a dark prison, the afflictions of a beloved cross; the shadows will bring you an eternal day. Eternal rest is the reward of the Cross. O, that day! O, that rest! Day to be deserved at whatever price, a thousand chains, a thousand torments, peace to be recovered from a thousand deaths!

Chorus

Adoration of the heart will sigh this, having conquered the body and freed the mind; noble love will desire, will breathe it.

Solo voice recitative

Put away your fleeing cares. The happy [hour] approaches, the blessed hour approaches. He comes to the beloved, to the desired. O, that brief delay. O that happy hour of the crown! Fighter, rejoice! A few moments separate you from fragile life. A tiny space separates you from the goal. He hastens to the fight, he rushes to the palm [of victory]. Sweet Jesus is your love, your life, and your health, your leader and your life. A precious laurel awaits your sacred head, native to the heavenly garden, it will surround it with wreathy leaves for ever.

Chorus

With Jesus looking down, and with Jesus as leader, the heavens rejoice, the sun wonders, and with God looking on, you conquer, you triumph.

Notes

1 John Bale, *The Vocacyon of Ioha[n] Bale to the Bishiprick of Ossorie in Irela[n]de his Persecucio[n]s in ye Same, & Finall Delyueraunce* (Rome: J. Lambrecht[?] for Hugh Singleton, 1553); William Camden, *Britannia siue Florentissimorum Regnorum, Angliae, Scotiae, Hiberniae, et Insularum Adiacentium ex Intima Antiquitate Chorographica Descriptio* (London: R. Newbery, 1586); John Speed, *The History of Great Britaine under the Conquests of ye Romans, Saxons, Danes and Normans* (London: [William Hall and John Beale], 1611).

2 Cf. Chapters 6 to 8 below; see also Peter Davidson, 'The Solemnity of the Madonna Vulnerata, Valladolid, 1600', in Peter Davidson and Jill Bepler (eds), *The Triumphs of the Defeated: Early Modern Festivals and Messages of Legitimacy* (Wiesbaden: Harrasowitz, 2007), pp. 39–54; 'Recusant Catholic Spaces in Early Modern England', in Ronald Corthell, Frances E. Dolan, Christopher Highley, and Arthur F. Marotti (eds), *Catholic Culture in Early Modern England* (Notre Dame, IN: University of Notre Dame Press,

2007), pp. 19–51; and '*Donec Templa Refeceris*: British Catholicism, Roman Antiquity, Historical Contention', in Cinzia Maria Sicca (ed.), *John Talman: An Early-Eighteenth-Century Connoisseur* (New Haven, CT: Yale University Press, 2008), pp. 77–96. An account of the cultural life of the English College at Valladolid can be found in Javier Burrieza Sánchez, *Una Isla de Inglaterra en Castilla: Exposición* (Palencia: V. Merino, 2000).

3 There are many examples out of the substantial repertory which survives: the anonymous *Psyche et Filii Eius*, performed at Valladolid in 1615, is an allegory of a family divided by religious and political faction; *Leo Armenus*, performed at Saint-Omers in the 1620s and revived at Rome in the 1640s, applies the iconoclast controversies in Byzantium allegorically first to the desecration of English religious houses under Henry, Edward, and Elizabeth and (in the 1645 revival) to iconoclasm by the English Parliamentarians.

4 Most famously in the engraved representations of the martyr paintings on the walls of the chapel of the English College in Rome: Niccolò Circignano, *Ecclesiae Anglicanae Trophaea ... Passiones, Romae in Collegio Anglico per N. Circinianum Depictae* (Rome: Bartolomeo Grassi, 1584). See also Gauvin Alexander Bailey, *Between Renaissance and Baroque: Jesuit Art in Rome 1565–1610* (Toronto: Toronto University Press, 2003), pp. 122–65.

5 A useful translation by R.F. Grady SJ can be found in *Jesuit Theater Englished*, ed. Louis J. Oldani SJ and Philip C. Fisher SJ (St Louis: Institute of Jesuits Sources, 1989), pp. 79–159. For advice on all this material I am indebted to Professor Alison Shell of University College London.

6 John Milton, *A Maske Presented at Ludlow Castle, 1634 on Michaelmasse Night, before the Right Honorable, Iohn Earle of Bridgewater, Vicount Brackly, Lord Praesident of Wales, and One of His Maiesties Most Honorable Privie Counsell* (London: [Augustine Mathewes] for Humphrey Robinson, 1637). In the context of Milton's imagination of the marches as the place where a dangerous, quasi-Catholic figure can operate, it is worth recollecting the degree to which the remoter territories of the marches provided a refuge to recusant Catholics. In 1605 the Anglican bishop of Hereford's men 'did make diligent search all that night, and daie following, from village to village from house to house, about thirtie miles compasse, neere the confines of Monmouthshiere, where they found houses full of alters, images, bookes of superstition, Reliques of idolatry, but left desolate of men and weomen, except here or there an aged weoman, or a child, all were fledd into Wales, and but one man apprehended'; see *Records Relating to Catholicism in the South Wales Marches*, ed. John Hobson Matthews (London: Catholic Record Society, 1906), p. 289.

7 These inscriptions are reproduced as illustrations in Floriano Grimaldi, *La Historia della Chiesa di Santa Maria di Loreto* (Loreto: Cassa di Risparmio di Loreto, 1993), pp. 500–10; Grimaldi also reproduces the texts of contemporary broadsheets which printed Corbington's inscriptions with woodcuts of the Holy House. All were printed at Loreto by Francesco Serafini. The English version is *The Miraculous Origin and Translation of the Church of our B. Lady of Loreto* (1634); the Welsh version is *Dechrevad a Rhyfedhvs Esmviad Eglwys*

yr Arglw y Dhes Fair O Loreto (1635); and the Scots version is *the Wondrus Flittinge of the Kirk of Our B. Ledy of Loreto* (1635). The Irish version, *Tosach Agus Aistriugha Miorbhuileach Thempoill Mhuire Loreto*, was printed in Irish type at Rome in 1707.

8 Aberdeen University Library, MS 2538, II, f. 48v.

9 The manuscript *Liber Alumnorum* or matriculation book in the archives of the English College at Valladolid lists 'Nicolaus Prichardus' as no. 51, 'Robertus Florus alias Corbingtonus' as no. 362. For a concise, and precise, summary of Corbington's career, see the entry on him in Thomas M. McCoog SJ, *English and Welsh Jesuits, 1555–1650* (London: Catholic Record Society, 1994), pp. 146–7.

10 Archivium Romanum Societatis Iesu (hereafter ARSI), MS Anglia 11, f. 27r, '1624. Rodolphus Corbingtonus in miss. Dunelmensi'.

11 ARSI, MS Anglia 11, f. 8r.

12 ARSI, MS Hist Soc 46, f. 47r.

13 ARSI, MS Anglia 10, f. 189v.

14 *Ibid.*, f. 94r; he is described as 'sanguine' in the report for the following year, on f. 121r.

15 Grimaldi, *La Historia della Chiesa di Santa Maria di Loreto*, p. 510.

16 One feature of the Scots grapholect, witnessed *passim* in the writings of his near-contemporary James Fraser, has eluded him: a Scot would have written 'quhilk', not 'whilk'. We might also expect 'chaulmer'.

17 ARSI, MS Anglia 42, f. 36r.

18 *Ibid.* 41, f. 251r, which records the sending of one Irishman into 'illam regni Scotici partem ubi sola Hibernica lingua in usu est' ['into that region of the kingdom of Scotland where Irish is the only language used'].

19 *Ibid.* 42, f. 36r, memorandum on the state of Scotland, early seventeenth century. Other reflections on language, including the Gaelic speech of the 'barbarian ... heretic' Argyll, can be found on ff. 20r–v, 41v–42r, 179r–80v.

20 *Ibid.* 24a, f. 9r et seq.

21 See Mgr Michael Williams, *St. Alban's College Valladolid: Four Centuries of English Catholic Presence in Spain* (London: Hurst, 1986), pp. 11–12. An independent Scots College was not established in Spain until 1623, and, before that, it is just possible that there were Scottish students at Valladolid.

22 There is no trace of the texts of any of these orations in the college archives at Valladolid. The Cornish Oration was probably delivered by Richard Pentreth, who joined the college in April 1600 and left for Douai in spring 1601, arriving there in July. *Registers of the English College at Valladolid*, ed. Mgr Edwin Henson (London: Catholic Record Society, 1930), p. 59.

23 Thomas Eclesal, *Relacion de un Sacerdote Ingles, Escrita a Flandres ... en la qual de la cuenta de la venida de su Magestad a Valladolid, y al Collegio de los Ingeses...Traduiza... por Tomas Eclesal Cavallero Ingles* (Madrid: Pedro Madrigal, 1592); Gregoria de Mediola SJ, *Historia y Milagros de Nuesta Señora La Vulnerata* (Valladolid: Bartolome Portiles, 1667), p. 24, also recalls the orations and verses 'en varias lenguas'.

24 I am grateful to Professor Maurice Whitehead, archivist of the Venerable English College, for drawing my attention to this manuscript, and to Professor Fr. Micheàl MacCraith of the University of Galway and to Geraint Evans of the University of Wales at Swansea for their expert advice on this manuscript. I am also profoundly indebted to my Oxford colleagues Professor Mark Williams of St Edmund Hall and Fr Brian MacCuarta SJ of Campion Hall for their most generous help and advice.

25 Professor MacCraith has kindly made available to me his seminar paper on the Irish verse in the manuscript, which also points out that Corbie was, potentially, not the only Irish speaker in the college in the later 1620s.

26 My Oxford colleague Professor Mark Williams thinks that Corbie is a more likely candidate as author of this verse than any Welsh resident of the college. He points out anomalous spellings – 'pen' for 'pan', 'pamywd' for 'pam wyd', 'cyphredinal' for 'cyphredinawl', 'wylofaint' for 'wylofain' – which he categorises as 'learner's errors'. He also identifies Latinisms: '[P]lural for singular, an attempt at apposition in a way that would be fine in Latin, but makes a genitive construction in Welsh.' Geraint Evans, who has also most generously communicated work in progress, will publish his own, different, deductions on authorship in a forthcoming article, ' "La Wallica": Welsh poems in the Farnese MS (Rome, 1626)' in *Studia Celtica.*

27 Translation most kindly supplied by Professor Mark Williams.

28 This text was rediscovered by my friend and colleague Christopher Archibald in the British Jesuit Archives, Mount Street, London (ABSI, Anglia V, f. 42v). I would like to emphasise his generosity in encouraging me to reproduce it here. It is the text of a cantata performed in Ralph Corbie's memory, in Rome, shortly after his death. The manuscript was formerly at Stonyhurst College, Lancashire. Henry Foley SJ, *The Records of the English Province of the Society of Jesus* (London: Burns and Oates, 1883), III, pp. 95–6.

3

Gentileschi and the ancestors

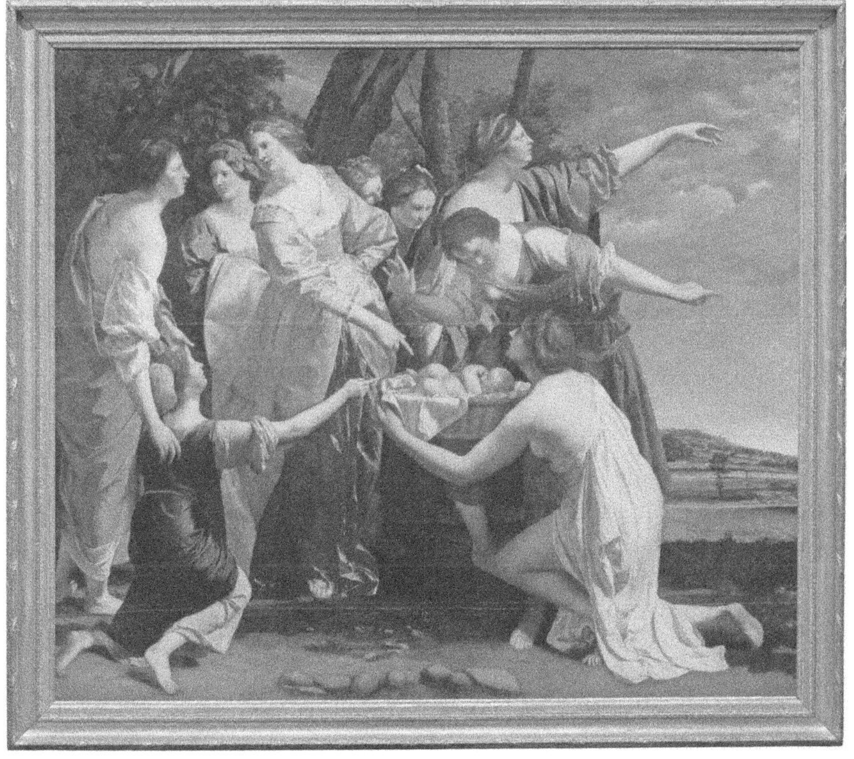

Figure 3.1 Orazio Gentileschi, *The Finding of Moses*, 1630–32, oil on canvas. © The National Gallery, London.

A haunting and elusive element, vital to a full understanding of Orazio Gentileschi's *The Finding of Moses*, recently purchased by the National Gallery, is the degree to which it is a dynastic, rather than primarily a religious, picture (shown in Figure 3.1). A crucial element of the court cultures of James I and Charles I, which appears to remain invisible to many interpreters, is the element of iconography, belief, and mythology which they brought with them from Scotland. This would seem to be the case with Gentileschi's painting, which hides in plain sight the imaginary portrait of the legendary ancestor of Charles I, and of the recently born future Charles II, namely the mother of the unbroken line of over one hundred kings of Scotland: Scota, the daughter of Pharaoh.

Aidan Weston-Lewis raised this possibility briefly in his excellent article published in *Apollo* in 1997, but few if any scholars have followed up the suggestions which that article presents. The current National Gallery interpretation of the painting suppresses the possibility entirely. It is the aim of this chapter to show that there is a vast hinterland of widely disseminated Scottish origin myth underlying the iconography of this painting, which Weston-Lewis dates convincingly to 1630–32, the two years after the birth of the heir, the future Charles II, on 29 May 1630. It seems highly likely, as he argues, that it was commissioned with the intention that it should hang in the then still incomplete Queen's House at Greenwich, and that its primary purpose is dynastic, celebrating a birth that adds another future king to the long line of Stuarts with their fabulous origin in Egypt. Weston-Lewis draws attention also to the currency of the mythical descent of the kings of Scots in the post-Restoration decoration of Holyroodhouse in Edinburgh for Charles II. It is the intention of this chapter to add to this excellent beginning a considerable quantity of detail about the origin myth and its dissemination, to bring forward the degree to which this myth was central to the iconography of the spectacle which welcomed Charles I to Edinburgh on 23 June 1633,[1] and to recall that the same spectacle exhibited a 'humanist Parnassus' of learned Scots, including two of the best-known disseminators of the myth: Hector Boece (Boethius) and the Latinist George Buchanan.[2]

I argue further that there is a quiet allusion to this origin myth in Thomas Carew's 1634 masque *Coelum Britannicum* and that the apotheosis at the end of that masque, together with the aspirations expressed by its concluding songs, inhabits an iconographic region very close indeed to that of the ceiling of *The Arts of Peace*, which was painted by Gentileschi for the Great Hall in Greenwich in 1635–38. I argue in conclusion that, taken together, the two Gentileschi paintings known to have hung in the Great Hall – *The Finding of Moses* and the more problematic *Lot and His Daughters* – can be read in harmony with the ceiling as a celebration of the present and future hopes of the Stuart dynasty, recently strengthened by the birth of a male heir.

Aidan Weston-Lewis's article offers a comprehensive survey of what is known of the date, commissioning, and purpose of *The Finding of Moses*.[3]

Reasoning from the commonwealth sale inventory, which begins its listing of the Queen's House from the Great Hall, he argues that 'the picture may have been painted for the Queen's House at Greenwich, and possibly with a predetermined location in mind'.[4] The placing of *The Finding of Moses* together with Gentileschi's *Lot and His Daughters* under the ceiling of *The Arts of Peace* is the most logical reading of the sequence of entries. He also draws attention to site-specific aspects of the picture:

> [This] offers further visual evidence to suggest that it was painted for a predetermined setting. If we imagine it hanging at right-angles to the left of a window facing the Thames, much better sense could be made of the otherwise somewhat histrionic and distracting gestures of the maidens at the right, since they would have a tangible focus beyond the picture frame (and indeed the building). It should be noted that the outstretched arms of both women ... directs the viewer's attention emphatically to the immediate right of the picture, not to the painted riverscape behind them ... [T]he west wall of the Great Hall would have offered just such a setting.[5]

He goes on to reason that, as a court painter on a salary, Gentileschi may indeed have been commissioned to paint a work intended to hang in a particular space in a still incomplete building, but for which precise plans already existed. He also observes that the reason for the localization of the landscape background of the picture in England 'might lie in the scope afforded by the subject for dynastic flattery'.[6] He suggests further that the most obvious point of reference would be the birth of the future Charles II in May 1630.

There is a simple sense in which both Gentileschi's Old Testament subjects express dynastic continuity: the infant Moses was saved from danger of death, and, more problematically, the incest of Lot's daughters carried on the human race when they believed all others might have perished. I would suggest, however, that the image of the Israelites in Egypt is not one which the Stuart court ever used of itself or of the Stuart dynasty, since until the 1640s the Stuarts never considered themselves as exiled nor in adversity. The iconography is one adopted, rather, by their opponents, the 'godly' English Calvinists, those who would become in time the Parliamentarians. At this point Weston-Lewis advances the Scottish traditional history, writing of 'a tradition of indeterminate origin, which held that the ancestry of the House of Stuart could be traced back through the Irish line to none other than Pharaoh's daughter herself'.[7] He goes on to draw attention to Jan Jakobz de Wet's 1670s work at Holyroodhouse (to which I return later), but says, mistakenly, that 'Stuart claims of descent from Pharaoh's daughter cannot, it seems, be documented as early as the 1630s', while stating perceptively that 'it was this tradition that prompted Gentileschi's choice of subject in the first place'.[8]

A rich context for Gentileschi's *The Finding of Moses* can be constructed if the whole history of the Scottish origin myth is investigated, particularly as there were multiple reasons why it was current in the circle of Charles I in the early 1630s. It is important also to demonstrate that this myth remained alive in Scottish consciousness until it died slowly – and, perhaps, reluctantly – with the publication of the first document-based critical history of early Scotland, by the Abbé Thomas Innes, in 1729.[9] Portraits of the fictitious Scottish kings were painted in all seriousness for Holyroodhouse in Edinburgh as late as the 1670s, and the pervasive myth of the ancient origins and continuous kingship of the Stuarts did much to sustain nascent Jacobite loyalties after 1688, as is witnessed by the incessant use of 'Fergusius' ('descendant of Fergus') as the name for the exiled James II (VII of Scotland) in the brilliant Jacobite Latin epic of the late 1680s, the *Grameid* by James Philip.[10]

Let us examine briefly the history of the complex story which the Scots evolved about their origins in the course of the late Middle Ages and perpetuated down to the eighteenth century.[11] This examination of the tradition of the myth and its persistence and endless reinvention is vital to form an understanding of how ubiquitous this material was in the minds and memories of early modern Scots. The late fourteenth and early fifteenth centuries constituted a period of notable historiographic activity in the Scottish kingdom. The second half of the fourteenth century saw the production both of John of Fordun's major Latin chronicle, *Chronica Gentis Scotorum* – the earliest attempt to write a continuous history of Scotland – and of John Barbour's vernacular verse epic, *The Bruce*. These were followed in the first decades of the fifteenth century by Andrew Wyntoun's rhyming, Scots-language *Orygynale Cronykil of Scotland*. Then, in the 1440s, there was another substantial addition to the burgeoning chronicle tradition, with Walter Bower's Latin *Scotichronicon*, a reworked, expanded, and amended version of Fordun's earlier *Chronica*.

These chroniclers of the fourteenth and fifteenth centuries extracted from the political turmoil and dislocation of the period after 1290, when the line of kings descended from Malcolm Canmore failed, a single story of overwhelming significance, namely the preservation of the Scottish kingdom and its institutions against the ambitions of the English Crown. Directly or indirectly, the works of Fordun, Wyntoun, Barbour, and Bower tended to justify and celebrate the success of the Bruce and Stewart royal line, which emerged victorious from the dynastic and civil wars of this period. They were politically consistent: devoted to the notion of Scottish independence and nationhood, however defined; they also used their texts to present exemplary models of behaviour.

The version of Scotland's origins given by the earliest of these chroniclers, John of Fordun, writing in the 1370s, is that a Greek called Gaythelos (later known as Gathelus) left his native land and went to Egypt, where he met and married Scota, the daughter of the Pharaoh Cenchres, oppressor of the Israelites. After Cenchres had been drowned in the Red Sea, pursuing Moses and his people, Gathelus and Scota left Egypt for Spain, where they settled at Brigancia. Two of their sons, Heber and Himec, went to Ireland and conquered it. Their son Micelius stayed in Spain, but three of his sons, Hibertus, Hermonius, and Partholomus, followed their uncles to Ireland. Finally, one of their descendants, Fergus, went to Scotland and became its first king.[12] This narrative is based on the Irish narrative of their own origins witnessed by the *Lebor Gabála Érenn* ('The Book of the Taking of Ireland') and other Irish-language texts.[13] Scottish chroniclers and romance writers relied heavily on the legend of Scota to construct their sense of collective history and challenge the myth redacted by English writers, which names Brutus as the original king with hegemony over the whole island.[14] The narratives upon which a collective English identity was built were the Trojan Brutus's founding of Britain and the legend of King Arthur; in every case, Scotland is figured as a subject kingdom.

Movement towards a more humanist perspective is suggested by John Barbour's lost poem, *The Stewartis Orygynale*. Unlike Fordun, who takes the genealogy of the Stewarts back to Adam, Barbour apparently takes them back to Troy (which may suggest that he had encountered the English legend of the Trojan Brutus during his studies in Oxford). Wyntoun in his *Chronicle* refers to *The Stewartis Orygynale* in terms which make it clear that the poem was available to him, so the text survived for a century or so.[15] Barbour was a loyal partisan of the Stewarts and a royal servant: it is partly thanks to his work that the Stewarts made themselves central to the history of Scotland – a fact that is important for the distant use which James VI (I of Great Britain) and Charles I would make of this material in England. Roger Mason observes, 'Part of the success of the Stewart dynasty ... lay in their willingness to identify themselves as the upholders and defenders of Scottish autonomy in the face of English aggression' – as they do in *The Brus*.[16]

When James IV's English queen, Margaret Tudor, made a joyous entry into Aberdeen in 1511, she was greeted by a series of pageants, first biblical, then scenes which were politically oriented. There are lacunae in the text, but it seems that a flourishing family tree was exhibited with Robert the Bruce as the heroic founder of the Stewart line; a similar object would be exhibited for Charles I in June 1633.[17]

The theologian John Major was far ahead of his time in doubting the whole Scottish origin story in his history of the island of Britain, published in 1521, saying shrewdly and wholly accurately:

As to this original departure of theirs out of Greece and Egypt, I count it a fable, and for this reason: their English enemies had learned to boast of an origin from the Trojans, so the Scots claimed an original descent from the Greeks who had subdued the Trojans, and then bettered it with this about the illustrious kingdom of Egypt.

He accepts that the Irish are descended from Spaniards: '[I]t is certain that the Irish are descended from the Spaniards and the Scottish Britons from the Irish – all the rest I dismiss as doubtful, and to me, indeed, unprofitable.'[18] He bases his account of early Scottish history on early medieval sources such as Bede and Gildas, but also asserts, on the basis of a couplet in rhyming hexameters which he quotes (presumably from a medieval chronicle), that Fergus was indeed the first king of Scotland, and took power in 330 BC:

Fergusius, primus dans jura et sceptra Britannis
Sub Christum centum ter terque decem fuit annis.[19]

[Fergus, first giver of the laws and sceptre to the Britons
Was three hundred and thirty years before Christ.]

Hector Boece (1465–1536), the first principal of the University of Aberdeen, published his *Gentis Scotorum Historia* in Paris in 1526. This was the point at which the fabulous history of Scotland passed into the form in which it was known internationally throughout the Renaissance. Boece's *Historia* formed part of a programme of state formation undertaken initially under the patronage of the Lord High Chancellor of Scotland and bishop of Aberdeen, William Elphinstone (1431–1514),[20] including the introduction of printing to Scotland, and the compilation of a distinctively Scottish Liturgy of the Hours, full of commemorations of Scottish saints: the *Breviarium Aberdonense,* published in Edinburgh in 1510.[21] Boece possessed copies of the *Scotichronicon* and Fordun's *Chronica*, but also drew on classical sources such as Tacitus's *Agricola*.[22]

He opens his first book with the story of Gathelus and Scota, and names Fergus mac Ferchar as the first king of Scotland, crowned in 330 BC.[23] Kenneth Mac Alpin, whom the medieval Scottish king lists typically name as the first king of Scotland, became king in 834.[24] Boece then produces a list of kings of Scotland, with their names, kinship, reign length, and deeds, from Fergus mac Ferchar to James III, who was 103rd in line. This list appears to be of his own devising. The sources he cites for his account of early Scottish history are Veremundus, his contemporary John Campbell, and Cornelius the Irishman. Not a word has survived from any of the three, nor are any of them mentioned by any writer earlier than Boece himself. He claims that Veremundus was an archdeacon of St Andrews, 'Spanish by nation, who composed in Latin a history from the origins of the people to the times of Malcolm III, known as Canmore, to whom he dedicated the work' (he was thus allegedly writing in the late eleventh century).[25] It is possible that Boece was deceived by a forged document; it is also possible that he made the whole story up, since the point of his lengthy list is to prove that the Scots had never been conquered since their arrival in Scotland in the fourth century BC, and to challenge English claims to primacy over the entire island. For good measure, he also asserts that the first Scottish king to be a Christian was Donald (V.48), who was converted in 203 AD, in advance of the conversion of England. Hector Boece's version of Scottish history was pre-emptive of the kinds of argument from origins which Henry VIII would advance in his *Declaration* of 1542, which 'deployed the whole panoply of British history (including Brutus and his progeny) in order to demonstrate his right to the sovereignty of Scotland'.[26]

Boece's *History* was extremely successful in Scotland, and it was also widely distributed outside Britain: some of it was translated into French by Jean Desmontiers, and into Italian by Petruccio Ubaldini (this latter was published in London).[27] The distinguished Italian historian Paolo Giovio also regarded Boece as a trustworthy authority.[28] In his own history of the Scots (1578), John Leslie, bishop of Ross, tells the story of Gathelus and Scota, their descendants, and the crowning of Fergus as the first king of Scotland, and then, from his book II onwards, gives a version of Boece's stories of the kings of Scotland, beginning with Fergus.[29] The *Historia Scotorum* (1582) of his Protestant rival, George Buchanan, although it is as sceptical about Scota and Gathelus as it is about the English origin legend of Brutus and his three sons, assumes that Fergus is a historical figure (I.18), and similarly offers a series of brief biographic sketches of his mythical successors, based on Boece (IV.5–V.58). With book VI, which begins with the reign of Malcolm, his account moves increasingly into historical time. Buchanan also cites the extreme antiquity of the Stewart line in his 1558 epithalamium for Mary Queen of Scots and the Dauphin:

> Haec una centum de stirpe nepotes
> Sceptriferos numerare potest, haec regia sola est,
> Quae bis dena suis includat secula fastis.

> [This royal house can reckon from its one stock a hundred descendants, who all successively bore the sceptre; this is the only house that covers in its historical records twice ten centuries.]

He also insists that it is the only European nation to have been continuously unconquered – a claim, in this context, obviously made to impress the French with the value of the alliance.[30] Buchanan's references to the mythical kings of Scotland are particularly important to the argument of this chapter: his works were read widely in the 1630s, being imitated by the royalist courtier Richard Fanshawe, among others.[31]

In Amsterdam, in 1602, John Johnson published an illustrated book, *Historical Inscriptions of the Kingdom of Scotland*, which is in fact a series of short Latin poems on what were by then the 107 kings of Scotland, prefaced by a king list beginning with Fergus. It was produced in the Netherlands on behalf of Andro Hart, the leading printer in Edinburgh, presumably because of the Dutch expertise in copperplate printing. The volume also includes a fragmentary Latin poem, by Andrew Melville, *Gathelus, or on the origin of the race*, which tells the story of Gathelus, Scota, and their descendants.[32] Melville was notorious for his outspoken reproof of James VI, so his poem is a witness to the importance he attaches to Scotland's long independent history, not to personal devotion to the Stuarts.[33] The volume concludes with engraved portraits of the Stuart kings, from Robert II to James VI. In the following year Johnson issued *Distinguished Heroes from the whole of Scottish History*, printed in Leiden, a collection of epigrams on distinguished Scots, beginning with Ferchard in 213 AD.[34]

In London, meanwhile, the arrival of James VI as the new king of England provoked inevitable curiosity about the northern kingdom. An anonymous guide to Scotland, which began with the list of Scottish kings, first published in Edinburgh with John Waldegrave in *c.* 1594, was reissued in London in 1603.[35] It was frequently reprinted in Scotland through the seventeenth century, but this is the only English edition. It was probably the work of John Monipennie, who, in 1612, introduced the London reading public to Scotland's legendary history – the first English-language version, other than Bellenden's Scots translation of Boece, which had been printed in Edinburgh in 1540.[36] Gathelus and Scota, Feredach and Fergus, were all introduced to the English, as was the assertion that the first Scottish king assumed the crown in 330 BC. There were two editions of this work in 1612, so it seems to have been modestly successful.

Ben Jonson's *The Masque of Blacknesse*, performed first on Twelfth Night 1605, with its fable of the Daughters of the river Niger travelling north to 'Albion the fair', is an oblique echo of the mythical origin of the Scots in Egypt. The route of the travels of the Scottish ancestors more or less match those of the Daughters of the Niger in the masque. There was a (false, but widely repeated) etymology of the word 'Scot' from the Greek *skotos* meaning 'black', which seems to have generated 'moors' as stewards at Scottish royal entries – a shadowy presence in honour of the Egyptian ancestors.[37]

When James VI returned to Scotland in 1617, after 14 years' absence, he was greeted by a barrage of poems and loyal addresses, later collected as *The Muses' Welcome*. The first welcome after crossing the border, when 'His M. came from Berwik to Dunglasse the xiij of May', was a Latin speech by Alexander Hume, which told him the story of Fergus, the first king of Scotland, and his successors, not omitting to remind him that Robert the Bruce 'had restored the pristine liberty of Scotland' from the English attempt at conquest under Edwards I and II.[38] A long Latin poem by David Hume, 'Regi suae Scotiae gratulatio', also reminds James about Fergus and the lengthy line of Scottish kings:

> Ingens Fergusii, primus qui Scotica sceptra
> Fundavit, soboles sexta et centesima, regnis
> Felix illucesce tuis, parilique vigore
> Fortunaque pari, regnum fundato Britannum,
> Atque pari fato regnum firmato Britannum,
> Et firmum in seros totidem transmitte nepotes …
> (Parva habita, haud parvis olim fundamina rebus)
> Transtulit, huc ades, et patrios agnosce penates,
> Fatalis soboles, fatali ab origine nona,
> Debita tot regnis, Scoti, Anglo Franco et Hiberno …[39]

> [Being the hundred and sixth great offspring of Fergus, who first established the sceptre of Scotland, happily shine on your realms, with equal vigour and equal strength found the British kingdom, with equal destiny confirm the British kingdom, and bequeath it, confirmed, to your progeny … (once thought small, but the foundation of things hardly small) Come hither and acknowledge your national household gods and your destined descendant, the ninth of his fated line, fated to govern so many realms, those of Scotland, England, France, and Ireland …]

In 1627 John Barclay published a compendium of Scottish history with Elzevier in Leiden, taken from a variety of sources both Scots and English, called *The Republic, or the status of the kingdom of Scotland and Ireland*: 24 years after the union of the Crowns, it seems to have been important to him to emphasise the political and cultural separateness of the Celtic countries. Boece's Scottish king list clearly remained a politically useful document, since the little work includes 'a catalogue of the kings of Scotland, from Hector Boece and George Buchanan', beginning with Fergus.[40] We will see that the king list, and the figures of Boece and Buchanan, all make appearances in the spectacle of state which accompanied Charles I's Scottish coronation in June 1633.

This account so far confirms in some detail that the mythical descent of the Stuarts was current in every generation in the sixteenth and early seventeenth centuries, down to the time when Charles I commissioned Gentileschi's *The Finding of Moses*, in the early 1630s – a commission which almost certainly related to the birth of the future Charles II, which birth of course added a further potential king to the Scottish line. It is important, too, to emphasise that this material was familiar to Charles I himself, demonstrably so after his northern coronation in 1633.

When Charles I came to Edinburgh in 1633 he was greeted by a series of pageants.[41] One of these was a show of the mythical ancestors:

> At the approach of the King, the Theatre (a Courten drawne) manifested Mercury with his feathered hat and his *Caduceus*, with an hundred and seven Scottish Kings, which he had brought from the Elisian Fields, *Fergus* the first had a speech in Latin …[42]

Charles was also presented with a *tableau vivant* of Scottish Humanists, including several of those writers who had been instrumental in disseminating the Scottish royal myth:

> In the midst of the streete, there was a Mountaine dressed for *Parnassus*, where *Apollo* and the *Muses* appeared, and ancient Worthies of Scotland, for learning was represented; such as *Sedullius, Ioannes Duns,* Bishop *Ephinstoune* of *Aberdeen, Hector Boes*, *Ioannes Maior*, Bishop *Gawen Douglasse, David Lindsay, Georgius Buchananus*; the word over them was *Fama super aethera noti.*[43]

Having added this rich Scottish background to the suggestion that Gentileschi's *The Finding of Moses* could well prove a dynastic painting, it is time to return to the puzzle pointed out by Aidan Weston-Lewis as to why the right-hand figures in the composition are gesturing emphatically to something beyond the picture to their left. In the later, Madrid version of the composition, all the figures face inwards, there are no pointing arms, the river landscape is generic, and the focus of the right-hand side of the Madrid picture is the carefully realised evening sky. The emphatic, strange gestures must therefore be bearers of meaning. As Weston-Lewis observes, they are not pointing to the British-looking river in the picture as the place where Moses was found. The woman in blue might possibly be pointing beyond the river to somewhere on the far bank, just to the left of the visible landscape. The woman in gold and purple is pointing high, with a curved hand, as though indicating something far away. Both are pointing left – that is, if we accept Weston-Lewis's convincing conjecture that the picture was hung on the west wall of the Great Hall, they are pointing to the Thames and beyond it, away to the north. Are they pointing to the direction from which Charles derives his original, Scottish kingship, as the present representative of a royal line extending back into the past in unbroken succession to the distant mythical figure of King Fergus?[44]

Both *The Finding of Moses* and *Lot and His Daughters* represent the founding or continuity of a dynasty, the latter by means excusable only by the belief that the three figures in the cave were the last living humans. *The Finding of Moses* represents the dawn of what would become the Stuart royal line. If this painting is read with Gentileschi's (now *ex situ*) ceiling painting of *The Arts of Peace* (1635–38, installed 1638), a coherent scheme emerges for the whole room. The birth of Charles II, like the birth of the royal child in Virgil's fourth *Eclogue*, not only adds another Stuart to the ancient line but ushers in a Stuart golden age, in which the Muses and the Arts of Peace flourish in the figures on the ceiling. The circle of female personifications above forms a counterpoint to the circle of women around Pharaoh's daughter; the colours of their robes complement and mirror each other, and the paintings on wall and ceiling carry forward different aspects of the same narrative – the same celebration of the first Stuart to be born in England.[45]

Inigo Jones is the most likely candidate for the iconographer of the ceiling; the message of its allegory is closely related to a contemporary court masque devised by Jones with the poet Thomas Carew, *Coelum Britannicum*, which was first performed on Shrove Tuesday 1634. This came at a pivotal moment, when it can be conjectured that the easel painting was completed, and the ceiling was just about to be started: several element of the masque's imagery relate to the messages conveyed by Gentileschi's work for the Queen's House.

The fable of the masque is concerned with British histories and distant ancestors: at one point Mercury, calling forth the Masquers, invokes

> Those antient Worthies of these famous Isles,
> That long have slept.[46]

Mercury had also led forth the figures of the ancient Scottish Kings in the 1633 Edinburgh pageant. There follows a 'grave antimasque' of the ancient inhabitants of Britain: 'Picts, antient Scots and Irish' dancing a 'Perica or Marshall dance', and personifications of England, Scotland, and Ireland follow.[47] After this there is a sky-borne pageant of cloud-throned virtues:

> Out of the further part of the heaven beginnes to break forth two other Clouds, differing in colour and shape; and being fully discovered there appeared sitting in one of them, Religion, Truth, and Wisedome … In the other Cloud sate Concord, Government, and Reputation …
>
> The great Cloud beginning to breake open, out of which stroake beames of light; in the midst, suspended in the Ayre, sate Eternity on a Globe … in the firmament about him was a troope of fifteene stares, expressing the stellifying of our British Heroes …[48]

Thus both the themes of the Great Room at Greenwich make an appearance in the masque: the mythical ancestors and the personifications of Concord and Wisdom, the fruits of peaceful government enthroned. Indeed, the whole mood and message of the iconography of the Great Hall of the Queen's house (dynastic stability, the Golden Age restored, the arts of peace) can be summarized in the closing verses of *Coelum Britannicum*:

Then from your fruitful race shall flow,
  Endless succession,
Sceptres shall bud and laurels blow
  'Bout their immortal throne.
Propitious stars shall crown each birth
  Whilst you rule them, and they the earth.

And perhaps these hopes are echoed as strongly in the last stage direction, the silent expression of royal aspiration:

> *The song ended, the two clouds with the persons sitting in them ascend; the great cloud closeth again and so passeth away overthwart the scene, leaving behind it nothing but a serene sky.*[49]

Epilogue

The work commissioned for the decoration of the Palace of Holyroodhouse in the 1670s and 1680s constitutes a later echo of the still current ancestral iconography which has been advanced for Gentileschi's *The Finding of Moses*. In the 1670s the Dutch artist Jan Jacobz de Wet (1641–1697) was working at Holyroodhouse in Edinburgh, under the supervision of the Scottish Baroque architect Sir William Bruce of Kinloss (1630–1710). In February 1673 he signed a two-year contract to provide decorative paintings for Charles II.[50] In these two years he painted allegorical and decorative pieces for the Palace. The overmantel painting in the king's closet is dated to the years included in this contract.[51] It shows *The Finding of Moses* (see Figure 3.2). In the context of a refurbished Scottish royal palace, there can be no doubt that the intended primary significance of the subject is dynastic rather than scriptural, perhaps acquiring new weight and solemnity from the recent wars of the three kingdoms. As at Greenwich, the setting of this *Finding of Moses* is almost certainly localised: while de Wet's landscape could pass for generally classicising and Italianate, there is a strong feeling of Scotland to the bare-sloped volcanic mountain beyond the river which dominates the left-hand side of the composition.

This *Finding of Moses* pre-dates the installation of the Gallery of Kings painted by de Wet by some ten years. It was not until 1684 (after a possible intermission in the Netherlands)[52] that he signed a contract for the arduous task of providing likeness of every member of the succession of kings described by Boece and Buchanan, which, in due course, filled the Gallery of Kings.[53] This work was commissioned by the Scottish Privy Council, another weighty piece of evidence for the seriousness with which Scotland at all levels of Society still took the old myths of origin. Charles II never visited his palace in Edinburgh, but he was consulted in some detail about the

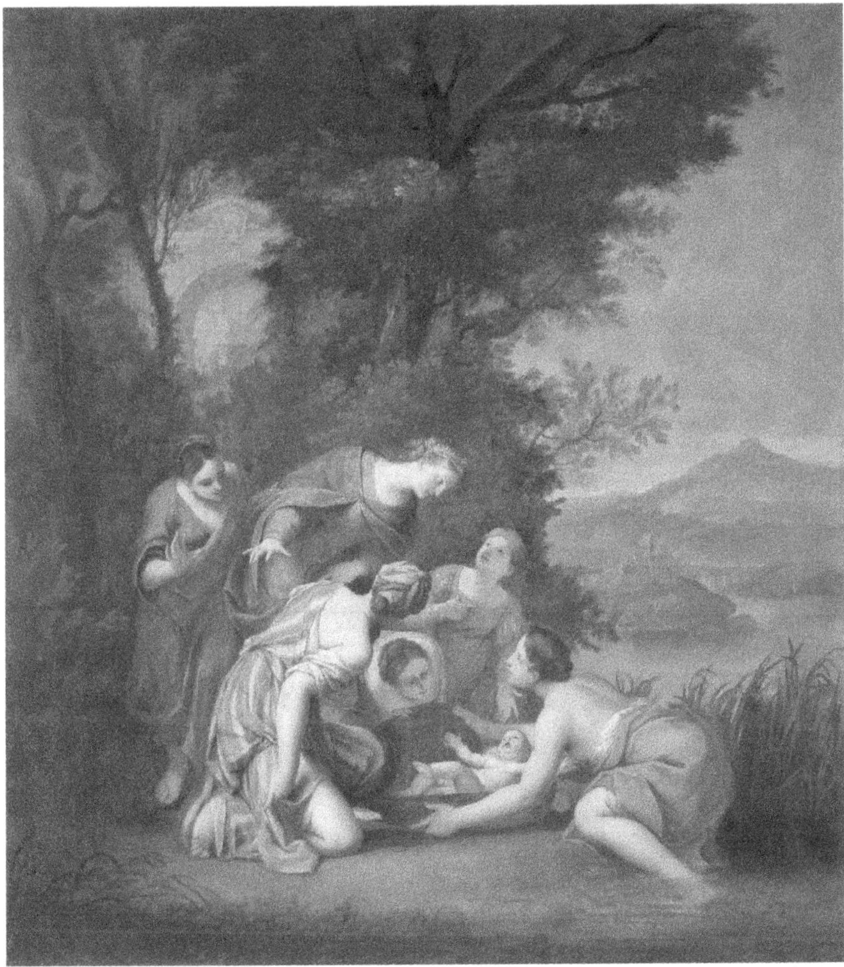

Figure 3.2 Jan Jakobz de Wet, *The Finding of Moses*, 1670s, oil on canvas, Royal Collection, Holyroodhouse, Edinburgh.

restoration and expansion of Holyroodhouse, and was clearly happy that he should be represented publicly by the old myths of the successors of Fergus and of Scota, the daughter of Pharaoh.

As late as 1685, at the very end of the reign of the restored Charles II, Boece's history was still being retold. William Alexander's *Medulla historiæ Scoticæ* includes a list of 110 kings from Fergus to Charles II. His text begins with this assertion: 'The Scots by the most judicious Writers, and by those who have most carefully studied, not only their own Antiquities, but those of other Nations are acknowledged (although they be not of the greatest) to be undoubtedly among the most antient People in Europe.'[54] He assigns their ultimate origin to Spain, though he does not include the story of Scota and Gathelus. Interestingly, this was published in London. An English translation of Buchanan's *History*, published in London in 1690 and thus in the aftermath of the Glorious Revolution, perhaps reflects a wary English interest in the history of the Scottish Stewarts at that particular historical moment. Certainly, the emphasis which the firebrand, beautiful, Jacobite Latin epic *The Grameid* places on belief in those origin myths which give James VII and II an unshakeable claim to the Scottish throne are an index of just how seriously they were still taken in the north.[55]

Notes

1 *The Entertainment of the High and Mighty Monarch Charles, King of Great Britane, France and Ireland, into his auncient and royall City of Edinburgh, the fifteenth of June, 1633* (Edinburgh: John Wreittoun, 1633).
2 Elizabeth McGrath, 'Local Heroes: The Scottish Humanist Parnassus for Charles I', in Edward Chaney and Peter Mack (eds), *England and the Continental Renaissance: Essays in Honour of J. B. Trapp* (Woodbridge: Boydell, 1990), pp. 257–70.
3 Aidan Weston-Lewis, 'Orazio Gentileschi's Two Versions of *The Finding of Moses* Reassessed', *Apollo*, 145 (1 June 1997), pp. 27–34.
4 *Ibid.*, p. 29.
5 *Ibid.*, pp. 30–1.
6 *Ibid.*, p. 31.
7 *Ibid.*, p. 32.
8 *Ibid.*
9 Thomas Innes, *A Critical Essay of the Northern Parts of Britain or Scotland* (London: William Innys, 1729).
10 James Philip, *The Grameid: an heroic poem descriptive of the campaign of Viscount Dundee in 1689 and other pieces*, ed. Alexander Murdoch (Edinburgh: Scottish History Society, 1888).
11 The account that follows is very much indebted to Professor Jane Stevenson.
12 John of Fordun, *Chronica Gentis Scotorum*, ed. William F. Skene, 2 vols (Edinburgh: Edmonton and Douglas, 1871), pp. 9–19 (Gathelus, Scota, and their descendants), p. 45 (Fergus); Walter Bower, *Scotichronicon*, ed. David Watt, 9 vols (Aberdeen: Aberdeen University Press, 1993), I, pp. 27–57.
13 John Carey, 'The Irish National Origin-Legend: Synthetic Pseudohistory', Quiggin Pamphlet no. 1 (Cambridge: University of Cambridge, 1994); Dauvit Broun, *The Irish Identity of the Kingdom of the Scots* (Ipswich: Boydell Press, 1999), pp. 11–19.
14 R. James Goldstein, '"I Will My Proces Hald": Making Sense of Scottish Lives and the Desire for History in Barbour, Wyntoun and Blind Hary', in Priscilla

Bawcutt and Janet Hadley Williams (eds), *A Companion to Medieval Scottish Poetry* (Cambridge: D.S. Brewer, 2006), pp. 39–40; Roger Mason, 'Scotching the Brut: Politics, History and National Myth in Sixteenth-Century Britain', in R. A. Mason (ed.), *Scotland and England, 1286–1815* (Edinburgh: John Donald, 1987), pp. 60–84.

15 E.g., *Androw of Wyntoun's Orygynale Cronykil of Scotland*, ed. David Laing, 3 vols (Edinburgh: Edmonston & Douglas, 1872–79), II, p. 320. See John Barbour, *The Bruce*, ed. A. A. M. Duncan (Edinburgh: Canongate, 2007), p. 3.

16 Roger A. Mason, 'Scotland, Elizabethan England, and the Idea of Britain', *Transactions of the Royal Historical Society*, 6th ser. 14 (2004), pp. 279–93, at p. 281.

17 *The Poems of William Dunbar*, ed. Priscilla Bawcutt, 2 vols (Glasgow: ASLS, 1998), I, p. 65.

18 *Historia Majoris Britannae tam Angliae quam Scotiae* (Paris: Judocus Badius, 1521), I.9, p. 37. Nicola Royan comments, 'Mair's political agenda, of encouraging union between Scotland and England, could not permit a comparison of the rival origin myths, lest one be seen to be better. It was more effective, then, for him to deny both absolutely' ('Hector Boece and the Question of Veremund', *The Innes Review*, 52.1, pp. 42–62, at p. 42). This theme is central, and will recur.

19 *Historia Majoris*, I.11.

20 Leslie Macfarlane, *William Elphinstone and the Realm of Scotland* (Aberdeen: Aberdeen University Press, 1985).

21 Jane Stevenson, Iain Beavan, and Peter Davidson, 'The Breviary of Aberdeen', *Journal of the Edinburgh Bibliographical Society*, 6 (2011), pp. 11–41.

22 Royan, 'Hector Boece', p. 49.

23 *Scotorum Historia*, I. 19.

24 On medieval king lists, see M. O. Anderson, *Kings and Kingship in Early Scotland* (Edinburgh: Scottish Academic Press, 1980).

25 Royan, 'Hector Boece', p. 45.

26 Roger A. Mason, '"Scotching the Brut"; The Early History of Britain', *History Today*, 35:1 (1985), pp. 26–31, at p. 27.

27 *Le Sommaire des antiquitez & merueilles Descosse*, redige & mys par escript par Iehan des montier (Paris: Anthoine Bonnemere pour Jehan Andre & Vincent Certenas, 1538); Petruccio Ubaldini, *Descrittione del Regno di Scotia et delle Isole sue Adjacente* (Anversa [i.e. London: John Wolfe], 1588).

28 Paolo Giovio, *Descriptio Britannae, Scotiae, Hyberniae, et Orchadum* (Venice: Tramezinus, 1548), f. 27v.

29 *De origine, Moribus et rebus gestis Scotorum* (Rome, in aedibus Populi Romani, 1578), pp. 42–9.

30 George Buchanan, ed. Thomas Ruddiman, *Opera Omnia* (Leiden: J.A. Langerak, 1725), II, p. 335, ll. 155–7.

31 *The Poems and Translations of Sir Richard Fanshawe*, ed. Peter Davidson (Oxford: Oxford University Press, 1997), I, pp. 143–4.

32 *Inscriptiones historicae regum Scotorum: continuata annorum serie a Fergusio primo regni conditore ad nostra tempora. Præfixus est Gathelus, sive de gentis*

origine fragmentum An. Melvini. Additæ sunt icones omnium regum nobilis familiæ Stuartorum in ære sculptae (Amsterdam: Cornelius Claesson for Andro Hart, 1602).

33 On *Gathelus*, see Paul J. Mcginnis and Arthur H. Williamson, 'Politics, Prophecy, Poetry: The Melvillian Moment, 1589–96, and Its Aftermath', *The Scottish Historical Review*, 89.1 [227] (2010), pp. 1–18, at pp. 7–8.

34 *Heroes ex omni historia Scotica lectissimi* (Leiden: Christophe Guyot for Andro Hart, 1603), pp. 2–3.

35 *Certeine matters concerning the realme of Scotland, composed together The genealogie of all the kings of Scotland, their liues, the yeeres of their coronation, the time of their reigne, the yeere of their death, and maner thereof, with the place of their buriall. The whole nobilitie of Scotland, their surnames, their titles of honour, the names of their chiefe houses, and their mariages. The archbishopricks, bishopricks, abbacies, priories, & nunries of Scotland. The knights of Scotland. The forme of the oth of a duke, earle, lord of Parliament, and of a knight. The names of barons, lairds, and chiefe gentlemen in euerie sherifdome. The names of the principall clannes, and surnames of the borderers not landed. The stewartries and baileries of Scotland. The order of the calling of the Table of the Session. The description of whole Scotland, with all the iles, and names thereof. The most rare and woonderfull things in Scotland. As they were anno Domini, 1597* (London: A. Hatfield, for Iohn Flasket, 1603). Roger A. Mason, 'Certeine Matters Concerning the Realme of Scotland: George Buchanan and Scottish Self-Fashioning at the Union of the Crowns', *The Scottish Historical Review*, 92.1 [233] (2013), pp. 38–65.

36 *The abridgement or summarie of the Scots chronicles with a short description of their originall, from the comming of Gathelus their first progenitor out of Græcia into Egypt. ... with a true chronologie of all their kings. Their reignes, deaths and burials, from Fergusius the first king of Scotland, vntill his Royall Maiestie, now happily raigning ouer all Great Brittaine and Ireland* (London: John Budge [and Simon Stafford], 1612).

37 Peter Davidson, 'The Edinburgh Entry of Mary Queen of Scots and Other Ambiguities', *Renaissance Studies*, 9.4 (1995), pp. 416–29.

38 *The Muses Welcome to the Kings Majestie, at his happie return to his old and native kingdome of Scotland* (Edinburgh, 1617), pp. 1–5, at p. 4.

39 *The Muses Welcome*, pp. 10–14.

40 *Respublica, sive status regni Scotiæ et Hiberniæ. Diversorum autorum*, ed. John Barclay (Leiden: Elzevier, 1627), pp. 111–36.

41 David M. Bergeron, 'Charles I's Edinburgh Pageant (1633)', *Renaissance Studies*, 6.2 (1992), pp. 173–84, at p. 107; *The Entertainment of the high and mighty monarch Charles King of Great Britaine, France, and Ireland, into his auncient and royall city of Edinburgh, the fifteenth of Iune, 1633* (Edinburgh: John Wreittoun, 1633), p. 13.

42 *The Entertainment*, pp. 12–13.

43 *Ibid.*, pp. 13–14.

44 Yet another aspect of Weston-Lewis's acute reading of the picture is the attention which he pays to the mysterious, apparently castellated, building shown

on the far bank of the river. He doubts very much that it represents any building known to have existed on the lower Thames. The unprovable possibility exists that it could represent a Scottish royal palace, just possibly Dunfermline Palace, where Charles I was born. There is not enough visual evidence, but the configuration seems to match, as does the relation of building to the slope of the hill.

45 It might be conjectured that the strange allegory of *Truth as Patron of Learning and the Arts*, which Robert Streeter painted for the ceiling of Wren's Sheldonian Theatre in Oxford, as well as some debts to prints or drawings of Correggio's ceilings in Parma, is chiefly indebted to Gentileschi's Greenwich ceiling.

46 'Coelum Britannicum', in Rhodes Dunlap (ed.), *The Poems of Thomas Carew with His Masque Coelum Britannicum* (Oxford: Oxford University Press, 1949), pp. 154–219, at p. 175.

47 *Ibid.*, p. 176.

48 *Ibid.*, p. 182.

49 *Ibid.*, p. 185.

50 See https://rkd.nl/en/explore/artists/83917 (retrieved 7 May 2023).

51 See www.rct.uk/collection/401241/the-finding-of-moses (retrieved 7 May 2023).

52 See https://ecartico.org/persons/8230 (retrieved 7 May 2023).

53 See www.rct.uk/collection/search#/1/collection/403275/eugenius-iii-king-of-scotland-535–58 and htts://rkd.nl/en/explore/artists/83917 (retrieved 7 May 2023).

54 *Medulla historiæ Scoticæ being a comprehensive history of the lives and reigns of the kings of Scotland, from Fergus the First, to Our Gracious Sovereign Charles the Second* (London: Randal Taylor, 1685), front matter and p. 2.

55 *The history of Scotland written in Latin by George Buchanan; faithfully rendered into English* (London: Edw. Jones for Awnsham Churchil ..., 1690); Philip, *The Grameid*. This work, too incendiary for print, was circulated extensively in manuscript from 1690 onwards, especially in the Jacobite heartlands of north-east Scotland.

4

Pope's recusancy

That Alexander Pope (1688–1744) was, throughout his life, a Roman Catholic in a militantly Protestant England is well known: Maynard Mack's standard biography offers substantial documentation of Pope's religion, from his upbringing in a devout Catholic family, to his refusal of the considerable social and financial advantages which would have attended his conformity to the Protestant Church of England, to his receiving of the Catholic sacraments on his deathbed.[1] It is also absolutely established that *The Rape of the Lock* is (in its origins) a coterie poem of a circle of élite recusant Catholics.[2] Mack is careful to balance the fact of Pope's Catholicism with the matured observation that Pope's spirituality (as opposed to religion) was not at the centre of his life: 'This is not to say that, at this or any other time, Pope was filled with religious zeal' – an absolutely just assessment based on incomparable knowledge of the man and his works. So we are left with a genuine conundrum, of a man not profoundly religious in himself simultaneously willing to embrace discomfort, danger, and humiliation for his adherence to the religion of his parents. 'Recusancy' is the word normally used to designate the position of those Catholics within Britain who chose the marginalised and disempowered lives forced on them by penal legislation if they refused the outward signs of conformity to the state religion; in itself, 'recusancy' means 'refusal'. Recusancy does not seem a particularly apt way of describing Pope's own position of tolerance and moderation in religious matters, but it describes precisely his ultimate *refusal* to conform, to abandon the religion of his family, of the social circle in which he had come to maturity, of his oldest friends.[3]

There has been much excellent work on the degree to which Pope's intellectual world was the intellectual world of a post-Tridentine Catholic, for all that his education did not include a formation in the rhetorical and devotional world of the Jesuit colleges.[4] Patricia Brückmann in particular traces the devotional and mystic reading which shadows the apparently fantastical 'Rosicrucian' machinery of *The Rape of the Lock*. In the course of her essay, she also traces the books which would have been available to Pope as

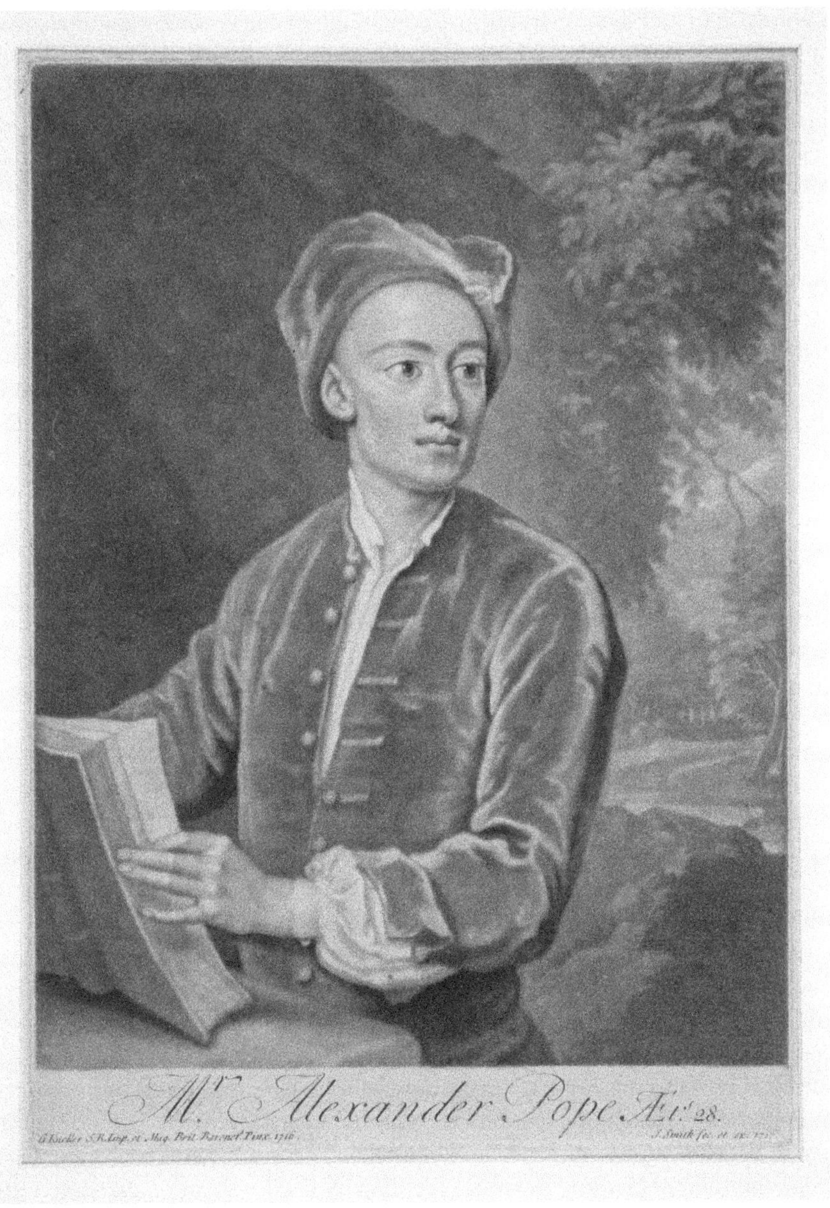

Figure 4.1 John Smith, *Alexander Pope*, 1717, mezzotint.

a young man and demonstrates just how much of the visionary and mystical literature of contemporary Catholicism was in the libraries of the circles of recusants, internally exiled by penal legislation to the upper reaches of the Thames near Windsor.[5] After reading her work, there can be no doubt of the very Catholic frame of reference of Pope's poem, and it becomes clear that this is an area in which further speculations yet might be ventured.

The purpose of this chapter is to develop facts, hints, and illuminations in the published works of Mack, Brückmann, and others into a necessarily brief investigation of the degree to which Pope's position as a recusant Catholic provides a central element in his work and life (see Figure 4.1). It is a surprising index of the post-Whig nature of the unexamined assumptions of the English-speaking academy that, despite the works of these scholars, there has not been a wider consideration of the way in which Pope's membership of an 'un-English' minority informs his work. Until recently, perhaps, the desire to claim Pope for the central tradition of English letters has precluded recognition of his continual negotiation, in work and life, with social marginality.

The climate has been changed by recent work on the cultural and literary history of the British Isles, particularly Alison Shell's superb *Catholicism, Controversy and the English Literary Imagination*, which has brought back an awareness, hitherto found more in confessional than in mainstream scholarship, of the extent to which recusant Catholic culture was an achieved and complete system, capable of challenging the Protestant ascendancy not only in terms of religious controversy but in claims to an essential and profound Englishness or Scottishness.[6] Arthur Marotti's collection of essays on the subject stresses the degree to which there were two cultures in early modern England, and the fact that Catholic culture was neither exhausted nor exclusively reactive.[7]

It is with awareness of the Catholic culture of the seventeenth century that I would like to approach Pope's work of the early eighteenth century, and show that, however moderate Pope's own religious position may have been, he was culturally very much an English Catholic and the inheritor of specifically recusant cultural traditions. It is an essential piece of historical nuancing to realise that people not in a modern sense 'religious' could, in the penal times of the seventeenth and eighteenth centuries, still make a choice to define their social and personal identity by their refusal of the state religion. Crucially, this refusal was associated in the eighteenth-century official mind (and, indeed, in the minds of pamphleteers who wrote against Pope in his lifetime) with at least the suspicion of Jacobitism – support for the exiled Stuart pretenders to the throne – and with a sense that a Catholic could not be a proper Englishman, because his education and religion alike were tainted with foreignness. He was thus in his lifetime in the invidious position of being assumed to be a potential traitor, and not just by his literary enemies, as Maynard Mack records:

> Pope had to give as much consideration to what he was perceived to be as to what he was. His position as Roman Catholic, with what ardor or lack of ardor held, made him only more vulnerable. Owing to that position it was still expedient for him, when Court was kept at Hampton Court, to decamp from his villa and go elsewhere.[8]

In asserting that Pope was a victim of both prejudice and penalty, I am very much developing existing work; indeed, part of my project in this chapter is to do justice to a genuinely innovative article on these topics which has not had perhaps the exposure which it deserves: Paul Gabriner's study of Pope and the English penal laws, which he published as long ago as 1990.[9]

This article, to which I make frequent reference, argues persuasively that Pope's recusancy was a central part of his experience. As well as reminding us that Pope suffered anxiety, financial loss, and humiliation as a result of his religion, Gabriner stresses that it had more serious consequences. He was very dependent, for all the powerful friends made in his maturity, on the circles of Catholics among whom he had grown up, whose experiences and difficulties he shared. An index of the seriousness of Pope's suffering under penalty is that he was unable, because of the laws forbidding a Catholic to reside within ten miles of central London, to go to London in his last illness for medical treatment.[10] The most important result of Pope's recusancy, according to Gabriner (and I find myself very much in agreement with him), is that he was excluded by penalty from owning – and, what is more, from inheriting – property or land.

The implications of this were very considerable in a century in which the improvement of house and grounds was a prevailing élite concern, and in which the neoclassical consensus emphasised endlessly the desirability (indeed, the moral beauty) of the one thing which Pope never had: an *inherited* estate, however modest. Contemporary legislation condemned Pope never to have the *paterna rura* which Horace's second epode defined as the summit of felicity. The house at Binfield in which Pope spent his youth was owned in fact by his father (and, as the penal laws tightened their net on recusants, even *having owned* the house appeared at one point likely to get Pope's parents into trouble) but had to be owned as a legal fiction by friendly Protestant cousins. The Binfield house, as Gabriner demonstrates, was sold in panic, as were many proximate Catholic estates, in 1716, when the laws against Catholics were rendered yet more stringent in the wake of a failed Jacobite rising.[11] Pope's father had been noted in his community as a gardener, a participant in a modest way in the élite fascination with gardening and garden layout of his day. Yet, after the enforced removal from Binfield,

Pope gardened with passion, and made his celebrated grotto, but all of it on rented land, and on rented land which he had occasionally to vacate on account of the laws against Catholics. It was only at the very end of his life that he began to purchase a house in London, and, indeed, the sale was carried through posthumously for Martha Blount, the residuary beneficiary of his will. Gabriner observes precisely the weight which the line imitated from Horace would have had for Pope: 'My lands are sold, my Father's house is gone.'[12] Thus Pope, excluded from one of the central Augustan myths of how to live a decorous and manly life, had to invent alternatives for himself, and for his community. There is a sense in which the grotto and the range of associations with which he surrounded it represent an alternative mythology, a mythology of virtue in internal exile, an embracing of shadow and ruin as though they were choices freely made.

Pope's letter to his friend Francis Atterbury (1663–1732), giving his reasons for remaining a Catholic after the death of his father, is well known and has been extensively discussed. This is not the place for a reiteration of the letter's reasonable, almost anachronistic professions of moderation and tolerance in religious matters, nor for a repetition of its repudiations of superstition and the temporal aspect of the papacy. Pope is making the profession of the loyal English Catholic, which was a recognisable way of being a recusant within English society from the late sixteenth century onwards. What I would like to focus on here is the image which Pope uses for the whole world of acceptance by the ascendancy, the whole world of preferment and public office which he is refusing in this letter: 'It is certain, all the beneficial circumstances of life, and all the shining ones, lie on the part you would invite me to.'[13] The use of the word 'shining' here sets up a powerful contrast: the shining world is everything that goes with public life, benefices (and apostasy); Pope's construction of an environment for himself is in the shadows, particularly in the shadows of his grotto, the obscurity of the loyal subject (the loyal Catholic) placed outside the law. The grotto – enchanter's cave, fane of justice – is a substitute for the inherited gardens which Pope can never own nor transmit.

The imagery of light and shade with which Pope attends his grotto (and with which he expresses the retired life of the recusant, as opposed to the active life of the conformist) appears throughout his verses in related contexts. As early as *Windsor Forest*, his pastoral of an intermission in the application of the penal laws, the lines which open the poem offer the retreat of Pope's parents as well as of the conventional nymphs: 'Unlock your springs, and open all your shades ... / Here waving groves a chequered scene display/ And part admit, and part exclude the day.'[14]

Again, eminence and brightness come together in the first of the ethic epistles to Bolingbroke: 'The few that glare, each Character must mark, /

You balance not the many in the dark.'[15] In the third epistle, the shadowy, ancient country house of the fasting miser Cotta (a place, 'like some lone Chartreuse', with a strong suggestion of the retired houses of the recusants, the kind of house which might have been ornamented with the sculptured stones later used at the entrance to Pope's grotto – a suggestion of 'the gloomy verdure' of Stonor Park) is thrown open to the day as the woods are felled by his spendthrift false-patriot son: 'Last, for his Country's love, he sells his lands, / To town he comes, compleats the nation's hope, / And head the bold Train-bands, and burns a Pope.'[16]

In epistle four, the good Genius of the place, calls the country into the garden, washing the gardens with 'shades from shades', as opposed to the (Dutch-style) gardens of Villario, where 'strength of Shade contends with strength of light: / His bloomy Beds a waving Glow display, / Blushing in bright diversities of day'.[17] So here, too, shade is associated with wisdom and consideration, brilliance with the passing fashions brought in with the Revolution. It is no exaggeration to say that the careful tracing of the imagery of shadows and shining is in itself a key to unlock one particular and deep-seated train of thought running throughout Pope's work.

In this chapter it is my intention to treat only two aspects of Pope the recusant in any detail, but with the hope that others will be encouraged to investigate this aspect of his works further. I hope to advance an argument that *The Rape of the Lock* could be read, particularly in its recurrent figures of bathos, as a poem closely concerned with the state of men living under the assault on élite selfhood deliberately contrived by the penal laws. This is yet another way of following the interpretative lead given by Patricia Brückmann in her essay on the Catholic sources of the poem's machinery. In conclusion, I would like to consider the grotto as a constructed recusant location, declaring its nature not only by inscription but also by its prominent display of reused stone carvings of specifically recusant origins.

To understand *The Rape of the Lock* as a recusant epic, a poem of identity and consolations, it is essential to understand the abnormality of the daily life of the families of Pope's Baron and Belinda. It is universally known that Pope undertook the first version of the poem as part of a project initiated by his friend John Caryll, to reconcile the quarrels between the Fermors and Petres caused by the incident which gives the poem its subject – an incident which was a 'serious breach in the small circle of Roman Catholics to whom unity was so important', as Patricia Brückmann puts it.[18]

If we look briefly at the penal laws against Catholics and the restrictions which they placed on even aristocratic members of Pope's circle, we get a sense of legislation designed to undermine or restrict all those areas of life to which a member of the eighteenth-century élite would look to define their identity and standing. Pope has a bitter two-line summary of the penal laws, which were renewed from 1688 onwards and then augmented continually through the whole period of Jacobite conspiracy: '[C]ertain laws, by suff'rers thought unjust/ Deny'd all posts of profit or of trust.'[19] What the penal laws did effectively was to remove Catholics from the mainstream of British life, so that they could not worship openly, occupy any public office, engage in litigation, be executor of a will, sit in Parliament, or practice as a lawyer or a doctor. They were forbidden at various times to own or bequeath property, to assemble in groups of more than 12, to carry arms, or to own a horse worth more than £5.[20] (Pope himself fell foul of this last enactment, and, after considerable anxiety and trouble, had to sell a horse which had been valued at five guineas.) All of this was in addition to the main provision of these laws, which enforced double land taxes on Catholics and subjected them to arbitrary fines. There was also particularly invidious legislation tempting the sons of Catholics to apostasy in return for an immediate share of the family estate.

If we consider the things by which a member of the eighteenth-century élite would have defined themselves, we see the extent to which the penal laws were designed to cause the greatest possible distress. Landholding and hereditary property are rendered problematic – at the least, ferociously expensive. Hospitality (an essential part of élite life) is restricted by the laws governing assemblies. Hunting is made difficult by the restrictions on horses. All avenues of augmenting income from parliamentary or other government office are closed. In an age when the wearing of a sword was the precise visual signifier of élite status, the Catholics are disarmed and subjected to searches of their houses for weapons. Their places of residence, as we have already seen, are restricted by the 'ten-mile act', so they are excluded from London, forced to keep their distance from the court. The effect of the legislation is meant to be attritive: to wear down the resistance of the recusants by daily harassment, to make the temptation to effect a change of religion as great as possible.

Maynard Mack quotes the first Marquis of Halifax on the situation of the élite recusant, a precise summary of the psychological damage which the Penal Laws were designed to inflict on an early modern sensibility:

> To have no share in the business, no opportunity of showing his own value to the world; to live at best an useless, and by others to be thought, a dangerous member of the nation where he was born, is a burden to a generous mind that cannot be taken off by the pleasure of a lazy unmanly life, or by the nauseous enjoyment of a dull plenty that produceth no food for the mind, which will ever be considered in the first place by a man that hath a soul.[21]

I would argue that this is, in effect, a summary of the world of *The Rape of the Lock*: a vital part of Pope's strategy in the poem is to reconcile the divided community by attempting to put their quarrel in the perspective of time, of the scale of the offence, of the smallness of the present compared to the giants of antiquity. As such, the dominant figure of the poem has to be bathos, the yoking of the noble and large with the quotidian and the small. But bathos has a completely independent life as a figure if we consider the circumstances of the coterie for whom the poem was initially written.

Living under penalty, they are condemned to the 'lazy unmanly life' of which Halifax wrote: they cannot augment estates, take any part in the government, bear arms, hold office. The men of the circle are feminised, deliberately emasculated, deprived of all things which build male élite identity, by the laws. If this is borne in mind, a reading of the poem emerges which disposes for ever of the vague critical consensus which would have the poem, as numberless undergraduate essays have parroted without a moment's reflection, 'satirize' the 'superficiality of the fashionable world'; instead, the poem, particularly in its original two-book form, emerges with a tone rather of warning, urgency, and reminder. Pope addresses his co-religionists continually in the figure of bathos, reminding them of their circumstances and of the real dangers of expropriation, exile, and imprisonment which potentially await them, as well as of the absolute need for unity within their community.

In this light, there are details of the poem which take on the characteristics of reminders of the true condition of the characters of the poem, such as 'And lodge such daring souls in *Little Men*'; Pope's choice of the mock-heroic expresses the enforced condition of mock heroism of the coterie to whom the poem is initially addressed.[22]

This point does not need to be developed at excessive length, but a few phrases gain considerable weight when seen in this context. In the first canto it is quietly underlined that the assembly is not attending the real court, from which they are excluded, but that they are assembled (presumably in one of the many lodgings within the complex) at Hampton '[t]o taste awhile the Pleasures of a Court', and that their pleasure of this kind is strictly limited: 'a court', not 'the court'.[23]

The mock-heroic serves also to stress the disarmed state of the ironically identified 'heroes' of the poem.

> Just then, *Clarissa* drew with tempting Grace
> A two-edg'd weapon from her shining Case;
> So Ladies in Romance assist their knight,
> Present the Spear and arm him for the Fight.[24]

The baron's speech of mock triumph after the severing of the Lock is no less a definition of a reduced and circumscribed world (and a clearly Catholic one) than it is an unerring travesty of classical tropes of eternal fame:

As long as *Atalantis* shall be read,
Or the small Pillow grace a Lady's Bed,
While *Visits* shall be paid on solemn Days,
When num'rous Wax-lights in bright Order blaze,
So long my honour, Name and Praise shall live![25]

This is absolutely precise: the immortality matches the action; but the immortality is clearly defined as being confined within the limits of the coterie.

Again, the bathos of the opening of the second canto is an underlining of the reduction of large feelings – or large potential – to a small compass by circumstances:

Not Tyrants fierce that unrepenting die,
Not *Cynthia* when her *Manteau*'s pinn'd awry,
E'er felt such Rage, Resentment, and Despair,
As Thou, sad Virgin! for thy ravish'd Hair.[26]

And the culminating expression of the circumscribed lives of his characters comes in the battle for the Lock, when men and women alike have to improvise arms from hatpins and snuffboxes. This non-weaponry is emphasised even further in the five-canto version of the poem by an elaborate history of the bodkin. Sir Plume indeed has to concentrate on the conduct of a clouded cane, since a sword is potentially forbidden to him: 'No common weapons in their Hands are found, / Like Gods they fight, nor dread a mortal Wound.'[27] For Pope's original audience, this would have carried resonances of the battles which they could never take part in – except in a Jacobite rising or the service of a foreign king – and of the provisions which would render it difficult for them so much as to fight a duel, which might be imagined the more likely consequence in reality of such a narrative of insult and feud.

In the context of my assertion that the bathos of the poem creates a not particularly coded series of messages to the recusant community, what are we to make of the laborious over-interpretations of the *Key to the Lock* of 1715 (a year of anti-Catholic scares in the face of another Jacobite rising), which, while getting everything wrong, still call at the end for the penal laws to be set into motion against Pope and his publisher, for having set forth a coded papist poem? In short, I would suggest that the *Key to the Lock* has something of the nature of a double bluff in offering a paranoid interpretation of the poem which flits from external to external using outdated tools of essentially allegorical interpretation, to produce a vague, uneasy sense of something Catholic having been put forth in disguise. This serves, of course, to ridicule such interpretations – and, indeed, to ridicule anti-Catholic paranoia – but it also deflects the outsider from the subtle poising of scale which gives the poem its coterie meanings, at the same time as it reiterates the presence of those meanings for those who have the genuine key of shared experience. In Pope's own summary of his position as poet and Catholic, he explains: 'Yet like the Papist's is the Poet's state, / Poor and disarm'd and hardly worth your hate.'[28]

It would be presumptuous to write at any length of Pope's grotto, in the cellars of his riverside villa at Twickenham, as a location which embraced shadow and obscurity, which set itself forth as a place of withdrawn virtue in opposition to the prevailing brutality and veniality of Walpole's England. Maynard Mack has written superbly and at length of this aspect of the grotto, on the Horatian inscription dedicating it – *secretum iter et fallentis semita vitae* – and on Pope's verses on the status of the grotto as the 'Aegerean Grott' of virtue in opposition, the symbolic headquarters of Pope and his friends.[29]

I would like here to add just one, possibly recusant, footnote to Mack's full discussion of the grotto, its construction, use, and associations. That is to return to the word which Pope used of the public world, which he rejected when he rejected Atterbury's tactfully phrased suggestion that he should apostatise on the death of his father – the word 'shining' – and simply to observe that the words which are associated by Pope with his grotto are all indeed oppositions to the shining world: shadows, recesses, retreats. The only shining in Pope's verses on his grotto is the sunlight on the river Thames, and that is specifically mentioned in opposition to the 'drops' and 'crystals' of the 'shadowy cave'.[30] The imagery of the nymph Egeria which Pope attaches to his grotto connotes supernatural wisdom instructing politicians (the legend is of the instruction of the primitive king of Rome, Numa) from the cave and grove just outside the city.[31] I would only wish to add here the thought that Pope's writings about his grotto will also bear, among their many meanings, the identification of the grotto as the location of the integrity which refuses compromise in religious as well as in political matters. There are many senses in which we can take the word shadowed (*umbratus*); 'removed to the margins by legal disability' cannot be discounted among them, any more than we can rule out a further implication in the famous couplet which concludes Pope's verses on the grotto: 'Let Such, Such only, tread this Sacred Floor, / Who dare to love their Country & be poor.'[32] There is a special sense in which a recusant would write these lines: an implication of having chosen an English life under penalty to the easier life of an exile on the Continent.

When we try to take these speculations further we have to proceed with considerable caution: there is no full documentation of the remodellings of the grotto even in Pope's lifetime, although the descriptions of it published shortly after his death offer at least impressions and a list of minerals.[33] The official documentation of the site as a listed monument is extremely cautious in dating any element of the grotto.[34] This is important here, because of the presence of two carved stones of unmistakably recusant origin and because their placing would appear to claim the grotto as a recusant space, by analogy with numerous sixteenth- and seventeenth-century recusant significations of place.[35]

Even in its present dilapidation, the roof of the grotto still bears these two carved slabs apparently dating from the seventeenth century.[36] These show respectively the crown of thorns and the Passion Shield or *Arma Christi*, that arrangement of the Five Wounds which constituted the badge of the last Catholic rising, the Pilgrimage of Grace in 1536, which retook York for Catholicism. These stones seem, at a reasoned guess, to be from the north, and definitely from the recusant north: the nature of the 'raised and sunk' lettering of the 'AK 1626' at the top of the Passion Shield is of a kind much more frequently encountered in the north than the south of Britain. We can presume that these are remnants from a northern recusant house, just possibly a house associated with the family of Pope's mother. The placing is highly significant: these stones are at the entrance to the grotto. This echoes the use of the Passion Shield as a discreet (or sometimes deliberately indiscreet) visual signifier of a Catholic house. Alison Shell, in a private communication, has associated the Passion Shield with the mysterious line 'Five for the Symbols at your Door' in the British counting song 'Green Grow the Rushes', and certainly the figures '5555' are inscribed above the door of Sir Thomas Tresham's oppositionally recusant Triangular Lodge at Rushton in Northamptonshire.[37] The Passion Shield itself is found in the recusant chapel of 'Skene's House' in the Guestrow at Aberdeen and on recusant castles across the north of Scotland. In this sense, the grotto is associated with the Catholic tradition of houses such as Harvington, Stonor, Rushton, and Hutton John, all of which declare their Catholic loyalty by carved stonework at an entrance or over a chapel window.

Finally, it might be possible to argue that Alexander Pope's Twickenham grotto (perhaps more in its original form with shells and mirrors than the refashioned geological grotto which survives today) may have been connected with a very early surviving grotto in Gloucestershire, supposed to have recusant associations, as well as drawing, in its function as a *camera obscura*, on the work of the Jesuit polymath Athanasius Kircher.[38] The little grotto in the garden of Bleby House in Winchcombe in Gloucestershire has been dated to the opening decade of the eighteenth century. (Again, there seems to be no documentation of any sort, and the information in the National Monuments Record preserves no clues as to date or function.) If indeed it is a recusant structure, then it possibly constitutes a precedent for Pope's revival of the grotto as a garden building after a period of neglect. Only local memory and oral tradition connect the Bleby House grotto with the finding of the relics of St Kenelm at Winchcombe.

The little grotto is certainly on the site of part of Winchcombe Abbey, and the relics of the boy-saint Kenelm were certainly exhumed from the abbey site where they had been buried at the Reformation. (Before the Reformation the relics had been venerated in the abbey itself.) Another oral tradition says that the relics were placed in the grotto temporarily after being exhumed in the early nineteenth century; at the moment it is very difficult to judge: the available sources, including the entry in the government register of buildings of architectural interest, all appear to derive from the description of the little grotto in Barbara Jones's inventory of follies and grottoes.[39]

This charming little structure is listed as of very early eighteenth-century date, antedating the construction of Pope's grotto, or of the grottoes of any of his friends. Inside it was clearly originally covered entirely with oyster shells, snail shells, and reflective glass. There is a suggestion that oyster shells set into a panel in a wall were another discreet sign of a recusant house, like the Passion Shield (my informant quoted the story as told of Mapledurham).[40] If this is the case (and I have yet to find another source for it), then Pope may have had an awareness of the associations of these shells, and the original form of his grotto may indeed have owed something to the grotto at Winchcombe. Certainly, there is no doubt that there was a recusant cult of St Kenelm and other British saints, as the naming of the celebrated Kenelm Digby would suggest.

Another name which recurs in recusant circles is that of Winifred, the tutelar of St Winefride's well in Flintshire, a perpetual site of pilgrimage (indeed, a recusant space deliberately maintained) throughout the penal times.[41] Alison Shell has also discovered that at least one contemporary of Pope's (Thomas Gent of York) appears to have associated Pope's grotto with this recusant pilgrimage site in his *British Piety Display'd* published at York in 1742.[42] Again, this identification is speculative (although it is very hard to see who apart from Pope could be the addressee in these lines), but it adds another recusant possibility to the associations of Pope's house and grotto, very much of a piece with the consistent recusant identity which this chapter has attempted to investigate.

Notes

1 Maynard Mack, *The Life of Alexander Pope* (New Haven, CT: Yale University Press, 1985), esp. pp. 338–9, 655, 810.

2 This is strongly asserted, if not particularly clearly demonstrated, in the edition in the 'Bedford Cultural Editions' series, *The Rape of the Lock*, ed. Cynthia Wall (Boston: Bedford Books, 1998).

3 The first version of this chapter was published some time before Joseph Hone's *Alexander Pope in the Making* (Oxford: Oxford University Press, 2021). It also long preceded Gašpar Jakovak's splendid assessment of the Catholic country house, 'The Catholic Country House in Early Modern England: Motion, Piety and Hospitality, *c.*1580–1640', in Kimberley Skelton (ed.), *Early Modern Spaces in Motion: Design, Experience and Rhetoric* (Amsterdam: Amsterdam University Press, 2020), pp. 81–110. I cite these works here to indicate how the trains of thought raised here developed in the next decade.
4 See particularly Mack, *Life*, pp. 48–9.
5 Patricia Brückmann, 'Virgins Visited by Angel Powers: *The Rape of the Lock,* Platonic Love, Sylphs and Some Mystics', in G. S. Rousseau and Pat Rogers (eds), *The Enduring Legacy: Alexander Pope Tercentenary Essays* (Cambridge: Cambridge University Press, 1988), pp. 3–20.
6 Alison Shell, *Catholicism, Controversy, and the English Literary Imagination, 1558–1660* (Cambridge: Cambridge University Press, 1999).
7 *Catholicism and Anti-Catholicism in Early Modern English Literature*, ed. Arthur Marotti (Basingstoke: Macmillan, 1999).
8 Mack, *Life*, p. 655.
9 Paul Gabriner, 'The Papist's House, the Papist's Horse: Alexander Pope and the Removal from Binfield', in C. C. Barfoot and Theo d'Haen (eds), *Centennial Hauntings: Pope, Byron and Eliot in the Year 88* (Amsterdam: Rodopi, 1990), pp. 13–63.
10 Gabriner, 'The Papist's House', p. 47, quoting *The Correspondence of Alexander Pope*, ed. George Sherburn, 5 vols (Oxford: Clarendon Press, 1956), IV, pp. 504–5.
11 Gabriner, 'The Papist's House', p. 30.
12 *Ibid.*, p. 25.
13 *Correspondence of Alexander Pope*, I, p. 454.
14 Alexander Pope, 'Windsor Forest', in *The Works of Mr Alexander Pope*, I (London: Lintot, 1717), pp. 47–72, at pp. 50–1.
15 Alexander Pope, 'Ethic Epistles', in *The Works of Mr Alexander Pope*, II (London: Gilliver, 1735), pp. 1–93, at p. 51.
16 Alexander Pope, 'Ethic Epistles, III', *Works*, II, p. 18.
17 Alexander Pope, 'Ethic Epistles, IV', *Works*, II, pp. 42–3.
18 Brückmann, 'Virgins Visited', p. 5.
19 Alexander Pope, 'The Second Epistle of the Second Book of Horace', *Works*, II, p. 55, ll. 60–1.
20 The penal laws are concisely described in Gabriner, 'The Papist's House', p. 47.
21 Mack, *Life*, pp. 43–4.
22 All my references are to the earliest published version of the poem: *The Rape of the Locke. An Heroi-Comical Poem* (London: Bernard Lintot, 1712), printed as part of *Miscellaneous Poems and Translation by Several Hands* (London: Bernard Lintot, 1712), pp. 355–76.
23 Pope, *The Rape*, p. 359
24 *Ibid.*, p. 361.

25 *Ibid.*, p. 363.
26 *Ibid.*, p. 364.
27 *Ibid.*, p. 370.
28 Alexander Pope, 'The Second Satire of Dr John Donne', in *The Works of Mr Alexander Pope*, II, pp. 13–64, at p. 41, ll. 11–12. Quoted with excellent contextual discussion in Gabriner, 'The Papist's House', p. 33.
29 Maynard Mack, *The Garden and the City: Retirement and Politics in the Later Poetry of Pope, 1731–1743* (Toronto: University of Toronto Press, 1969), pp. 41–77.
30 These verses are first found in a letter to Bolingbroke of 3 September 1740; *Correspondence of Alexander Pope*, IV, p. 262, ll. 2–4.
31 Ironically, or appositely, the structure which the era of the Grand Tour identified as the grotto of Egeria was in fact a garden building, the Nymphaeum of the Villa of Herodes Atticus, lying between the Via Appia Antica and the Via Appia Nuova.
32 *Correspondence of Alexander Pope*, IV, p. 262, ll. 13–14.
33 A very full and informative discussion of the stages of the evolution of Pope's grotto can be found in Anthony Beccles Willson, *Alexander Pope's Grotto in Twickenham* (London: Garden History Society with the Twickenham Museum, 1998).
34 The register of listed buildings in England and Wales and the information held at the National Monuments Record at Swindon (a division of English Heritage) do not even conjecture dates for any of the elements of the grotto as now surviving. In the light of this, my paragraph about the reused recusant stones must be read with caution. They could have been imported after Pope's death; the statues now in the grotto certainly were.
35 See Davidson, 'Recusant Catholic Spaces', pp. 19–51.
36 See Mack, *The Garden and the City*, pp. 63–5.
37 See Nicolaus Pevsner and Bridget Cherry, *The Buildings of England: Northamptonshire* (London: Penguin, 1973), p. 400.
38 For Kircher's *Camera Obscura*, see especially Eugenio Lo Sardo, *Athanasius Kircher: Il Museo del Mondo* (Rome: De Luca, 2001), pp. 239–41.
39 This information and access to the grotto were given by the present owner, Duncan Michie, Esq. For the original printed assertion of the recusant associations of the grotto, see Barbara Jones, *Follies and Grottoes*, 2nd edn (London: Constable, 1974), p. 327.
40 John Seward, Esq., at Pluscarden Abbey, Moray, November 2002, personal communication.
41 For a long time the English Jesuits appear to have acted as the guardians of the well, a fact crucial to the understanding of Gerard Manley Hopkins's dramatic fragment *St Winifred's Well*. Their stewardship is attested in the manuscript at Stonyhurst College, Lancashire, Stonyhurst MS. AII, 8, which contains not only a mediaeval life of St Winifred but also records of early modern cures of pilgrims at the well.

42 Shell's discovery is what seems a clear allusion to Pope in Thomas Gent's work tracing the history of St Winefride's Welle: Thomas Gent: *British Piety Display'd in the Glorious Life, Suffering, and Death of the Blessed St Winefred ... Part the Fifth* (York: Printed by the author Thomas Gent, 1742), p. 12. She has also kindly communicated to me Gent's verses:

Hail, *publick* FRIEND! Lov'd by fair *B-rl-ngton,*
Since I must call You by no other Name;
Behold St. *Win'frid*'s Life, which, when begun,
Kind, you approv'd – that set my Soul a-flame!
May Your's when Death in Swan-like Strains you sing,
'Mid'st Joys expressless, mount on Angel's Wing!
May bless'd *ELIZA*, comfort of your Breast
When living, meet you with St. *Winfred*'s Ghost;
And never part until YE all find Rest,
Thro' Seas of Air, upon the heav'nly Coast;
Unless it be, thro' GOD'S Command, to do
A Guardian's Part, as Angels do for You.
Let not my wand'ring Thoughts the least offend,
Since to learn'd Judgments I shall e'er give Place.
The *Soul's* Extension blissful Hopes attend,
Swift, as on Turtle's Wings, that fly to Peace.
Err sure *mine* may; like those who rove thro' Dark;
'Till, with Faith's Branch, it finds Religion's Ark.

5

Mr Gibbon's shadow, or 'the parent of the arts'

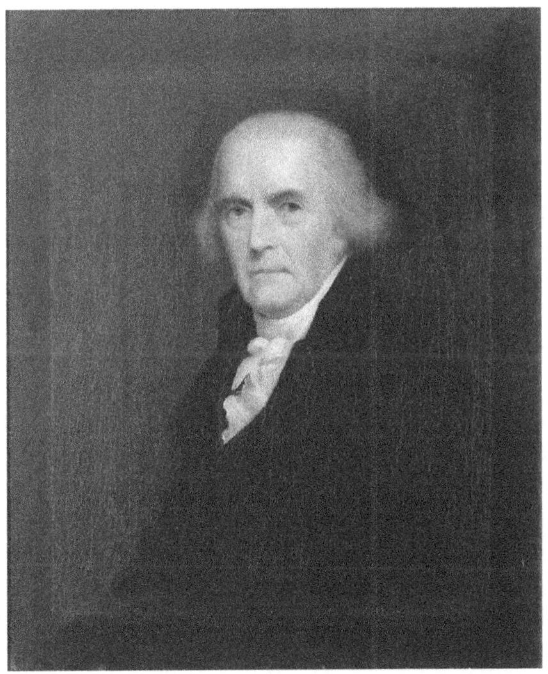

Figure 5.1 Anon., *James Byres of Tonley*, 1810, oil on canvas, National Trust for Scotland, Castle Fraser Garden & Estate, Aberdeenshire.

One of the most celebrated passages in Edward Gibbon's autobiography identifies the moment when the idea for what would become his magnum opus, *The History of the Decline and Fall of the Roman Empire*, first came to him: 'It was at Rome, on the 15th of October 1764, as I sat musing amidst the ruins of the Capitol, while the barefoot friars were singing vespers in the Temple of Jupiter, that the idea of writing the decline and fall of the city first started to my mind.'[1]

It is a carefully staged scene which almost certainly never happened: the citizen of the new world empire musing alone at the ruined heart of the world empire of antiquity, hearing the faint sound of vespers from a church whose fabric is itself a palimpsest. The meditation is in English; the power of Rome has passed to Britain. But we must doubt that this haunting collocation of time and place is real in any simple sense. Gibbon's editors point out that his first editor, his friend Lord Sheffield, chose this version from a late draft of the *Memoirs* and that in any case the church is built on the site of the temple of Juno Moneta, not Jupiter, thus upsetting Gibbon's neat rhetorical progression of male deities.[2] An earlier draft of the *Memoirs* does not place the scene outside amidst the ruins at all, but inside the Franciscan church of Santa Maria in Aracoeli.[3] In sober fact, the journal of Gibbon's travelling companion, William Guise (1737–83), reports that it rained (at least in the morning) of that famous day, and that they visited no ruins, but went instead for a second look at the pictures offered for sale by the dealer Thomas Jenkins.[4]

This being the case, even allowing that the weather might have cleared by the time that vespers were being sung in Santa Maria in Aracoeli, we have to consider this moment on the Capitol as most probably a composite, symbolic, and expressive fiction. Such a fiction naturally demands that the protagonist should be doing his musing in solitary communion with the past; in fact, Gibbon's interaction with the Roman past in those crucial days of October was mediated by the company and opinions of the expert who Gibbon and Guise had hired as their *cicerone*, an expert who by the 1760s was himself composing an ambitious historical narrative with analogical resonances for the third quarter of the eighteenth century.

Almost the first things that Gibbon and Guise did on arrival in Rome in the autumn of 1764 was to club together with a Mr Ponsonby to engage this guide to the history and artistic treasures of the city. As early as the middle of the seventeenth century, being a *cicerone* (or, as they preferred to call themselves, antiquary) was a distinct profession in Italian cities such as Rome, Venice, and Florence. James Byres, son of the laird of Tonley in Aberdeenshire (1733–1817), was an antiquary, architect, archaeologist, historian, and man of taste, and a member of the shadowy community of British exiles in Rome (see Figure 5.1). In fact, Byres was a citizen of a rich cluster of shadow communities: a British Catholic, a homosexual, a defeated Jacobite. An inhabitant of the modern Rome of clerics, exiles, spies, and *virtuosi*, he too thought much about the rise and fall of empires, ancient and modern. What engages my interest particularly here is that Gibbon would have had his first sight of the antiquities of Rome in the company of this shadow compatriot, this oppositional historian who thought of himself as a subject of the still living James Francis Edward Stuart.[5]

Byres was born into an old Aberdeenshire family who were mostly Episcopalians, within a mostly irenic society where Roman Catholics and Episcopalians intermarried and lived peaceably together, united in their loyalty to the house of Stuart. His parents and siblings went into exile in 1746 after the Jacobite defeat at Culloden, going to France (where they had relatives, including the Jacobite George Gordon, d. 1757, son of Robert Gordon of Esselmont and Hallhead, wine merchant at Bordeaux)[6] before gravitating to the court of James Francis Edward Stuart at Rome. Byres studied art and architecture at the Academy of St Luke in the city, with some success:[7] he made fine architectural designs, including those for Sir Watkin Williams-Wynn's palatial house at Wynnstay in Denbighshire, now in the National Library of Wales.[8] Many of Byres's other plans for country houses survive, in a refined late baroque style with a fascinating admixture of Vanvittelian classicism. None appear to have been built.[9] Byres was also involved, with his fellow Catholic *virtuoso* John Thorpe SJ,[10] in the furnishing of the Weld family's Catholic chapel at Lulworth in Dorset, the first substantial free-standing structure to be built for Catholic worship in England since the Reformation.[11] He dealt in pictures, including Poussin's *Seven Sacraments*, now in the National Galleries of Scotland, as well as coins, medals, and intaglios.[12] A manuscript from the middle of the eighteenth century survives at Stonyhurst College,[13] titled *Some Observations on Rome etc.*, which contains a list of the author's drawings, as well as minute observations of architecture and inscriptions. It is clearly a *cicerone*'s notebook, and the hand is very similar to Thorpe's; I would advance the conjecture that it is his, and that it offers further insight into the profession of antiquarian.

It is fascinating to insert Byres, with his knowledge and his distinctly counter-cultural apprehension of the past, into Gibbon's Roman narrative, as Gibbon himself gives him only one sentence, albeit one which implies that Byres taught him a great deal:

> [M]y guide was Mr Byers, a Scotch antiquary of experience and taste; but, in the daily labour of eighteen weeks, the powers of attention were sometimes fatigued, till I was myself qualified … to select and study the capital works of ancient and modern art.[14]

This sentence implies being constantly in each other's company, however, and that Gibbon conversed constantly with Byres for many weeks. Guise, Gibbon's companion, confirms that Byres had been 'much recommended to us'.[15] He also confirms incidentally, in his entry for Saturday 6 October, that it was Byres who supplied the erroneous 'fact' that the Aracoeli was built on the ruins of the temple of Jupiter Capitolinus.[16] Gibbon's attitude to Byres cannot be reconstructed beyond the sincere praise which he briefly implies. Gibbon was not unaware of the plight of the Catholic exiles from Britain: he knew the ferocity of English anti-Catholicism from the response to his own brief, undergraduate conversion; he also had fresh in his mind an encounter with Commander Richard Acton, a Catholic convert, distant relative living in exile, which had taken place at Pisa on 24 September 1764, for whose stranded state Gibbon felt sincere pity.[17]

We cannot know what happened on 15 October to cause Gibbon to attach such retrospective significance to the day. One heterodox suggestion might be that the plan of writing a Roman history came to Gibbon while viewing the pictures offered for sale by Thomas Jenkins. Although Gibbon is alone on his probably fictitious crepuscular visit to the Capitol, Guise's *Journal* conforms that that Byres, Guise, and Gibbon had visited it daily together in the course of the earlier part of their tour.[18]

Frequent visits to the Capitol early in the 'course of antiquities' also formed part of Byres's documented curriculum for two young Americans, Samuel Powel and John Morgan, who had explored Rome with him earlier in 1764,[19] and they seem to have focused on the Capitol in their second week.[20] Inevitably, this site was an early point in most Grand Tour itineraries, as the history and topography of Rome can be most conveniently expounded from its unique point of vantage. It is fruitful, in the light of Byres's own writings from the 1760s, to conjecture what form his instruction would have taken: he was interested in Mediterranean origins and deep time, but his customary discourse on Roman history was surely tailored to the educations and expectations of the English-speaking Grand Tourists; we may conjecture, from his manuscripts, that it was delivered with substantial Jacobite and Catholic mental reservations.

When Byres was guiding Gibbon round Rome, he had already begun work on his illustrated book on the arts and civilisation of the Etruscans which will form the main subject matter of this chapter. Silent, unfinished, and its text unpublished, it is a sort of ghost-ancestor of Gibbon's *Decline and Fall*: a history of an ancient defeated people written by a member of a defeated community.[21] The Etruscans were Byres's private passion, in part because he saw their relations with the belligerent Romans as analogous to those of the Jacobite northern Scots with the aggressive Whigs of England and Lowland Scotland. There can be little doubt that he was also interested in them as a lost gay culture, given the explicitly homoerotic nature of those Etruscan tomb paintings which Byres chose to study and have drawn.[22] What Byres really thought of the Romans (and it might be conjectured, by extension, of the English Whigs, including Gibbon) can be reconstructed from his manuscript notes. They were uncultured people of 'ignorant vanity … living on the spoils of their neighbours'.[23]

Perhaps Byres had imparted some of his views to Gibbon by the end of their tour, if not by the evening of 15 October 1764. In a celebrated apopthegm, Gibbon allowed that that '[a]ll superfluous ornament is rejected by the cold frugality of the Protestants; but the Catholic superstition, which is always the enemy of reason, is often the parent of the arts'.[24]

'The parent of the arts'

The group of expatriate British Catholic intermediaries, of which Byres was a prominent member, was essential for the Grand Tour to function. The young Protestant *milordi* were not wholly welcome in Rome, as the Scottish architect Robert Adam found to his embarrassment in 1755, when he had to rely on introductions from his Catholic and Jacobite compatriots to obtain access to palaces, museums, and society.[25] The activity of this group forms a significant thread of expatriate Catholic activity, one that contributed substantially to the mainstream culture of Britain. If we imagine the Whig 'Earls of Creation' in the eighteenth century drinking claret under the painted ceilings of their Palladian villas, surrounded by works of art ancient and modern bought on their tours of the Continent, looking out over grounds designed with the indispensable advice of Alexander Pope, it is likely that many of these refinements were supplied to them by members of the penumbral world of Catholic intermediaries, art dealers, and men of taste, many of them living in exile abroad, or seclusion at home.

This activity by British Catholics as connoisseurs, art dealers, and 'tastemakers' is summarised here for the period between the 1560s and the end of the eighteenth century. It is to be conjectured that the phenomenon of the Catholic 'man of taste' had its origin in the first decade or so of the reign of Elizabeth: by contrast to a society that had grown notably anxious about many kinds of images and generally averse to foreign travel, Catholics perforce developed continental connections and affinities. Gerard Kilroy, in his biography of the cosmopolitan intellectual and Jesuit martyr St Edmund Campion, points to the flight of the Catholic fellows from Oxford in 1571, and the subsequent strengthening of the borders of England, amid a general discouragement of travel, as the point at which England began to drift away from Europe, and from international learning, as well as from visual modes of devotion of the emerging baroque.[26] This had a great deal to do with Elizabethan policy, and less to do with religion. Certainly, Scotland in the same period was a divided polity, but Lowland Calvinists, and northern Episcopalians and Catholics alike, travelled widely, albeit in different regions of Europe. Scotland was a participant in the northern Renaissance, and international baroque, in a way that carried the names of the writers Buchanan and Barclay to just about every state in the world where there was a printing press, or a bookseller.[27]

It is notable that, in the first generation of Catholicism under penalty, the survival of Marian links to the Continent went hand in hand with contact renewed through the exiled colleges and religious houses that were being founded or refounded there. Thus, Sir Thomas Tresham, inheritor of a mid-sixteenth-century recension of the international Renaissance, naturally incorporated the 'hieroglyphics' that he had learned (most probably from such texts as the *Hypnerotomachia* of Francesco Colonna) into the speaking architecture of his symbolic Banqueting House at Lyveden in Northamptonshire. He had copies of Palladio and Serlio in his library. It is perhaps the intensity of religious meditation which Tresham's symbolic buildings incorporate which marks them out as very early English manifestations of what would become the Counter-Reformation tradition of meditation on emblems and 'speaking pictures'.[28]

Alexander Seton, first Earl of Dunfermline, was a very early product of the Counter-Reformation, having studied in Rome at the Collegium Germanicum and the Collegio Romano, and he commissioned an extraordinary painted gallery for his villa just outside Edinburgh.[29] Seton had copies of Serlio, Palladio, and the Catholic antiquary Baronius in his library.[30] Seton was a representative of a more modern, Tridentine, Jesuit tradition: he had ideas of Scottish and Catholic antiquity (for example, he conserved the Book of Scone in his library),[31] and was a member of that aristocratic group with developing Jesuit connections who built fortified houses with very large chapels to serve as parish churches in Aberdeenshire just before the official reformation of 1560.[32] The learning transmitted in Seton's houses, and in the castle of his neighbours the Hays of Delgaty, was Jesuit, rhetorical, and emblematic – in a word, baroque – a fact confirmed by the adult writings of those, scattered across learned Europe, who apparently had their school education in northern Aberdeenshire.[33] Of the Scottish Catholic families, only the Counts Leslie, enriched and ennobled for effective mercenary soldiering in the Holy Roman Empire, seem to have had a policy of conserving as many material relics of the Catholic past as they could.

Tresham and Seton are, to some degree, emblematic of two different British Catholic ways of relating to the international world of taste and the arts. Tresham looked to the past – or, at least, to the fairly recent past – but the way which he used *imprese*, sacred heraldry, and emblems was articulated by his contact with the cosmopolitan Jesuit St Edmund Campion – so that Tresham's last layout at Lyveden New Beild, which remained unfinished at his death in 1605, became a complex paradise, anticipatory of the interior (and real) gardens created by Jesuits in the middle of the seventeenth century, such as the Marian paradise of Henry Hawkins and the Sodality gardens in the English College at Saint-Omer.[34] At Lyveden, a long course of labyrinths and canals and orchards articulates the approach to the banqueting house whose number symbolism of threes and fours contemplates the crucifixion, while the 'hieroglyphics' carved in its frieze commemorate the English priests who have died for Christ, and Tresham's own worldly sufferings.

Retrospective salvage would become an important way of being Catholic in Britain in the following century: conserving objects, charters, muniments; existing on the leading edge of the nascent antiquarian and archaeological movements.[35] Generally, it is a mistake to assume that post-Reformation Catholics were looking with hopeless longing to the past, for they were also post-Tridentine Catholics. Much of the pattern of conservation of past artefacts by the English Catholic community – manuscripts as well as textiles and works of art – can be seen to be as much antiquarian (or even aesthetic) as devotional. And, of course, vestments were conserved for use. The Townleys conserved the fifteenth-century Whalley Abbey vestments, presumably for practical use in their chapel, since the chasubles have been retailored to be less voluminous, as well as the text of what used to be called the 'Townley' mystery plays.[36]

As the seventeenth century progressed, a key distinction or division that seems to emerge involves the use of the visual in education and devotion. Protestant education was, unsurprisingly, verbal in focus. Its Catholic counterpart, especially as clearly documented in the *Customs Book* by the rector of the English Jesuit College at Saint-Omer in what was then the Spanish Netherlands, instead used place, spectacle, theatre, gardens, and installations and arrangements of relics as an immersive environment for young recusant Catholics being fortified for the almost inevitable trials of their adult lives.[37] Jesuit pedagogy is intensely visual, not least because much of it is focused on *visualisation* of scripture, on making emblems, and on reading iconographies.[38] Perhaps the most important element of this English schooling in exile was that it was fully participant in those international movements in the visual arts, from which much of Britain was excluded.

This simple idea explains much about the importance of the international sophistication of the courts of Charles I and Henrietta Maria.[39] A high proportion of the members of the queen's court, self-selected by their ability to speak French, the queen's only language for her first few years in England, were Catholic gentry who had travelled or been educated abroad. The Earl of Arundel, being a Catholic, was not only one of the early collectors in England but also travelled widely on the Continent and drew into his circle Inigo Jones, who underwent vital elements of his visual education in the earl's company, moving in circles overlapping with such young travellers and *virtuosi* as Kenelm Digby.[40] The nuncio to the queen's court, George Conn, had his education in Catholic Aberdeenshire, a few miles from Seton's estate at Fyvie, before he moved to the English College in Rome.[41] He was a published poet and controversialist in Latin.[42] Conn's family seem to have been the very same gentlemen architect-masons who built the new Aberdeenshire Catholic fortress-chapels from the late 1550s to the 1590s; and his tomb in Rome, in San Lorenzo in Damaso, is in the manner of Bernini.[43]

It seems safe to assert that no multisensory or immersive education of the sort described above for the College of Saint-Omer was available in England. When John Aubrey documented an innovative schoolmaster in Durham who taught grammar by means of spatial visualisation, pasting up prints of Roman emperors and arranging grammatical components in the imagined space under each print, he was implying that this was an unusual, as well as a highly effective, means of teaching. He also noted that it derived from the kinds of pedagogic technique commonly used by the Jesuits. And Aubrey would have known: he had Jesuit friends, among his astonishingly wide circle; and, in one crisis of his fortunes, he wondered if he might be received as a kind of gentleman pensioner in a monastery.[44] No better example could be given of the non-visual nature of an English upbringing than the account of his own childhood given by Aubrey in his *Life of Himself*. Wanting to learn to draw, he had to do so by copying the few pictures available in rural Wiltshire more or less in secret, continually discouraged from the enterprise. In mature life he did draw, producing rapidly sketched antiquarian surveys, as well as some touching self-taught drawings of places that had been important to him. He also made pioneering and attentive drawings of the progress of Gothic design as evidenced in English churches. One of his earliest antiquarian activities, in his student days, was to commission William Dobson's assistant Fr Jerome Hesketh (who later used painting as a cover for his ministrations to northern recusant families) to survey what little was left – Aubrey's own lovely word is 'umbrages' – of the ruins of Osney Abbey in Oxford.[45] Perhaps this visual sensibility, as well as the company he kept, caused the loutish 'Gape-Abouts' who hung around the gate of All Souls to point at him and whisper the dangerous accusation 'Romano Catholicus'.[46]

In the next generation, John Talman (1677–1726), who seems to have been a discreet convert to Catholicism from a cultivated family, collected drawings on the Continent, especially in Italy, and disseminated contemporary continental design in England. He lived mostly in Rome from 1708 to 1717, and prospered there, collecting mightily and being elected a member of the Arcadian Academy.[47] As an exiled Catholic resident of Rome, he became a pivotal figure in the early stages of the Grand Tour, a forerunner of the expatriated men of taste of the mid-century such as Byres, or the Jesuit John Thorpe, who negotiated entry, access, and introductions for the English Grand Tourists.[48] This function of the expatriated Catholics was essential if the Grand Tour was to function smoothly. The young Protestant gentlemen were not invariably welcome in Rome, and were not automatically granted access to monuments and museums without a local introduction, as Robert Adam's above-mentioned difficulties in the 1750s attest. Adam's wonderfully self-justifying letter home, excusing his dining with Jacobites because otherwise all doors were closed to him, has a particular force, in that the Adam family firm had the contract to build the fortresses in northern Scotland that had been designed to keep the Highlanders down.[49]

In 1708, just before his departure for Rome, Talman provided designs for a recasting of the buildings of All Souls in Oxford, in a full-blooded continental baroque style, which would have in some ways have accorded well with James Gibbs's later Radcliffe Camera, although they would have lacked the fantasy and melancholy of the work by Nicholas Hawksmoor that was actually built. In Talman's will, he directed his executors to identify his great folders of drawings by the motto which is inscribed upon them 'with this inscription on the front of each booke (viz) Delicta majorum et meritus Lues Britan[n]e donec Templa refeceris'. This Horatian motto itself had been a highly charged phrase in the two centuries following the Reformation. Its history and applications emphasise that the formation of an antiquarian and aesthetic 'paper museum' such as Talman's could not be a politically neutral activity as late as the 1720s. Assuming that Talman himself intended the motto on his folios of drawings to be a clue to their nature, let us consider the implications of these two opening lines of the sixth ode of the third book of Horace:

> Delicta majorum et meritus lues
> Romane donec Templa refeceris

> [You will expiate the sins of your ancestors, as you deserve to, Romans, until you have rebuilt the temples.]

To a British Catholic writing in the 1720s, these lines would have allegorised themselves instantly almost without conscious mental effort, and their contemporary application seemed unequivocal. Talman emphasised this by substituting *Brittane*, 'O Briton', for *Romane*, 'O Roman'. So the text which he wrote on his albums read

> Delicta majorum et meritus lues
> Brittane donec Templa refeceris

This is particularly clear in its implications if we consider the two lines which follow in Horace: '[A]nd the fallen houses of the gods and the statues fouled with black smoke.' The destruction and spoliation of the churches, cathedrals, and religious houses of Britain since the Henrician schism, through the Elizabethan iconoclasm and the depredations of the wars of the three kingdoms in the mid-seventeenth century, are wrongs which are as yet unrighted. A Catholic was certainly not of necessity a Jacobite in the 1720s, but the two groups were certainly associated in the eyes of the Protestant government of an island whose Catholic former sovereigns were in exile after the short-lived and disastrous attempt to restore public Catholic worship under James II. Catholicism was still illegal and penalised outside the extra-territorial chapels of the foreign embassies; indeed, a possible reason for an English Catholic to go abroad in 1709, as Talman did, was the intensification of the financial sanctions against Catholics in the wake of the Jacobite rising of 1708/09. It is important not to over-interpret the dates of Talman's continental travels – he had excellent reasons to be in Italy, including commissions for those in power in London – but his sojourn abroad from 1709 to 1717 placed him beyond the reach of a further series of anti-Catholic measures in response to the Jacobite rising of 1715.

From the perspective even of a moderate Catholic obedient to the government in London, the temples ruined by Henry and Elizabeth, the images of the saints pulled from their niches and destroyed, are a reproach to Britain and Ireland, and the long century of religious strife, risings, and civil wars a divine punishment for this impiety. A sombre reading of Talman's Horatian motto is borne out by the famously grim conclusion of Horace's ode:

> Aetas parentum, peior avis, tulit
>   Nos nequiores …
>
> [Our parents' time was worse than that of our grandparents, and we are worse still and our children will be worse yet.]

The reading of the first line which Talman chose – the version of Horace's lines which he wrote on his albums – emphasises the guilt of his contemporaries. He chose *et meritus*, 'we deserve to pay for the sins of our fathers', rather than the softer *immeritus*, the alternative reading in circulation, which became the established reading: we pay for the sins of our fathers 'although we are ourselves innocent'.

And yet, for all this grimness, the verb in Talman's motto is in the future tense – *refeceris*, 'until you rebuild' – implying some level of belief that a time will come when there will be a true restoration and that the desecrated churches, and the proscribed church of which Talman was a discreet member, will be restored to their former beauty and honour. With this fascinating motto, inscribed on the great folios of drawings which combine superb architectural collections with detailed depictions of Catholic religious ceremonial, Talman is talking to the future: to an imagined generation of visually aware Catholic fellows of the 'College of the ever-blessed Trinity' in Cambridge to whom he originally left his great collection.

The poet Alexander Pope (1688–1744) began life in a cultivated Catholic and Jacobite circle upriver of Windsor,[50] and went on to a position of extraordinary influence as an arbiter of taste in gardens, garden structures, and inscriptions, as well as in literature.[51] Pope came to manhood in circles with strong connections to the continental Catholic colleges, with their traditions of symbolic and contemplative gardening. In his own formulation of the quasi-naturalistic English garden, he advised strongly programmatic, allusive, and associational gardens and designed landscapes; he combined these with an emphasis on informal layouts, and this culturally hybrid style characterises his contribution to the British (and global) garden arts of the eighteenth century.[52] It is notable that his lifelong Catholicism offers a particular inflexion of the commemorative element in the gardens which he made for himself and others: the focal memorial obelisk for his mother in his own Twickenham garden, a locus of prayer for the dead, shadows the urns and monuments to the memories of dead friends with which his advice enriched the gardens and landscapes of England.[53]

James Gibbs (1682–1754) was a lifelong Catholic, and certainly remained in contact with the Aberdonian networks of Jacobites and Catholics among whom he had grown up. Originally he had studied for the priesthood at the Scots College in Rome, but had rapidly turned to architecture, which he practised with success, being one of the few practitioners of his generation to have a genuine knowledge of contemporary continental styles.[54] Gibbs's will is a fascinating document: he left his house and its contents to the ferociously Jacobite painter Cosmo Alexander, and much of his collection to the Radcliffe Library in Oxford. Gibbs's will also tactfully directed money destined for Masses and for the support of the Roman Church, through the route of the wine trade, whose members were often British Catholics – in this case via Mr Ker, a Scottish wine merchant in Greek Street, Soho.[55] It is perfectly possible that Gibbs's money helped to fund the seminary and chapel at Aquhorthies in Aberdeenshire which James Byres designed on his return to Scotland from Rome.[56]

And there this hasty survey should come to a halt, even though there are many more names which could be added to those who took part in this category of Catholic activity over the penal centuries, activity which contributed substantially, invisibly, to the mainstream culture of Britain.

James Byres and the Etruscans

We turn now to a detailed examination of the surviving evidence about the book on Etruscan tombs that Byres was writing in the 1760s. Although its plates, engraved by Byres's partner (in the modern sense) Christopher Norton (1738–99), were published without commentary after his death, it never came to fruition, as we have seen. As an attempt to set that project in the twin contexts of Grand Tour archaeology and recusant analogical history, this section complements and extends the analysis previously advanced by David Ridgway concerning Byres's cultural background and his use of historical analogy, political and personal, and also suggests that Byres's homosexuality played a part in shaping his view of the Etruscans and the representations of Etruscan art that he commissioned.[57] I argue, however, that it is possible to know somewhat more about this lost book than Ridgway suggests. Although the engraved plates have been lost, the original sepias by Polish-Lithuanian artist Franciszek Smuglewicz (1745–1807) all survive in the von Wagner collection at Würzburg (see Figure 5.2); extensive notes are in the National Library of Scotland; and it would also seem possible that Byres lent his notes to Johann Joachim Winckelmann (1717–68), who appears to have drawn on them for the Etruscan section

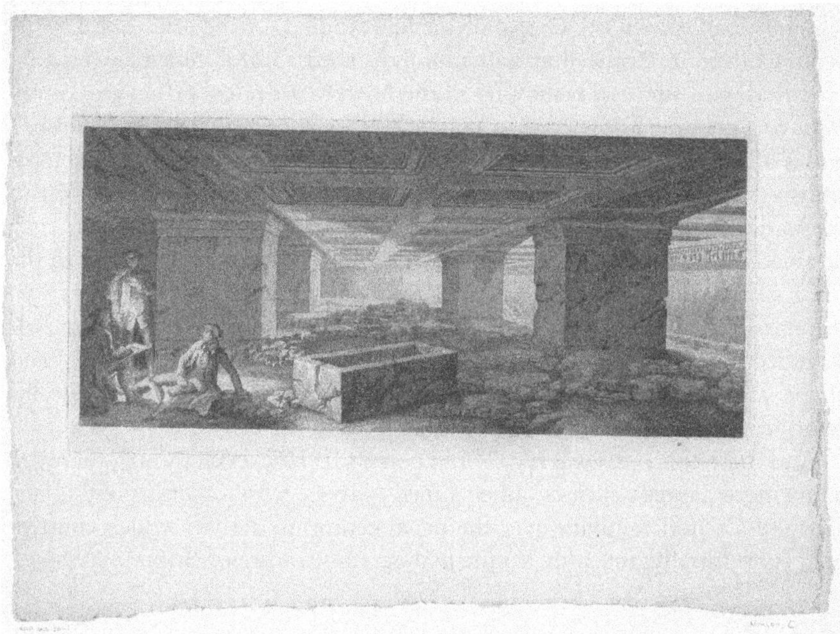

Figure 5.2 Franciszek Smuglewicz, engraved by Christopher Norton, plate of an Etruscan tomb in Tarquinia, engraved *c.* 1762–70, from James Byres, *Hypogæi, or Sepulchral Caverns of Tarquinia, the Capital of Antient Etruria* ..., ed. Frank Howard (London, 1842).

of his landmark publication, *The History of Ancient Art* (first published, in German, in 1763).

As well as Winckelmann, Byres's circle included the antiquarian Sir William Hamilton (1730–1803), British ambassador to Naples, and Giovanni Battista Piranesi (1720–78). He was closely associated, and may even have played a part in, the confection of those fabulous marble twins in the Ashmolean, known as the Newdigate Candelabra, whose inscriptions claiming imperial antiquity still preserve an echo of the claims made on their behalf by their seller. Piranesi dedicated his plate of one of them to Byres, just possibly as a coterie joke.

Like Thomas Dempster of Muiresk (1579–1625), also an exiled antiquarian, scholar, and Etruscophile, Byres came from a society in Aberdeenshire where many gentry families remained Roman Catholic after the Reformation. In a prosperous region, remote from central government and under the patronage of the powerful families of Gordon and Seton,[58] the sufferings of the Aberdeenshire Catholics were much mitigated by local toleration and accommodation. They were not the objects of any sustained political coercion or penalty until the Jacobite campaigns and risings that followed the 1688 flight from England of King James, VII of Scotland and II of England and Ireland, the last Roman Catholic monarch to reign over all (indeed, any of the) three kingdoms. Although military and professional careers in Britain remained theoretically closed to them, many Aberdeenshire Catholics prospered on the Continent, in the wine trade, and, most notably, as mercenary soldiers.[59] It was through such networks, partly based on kinship, that the parents of James Byres made their escape after the catastrophic defeat at Culloden of the Jacobite rising of 1745–46, and arrived eventually in Rome, where, as we have seen, Byres was to make his career as antiquarian, *cicerone*, and art dealer.[60]

The passing of the penal laws against those practising the Catholic faith and those who had supported the Jacobites had both direct and indirect effects. The aspect that Byres would have absorbed axiomatically and unconsciously from his background – just as he acquired the northern Scottish habits of speech still identifiably present in his adult orthography – would have been the habit of seeing the past, including the remote past, as having a particularly intense relationship to the present. This could take the form of looking to antiquity for precedent and authority. For instance, the Jacobite Latin epic the *Grameid*, by James Philip (1691), advanced the claim of James VII and II to his throne as unquestionable through one word: *Fergusius*, 'descendent of Fergus' – i.e. king of Scotland in unbroken succession from the mythical founder of the realm, King Fergus.[61] There was a deep-seated tendency throughout early modern Britain to read history analogically, and to present ancient events as direct parallels with the present.[62] This was particularly evident, in the case of the Catholic community, in the plays of the exiled Jesuit colleges on the Continent. These works represented contemporary persecution of the British Catholics as analogous to the pagan persecution of early British Christians, or to the Byzantine iconoclastic persecution of those who still honoured sacred images.[63] Christopher Highley has formulated a particularly clear form of words to describe these confessional and political apprehensions of the past:

> We should remember that antiquarian works are as much about the present as the past, and that like all text, their meanings are not fixed but contingent: as the cultural circumstances surrounding the production and reception of texts change, so texts accrue new meanings.[64]

Of course, no early modern history is free of contemporary allusion or implication, and no antiquarian discipline is immune from reading the past allegorically as a reflection on the present. This is perhaps particularly true of Scotland, as suggested by the comparatively late date of the foundation of the Society of Antiquaries of Scotland: 1780.[65] The Society of Antiquaries of London had been founded in 1707, but the anxieties surrounding the study of antiquities can be inferred from William Smellie's note on that foundation in the first volume of *Archaeologica Scotica*, as late as 1792.[66] In it, he implied that only the death, in 1766, of the last credible Stuart pretender to the thrones of England and Scotland, James Francis Edward Stuart, had cleared the way for licit antiquarian activity in Scotland:

> Till we were cordially united with England, not in government only, but in loyalty and affection to a common sovereign, it was not perhaps altogether consistent with political wisdom to call the attention of the Scots to the ancient honours and constitution of their ancient monarchy.[67]

Byres's position on the Etruscans was inevitably informed by Catholic and Jacobite historiography, and attracted him to continuities that began in the remote past.[68] In Dempster's *De Etruria Regali*, Dempster asserted that the ancient monarchy of Etruria has been revived in the rule of the Medici grand dukes of Tuscany.[69] Of Tuscany he wrote:

> Etruriam bello juxta, paceque olim florentem, ac bis mille annis Regibus parentem, variasque humanae vicissitudinis vices expertam, nunc tandem sub Serenissimis principibus Monarchio imperio restitutam ... a nomine exordium duco.[70]

> [I derive its origin from its name Etruria, once flourishing equally in war and peace, and, for two thousand years, nurturer of kings, and tested in the various alterations of human misfortune, yet, now, restored under the most serene princes to monarchical empire.]

In fact, local historical traditions attributed other origins to Florence: chiefly, that it was a Roman colony, founded either by Julius Caesar or by Roman veterans who had served with Sulla.[71]

In his 1766 manuscript *Journal of a Tour to Sicily*, Byres recorded a visit to the collection of the prince of Biscari, and made it clear that the relations between the cultures of Greece and Etruria in antiquity were only beginning to come into focus for his generation of antiquarians. In that process, his own work was to play a small, but not unimportant, part:

> He has an exelent colection of Etrusk Vases some very antient found at Comarina some with Etrusken, some Egyptian, and some with Greek figurs on them, and with Greek and Etrusken inscriptions which I think shows that the Nations had great communication together and boroud ther artes from one another.[72]

The subterranean Etruscan tombs at Corneto, now Tarquinia, had been known since the early eighteenth century, but interest in them was revived by etchings of their wall paintings published by Piranesi in 1765. It seems probable that Byres either accompanied him on the visit on which he made the drawings on which those etchings were based, or visited the tombs independently at some other point in the earlier 1760s. It seems likely that Byres made his manuscript drafts for a history of the Etruscans beginning around this time. These fragmentary drafts were possibly made over a considerable period: they contain a note referring to the Etruscan scholar Mario Guarnacci's *Origine Italiche* of 1767, and, indeed, by 1767 Byres was certainly canvassing for subscribers.[73] All the notes now in the National Library of Scotland are presumably drafts of text to accompany Byres's visual recording of the wall paintings from Corneto/Tarquinia, which survive as the sepias by Smuglewicz in Würzburg, and the engraved plates by Norton after Smuglewicz that were to wait so long for publication.[74]

By the end of the decade Byres had gathered as many subscribers as he thought he needed, but the etched copper plates were left behind when he returned to Scotland permanently in 1790, and were detained at Livorno for the duration of the Revolutionary and Napoleonic Wars and until 1817, in packing cases with other effects belonging to Byres's nephew, Patrick Moir. They were finally printed posthumously in London in 1842, in the folio entitled *Hypogæi, or Sepulchral Caverns of Tarquinia*, but with minimal text, and as a pendant to Mrs Hamilton Gray's *A Tour to the Sepulchres of Etruria in 1839*, published in London in 1841.[75]

Byres was fascinated by the achievements of this 'first people of Italy' and regarded their subjugation by the Romans as barbaric. As briefly noted above, within the historiographic tradition that Byres inherited, it would have been very easy to think of them as comparable to the Jacobite northern

Scots, menaced and defeated by an invasive southern neighbour. From the fragmentary drafts and notes in Byres's manuscript remains, it is clear that some parallel of this kind was at the centre of his thinking. He dwelt on the Romans as uncivilised, destructive conquerors in a draft headed 'History of the Etruscans/Section 1st/The antient state of Italy':[76]

> Nothing can be more incertin then the accounts left us by the antients of the first inhabitants. This is principaly owing in the first place to the Roman Conquestes and their ignorant Vanity in the arley time of the Republic when ignorant of letters they dispised al artes and sciences eccept that of Ware living principally on the spoils of their nibours in subduing the Etruscans and other nations ... [B]efor they had aquaired a teast for nolege themselves they put a stope to the Prograce of Science and the Vanity of apering the onely great nation probably indared them to destroy the Etruscan records which perhaps showed the meanes of ther origin which [they] probably wanted to Conceal.

He also began an argument for the closeness of the Gaels of Britain and Ireland, on the one hand, and the ancient inhabitants of Italy, on the other. This was part of a speculation about all of Europe being peopled from the same stock, scattered by the deluge; but it also reveals an undercurrent of hope that affinities between the Etruscans and the Gaels would emerge. Most of this discourse was based on very speculative guesses about language, embodying a wild hope that Gaelic or Welsh would prove the key to Etruscan:

> Ti or Ty in the Celtic signifies a House and Tan or Taen fire Titan the house of fire ... Celtic Alp or Alb white being generally coverd with snow. The Celtes in the asiatick provinces especially was verey earley called Titans which in Celtic signifies sons of the Earth and answers to Aborigines a neam assumed by the Umbriens a tribe of the same nation in Italy ... to endeavour to ... write down all the antient neams of Men and Pleses in Italy particularly Tuscany to get them explained by the Erse [i.e., Irish] or Welsh. To write down the Etruscan inscriptions in the Roman Character from the different Etruscan alfabets and see if they can be explained by the same language.[77]

It is to a British tradition of historical analogy among those living under penalty and in eclipse that Byres's Etruscans form an epilogue: civilised, skilled in the arts, indigenous to their territories, and in regular contact with the most cultivated peoples of the known world, yet silenced, defeated, and written out of history by their aggressive and victorious southern neighbours. The Catholic and Jacobite Scots of the north were particularly aware of the mythical origins of the Romans from their own endless appropriations of, and allusions to, the epic of the exiled hero, the *Aeneid*. In parallel with this, it is not difficult to see how the Etruscans might have come to resonate with their own mysterious ancestors who had left the north-east of Scotland rich in stone monuments, mostly pictorial representations without text.[78]

Byres had particular reason to champion Etruscan against Roman: for the enemies who had driven his family into exile, the Lowland Calvinist, the Presbyterian Whig, the whole story of Scotland's past was one of fragmentation and subjugation. Most important of all to those who negotiated the 1707 Union with England, and who subsequently fought off what they perceived as the Jacobite threat in 1715–16, 1719, and 1745–46, was a notion of their own *difference*, both from the Gaelic-speaking Highlanders from the north-west of the kingdom and the Catholic and Episcopalian Jacobites from the north-east. According to John Clerk of Penicuik, the Lowland Scots descended from the tribe of the Brigantes, whose geographic range was largely within present-day England. This made the Lowlanders a people distinct from the inhabitants of the north not only by origin but also by inclusion within the pale of Roman civilisation, to the south of the frontier of Empire that nascent archaeology was recognising in the structure now known as the Antonine Wall.[79]

Another parallel is worth considering, however. I would argue that James Byres was one of the first Scots to identify himself as gay in a modern sense, conscious of a lifelong orientation in himself and in others, and a member of a cultivated group of like-minded *virtuosi* in Rome. A reading of the lives gathered in Ingamells's prosopography of the Grand Tour indicates the existence of homosexual communities in eighteenth-century Rome and Florence, relatively discreet and rarely troubled. Winckelmann wrote all his work from an explicitly gay perspective. In a conversation piece of Byres with his household by Smuglewicz, now in the Scottish National Portrait Gallery, Christopher Norton is in the picture along with Byres's parents and sister.[80] The subject of the large oval bas-relief hanging on the wall behind the figures is unmistakably Ganymede with an eagle drinking from the shallow dish in his hands, a clear declaration of an affinity. Byres's will,[81] moreover, makes the closeness of the relationship between Byres and Norton explicit. The latter is listed as a major beneficiary, having been married to one of Byres's cousins – a venerable means of facilitating such a transfer of family capital.

This leads us to a reconsideration of one of the plates in the book which shows two antiquarians shown drawing a pilaster painting in a tomb, in one of the earliest images in both Smuglewicz's and Norton's sequences.[82] Although the figures may be generic scene-setting antiquaries, it is possible also to read them as Byres and Norton in the act of making their own records of the tombs, a gay couple making modern drawings of an ancient depiction of a near-naked youth. The plate seems to dramatise the rediscovery of these enigmatic 'ancestors'. The *Hypogæi* drawings reproduce many wall paintings of naked male figures, and the impression given by what survives of the project is of a discovery of a homosocial society delighting in homoerotic depictions.

I consider it highly likely that some of the research notes that governed the choice and sequence of illustrations for Byres's project (which he possibly made in the early 1760s, when Piranesi was making the drawings for his own Etruscan plates) were made available to Winckelmann when the latter was preparing his *History of Ancient Art* (1764).[83] In that work, Winckelmann alluded to 'a later discovery' of Etruscan tomb paintings than Buonarotti's, with 'more important pictures', before going on to list them. They coincide almost exactly with the material drawn and engraved for Byres's Etruscan project, to the degree that it is possible to consider these pages of Winckelmann's, with their emphasis on the male nude, further dispersed fragments of Byres's lost *Hypogæi* text.[84]

In summary, James Byres's thinking about the past, both in its fascination with origins and remotest antiquity and in a kind of analogical sympathy with the Etruscans (and disparagement of the Romans), conforms to strong patterns of Scottish historiography, with its emphasis on the wholly fictional integrity of an ancient Scottish kingdom ruled by an unbroken line of kings. Further, he shows signs of the kinds of analogical reading common in the Catholic and Jacobite communities, with a tendency to identify Lowland Scotland and England with the Romans – but sometimes, confusingly, the Stuarts and their adherents in the north with the Trojans of the *Aeneid* – and, on the other hand, the Etruscans by implication with the northern Stuart-loyalist Scots. So, via this implied identification, Byres claims the Etruscans as ancestors. Given that he considered a number of what we now know to have been Greek vases to have been Etruscan, and that these vases frequently depicted the male nude, as did the homoerotic paintings in Etruscan tombs, he may also have been claiming the Etruscans as ancestors in a more imaginative and personal sense, by identifying them as a society inclusive of gay sensibility and practice.

Notes

1 Edward Gibbon, *Memoirs of My Life and Writings*, ed. A. O. J. Cockshut and Stephen Constantine (Keele: Ryburn Publishing, 1994), p. 170.

2 *Ibid.*, pp. 411–12.

3 *Ibid.*, p. 412. Lord Sheffield's note confirms the identification of the church as Santa Maria in Aracoeli.

4 *Ibid.* Cf. *The Grand Tour Diaries of William Guise, from Lausanne to Rome*, ed. Paul and Jane Butler (Gloucester: Hobnob Press, 2022), p. 166.

5 Cf. Brinsley Ford, 'James Byres, Principal Antiquarian for the English Visitors to Rome', *Apollo*, 99 (June 1974), pp. 446–61; H. G. Slade, 'James Byres of Tonley (1734–1817): The Architecture of a Scottish Cicerone', *Architectural Heritage*, 2:1 (1991), pp. 18–28; and J. Ingamells, *A Dictionary of British*

and Irish Travellers in Italy, 1701–1800 (New Haven, CT: Yale University Press, 1997), pp. 169–72. The latter work also contains biographies of several of Byres's friends and associates: Andrew Lumisden, on pp. 616–17; Colin Morison, on pp. 679–82; Christopher Norton, on pp. 715–16.

6 See www.thepeerage.com/p39999.htm#i399981 (retrieved 7 April 2023).

7 There were more Scots than any other foreign nationals in the Roman Academy of St Luke: Keith Andrews, 'Scottish Artists in the Roman Circle of Winckelmann and Fuseli', in *Sind Briten Hier? Relations between British and Continental Art* (Munich: Fink, 1981), pp. 83–95.

8 Timothy Mowl, 'A Roman Palace for a Welsh Prince: Byres' Designs for Sir Watkin Williams-Wynn', *Apollo*, 142 (November 1995), pp. 33–41.

9 Although, in the estimation of Brinsley Ford, 'in the course of time it may well be discovered that one of them was actually built': 'James Byres: Principal Antiquarian', p. 450.

10 The majority of Thorpe's papers are at Stonyhurst College, Lancashire, and at the British Jesuits' ABSI archive, Mount Street, London. Stonyhurst holds his commonplace book, which he titled *Farrago*, which contains many items relating to the deposition of James II, and also to Scottish and Stuart affairs, Stonyhurst MS A V 34. A substantial collection of Thorpe's letters is in ABSI at Mount Street. These papers will form the subject of study in the near future, led by Dr Janet Graffius of Stonyhurst.

11 G. Holt, 'The Letters from Rome of John Thorpe S.J. to Charles Plowden, S.J., 1784–92', *Recusant History*, 28:3 (2007), pp. 434–57.

12 Paolo Coen, *Il Mercato Dei Quadri a Roma nel Diciottesimo Secolo: La domanda, l'offerta e la circolazione delle opera in un grande centro artistico europeo*, 2 vols (Florence: Leo S. Olschki, 2010), I, pp. 70–7, 218–19; William J. B. Paton, James Byres of Tonley, 1734–1817: The Self-Promotion of a Connoisseur, doctoral thesis, University of Aberdeen, 2022.

13 Stonyhurst, MS A 5 40.

14 Gibbon, *Memoirs*, p. 186.

15 Guise, *Journal*, p. 157.

16 *Ibid.*, p. 159.

17 'I feel very sorry for this poor old man. At the age of sixty he finds himself abandoned by the English for having changed religion: weighed down by infirmity, without hope of seeing his country again …' Acton was further isolated by his inability to learn Italian.

18 Guise, *Journal*, pp. 157–68.

19 K. O'Brien, *The Cambridge Companion to Edward Gibbon* (Cambridge: Cambridge University Press, 2018), p. 63.

20 J. D. Prown, 'A Course of Antiquities at Rome, 1764', *Eighteenth-Century Studies*, 31:1 (1997), pp. 90–100; 'A Course of Antiquities at Rome, 1764', in *Art as Evidence: Writings on Art and Material Culture* (New Haven, CT: Yale University Press, 2001), pp. 281–94.

21 National Library of Scotland, Edinburgh (hereafter NLS), MS Inv Dep 184B, unfoliated. See also Peter Davidson, 'James Byres: A Note on Catholicism,

Jacobitism and the Etruscans', in J. Swaddling (ed.), *An Etruscan Affair: The Impact of Early Etruscan Discoveries on European Culture* (London: British Museum Press, 2018), pp. 175–9.

22 James Byres, *Hypogæi, or Sepulchral Caverns of Tarquinia, the Antient Capital of Etruria*, ed. Frank Howard (London: P. & D. Colnaghi, T. Cadell, 1842).

23 NLS MS Inv Dep 184B, unfoliated.

24 *The Miscellaneous Works of Edward Gibbon*, ed. John, Lord Sheffield, 5 vols (London: John Murray, 1814), I, p. 159.

25 John Fleming, *Robert Adam and His Circle in Edinburgh and Rome* (London: John Murray, 1962), pp. 146–9; M. Cola, 'Scottish Agents in Rome in the Eighteenth Century: The Case of Peter Grant', in S. Bracken and A. Turpin (eds), *Art Markets, Agents and Collectors: Collecting Strategies in Europe and the United States, 1550–1950* (London: Bloomsbury, 2021), pp. 102–12.

26 Cf. Gerard Kilroy, *Edmund Campion: Memory and Transcription* (Aldershot: Ashgate, 2005); see also Peter Davidson, 'Alexander Seton, First Earl of Dunfermline: His Library, His House, His World', *British Catholic History*, 32:3 (2015), pp. 315–42; also, in this volume, pp. 231–244.

27 M. Tucker, 'Barclay, William [Guillaume] (1546–1608), Civil Lawyer', *Oxford Dictionary of National Biography* (retrieved online 16 March 2023); D. Abbott, 'Buchanan, George (1506–1582), Poet, Historian, and Administrator', *Oxford Dictionary of National Biography* (retrieved online 16 March 2023).

28 Nicholas Barker and David Quentin, *The Library of Thomas Tresham and Thomas Brudenell* (London: Roxburghe Club, 2006).

29 Maurice Lee, 'Seton, Alexander, First Earl of Dunfermline (1556–1622), Lord Chancellor of Scotland', *Oxford Dictionary of National Biography* (retrieved online 16 March 2023); Michael Bath, *Renaissance Decorative Painting in Scotland* (Edinburgh: National Museums of Scotland Publishing, 2003). For the painted gallery, see Chapter 14, p. 237.

30 See Chapter 14.

31 A major manuscript witness to John of Fordoun's fourteenth-century *Chronica Gentis Scotorum*, once conserved at the Abbey of Scone in Perthshire, and now probably the copy in Edinburgh University Library.

32 This sequence of fortified houses, from Towie Barclay to Delgaty, from the 1550s to the 1590s, the latter of which bear the Jesuit IHS, probably constitutes the earliest evidences of Jesuit activity in Britain.

33 A. Roberts, 'Hay, John (1547–1607), Jesuit', *Oxford Dictionary of National Biography* (retrieved online 16 March 2023).

34 Henry Hawkins SJ, *Partheneia Sacra, or The Mysterious and Delicious Garden of the Sacred Parthenes, Set Forth and Enriched with Pious Devices and Emblemes* (Rouen: Jean Coustourier, 1633); Janet Graffius, '"*Bullworks against the Furie of Heresie*": Relics, Material Culture and the Spiritual and Cultural Formation of the Sodality of St Omers English Jesuit College, 1593–1650', PhD dissertation, University of Aberdeen, 2020 (publication forthcoming).

35 See Peter Davidson, 'The Aberdeen Breviary: A Preliminary Census of Copies', *Journal of the Edinburgh Bibliographical Society*, 6 (2011), pp. 27–42; T.

Coletti and G. McMurray Gibson, 'The Tudor Origins of Medieval Drama', in K. Cartwright (ed.), *A Companion to Tudor Literature* (Oxford: Wiley-Blackwell, 2010), pp. 228–45.

36 *English Medieval Embroidery: Opus Anglicanum*, ed. Clare Browne *et al.* (New Haven, CT: Yale University Press, 2016), p. 250; Coletti and Gibson, 'The Tudor Origins of Medieval Drama', pp. 235–45.

37 G. Schondonch, *The Customs Book of St. Omers: Selections from the Original Manuscript*, ed. J. Reed, A. Callinicos, J. Browne, D. Höhr, and J. Graffius (Stonyhurst: St Omers Press, 2019).

38 J. Loach, 'Revolutionary Pedagogues? How Jesuits Used Education to Change Society', in J. O'Malley, G. Bailey, S. Harris and T. Kennedy (eds), *The Jesuits II: Cultures, Sciences, and the Arts 1540–1773* (Toronto: Toronto University Press, 2006), pp. 66–85; see also P. Shore, 'Baroque Drama in Jesuit Schools of Central Europe, 1700–1773', *History of Universities*, 20:1 (2005), pp. 146–79.

39 The Scottish elements in this court culture are investigated in Chapter 3; the Caroline court might be described as a revival of the Scoto-French courts of sixteenth-century Scotland.

40 Edward Chaney *The Evolution of the Grand Tour: Anglo-Italian Cultural Relations since the Renaissance* (London: Frank Cass, 1998), pp. 203–14; R. Smuts, 'Howard, Thomas, Fourteenth Earl of Arundel, Fourth Earl of Surrey, and First Earl of Norfolk (1585–1646), Art Collector and politician', *Oxford Dictionary of National Biography* (retrieved online 20 March 2023); M. Forster, 'Digby, Sir Kenelm (1603–1665), Natural Philosopher and Courtier', *Oxford Dictionary of National Biography* (retrieved online 20 March 2023).

41 R. Smuts, 'Conn, George (d. 1640), Diplomat', *Oxford Dictionary of National Biography* (retrieved online 20 March 2023).

42 *Præmetiæ, siue Calumniæ Hirlandorum indicatæ, et Epos, …* (Bologna: Nicolas Tebaldini, 1621); *Vita Mariæ Stuartæ Scotiæ reginæ, dotariæ Galliæ, Angliæ et Hiberniæ hæredis* (Würzburg: Stefan Fleischman, 1624 [and a Rome edition of the same year]); *Georgii Conaei de duplici statu religionis apud Scotos libri duo* (Rome: typis Vaticanis, 1628).

43 Peter Davidson and David Walker, 'Scottish Catholic Material Culture', in Robert Scully SJ (ed.), *A Companion to Catholicism and Recusancy in Britain and Ireland: From Reformation to Emancipation* (Brill: Leiden, 2021), pp. 303–38.

44 Aubrey, *Brief Lives*, I, p. 435.

45 A. Fox, 'Aubrey, John (1626–1697), antiquary and biographer', *Oxford Dictionary of National Biography* (retrieved online 20 March 2023); Aubrey, *Brief Lives*, I, p. 433.

46 Kelsey Jackson Williams, *The Antiquary: John Aubrey's Historical Scholarship* (Oxford: Oxford University Press, 2016), p. 117

47 G. Parry, 'Talman, John (1677–1726), antiquary and art collector', *Oxford Dictionary of National Biography* (retrieved online 20 March 2023); C. Giometti, 'John Talman and the Roman Art World', in Sicca, *John Talman*, pp. 159–87; Davidson, '*Donec Templa Refeceris*'.

48 Ingamells, *A Dictionary of British and Irish Travellers*, pp. 939–42.

49 Fleming, *Robert Adam and His Circle*, pp. 146–7.
50 Joseph Hone, *Alexander Pope in the Making* (Oxford: Oxford University Press, 2021).
51 Mavis Batey, *Alexander Pope, the Poet and the Landscape* (Barn Elms: Barn Elms Publishing, 1999); Morris Brownell, *Alexander Pope and the Arts of Georgian England* (Oxford: Oxford University Press, 1978).
52 See also an exemplary account of Pope and melancholy in the garden in David Coffin, *The English Garden: Meditation and Memorial* (Princeton, NJ: Princeton University Press, 1994), pp. 201–5.
53 See the last chapter of this book for a speculative meditation on the Congreve memorial at Stowe.
54 Cf. B. Little, *The Life and Works of James Gibbs 1682–1754* (London: Batsford, 1955), pp. 10–15; William Aslet, 'Il Ritorno di Signor Gibbi in Patria: James Gibbs's Training in Italy and Its Bearing on His Later Career', *Georgian Group Journal*, 27 (2019), pp. 1–13.
55 Will of James Gibbs, probate 16 August 1754, The National Archives, PROB 11/810/277, ff. 212–13; A. S. MacWilliam, 'James Gibbs, Architect, 1682–1754', *The Innes Review*, 5 (1954), pp. 101–3. Perhaps it is worth noting here that, when Robert Adam appeared as a force in architecture and connoisseurship in London, it was on the basis of his detailed Roman knowledge: John Fleming, 'Adam, Messrs. Robert and James: Art Dealers (I)', *The Connoisseur*, 144 (1959), pp. 168–71; Fleming, *Robert Adam and His Circle*, pp. 245–9. In Rome, Robert wrote to his family explaining his desire to construct an image as a dilettante, saying that 'my being an artist if I am discovered to be such may do me hurt': A. A. Tait, 'Adam, Robert (1728–1792), Architect', *Oxford Dictionary of National Biography* (retrieved online 24 March 2023).
56 Slade, 'James Byres of Tonley', pp. 26–7.
57 David Ridgway, 'James Byres and the Definition of the Etruscans', in J. Swaddling and P. Perkins (eds), *Etruscan by Definition: Studies in Honour of Sybille Haynes*(London: British Museum, 2009), pp. 2–8; David Ridgway, 'James Byres', in N. Thomson de Grummond (ed.), *Encyclopedia of the History of Classical Archaeology* (London: Routledge, 2015), pp. 211–12.
58 See Chapter 14.
59 A detailed prosopography is to be found in Tom McInally, *The Sixth Scottish University: The Scots Colleges Abroad* (Leiden: Brill, 2012); see also David Worthington, *Scots in Habsburg Service* (Leiden: Brill, 2004). Byres's uncle by marriage, Robert Gordon of Hallhead (d. 1737), was a wine merchant in Bordeaux and may well have acted as a banker for exiled Jacobites after the rising of 1715: Jacobite items, possibly left with him for safekeeping, or as securities, eventually found their way, via a Jesuit descendent, Fr. Pedro Gordon of Cadiz, into the collections of Stonyhurst College, Lancashire (personal communication from the curator).
60 The most important paper in the context of this chapter is Ridgway, 'James Byres and the definition of the Etruscans'. See also, however, Ford, 'James Byres, Principal Antiquarian'; Ingamells, *Dictionary of British and Irish Travellers*;

Slade, 'James Byres of Tonley'; and Prown, 'A Course of Antiquities'. For Byres as an antiquarian, see especially Ridgway, 'James Byres and the Definition of the Etruscans', which identifies the tombs illustrated by Byres as the otherwise unknown 'Biclinio', 'Ceisinie', and 'Tapezzeria', as well as the surviving, if damaged, 'Mercareccia' and 'Cardinale'.

61 Cf. Philip, *The Grameid.*

62 Judith Swaddling has pointed out to me the prevalence of this mode of thought in antiquity: most familiar in Plutarch's *Parallel Lives*, although, ironically, the practice seems to go back several centuries earlier to the Etruscans themselves, who placed characters who suffered similar fates or carried out similar deeds in juxtaposition on the backs of their bronze mirrors. See, for instance, J. Swaddling and S. Woodford, 'Lokrian Ajax and the New Face of Troilos: The Troilos Mirror in the British Museum', *Mediterranea*, 11 (2014), pp. 11–26; also 'Ajax and Amphiaraos', in Judith Swaddling, *Corpus Speculorum Etruscorum*, 1 (London, 2002), no. 28.

63 This subject is expertly handled in Alison Shell, *Catholicism, Controversy and the English Literary Imagination* (Cambridge: Cambridge University Press, 1999).

64 Christopher Highley, *Catholics Writing the Nation in Early Modern Britain and Ireland* (Oxford: Oxford University Press, 2008), p. 110.

65 The society received its charter in May 1783: see R. G. Cant, 'David Steuart Erskine, 11th Earl of Buchan: Founder of the Society of Antiquaries of Scotland', in A. S. Bell (ed.), *The Antiquarian Tradition in Scotland* (Edinburgh: John Donald, 1981), pp. 1–30.

66 Cant, 'David Steuart Erskine', p. 10.

67 W. Smellie, 'An Historical Account of the Society of the Antiquaries of Scotland', *Transactions of the Society of the Antiquaries of Scotland*, I (1792), pp. iii–xiii, at p. iv.

68 Peter Davidson, 'James Byres of Tonley: Jacobites and Etruscans', *Recusant History*, 30:2 (2010), pp. 61–74.

69 Completed in manuscript form in 1619, and printed by Thomas Coke, as edited and annotated by Filippo Buonarotti, in Florence in 1723–24. See Paolo Bruschetti (ed.), *Seduzione Etrusca: Dai segreti di Holkham Hall alle meraviglie del British Museum* (Geneva: De Gruyter, 2014).

70 See *Seduzione Etrusca*, p. 286. This translation by Jane Stevenson.

71 See H. Lamers, *Greece Reinvented: Transformation of Byzantine Hellenism in Renaissance Italy* (Leiden: Brill, 2015), p. 181.

72 NLS, MS 10339, f. 54r. His conclusions are, to a degree, in accord with those of Mario Guarnacci, in his *Origini italiche, o siano memorie istorico-etrusche: sopra l'antichissimo regno d'Italia e sopra i di lei primi abitatori nei secoli piu remoti*, 3 vols (Lucca: Leonardo Venturini, 1767–72), which Byres noted in NLS MS Inv Dep 184B that he had read and epitomised.

73 As witness the signed and dated receipt for a deposit for the subscription to Byres's work in Aberdeen University Library, 'Vouchers and receipts' file. The set of drawings by Byres for a refacing of King's College, in the MS 'K' series in Aberdeen, presumably date from the same visit to Scotland.

74 Ridgway, 'James Byres and the Definition of the Etruscans', p. 4.
75 Elizabeth Caroline Johnstone Gray, *Tour to the Sepulchres of Etruria, in 1839* (London: J. Hatchard and Son, 1841); Byres, *Hypogæi*.
76 The folder of manuscripts that relates to Byres's Etruscan project is not foliated, and consists of loose sheets as well as three stitched gatherings with different attempts at a discursive treatment of the subject. It seems counter-productive to invent a foliation that does not apply to visibly foliated leaves.
77 This passage seems to offer valuable confirmation that Byres did indeed transcribe Etruscan inscriptions.
78 George Henderson and Isabel Henderson, *The Art of the Picts: Sculpture and Metalwork* (London: Thames & Hudson, 2011).
79 The *limes* of the empire were often set at the Antonine Wall in Stirlingshire. Whig antiquarians tended to ignore Hadrian's Wall, or ascribe it to later builders. Hopeful apologists for Roman Scotland looked eagerly for Roman traces further north, interpreting indigenous earthworks and excavated artefacts in Angus and the Black Isle as Roman: see John Clerk, *Dissertatio de monumentis quibusdam Romanis in Boreali Magnae Britanniae Parte* (Edinburgh: T. and W. Ruddiman, 1750). The classic account of the assertion of the *Romanitas* of Scotland, by Sibbald as well as Clerk, is Stuart Piggott, *Ruins in a Landscape: Essays in Antiquarianism* (Edinburgh: Edinburgh University Press, 1976), especially pp. 133–59. An overview of the subject is provided by P. Davidson and D. MacCannell, 'The 1707 Union, Europe and the Culture of Scotland', in A. Mackillop and M. Ó Siochrú (eds), *Forging the State: European State Formation and the Anglo-Scottish Union of 1707* (Dundee: Dundee University Press, 2009), pp. 175–91.
80 The portrait dates from *c.* 1775–78. It is one of two versions, with variant backgrounds, this one in the Scottish National Portrait Gallery, Edinburgh, inv. no. PG2601.
81 This can be found in the same manuscript collection in the NLS as his notes on Etruscan history.
82 Byres, *Hypogæi*, pl. II.
83 Winckelmann's knowledge of Etruscan tombs from descriptions is noted in *Winckelmann, Firenze e gli Etruschi*, ed. P. Arbeid, S. Bruni, and M. Iozzo (Florence: Edizioni ETS, 2016), p. 154.
84 J. J. Winckelmann, *The History of Ancient Art* (Boston: Little, Brown & Co., 1856), pp. 357–9. It would be rash to claim that Byres is the *only possible* source of this information, but he remains a very likely one.

Part II

Materialities

6

The solemnity of the Madonna Vulnerata, Valladolid, 1600

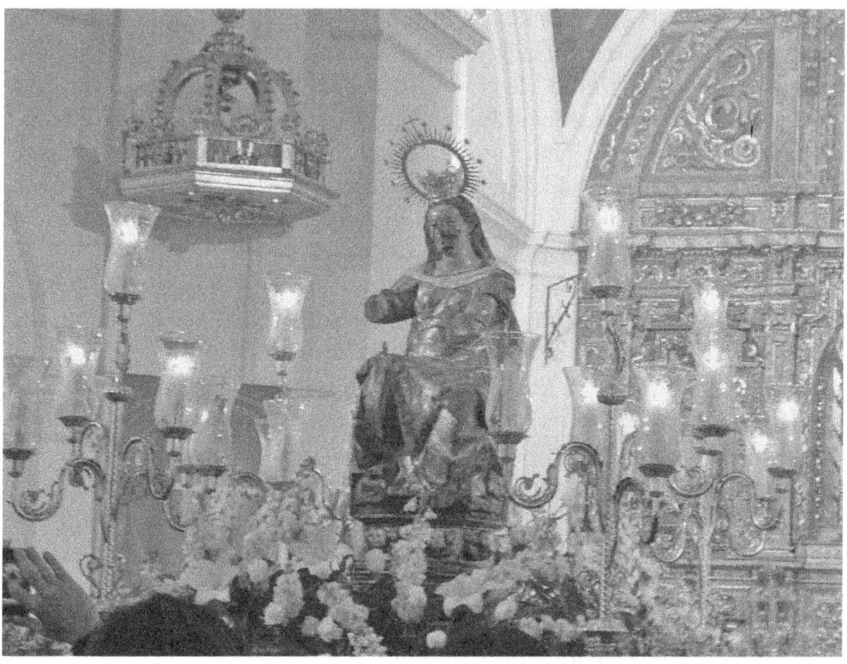

Figure 6.1 Anon. (southern Spanish), *Virgin and Child* (known as 'La Vulnerata'), polychrome wood, late sixteenth century, subsequently vandalised, Real Colegio de San Albano, Valladolid, Spain.

On 7 September 1600 a vandalised statue was processed with lights and music through the streets of the Spanish city of Valladolid to the English Catholic College of St Alban, where it was received by no less a person than the queen of Spain (see Figure 6.1). The college was decorated for the occasion with *affixiones* of symbolic pictures and verses, as was the custom of all Jesuit colleges on solemn days. What was particularly striking about the ceremonial on this day was the oppositional political message it was at pains to express, and the extraordinary way in which it utilised nearly all the resources of baroque communication – including word, image, emblem, oratory, and contemplation of the potentially to-be-tortured bodies of the students themselves – to convey a nexus of ideas about true and false religion and, more unexpectedly, about true and false national identity. The ritual was devised to act as a summary and reminder of these things, a complex act of positioning, which clearly retained its symbolic power for half a century at least and had distinct echoes even after that.

This chapter is concerned with the culture and ideas of a specific community of early modern exiles, the Roman Catholics chiefly from England, but also from Scotland, Wales, and Ireland, who formed colleges in Flanders, Italy, and Spain. As a response to the initially unpopular schism between the English and Roman Churches that had occurred under Henry VIII, the ancient English Pilgrim Hostel in Rome had mutated by 1579 into the Venerable English College within the Papal University, training priests for the dangers of the English mission.[1] New colleges for the same purpose were founded at Saint-Omer and Douai in Flanders (now northernmost France), both of which were then ruled by the Catholic kings of Spain, as well as at Valladolid and Seville.

These colleges functioned as active cultural centres. In direct opposition to the new order in England, the ones in Spain arrogated to themselves the right to award university degrees which, in the Spanish official mind, could no longer be awarded in England; the pseudo-universities of Oxford and Cambridge were disqualified both by their heresy and by the fiat of Philip II, crowned king of England as the husband of Mary Tudor, who asserted his sovereignty over England until his death. The exiles' colleges thus constituted themselves as a parallel and oppositional England. Alongside theological and philosophical study, all maintained a programme of literary and cultural production: plays, exhibitions of symbolic 'speaking pictures' or emblems, schemes of wall painting and easel painting, oratory, and even evening classes for exiled English-speaking laypeople.

The earliest evidence of an English college at Valladolid is from around 1588, by which time that city was regularly visited by the Spanish court, with an established and flourishing university. There was already a group of English and Irish exiles in the town. After the dynamic Jesuit Fr Robert Persons arrived in Spain in 1589, things moved swiftly: the College of St Alban was in being by early September that year, and soon obtained a royal charter and substantial endowments; and the now Royal College of St Alban received the dubious accolade of being mentioned by name in Elizabeth of England's proclamation against seminary priests in 1591.[2] Its bull of foundation was issued in 1592, and building must have commenced almost immediately, as Philip II and the princes visited its still incomplete structures on 3 August of that year. On that occasion the college site was decorated with Latin verses and speaking pictures, which are recorded in a printed account as well as in an album of inscriptions in the Biblioteca Nacional de España in Madrid.[3] The king's successor, Philip III, visited in August 1600, an occasion also marked by emblems and verse, recorded in an illustrated presentation volume, now BNE MS 2492.[4]

Both these royal visits were an opportunity for the new college to display its perceptions of its own status and identity, and of the condition of the country from which the students had been exiled. Not coincidentally, the prestigious early modern modes of communication with which they achieved this, emblems and oratory, were the ones that their curricula most strongly emphasised. It should also be stressed that, on both these occasions, the orations were in a multiplicity of languages, notably the minority languages of Britain and Ireland. In continuing to stress the multiplicity of cultures and languages of the three kingdoms, these festivals were ripostes to the exclusionary anglophone character of the Tudor regime.

By the time of 1600's Solemnity of the Vulnerata on 7 September (the date is significant), the emblems and orations were unequivocally oppositional. Indeed, they constituted that thing which so consistently eludes current critics of early modern literature: a genuinely subversive text, proposing a radical inversion of the existing order of things. Although the Elizabethan state was in fact quite easy-going about those social groups hitherto put forward by contemporary writers as 'subversive' (for instance, articulate women, discontented servants), its official reaction to the exiled Catholics – and especially to the Society of Jesus – indicates very clearly who it thought its most potent enemies were.

Specifically, the ritual surrounding the installation of the mutilated statue asserted the authenticity and antiquity of English Catholicism and the illegitimacy, in every sense, of the Elizabethan regime. But it went beyond this, to assert an ownership of English history and a claim of authentic Englishness to which geographical England was no longer entitled. This ceremonial is recorded in two sources: a manuscript in Rome, Venerable English College Liber 1422; and what seems to be a unique pamphlet in the library of St Alban, Valladolid: *Recebimento que se hizo en Valladolid a una imagen de nuestra Senora* (Madrid, 1600). It seems likely that this was printed as a companion piece to the account of the August visit of the royal family that was published by Andres Sanchez, also in 1600 at Madrid.[5]

To understand the context of this oration at the gate of the college in the presence of the vandalised statue, followed by its installation in the college chapel to serve as an image of self-wounded England, it is essential briefly to consider the iconography of the college at Valladolid, and then the parallel iconography of the Chapel of the Venerable English College at

Rome – an institution also much influenced by Persons. Both these highly charged places – and the ceremonial enacted in and around them in the early modern period – asserted a startling reversal of the status quo as it was perceived in Britain.

Indeed, the iconography of both Rome and Valladolid advanced a flatly contradictory version of reality, in which the true England was in exile, and these colleges were the sites of authenticity, the seedbeds – 'seminaries' in the literal sense – out of which true Englishness could be restored to England itself. Schismatic England was articulated as a partial, diminished place, lost and untrue to itself. It was no accident that the exiled English religious houses commissioned paintings of the Saxon sovereigns of England, for this constituted an explicit claim to authentic, historically continuous Englishness defined in terms of saintly royal Catholicism. Among the paintings at Valladolid are a sequence of saintly monarchs of England, painted at Seville by Francisco Pacheco in the early seventeenth century: Saints Lucius, Edilbertus, Sebbus, Oswald (whose facial resemblance to the usual portrait type of Philip II is unmistakable), Richard, Edmund, Edward the Martyr, and Edward the Confessor (carrying a lily, and with his hand to his breast).[6] In the corridors of the college, this sequence of martyred monarchs echoes a graphically painted series of martyred alumni, and is part and parcel of the construction of an alternative version of history. Similar ideas about history and martyrdom are put forward by the iconography of the Venerable English College in Rome, as well as that of Syon Abbey, Lisbon (about which we will hear more in Chapter 7).[7]

At Valladolid, the high altar was originally flanked by statues of the martyred king and archbishop, St Edmund and St Thomas Becket, with the representation of the proto-martyr of England, Alban, between them.[8] Nevertheless, historical circumstances presented the new college there with a ready-made emblem of the wounds that history had inflicted on the Church and on England as a whole. In the course of the Earl of Essex's abortive 1596 expedition against Spain, his troops had sacked a church at Cadiz, and ritually and publicly vandalised a statue of the Virgin and Child. This image, in its mutilated state, was transported to Valladolid and installed in the college chapel on the occasion that is the focus of this chapter.

There is an extraordinary (albeit slender) possibility that the vandalism during the Cadiz raid was intended to be symbolic, and ordered officially, perhaps even by Lord Burghley, in response to an incident at County Leitrim, Ireland, in the late 1580s. On that occasion, Sir Brian O'Rourke and his gallowglasses had ritually vandalised a statue of Queen Elizabeth, striking it with axes, insulting it verbally, and dragging it from a horse's tail. Burghley was informed about what had taken place, and the last report on it in his dossier dates from just three years before the attack on Cadiz.[9]

In a precise sense, the Vulnerata – as the Cadiz statue had come to be known by 1600 – served as an equivalent to the Martyrs' Picture in Rome. Placed at the centre of the reredos behind the high altar in Valladolid, it became an enduring reminder of the triumphs of the Queen of Heaven and of the wounded and disintegrated state of divided England under its heretical earthly queen. To the exiled community, the statue would have been intensely consoling, via its suggestion that, whatever worldly triumphs Elizabeth might enjoy, in the long run she could only be self-defeating. In this context, the Vulnerata emerges as the image of an England self-wounded by the ignorance and blindness of her children. Moreover, no elaborate framing devices are needed to convey this. Within the image itself, the Christ Child has been destroyed, implying a world with no Incarnation, and therefore with no hope; and the gashes that disfigure the Virgin's face reflect the disordered state of those who desecrated it. Tellingly, the students gathered regularly before this image to offer formalised prayers, both for forgiveness for the wrongs done in England and for the restoration of England to the Catholic faith.

Complex ideas of fall and exile are prominent in the ceremonial that accompanied the installation of the Vulnerata in 1600. Although this ritual was devised specifically for the occasion, it recognisably derives from three pre-existing types. The procession of images through southern European towns was, and in some places remains to this day, a vital expression of community. The display of emblems was standard on Jesuit colleges' celebrations of festal days, as were displays of oratorical skill. And, since the queen of Spain was the first to venerate the rescued image, there was an element of the ceremonial traditionally attending any royal visit or entry.

Indeed, the procession of the Vulnerata, first to the Carmelite church and then to the College of St Alban, followed the usual route of the *adventus* of any bishop or of any royal entry into the city, which was up until that time a regular fixture of the Spanish court's peregrinations.[10] We know that the procession was accompanied by music, because the *Gastos*, or accounts of the College of St Alban, record against the marginal note '*menestriles*' '*De oficiar dos bisperos y una misa y un salve y un procession los menestriles lel dia de la colocacion de nuestra senora seys ducados*' – a considerable sum.[11]

Turning now to the message of 7 September, as Alison Shell and I have both observed elsewhere, this date was Elizabeth of England's birthday, and meant to be kept as a festival in England as part of a concerted symbolic attempt to affirm the new Protestant order by overwriting the Virgin with the Virgin Queen. This phenomenon is particularly noteworthy in the printed account of the ceremony:

> [L]os hereges en Inglaterra han quitado la fiesta de la Natividad de Nuestra Señora, y en su lugar celebran con grande solenidad, y han puesto en su calendario con letras coloradas la natividad de la Reyna Ysabela.[12]

[The heretics in England have abandoned the feast of the Birthday of Our Lady and in its place celebrate with great solemnity, and have written in their calendars in rubricated letters, the birthday of Queen Elizabeth.]

Of course, 7 September is also the vigil of the feast of the Birthday of the Virgin, and as such is observed to this day in the *ferias* of Valladolid and of its sister university town of Salamanca. This was emphasised by the author of the printed relation as well as by the orator on the occasion, both of whom criticised not only Elizabeth's impious tampering with the sacred calendar but, more significantly, the superiority of the fruitful Virgin to the sterile queen. This comparison was also inevitably made in England, too, in such uneasily positive images as the monument to Elizabeth's governess Blanche Parry at Bacton in Herefordshire, where an improvised parody of a mediaeval chantry chapel sculpture places the figure of Parry uneasily on her knees before the seated figure of Elizabeth herself.[13]

Further assertion of the illegitimacy of the prevailing regime in England was conveyed explicitly by the content of the oration at Valladolid, and implicitly by the presence in the college, at least by the year 1610, of the portraits of the earliest English kings. The painting of the martyrdom of St Alban in the refectory, which appears to date from the first years of the college, is a very strange artefact, depicting Alban's executioner as an Amerindian. I strongly suspect that this was meant to express the 'barbarism' of the English by a kind of parallelism, just as the drama *Titus or the Palm of Christian Courage*, performed at the Jesuit College at Kilkenny in 1644, depicts the English allegorically as Japanese persecutors of the Christians.[14] And, soon enough, the Valladolid college would begin commissioning a series of formal commemorative portraits of martyred former students; but, for the present, it should be remembered that martyrdom was the leading theme of the oration made on this occasion.

Philip III, though present in late seventeenth-century pictures of the Vulnerata procession now in the college chapel at Valladolid, had in fact been called away to Madrid in September. In a sense, however, the event 'worked better' without him: the queen of Spain, ritually placing herself as lower in the hierarchy than the statue – i.e. as the hostess who receives the royal visitor – both sufficiently embodies the royal power that sustains the college and also offers an image of legitimate, pious female royalty which contrasts perfectly with the absent female royal heretic.

The clearest medium used on this occasion to articulate this message was that of the emblems, however. The manuscript in Rome and the very similar printed pamphlet at Valladolid both record nine emblems as having been displayed on the day of the ceremony. They clearly develop themes from earlier emblematic exhibitions for the two previous royal visits to the college; for instance, an emblem of Noah's Ark was displayed in both 1592 and September 1600. But, in 1592, its message was the contrast between the dove, the martyred English priest who carries souls home to God, and the Protestant clerical raven, who feeds on the bodies drowned in the flood.[15] In 1600 the image is of a voyage home to an England restored to itself, attended by a dove and an olive branch. There are also strong echoes of the kinds of emblem displayed during Philip III's visit earlier in 1600. Thanks to the present writer's re-identification of BNE MS 2492 as the presentation volume from the occasion of the king's visit, we can see a few of the pictures that make explicit the political as well as religious oppositions celebrated by these festivals. This manuscript includes an image of Philip as the life-giving sun, begging him to thaw the frozen waters of the lost north.[16] The lostness – and, indeed, the horror of the north – is of course the subject of the last work by Miguel de Cervantes, the impossible *Trabajos de Persiles y Sigismunda, historia setentrional*, first published in 1617, which likewise closely reflects the world view of Catholic Spain that the north was the source of dangers, heresies, and hostile armies.[17]

Later in the collection of manuscript emblems, Philip appears as the day star who will shine to illumine the darkness in England.[18] Similarly, on folios 12v and 13r, we find the emblem of the rose and sun, which draws a comparison between the true England, the rose, now withered by an unnatural winter, and expresses the hope that the future work of the seminarians under the benign sun of Spain will cause the whole island to be strewn with roses.[19] This resonates strongly with the rose emblem displayed for the Solemnity of the Vulnerata in September 1600.

No pictures of the Vulnerata ceremony's emblems appear to have survived. From contemporary written descriptions, however, we can conclude that many of the same messages were being conveyed. The writing of the *affixiones* set up in the college is recorded in the expense book as having cost ten reales, but another 30 were spent on 'German Guards' for them and the other papers displayed in the college, so large was the crowd that came to see them. The mutilated statue itself is at first compared to the enduring palm tree, as a symbol of both resilience and ultimate victory. Then, its devout rescuers – specifically, the English students – are represented as the priests carrying the Ark of the Covenant through Jordan. England is a vineyard untended for want of priests and, finally, the brightness of the Star of the Sea guides the ship of the Church back to the haven of England. These beautifully devised emblems represent a distinctively English contribution to a genre usually associated with the Catholic seminaries of the Low Countries, to which the English College of Saint-Omer was to contribute in the course of the seventeenth century.[20]

The emblem that makes the strongest political statement, however, is that of the rose which nourishes the productive honeybees and kills the sterile bumblebees. The initial, obvious interpretation of this is that the Virgin, the Mystic Rose, is death to the heretics and life to the faithful. Beyond this, there is a sense that England has become a sterile land, but one that could yet be restored to fruitfulness. The childless Elizabeth is clearly figured in the sterility of the bumblebee, as opposed to the literally and spiritually fruitful Virgin. In the same way, Elizabeth's barrenness had been figured 30 years earlier in the emblem of the fruitful and fruitless vines sewn by Mary Stuart in her captivity, an emblem produced as evidence in the trial of the Catholic Duke of Norfolk in 1572.[21] As well as emblems, poems were attached to the temporary hangings that decorated the college. The last of these again makes the same point: that there has been an alteration in England itself, such that the country which had been the dowry of the Virgin Mary had sunk to the condition of Athens after it was deserted by the goddess Athena.[22]

But let us return to the ceremonial of September 1600 itself. When the image had been venerated first by the queen and then by the rest of the company, an oration in English and/or Latin drew together the whole symbolic importance of the ceremonial of the day, playing on the themes of exile and martyrdom, and of the lostness of contemporary England:

> Enter O triumphant queene of martyrs enter into this your college as into a fertill soyle of martyrdome, that by your coming the number of those victorious martyrs may daily encrease. Remayne with us, most gratious lady, in this our solitude and tyme of banishment until the clouds of heresy be dispenced and the desryed day appear. That day I meane when our England shall be lightened again and renewed againe with the true sonne of the catholicke religione and you returning tryumphant and victorious with us to take possession of your ancient dowry.[23]

Then, fascinatingly, the orator positioned his own and the other students' bodies in relation to the wounded body of the statue.

> [I]f the sword of Gods justice be already drawne behold us here ready to be sacrificed for the sinnes of our people lett the word of revenge take it upon our bodies, let us suffer imprisonment, rack, banishment and death we only desire the lives of our bretheren.[24]

Soon enough, the corridors that led to the chapel where the Vulnerata would be venerated were to be filled with commemorative portraits of the alumni of the college – including Garnet, Walpole, and Palleser – carrying their martyrs' palms before the scenes of their respective tortures and deaths.

Thus, in the oration for the Vulnerata, like the trophies for the faith in the English College in Rome, the students' potentially tortured flesh and potentially shed blood become England; the peroration that concludes the oration makes this point clear:

> Cherish, o Sacred Virgin, these your children, your souldiers, your servants, instruct them with heavenly discipline, indue them with holy armour, inflame them to this your combate with the desyre of everlastinge felicitie, that having vanquished with their valour and vertue the blind barbarous impietie wherewith their countrie is oppressed, you may returne at laste after so many years of exile to your England, your kingdome, your auncient and dearly beloved dowry. [25]

This is perhaps the point to emphasise: the whole intellectual enterprise of exiled Catholicism is a passionate argument for Englishness and for possession of the true heritage of Catholic England. These points are argued allegorically again and again in the Latin drama of the exiles' Catholic colleges.

Early in 1600 the accounts for the college in Valladolid record the expense of binding 'quince libros de la historia Anglicana'. To this day, the college's library contains Protestant histories of Britain with manuscript erasures and refutations, which are particularly savage on the pages of William Camden's *Annales* and John Speed's *The Historie of Great Britaine*.[26] In the Valladolid copy of Camden's *Annales*, which bears a charming *probatio pennae* on the flyleaf: 'We be three Lancashire lads', all royal titles applied to Elizabeth have been obliterated. Throughout the book there are passionate marginalia presenting the Catholic viewpoint on the history and topography of England. Whoever wielded the pen clearly hated Burghley with a passion, for, wherever his name occurs, the paper has been all but scored through. This is a fascinating artefact, at once recognising Camden as an expert who cannot be ignored and controverting absolutely the content of his expertise. A copy of his *Britannia* has also been heavily expurgated and annotated, beginning with an elegantly written 'auctore damnato' beside his name on the title page; and Speed's *Historie* has received much the same treatment.

In the later seventeenth century clear remembrances of the Vulnerata and the symbolic force given to the vandalised statue by the 1600 ceremonial can be identified within the culture of the English colleges. The occasion, in other words, had a long life in both Spanish and exiled British memory. The first of these clear echoes can be found in one of the Latin plays written for performance in the colleges, *Leo Armenus*. As was frequently the case, this play drew on history to find a parallel to the present state of England: here, the struggle in Byzantium between those who gave honour to sacred images and those who destroyed them, known as the civil wars of iconodule and iconoclast.

Leo Armenus was performed in the 1620s in Saint-Omer in Flanders and in 1645 at the Venerable English College in Rome. Its scene that most clearly recollects the Vulnerata and all that the statue stands for – serving as a reminder to the exiles that conditions have changed, if anything, for the worse since 1600 – is one in which the iconoclast Sabatius bursts out of hiding and defaces an image of the Virgin under the horrified eyes of the good Theophilus, who then voices the following lament for the injury done to the statue and to the sacred person it represents: 'Perite flores: Laesa jam florum est parens. / Marcescite rosae, coelitum elanguet rosa.'[27] The play was revived in 1645 at Rome, where a large influx of travellers and royalist exiles from Britain created a new audience for the English College's plays; intense iconoclasm had returned to England, and the whole problem of the three kingdoms and of what it meant to be English (or Scots, or Irish, or Welsh) had been brought to the forefront of people's consciousness by civil war. Many Protestants had come to share the established Catholic sense of a native land grown strange to itself: violent, usurped, self-wounding, and diminished. In this context, *Leo Armenus* attained a new set of topical resonances as the rules of what constituted England and not-England had changed again.

The history and memory of the Vulnerata persisted to the end of the century, and beyond. The Spanish rector of St Alban, Manuel de Calatayud, rebuilt its chapel in the late 1670s, at great expense and with no little controversy, into what could be described as an imitation of the Gesú at Rome, but so confined by its narrow site as to have caused the nave to implode into an octagon. Around the dome thus created, de Calatayud commissioned grand processional canvases from Diego Diez Ferreras. These are remarkable works, not least because they appear to be using prints from the 1600s as the basis for their likenesses of Philip III, Robert Persons, and other historical figures, some of whom were in fact not present in Valladolid in September 1600. This sequence of paintings takes us through the whole history of the Vulnerata, from the sack of Cadiz, through its transport on a triumphal car, to the solemn procession through the streets of Valladolid to the chapel of the English College. These are exceptionally interesting documents, both as a late seventeenth-century imagining of what happened in 1600 and an underlining of the crucial symbolic force that the vandalised statue had retained throughout the intervening period, almost up to the brief reign of the Catholic James II and VII.[28]

The last echo of the triumphs of the Vulnerata came from half a world away in 1680. The Mexican savant Carlos de Sigüenza y Góngora, in his wonderful and complex exposition of the history and mythology of Mexico for the entrance of its viceroy into Mexico City in 1680, wrote of another church profaned by the English and of the miraculous sequel to the event (for we should remember that many miracles were attributed throughout the seventeenth century to the power of prayers offered before the Vulnerata). Celestial music emanated from a church in the province of Tabasco, profaned by the English heretics commanded by 'a pirate';[29] and these other-worldly sounds then proceeded in front of the Mexican troops for many leagues:

> Al pasar por un iglesia que profaneron con impiedad los herejes, oyeron nuestros soldatos músicas celestiales que les antecedieron en el camino por muchas leguas, como consta de información plenísima que de ello se hizo.[30]
>
> [Passing a church which had been impiously profaned by the heretics, our soldiers heard celestial music, which preceded them on the road for many leagues, as to make absolutely clear from whom the music came.]

What especially intrigues me about this account of another English raid and its sequel is that Sigüenza y Góngora ultimately related it to the festival he was orchestrating in the capital: celestial harmony echoing the earthly harmony of the Western Paradise, in a last echo of the Solemnity of the Vulnerata.

In the time of James II and VII, the oppositional and confrontational ceremonial of the exiled Catholics was revived. The newly Catholic regime – apparently possessed of tact and political acumen in equally negative quantities – published, first in Rome and then in London, an account of the Catholic Earl of Castlemaine's embassy to the pope. Although the plates in this volume contained various symbolic images of Protestantism trodden underfoot by Catholicism, and of Britain's return to the true Church, its frontispiece was perhaps particularly incendiary: it showed the English ambassador in the act of kissing the papal foot, in an attitude of prostrate submission, iconographically parallel to other paintings of homage being shown by subject provinces to an emperor. Seldom, I would suggest, since the *blijde inkomst/joyeuse entrée* on which the Netherlands based its claim of secession from Spain, has a festival text caused so much trouble.[31]

There is still some historical debate as to precisely what ignited the rebellion that removed James from the throne. It seems unlikely that it was *only* the birth of Prince James Francis Edward, as there had been several royal children before him, none of whom had survived infancy. I would suggest that one of the sparks which caused the explosion – and thus the Jacobite exile, and the exiled festivals of the Jacobites – was quite possibly the publication of this tactless and oppositional book, with its reassertion of the truth of that alternative, Catholic, reality which had been symbolically articulated in the Valladolid festival of 7 September 1600.

Notes

1 Michael Williams, *The Venerable English College Rome* (London: Associated Catholic Publications, 1979). This whole project is much indebted to Mgr Williams; to Dr Javier Burrieza Sánchez, archivist at Valladolid; to Fr T. M. McCoog SJ, archivist of the British Province of the Society of Jesus; to Andrew Nicoll, archivist of the Catholic Church in Scotland; and to Mgr Denis Carlin, rector of the Royal Scots College in Salamanca.

2 See Michael Williams, *St. Alban's College Valladolid: Four Centuries of English Catholic Presence in Spain* (London: Hurst, 1986); Javier Burrieza Sánchez, *Una Isla de Inglaterra en Castilla* (Palencia: V. Merino, 2000).
3 BNE, Madrid, MS 6001; Thomas Eclesal, *Relacion de un Sacerdote Ingles … in la qual le da cuenta de la venida de su Magestad a Valladolid, y al Colegio de los Ingleses* (Madrid: Pedro Madrigal, 1592).
4 *Relacion de la venida de los Reyes Catholicos, al Colegio Ingles de Valladolid, en el mes de Agosto, Año de 1600* (Madrid: Andreas Sanchez, 1600). Copies of these rare publications have been found with the kind help of Dr Javier Burrieza Sánchez, archivist of the Royal College of St Alban, Valladolid.
5 The title page of the longer work advertises, after the main title, '*la collocacion y fiesta hecha en el mesmo Collegio, de una Ymagen de Nuestra Señora mal-tratada de los hereges*'.
6 In these identifications, I am again grateful for the kind help of Dr Burrieza Sánchez. Now preserved at King's College, Aberdeen, is a depiction of a Scottish king, similarly dressed, who may be St King David, dating perhaps from the Catholic refitting of the Trinity Church in Aberdeen for James II and VII, perhaps from the Scottish abbey at Regensburg, where there was a painting of King Achins, mythical founder of the house.
7 Michael Williams, 'Paintings of Early British Kings and Queens at Syon Abbey, Lisbon', *Birgittiana: Rivista Internazionale di Studi Brigidiani*, 1 (1996), pp. 123–34. These paintings are now all at Oscott College, Birmingham.
8 The present arrangement of the high altar, dating from the later seventeenth century, preserves the flanking figures of archbishop and king, removing Alban to the pediment of the retablo to make way for the central figure of the Vulnerata.
9 Alan J. Fletcher, *Drama and the Performing Arts in Pre-Cromwellian Ireland: A Repertory of Sources and Documents from the Earliest Times until c. 1642* (Cambridge: D. S. Brewer, 2001), pp. 436–9.
10 See Sánchez, *Una Isla de Inglaterra en Castilla*, especially pp. 29–33.
11 The college had no music of its own, it would seem: a letter from Persons to Fr Joseph Cresswell dated June 1600 stated that all the instruments in the house had been taken away except for a lute: copy in the Jesuit Archives, Mount Street, London.
12 *Recebimento que se hizo en Valladolid a una imagen de nuestra Senora* (Madrid, 1600), p. 6.
13 Discussed and illustrated in Nikolaus Pevsner, *The Buildings of England: Herefordshire* (London: Penguin, 1963), pp. 69–70.
14 Fletcher, *Drama and the Performing Arts*, pp. 489–91.
15 BNE, MS 6001, ff. 40r–v; *Recebimento de la Imagen de Nuestra Señora*, sig. H1v–H2r.
16 BNE MS 2492, f. 23r: '*[S]ic te Solem in Hyperboreis ipse creabis aquis*' ['You are like the sun that thaws the frozen waters of the north'].
17 Miguel de Cervantes Saavedra, *Persiles y Sigismunda*, ed. Rodolfo Schevil and Adolfo Bonilla (Madrid: B. Rodriguez, 1914), esp. pp. 281, 297. Throughout Cervantes's romance the north is imagined as a place of darkness, death,

treachery, and separation; nor is there any good reason to suppose that Cervantes was wholly unaware of the English College and its activities.

18 BNE, MS 2492, ff. 10v–11r:

Spes est agricolis pulsandi Tristia noctis
  Lucifero assueto more trahente diem.
Nos simili, princeps, relevas spe, lumina nostris
  Dum facis ut fidei laeta feramus agris,
Namque ha[e]c nostra fovet fidei spes pectora, nempe
  Luciferos mittis mox erat alma dies.

[It is the hope of labourers that the sorrows of the night will be conquered, and Lucifer in his accustomed way, will bring the day: For us, similarly, o prince, you ease our lights with hope, since you make it that happy, we will till the fields of faith, for this hope comforts the breast of faith, that truly, you send Lucifers/ light-bringers, and soon it will be clear day.]

19 BNE, MS 2492, ff. 12v, 13r:

Stare diu, rosa pulchra nequit, nisi pulchrior ipsam
  Candens vitali lumine phoebus alat.
Phoebo abeunte cadit, phoebo redeunte virescit,
  Vitam ex phoeba luce caduca trahit.
Sic rosa flagrantes quondam spargebat odores
  Anglica, purpureas ambitiosa comas.
At postque Hesperio cepit se tollere soli.
  Frigoreque haeretico Terra Britanna premi.
Tum rosa defecit, neque enim sine sole vivere,
  Aut gelido potuit crescere pulchra solo.
At modo foelici campos deus irrigat imbre,
  Sanguine, faecundo semine, terra madet.
O sol Hesperiae princeps tua lumina sparge,
  Fundet odoriferas Anglia tota rosas.

[For a long time, a beautiful rose was not able to stand, unless a more beautiful sun nourished it shedding the light of life. Once the sun was gone, it fell; with the return of the sun, it flourishes, drawing life from the failing light. Thus the English rose once used to shed sweetest scents, encircled with lush foliage. But after the Evening Star began to drag the sun to itself, the Land of Britain was oppressed with a heretic frost. Then the rose failed, for it was not able to live without sun, or beauty to flourish by ice alone. But then, God watered the fields with a happy shower of blood, and to wet the earth with life-giving seed. O sun, prince of the Western Land, shed your light, strew all England with sweet-scented roses.]

20 See especially Karel Porteman, *Emblematic Exhibitions (Affixiones) at the Brussels Jesuit College (1630–1685): A Study of the Commemorative Manuscripts (Royal Library, Brussels)* (Turnhout: Brepols, 1996).

21 See Michael Bath, *Renaissance Decorative Painting in Scotland* (Edinburgh: National Museums of Scotland Publishing, 2003), pp. 36–7. The duke's death, incidentally, is lamented in a passionate marginal annotation in the copy of Camden's *Annales* now at Valladolid.

22 *Recebimento*, p. 6.

23 Archivum Venerabilis Collegii Anglorum de Urbe, Rome (hereafter VEC), MS Liber 1422, f. 59v. The Latin text (*Recebimento*, p. 12) reads:
'Utinam licuisset nobis (o clarissima caelorum Regina) capita nostra subijecere nefarijs sceleratorum ensibus, & obiectis pectoribus excipere haec vulnera quae in sacram tuam imaginem inflixerunt ... Ingredere (o Regina Martyrium) in hoc tuum Collegium, veluti in clarissimum martyrii thalamum, ut Christo & Ecclesiae novos quotidie Martyres parias.'

24 VEC, MS Liber 1422, f. 59v. The Latin text (*Recebimento*, p. 14) reads:
'Quod si iam divinae gladius districtus est, ecce nos piacula &anathemeta esse pro populo nostro: in nos ille mucro dissaeviat: patiamur carceres, eculeos, carnificinas, lanientur nobis corpora, distrahantur artus, evelantur viscera, tantum illi non pereant in eternum.'

25 VEC, MS Liber 1422, f. 59v. The Latin text (*Recebimiento*, p. 14) reads:
'Fove hos tuos Alumnos (o Virgo) tuos milites imbue coelestibus disciplinis, indue sanctissimis armis, accende eternis premiis ad pugnam, ut foelicissima eorum virtute, victa impietate, tandem in Angliam, tuum illud regnum, tuam dotem, longo post liminio revertaris.'

26 For these marginalia, see Davidson, '*Donec Templa Refeceris*'.

27 'Die, flowers, the mother of the flowers is wounded, roses fall, the rose of the heavens is hurt'; see Shell, *Catholicism, Controversy, and the English Literary Imagination*, pp. 207–9.

28 See particularly Sánchez, *Una Isla de Inglaterra en Castilla*, pp. 30–1.

29 Sherlock is the name suggested by the expert on pirates of this period, Dr James Kelly (personal communication).

30 Carlos de Sigüenza y Góngora, *Seis Obras*, ed. William G. Bryant (Caracas: Biblioteca Ayacucho, 1984), p. 217.

31 John Michael Wright, *An Account of His Excellence Roger Earl of Castlemaine's Embassy from His Sacred Majesty James II ... to His Holiness Innocent XI* (London: Thomas Snowdon for the author, 1688). This had been published in Italian the year before as Giovanni Michele Writ, *Raggvaglio della Solenne Comparsa, Fatta in Roma gli otto di gennaiao MCCLXXXVII dall' Illvstrissimo, et Eccellentissimo Signor Conte di Castelmaine Ambasciadore Straordinario della Sagra Real Maesta di Giacomo Secondo* (Rome: Domenico Antonio Ercole, 1687). There is also, in the MacBean Jacobite collection in Aberdeen, a single leaf recording the papal nuncio's entry into Windsor on 3 July 1667 [*sic* for '1687'?].

7

Opposing Elizabeth

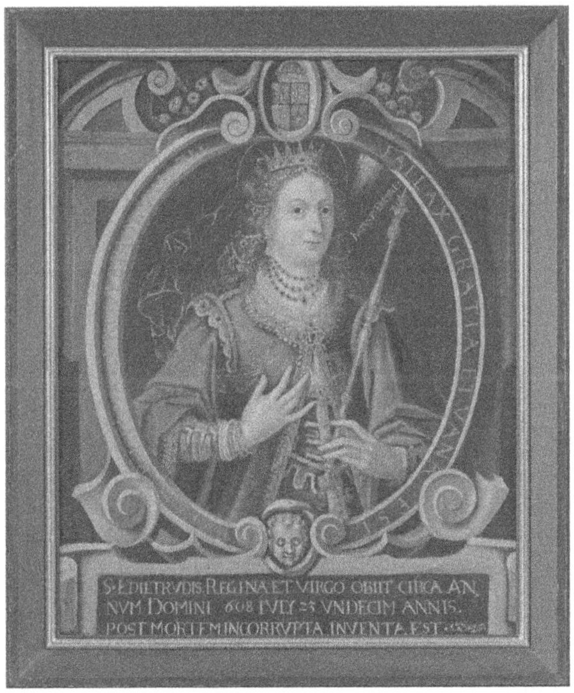

Figure 7.1 Studio of Francisco Pacheco, *St Ediltrudis*, early seventeenth century, oil on canvas, St Mary's College, Oscott, Sutton Coldfield, England.

Elizabeth I of England was cordially detested in Catholic Europe, as well as by many of her own subjects, particularly English and Irish Catholics marginalised at home or driven into exile by her religious policies. This chapter suggests, perhaps controversially, that the literal and symbolic images with which the persecuted Catholic community opposed Elizabeth were as cogent as the improvised, albeit magnificent, iconography that was set forth in her praise (see Figure 7.1).

Scholarship on the presentation of the image of the queen continues to develop and deepen. By its sheer size and authority, this scholarly literature tends to suggest that depictions of Elizabeth were accomplished English manifestations of an international symbolic language.[1] It has broadly failed, however, to capture the degree to which the presentation of the image of the queen had to be invented, almost without precedents, by the ingenious circle of Protestant humanist 'new' men and women who surrounded her. Indeed, a proclamation from very early in Elizabeth's reign explicitly *forbidding* the circulation of unlicensed images of the new monarch would appear to reflect anxiety on this score in her immediate circle. This proclamation, of which a manuscript draft survives with corrections in William Cecil's hand, outlaws the circulation of all representations of the queen, until

> some cunning person shall shortly make a portrait of her person or visage to be participated to others for satisfaction of her loving subjects; and furthermore commandeth all manner of persons in the meantime to forbear from painting, graving, printing or making of any portrait of her majesty.[2]

Within the systems of signs and symbols that prevailed in the sixteenth century, required by every aspect of early modern monarchy from portraiture to civic festival, it was not at all easy to find ways of depicting a ruler as 'edgily' placed as Elizabeth. An unmarried woman ruler, whose legitimacy was open to question in the light of the wills of her Protestant father and brother, childless and unwilling to identify a successor, committed to a religious policy that filled the upper ranks of her Church with ambitious new men: all this exists at a sharp angle to late Renaissance repertories of images of authority, stability, and continuity. Such conventional ideas, beliefs, and images would have been much more easily applied to Mary Stuart, the unequivocally legitimate descendent of English kings and mother of a son, or even to Philip of Spain, crowned king of England in 1554 and ruler of half the world from 1556, who was also the father of a living heir.

Considering the reign of Philip and Mary brings the central problem into focus: religion. Put simply, Elizabeth's position led her to favour an innovated Protestant settlement that nonetheless claimed both divine authority and ancient precedent. Escalating hostility on both sides caused that settlement – and much of Elizabeth's governance – to be defined essentially in opposition to international Catholicism. Over time, as English Catholics came to be treated as potential or actual traitors, many of them would advance a passionate scrutiny of Elizabeth's title and style, as proclaimed at her accession:

> The most high and mighty Princess … by the grace of God Queen of England, France and Ireland, defender of the true, ancient and Catholic faith, most worthy Empress from the Orkney Isles to the Mountains Pyrenée.[3]

One of the languages in which they could respond was the international discourse of images. If the symbolic presentation of Elizabeth is studied in isolation, by reference to English tradition alone, it appears far less strange or ingeniously improvised than in fact it was. In particular, the work of Roy Strong and the many excellent exhibitions of Tudor painting that have followed in its wake have so familiarised the scholarly community and interested public with Elizabeth-as-Peace/Chastity/Cynthia, Elizabeth-with-Phoenix, and so on that these allegorical or *impresa* portraits seem to define a norm, rather than constituting an evolving exception.[4] I would argue that, within the terms and constraints of late Renaissance public discourse, the case against Elizabeth was actually far easier to put than that in her favour. Yet, if we ignore the rest of Europe, this paradox remains invisible. *Dissing Elizabeth*, the thoughtful collection of essays edited by Julia Walker, focuses only on English and Ireland, and thus inevitably misrepresents publicly articulated opposition to Elizabeth. The ingenious iconographies of power devised in the Cecil circle, and by the Queen's Champion Sir Henry Lee, would subsequently provoke a consistent series of contrary, Catholic iconographies which criticised Elizabeth by contrasting her with her cousin Mary Queen of Scots, with the saintly Saxon queens of English history, and with the Blessed Virgin herself. As I have already suggested, it was much easier to dispraise than praise Elizabeth within the bounds of early modern public discourse. In an age that upheld male authority, tradition, royal legitimacy, and the uncontroversial succession of natural heirs, Elizabeth could be straightforwardly represented as an aberration. The claim to tradition and antiquity was one of the central battlegrounds of controversy between Protestants and Catholics. Much polemical writing sought to legitimise the Protestant monarchies and the Reformation itself as a return to a pristine form of Christianity, in ways that were no less forceful that Catholic assertions of their continuity with the Church of the catacombs.[5]

I would like to present three examples of this form of controversy. The first is the oppositional statements about Elizabeth that were included in the needlework pictures made by Mary Queen of Scots during her long captivity in England. Although what survives of these has been discussed in some detail elsewhere, this chapter discusses needlework by Mary which is known but no longer extant.[6] Second, there is the observation that the altarpiece in the chapel of the Venerable English College in Rome, completed in 1580 and subsequently circulated as an engraving, may have elicited, in response, the glorification of Queen Elizabeth in the iconography of the 1590s 'Ditchley' portrait.[7] The third and final example concerns the portraits of saintly Saxon monarchs that were displayed in the exiled Catholic colleges and religious houses on the Continent.

For a detailed description of the now lost emblematic bed hangings embroidered by Mary Stuart, we are indebted to the following passage by William Drummond of Hawthornden, written in the early seventeenth century:

> I have been curious to find out for you, the *Impresa*'s and Emblems on a Bed of State, wrought and embroidered all with Gold and Silk by the late Queen *Mary*, Mother to our sacred Sovereign, which will embellish greatly some pages of your Book, and is worthy [of] your Remembrance. The First is the Loadstone turning towards the Pole; the Word is her Majesty's Name turned into an Anagram, *Maria Stuart, Sa vertue m'attire*, which is not much inferiour to *Veritas armata*. This hath Reference to a Crucifix, before which with all her Royal Ornaments she is humbled on her knees most lively, with the Word *undique*. An *Impresa* of *Mary of Lorrain* her Mother, A *Phœnix* in Flames, the Word *en ma fin git mon commencement*. The *Impresa* of an Apple Tree growing in a Thorn, the word *per vincula crescit*. The *Impresa* of *Henry* II the French king, a *Crescent*, the Word *donec totum impleat orbum*. The *Impresa* of King *Francis* I, a *Salamander* crowned in the Midst of Flames, the Word *Nutrisco et extinguo* ... Two Women upon the Wheels of Fortune, the One holding a *Launce*, the other a *Cornucopia*: which *Impresa* seemeth to glance at Queen Elizabeth and her self; the word *Fortunae comites*. The *Impresa* of the Cardinal of *Lorrain*, her Uncle, a Pyramid overgrown with *Ivy*, the vulgar word *Te stante virebo*; A Ship with her Mast broken and fallen in the Sea; the Word *Nunquam nisi rectam*. This is for her selfe and her Son, a big *Lyon* and a young Whelp beside her, the Word *unum quidem sed Leonem*. An Emblem of a Lyon taken in a Net, and Hare wantonly passing over him, the Word, *Et lepores devicto insultant Leoni* ... A Palm Tree, the Word *Ponderibus virtus innata resistit*. A Bird in a Cage, and a Hawk flying above, with the Word *il mal me preme et me sparenta peggio* ... A Porcupine amongst Sea Rocks, the Word, *ne volutetur*. The *Impresa* of King Henry VIII, a *Portcullis*, the Word, *altera securitas* ... A Tree planted in a Churchyard environed with dead Men's bones, the Word *Pietas revocabit ab orco*. Eclipses of the Sun and Moon, the Word *Ipsa sibi lumen quod invidet aufert*; glancing as may appear at Queen Elizabeth ... A Vine-tree watred with Wine, which, instead of making it spring and grow, maketh it fade; the Word, *Mea sic mihi prosunt*. A Wheel rolled from a Mountain into the Sea, *Piena oh dolor roda de Speranza*; which appeareth to be her own, and it should be *Praecipito senza speranza*. A Heap of Wings and Feathers dispersed; the Word *Magnatum Vicinitas*. A Trophie upon a Tree, with Mytres, Crowns, Hats, Masks, Swords, Books and a Woman with a Vail about her Eyes or muffled, pointing to some about her with this Word, *Ut casus dederit*. Three crowns, Two opposite and another above in the Sky, the Word, *aliamque moratur*. The Sun in an Eclipse, the Word, *Medio occidit die*.[8]

Let us be highly selective in considering only a few of the images described by Drummond. First of all, there is a reminder of Mary's status: the arms of Scotland, England, and France, which make an implicit claim to the throne of England. Those emblems that Drummond interprets as 'glanc[ing]' at Elizabeth are more directly expressive of hostility to the English queen. The image of women standing on the wheel of fortune conveys an explicit threat. The image of moon and sun is starkly hostile: the moon of Elizabeth has temporarily eclipsed the rightfully ruling sun, but, like any eclipse, will not last for long. It recalls how Elizabeth's own iconographers liked to present her as the virgin-goddess Cynthia, with the crescent moon in her hair. In these emblems, Mary expresses her sense not only of injury but also of her own worth and significance. It is important to recognise just how unequivocal and confrontational a statement the lost state bed made, in the terms of a discourse that was deadly serious in the sixteenth century. A French-language description of the same bed, possibly made by a member of Mary's household at Fotheringhay, is found in a British Library compilation manuscript.[9] Although this account differs in some details from Drummond's, it seems clear that they are describing the same object. The French list includes more emblems than Drummond does – it is possible that a pair of curtains had been lost from the set of furnishings before Drummond saw them – but the additional emblems, including a repeat of the palm tree and tortoise, all convey very much the same messages. That is, they assert Mary's rights and worth, and imply that the world has cast her down only that she might be rewarded with an earthly and/or heavenly crown. Elizabeth, had she been aware of this list or the object it described, would probably have felt vindicated in her decision to eliminate such an obdurate and confrontational opponent.

Before moving on, it is important to note that Mary's oppositional images had an immediate currency and were used as part of the public opposition to Elizabeth, discreetly in England, but openly on the Continent. These images, along with others that had been used by Mary in her captivity, were taken up by the great Jesuit poet St Robert Southwell immediately after her execution in 1587. With great skill and eloquence, Southwell weaves this iconography into an argument in favour of Mary as a divinely favoured martyr for the Catholic faith, and against Elizabeth as little better than a murderess. These verses caused enough alarm in the highest circles of Elizabeth's administration for the Bacon family to seek and obtain a copy soon after their composition.[10] From the point of view of these hostile readers, the crucial and most provocative lines must have included:

> Alive a Queen, now dead I am a Saint
> Once M. called my name nowe Martyr is
> From earthly raigne debarred by restraint
> In liew whereof I raigne in heavenly bliss
> […]
> Rue not my death rejoyce at my repose

It was no death to me but to my woe
The budd was opened to let out the Rose
The cheynes unloo'sd to lett the captive goe.[11]

There is a strange correspondence between one of the most celebrated English portraits of Elizabeth and the altarpiece of an institution that might be considered an intellectual epicentre of opposition to her: the Venerable English College in Rome. Before it was rebuilt in the nineteenth century, the walls of the college chapel were painted with scenes of all the martyrdoms suffered for the sake of the Christian religion in England, from St Alban down to the reign of Henry VIII.[12] The chapel altarpiece, painted by Durante Alberti and installed in 1580, is a complex expression of both the nature of the exiled Catholic project and the purpose of the English mission. The Trinity are above in the heavens, while Christ's blood falls down onto a dim map of England, below which an angel holds up a banderole with the defiant motto 'I come to set the world on fire'.

In Alberti's altarpiece, Christ's blood falls from his wounded side onto a representation of England on the globe below him: I would like to advance the possibility that the audacious and extraordinary iconography of the 'Ditchley' portrait of Elizabeth, which Sir Roy Strong dates to the early 1590s, constitutes, to some degree, a response to the symbolic map on the altarpiece of the *Venerabile*. This portrait was painted for Henry Lee, the retired Queen's Champion, who entertained her at Ditchley in 1590.[13] He may well have devised the iconography himself; certainly, he was no stranger to this mode of expression, having devised the iconographic schemes for the annual Accession Day tournaments. The painting depicts Elizabeth as a titan, standing on the map of England with a stormy sky about her head. There are inscriptions, Latin mottoes, and a sonnet in English that compares the queen's divine powers with those of the natural elements. One of the Latin texts reads 'Potest nec ulcistur' ['She could take revenge but does not'], and the sonnet begins with the assertion that the sun 'hath no such glorye'. It is an iconography so audacious as to appear hubristic, certainly more grandiose than that of any contemporary continental monarch. The last couplet of the sonnet, now mutilated, hints at a divine source for Elizabeth's power: 'Riuers of thancks still to that oc[...] / Where grace is grace aboue, power pow[...].' As a response to Alberti's altarpiece, this is direct and confrontational. The blood of Christ falling on the wounded land is countered by the giant figure of Elizabeth standing on the same landmass, which, moreover, is made to appear further from Europe's shores than was geographically the case.

As Chapter 6 has noted, it was no accident that the exiled Catholic colleges and religious houses commissioned paintings of the Saxon sovereigns of England; this was part of an explicit claim to authentic, historically continuous Englishness, defined in terms of saintly royal Catholicism, and an implied rebuke to the saints' degenerate royal successors. Among the paintings at Valladolid there is a sequence of holy kings of early England, painted in the early seventeenth century.[14] Here, I argue that the parallel series of Saxon kings, queens, and princesses from the English Syon Abbey in Lisbon, now held by Oscott College, Birmingham, includes specific, as well as general, responses to images of Elizabeth; and that the fictive architectural framing, common to both the Lisbon and Valladolid sequences, is a considered reply to published images of Elizabeth.

The Valladolid kings and the Lisbon kings, queens, and princesses all appear to come from the Seville workshop of Francisco Pacheco.[15] The set at Valladolid arrived there in 1602, and evidence mustered by Mgr Michael Williams would suggest that the Lisbon series, clearly from the same workshop, were dispatched to Portugal by 1616, possibly at the instigation of the Conde de Luna y Mayorga.[16] Before we trace the exact connection between these two sequences of portraits and a depiction of Elizabeth, it is important to consider the larger context, in which these images of Saxon monarchs functioned as an explicit challenge to the queen's authority.

As we have seen, the iconography of Elizabeth was necessarily an improvisation, and thus innately ill suited an age that valued stability, antiquity, and continuity. Catholic controversialists appealed to antiquity in their disputes with England (among other Protestant nations) and incessantly asserted their continuity with the Church of the Apostles. In response, Protestants also appealed to antiquity, claiming that theirs was a Church of apostolic purity, purged of medieval errors and innovations. In the seventeenth century the Protestant archbishop of Armagh in Ireland, James Ussher, devoted prodigious energies to the recovery of an autochthonous Celtic Church that was essentially independent of Rome. Much the same argument was made in England, for the autonomy and antiquity of the 'British Church'.[17]

It is only in this context that one can properly understand the counter-argument, advanced by the exiled Anglo-Dutch Catholic antiquary Richard Verstegan, that the real origins of the English lie with the continental Saxons, and not with British indigenes.[18] The summary of his position by Counter-Reformation historian Anne Dillon cannot be bettered:

> The reformers claimed a specifically British pedigree as opposed to a Saxon one ... The Catholics embraced and extended this Protestant construction of Catholic Saxon origins ... [Fr Robert] Persons, referring to 'our predecessors the English Saxons', exploited what, at first sight, might appear a loss of birthright.[19]

As such, nearly any reference to Saxon monarchs constituted an implicit challenge to Elizabeth and to the post-Reformation English Church. But there is also an explicit challenge expressed in the way the design of the Saxon portraits answers one of the most audacious engraved depictions of Elizabeth. The title page of the 1568 English Bible, known as 'the Bishops' Bible', consists of an engraved strapwork cartouche, enclosing a feigned oval containing a portrait of Elizabeth with crown and sceptre, with her titles inscribed on its frame. The contemporary arms of England are at the top centre.[20] Both the Valladolid and Lisbon sequences have the same oval framing and very similar feigned-stone strapwork surrounding the portraits – a resemblance that goes beyond mere coincidence.[21] Every one of the Valladolid and Lisbon portraits, all of which also bear the contemporary arms of England at top centre, is thus a reproach to the arrogance and impiety that has placed the queen's image on the title page of the Bible. Thus, too, the saintly virtues of charity, piety, and endurance which are conveyed by inscriptions and quasi-*imprese* on the Saxon portraits are not only appropriate moral examples for English religious houses with royal connections but also accusations directed against Elizabeth's person and polity.[22]

This is especially clear in the Lisbon depiction of St Ediltrudis (probably, more correctly, Etheldreda), whose facial type and pose are very close indeed to the engraving of Elizabeth on the Bishop's Bible's title page.[23] Crucially, however, Ediltrudis is shown as subordinate, and attentive, to God: a ray of light from above touches the right-hand side of her head, and an inscription, rendered as if it is her speech, reads 'Justus es Domine' ('Lord, you are just'). The text from the Vulgate inscribed on the feigned oval, from Proverbs 31:30, 'Fallax gratia et vana est pulchritudo' ('Charm is deceitful and beauty empty'), calls to mind the second part of the Biblical verse: '[M]ulier timens Dominum ipsa laudabitur' ('[T]he woman who fears the lord is to be praised'). The inscription below the portrait describes Ediltrudis as 'Regina et virgo', and asserts that, 11 years after her death, her body was still incorrupt (this assertion was based ultimately on Bede's *Ecclesiastical History*).[24] This, too, could have been seen as yet another rebuke to the earthly monarch of England, enveloped as she was by chivalric imagery praising her unfading beauty.

These examples of the use of the visual and symbolic discourses of the late Renaissance to make statements in opposition to Elizabeth demonstrate that, paradoxically, oppositional utterances were securely located within a continuous tradition of royal and public imagery. It is the public and visual articulation of Gloriana, Diana, Cynthia, the Faerie Queene, the Phoenix, the Vestal, the Virgin Queen – the whole 'cult of Elizabeth' – that constituted a desperate, if sumptuous, improvisation.

Notes

1 The classic work is Roy Strong, *The Portraits of Queen Elizabeth* (Oxford: Clarendon Press, 1963), which was further developed in his *The Cult of Elizabeth* (London: Thames & Hudson, 1977). Strong's rehang of the National Portrait Gallery and the programme of exhibitions he initiated there also served to focus scholarly attention on the iconography of Elizabeth's court, to the extent that many subsequent scholars have perceived that iconography as typical and canonical, rather than as an adroit local improvisation within an international symbolic language.

2 Proclamation draft dated at Westminster, December 1563, 6 Elizabeth I; *Tudor Royal Proclamations*, ed. Paul L. Hughes and James F. Larkin, 2 vols (New Haven, CT: Yale University Press, 1969), II, pp. 240–1.

3 Proclamation dated Westminster, 15 January 1559, 1 Elizabeth I; *Tudor Royal Proclamations*, II, p. 103. This claims all territory ever held, even conjecturally, by any English monarch, and a good deal more; such historical inconveniences as the defeat at Bannockburn and the loss of Calais are simply elided.

4 There was a particularly splendid group of portraits of Elizabeth exhibited at the Tate Gallery, London, in the *Dynasties* exhibition of 1995/96; see *Dynasties: Painting in Tudor and Jacobean England, 1530–1630*, ed. Karen Hearn (London: Tate Gallery, 1995), pp. 78–90.

5 There is much useful discussion of these controversies in Shell, *Catholicism, Controversy, and the English Literary Imagination*.

6 Mary's needlework has been discussed in a superbly detailed article by Michael Bath, 'Embroidered Emblems: Mary Stuart's Bed of State', *Emblematica*, 15 (2007), pp. 5–32. In brief, Mary's embroideries should not be regarded as time-filling craftwork but as artefacts designed to communicate meaning. Much of her work on small panels is based on identifiable and internationally known literary sources, such as a book of the *imprese* adopted by royal and noble individuals in France (Claude Paradin, *Devices Heroqiues* [Lyon: Jean de Tournes, 1551]), and, inevitably, each picture-plus-motto communicated a political message. Attacks on Elizabeth are sometimes explicitly present, as in the vine imagery in Mary's Oxburgh hangings. A vine will fruit only on wood that is one year old – this year's growth – so an unpruned vine is a sterile one that can bear no fruit. Mary is fertile, Elizabeth sterile. This is also a reference to John 15:1–8, which alludes to Christ's image of Himself as the true vine, and the division of humans into fruitful and sterile branches – the virtuous and the vicious – and makes it explicit that the sterile branches will be lopped and burned: 'If a man abide not in me, he is cast forth as a branch, and is withered; and men gather them, and cast them into the fire, and they are burned.' The emblem image in Mary's textile therefore not only criticises Elizabeth but threatens her with divine – and perhaps earthly – punishment.

7 For the altarpiece, see Chapter 6 and Davidson, 'Recusant Catholic Spaces in Early Modern England', pp. 23–7; it was reproduced in a volume of engravings

of martyrdoms for the Catholic Church in England, from St Alban down to the English Reformation, a work of violent hostility to Elizabeth's governance and religious settlement: Niccolò Circignano and G. B. di Cavallieri, *Ecclesiae Anglicanae Trophaea* (Rome: Bartolomeo Grassi, 1584). There is an exemplary discussion of this work in Anne Dillon, *The Construction of Martyrdom in the English Catholic Community 1535–1603* (Aldershot: Ashgate, 2002), pp. 70–242.

8 Drummond's letter is printed in Ben Jonson, *Works*, ed. H. C. Hertford and Percy Simpson, 2 vols (Oxford: Clarendon Press, 1925), I, p. 208. Again, the reader is referred to Bath's comprehensive 'Embroidered Emblems', which also considers how this text relates to National Library of Scotland, Hawthornden MS 2064, f. 21 – a somewhat random collection of papers associated with William Fowler, which begins a list very similar to that given by Drummond in the words, '5 April 1603 after the kings departeur I did observe these devyces vpon the queenes his mothers bedd'. Drummond's letter 'To his worthy friend Master Benjamin Johnson' first appears in print in *The Works of William Drummond of Hawthornden* (Edinburgh: James Watson, 1711), p. 137.

9 British Library, MS Cotton Caligula D. I., f. 142r–v.

10 A manuscript copy of 'Decease Release' among the papers of Anthony Bacon is marked in French, 'Some verses by Mr Southwell on the Scottish Queen, received the month of February, 1586' (1587 n.s.): Lambeth Palace Library, MS 655. Elizabeth's enemies also continued to advance the claims of Mary Stuart after the latter's death; memorial portraits and the (abandoned) canonisation process are discussed at length in my article 'Saint Mary, Queen and Martyr', *History Scotland*, 2.1 (2002), pp. 32–7.

11 Stonyhurst College, Lancashire, MS Anglia v. 27, edited in Peter Davidson and Anne Sweeney (eds), *The Collected Poems of St Robert Southwell SJ* (Manchester: Carcanet Press, 2007), pp. 41–2.

12 There is a detailed and illuminating account of the original mural paintings in Bailey, *Between Renaissance and Baroque*, pp. 153–65.

13 Hearn, *Dynasties*, pp. 89–90. This idea has also been advanced independently by Jason A. Nice in 'Cross-Confessional Features of English Identity: The Ditchley Portrait of Queen Elizabeth I and the High Altarpiece of the English College in Rome', in Philip M. Soergel (ed.), *Nation, Ethnicity and Identity in Mediaeval and Renaissance Europe* (New York: AMS Press, 2006), pp. 185–209.

14 For identifications, I am grateful for the kind help of Dr Burrieza Sánchez. There is a depiction of a Scottish king, similarly dressed, preserved at King's College, Aberdeen, who may represent King Achins, mythical founder of the Scottish monasteries in Bavaria, and thus may have come from the Scottish Benedictine abbey at Regensburg.

15 As there are excellent accounts of both these series, I will be economical with detail: the Valladolid kings are discussed in Sánchez, *Una Isla de Inglaterra en Castilla*, and the Lisbon series in Mgr Williams, 'Paintings of Early British Kings and Queens'. I am much indebted to the kindness of Mr Gerard Boylan, librarian at Oscott College, who has given me access to study photographs

of the Lisbon series. See Enrique Valdivieso, *Francisco Pacheco (1564–1644)* (Seville: Caja San Fernando, 1990).

16 Williams, 'Paintings of Early British Kings and Queens', p. 130.

17 Donna B. Hamilton, 'Richard Verstegan's *A Restitution of Decayed Intelligence* (1605): A Catholic Antiquarian Replies to John Foxe, Thomas Cooper, and Jean Bodin', *Prose Studies*, 22.1 (1999), pp. 1–38.

18 Richard Verstegan, *The Restitution of Decayed Intelligence* (Antwerp: Robert Bruney, 1605).

19 Dillon, *Construction of Martyrdom*, pp. 333–4.

20 Elizabeth is placed between female personifications of Faith and Charity, and therefore, by implication, is herself presented as the personification of Hope. For this history of the Tudor Monarch's image on the Bible and for later Elizabethan use of personifications of the virtues in this context, see John N. King, 'The Royal Image 1535–1603', in Dale Hoak (ed.), *Tudor Political Culture* (Cambridge: Cambridge University Press, 1995), pp. 104–32.

21 This acute observation is that of Dr Daniel MacCannell.

22 The Scottish Benedictine Monastery at Regensburg is recorded in Aberdeen University Library, MS 2538, vol. III, f. 10r, as also having displayed three portraits of ancient Scottish monarchs in 1659, but the context was wholly different. The historiography of Scotland (both Protestant and Catholic) accepted more or less the same version of Scottish royal succession from legendary times down to the Stuarts; and the legendary kings were claimed as founders of what were in fact originally Irish religious houses in Franconia.

23 Williams, 'Paintings of Early British Kings and Queens', p. 128.

24 Bede, *Ecclesiastical History of the English People*, ed. B. Colgrave and R. A. B. Mynors (Oxford: Clarendon Press, 1969), pp. 394–5.

8

Relics and memorials of Mary Stuart in the Low Countries

Among the most compelling objects of memory and veneration created or preserved by the exiled British Catholic community are those created posthumously in honour of Mary Queen of Scots (1542–1587) as a Catholic martyr. What is particularly compelling about this group of powerful and politically confrontational objects is that they were created in the material vacuum left by the Elizabethan state's extreme care that no physical relic of Mary Stuart should leave the site of her execution. Originating on either side of the turn of the seventeenth century, these objects relate closely to the intellectual and historical narratives implicit in the display of relics and memorials at such institutions as the English College of Saint-Omer, founded by Robert Persons SJ in 1593. Indeed, it seems probable that some of the fragmentary relics that make up the composite gilt and polychrome card reliquary now known as the Blairs Jewel (since it was long located at Blairs College, Aberdeenshire) were once part of the relic collection of Saint-Omer (see Figure 8.1). In any case, like the relics arranged at Saint-Omer in the early modern period, which are now substantially preserved at Stonyhurst College in Lancashire, the Blairs Jewel relics not only emphasise the antiquity and continuity of the Roman Church – as manifested in the series of martyrs from ancient Rome down to the Tudor and Stuart present which are represented in it – but also advance new claims of connection between Mary Stuart and the Jesuit martyrs of England. This pattern of a demonstration of continuity is also the leading theme of the most celebrated illustrated martyrology produced by the English Counter-Reformation: *Ecclesiae Anglicanae Trophea* (Rome: Bartolomeo Grassi, 1584), which ends with the martyrdom of St Edmund Campion and his companions; the account of contemporary atrocities against Catholics, the *Theatrum Crudelitatum Haereticorum Nostri Temporis* (Antwerp: Adrian Hubert, 1587), ends with the execution of Mary Queen of Scots. This latter work emerged from the same exiled circle in Antwerp which produced the objects discussed here, and is closely related to them.

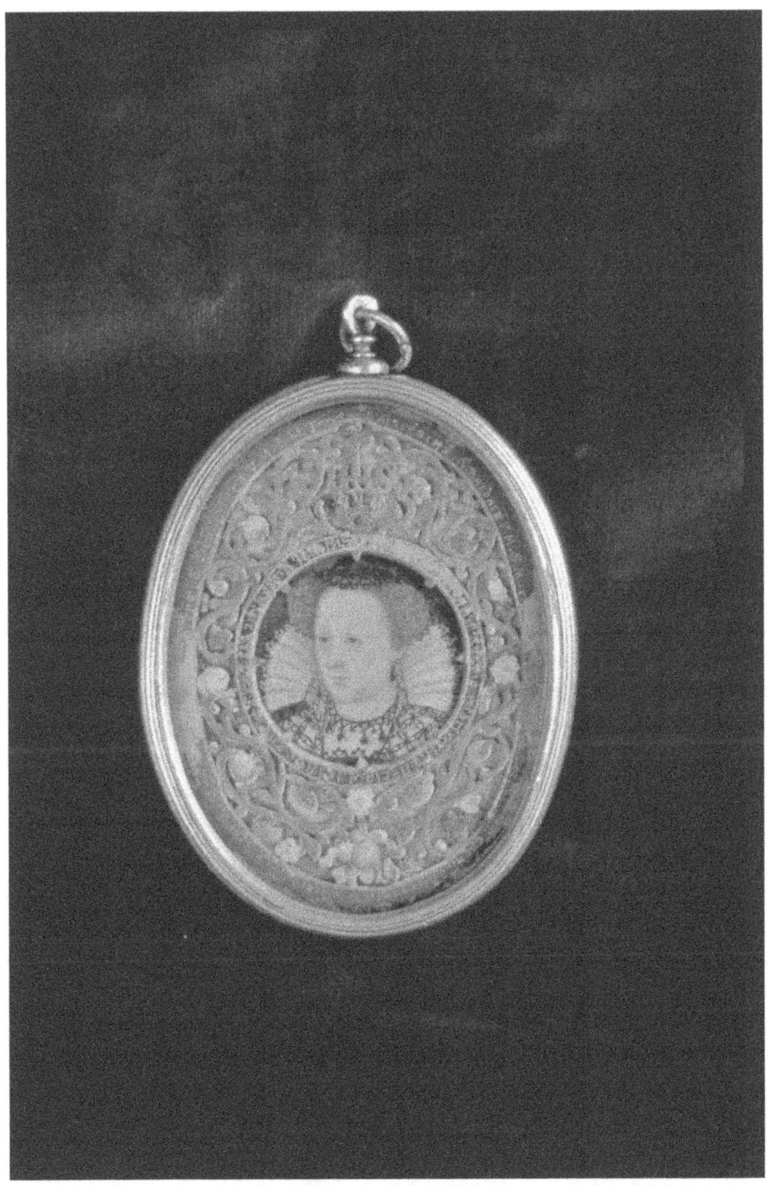

Figure 8.1 Anon. (*Klosterarbiet?*), Low Countries, *c.* 1620, *The Blairs Jewel*, miniature, cut-paper work, relics, framed under glass. Formerly Blairs Museum, Aberdeen, to be transferred to Scottish Catholic Museum, Glasgow. © Trustees of the Blairs Museum.

This chapter focuses on a set of objects which were all either preserved by, or newly created for, members of the Curle family: closely connected to Mary Stuart, these Catholic refugees had moved to Antwerp within a few years of her death. A copy of the testament in which Hippolytus (or Hugh) Curle SJ (*c*.1590–1638) disposed of his family property before joining the Society of Jesus in 1618 has been preserved in the Scottish Catholic Archives, and is currently on loan to the University of Aberdeen.[1] This document, which has been comprehensively analysed and partially transcribed in an article by Fr Jos Vercruysse SJ, provides important evidence for the origin of these objects in the household of Hippolytus's mother Barbara Curle, née Moubray (1559–1616), and her sister-in-law Elizabeth Curle (1560–1620) and on the initiative of Hippolytus Curle himself.[2] This testament also offers a date for the memorial and cenotaph in St Andrew's church in Antwerp, which is discussed below, and identifies Hippolytus Curle SJ as its patron and, presumably, iconographer.

Both these women had been attendants to Mary Stuart, Elizabeth Curle remaining with her up until the moment of her execution; and Barbara Curle's husband Gilbert had served as Mary's confidential secretary. They had a pension settled on them by the Spanish Crown, on the condition that they should live in France or the Spanish Netherlands – a stipulation that carries the undertone of the protective custody of witnesses.[3] The Curles could reasonably be expected to offer significant (and potentially politically explosive) testimony, should moves be made to beatify or canonise the dead queen.[4]

This group of objects and memorials leaves little doubt that Barbara and Elizabeth Curle considered Mary unequivocally to have been a martyr; they were programmatically forming a material legacy that both presented her in this light and embodied their loyalty and devotion to her, as well as highlighting their own status as witnesses to her potential sanctity. It is no coincidence that these activities mirrored the controversialist and propagandist publications of London-born antiquary Richard Verstegan (*c*.1550–1640), who moved to Antwerp around 1585, and whose illustrated account of Mary's execution was published as the culmination of his *Theatre of the Cruelties of the Heretics of Our Time*.[5]

In this group of objects and memorials, almost the whole repertory of baroque art and ceremonial is represented. There is a portrait designed as an object of veneration and a record of martyrdom. There are funerary and commemorative inscriptions and imagery; a book whose binding is of Kunstkammer quality, preserved as a secondary relic; objects created *ex nihil* as tangible embodiments of memory; a composite reliquary, incorporating relics from different periods of the history of the Church to produce a narrative of Roman Catholic continuity; and objects implying other specific historical and theological narratives. Together with objects now lost, these items all advanced the posthumous reputation of Mary Stuart – beyond doubt, a central preoccupation of the Curle family. The shaping of the collection's overarching narrative would fall to the next generation of the family, however, particularly Hippolytus Curle, whose education at Douai and membership of the Society of Jesus would crucially inform how the reliquary and monument express their narratives. It is from his testament, made just before he became a Jesuit and signed on 1 September 1618, that we can date the transfer of ownership to the society of what has come to be known as the *Memorial Portrait of Mary Queen of Scots*, and also date the Antwerp cenotaph.

Let us now consider the objects, roughly in the chronological order of their creation. The oldest is a mid-sixteenth-century red velvet-covered prayer book which belonged to Mary Stuart but which was originally made for Mary Tudor, brought from Fotheringhay by the Curles. Given to the Jesuits by Hippolytus Curle, presumably around the time he joined the society (it is not specifically mentioned in his testament), it is now at Stonyhurst. The next object chronologically is the first version of the *Memorial Portrait* long at the Blairs Museum, Aberdeen, probably painted in Antwerp in the 1590s. Closely related to this object is the monument to Barbara and Elizabeth Curle erected by Hippolytus in 1620 in the Church of Sint-Andries, Antwerp, with its painted inset portrait of Mary Stuart on a copper panel; this is a variant of the portrait type of the *Memorial Portrait*, both deriving from the miniature which would form the centrepiece of the Blairs Jewel.[6] The relic of the Holy Thorn, once the possession of Mary Stuart, also came eventually to the English Jesuits, but by a wholly different line of transmission via Thomas Percy, Earl of Northumberland.[7]

The composite reliquary, known as the Blairs Jewel, is structured around a sixteenth-century miniature of Mary, which was almost certainly brought from England by the Curles. The arrangement of the reliquary appears to date also from around 1620. The most plausible explanation for its creation is that Hippolytus Curle directed it to be made, with assistance from other British Jesuits in the Low Countries. One of its many strands of implicit narrative is a continuation of the act of commemoration expressed in both the portrait and the monument. We know from Hippolytus's 1618 testament that he also gave the Jesuits a white and black encaustic *Agnus Dei* on a golden chain, with an image of St Ignatius of Loyola painted on a crystal on one side, and various relics on the reverse.[8] This is lost; but its very nature as a Jesuit composite reliquary, double-sided and under glass, relates it closely both to the Blairs Jewel and to the 'Sichem' composite reliquary now at Stonyhurst.[9] Both of these reliquaries drew on holdings of relics whose range closely matched that of the relic collections known to have been owned by the exiled British Jesuits at Saint-Omer and Watten.[10] In a sense, it is possible to read a composite reliquary like a text with a textual history, if the points of origin of the constituent relics can be reconstructed – which, for the greater part, they can be here.

A silk gauze veil, allegedly worn by Mary at her trial, also survives, in a private collection in England, and it is embroidered in gold thread with authenticating details.[11] The fine gauze of the veil itself has been bordered with a slightly more robust silk, supporting the embroidery, and edged with gold lace, with little gold lace IHS Jesuit badge pendants at the four corners. The inscription, in capitals, runs: [top] 'VELUM SERENISS. MARIAE. SCOT. ET GALLIAE REGIN. ET MART. QUO <VERATUR?>'; [bottom] 'DUM AB HERET. AD MORT. INIUSTISS. CONDEMNATA FUIT ANNO SAL. MDLXXXVI'; [right] 'A NOBILISS. MATRONA DIU RELIGIOSE CONSERVATUM'; [left] 'ET TANDEM DEVOT. ERGO DEO ET SOCIET. IESU CONSECRATUM'.[12]

> [The veil of the most serene Mary, Queen of Scotland and France and martyr, which [was worn?] when she was condemned by the heretics to a most unjust death in the year of our Lord 1587, religiously kept for a long time by a most noble lady, and eventually solemnly consecrated to God and the Society of Jesus.]

It is highly likely that this came into the possession of the Jesuits (and, eventually, that of Henry Benedict Stuart, Cardinal York, who gave it to the ancestor of the family who now own it), also by way of the Curles in Antwerp.

At some point, possibly in the 1640s or even 1680s, a second version of the *Memorial Portrait* was created; this is now in the Royal Collection and displayed at Holyroodhouse, Edinburgh. Clearly deriving from the *Memorial Portrait* archetype then in the Scots College at Douai, this second portrait had different inscriptions, which are discussed further below, and was generally much coarser in execution – notably, in the handling of the background elements.

The portrait of Mary Queen of Scots that Hippolytus Curle presented to the Scots College in Douai as its inalienable property was characterised by him as 'the representation of the Queen of Scotland, Mary Stuart, dressed as she was at her martyrdom, on which the two gentlewomen, Jane Kennedy and Elizabeth Curle, are represented by name' (see Figure 8.2).[13] This description indicates beyond any doubt that Hippolytus was referring to the portrait now at the Blairs Museum, which was preserved during the French Revolution – when most of the other possessions of the Scots College in Douai seem to have been lost – and donated to the seminary at Blairs in 1833.[14]

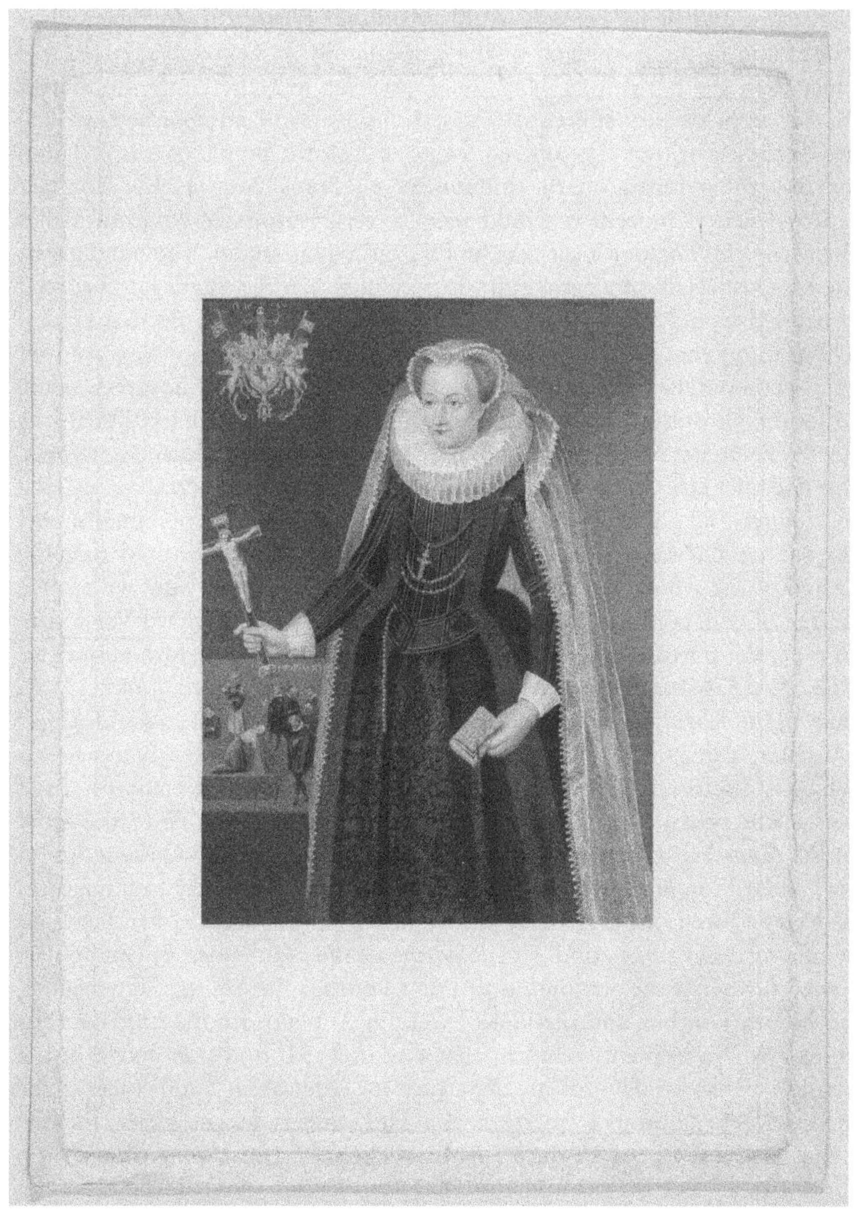

Figure 8.2 Edward Francis Finden (1791–1857), *Mary, Queen of Scots*, undated stipple engraving (after Frans Pourbus the Younger's 1590s oil *Memorial Portrait of Mary Queen of Scots*, formerly Blairs Museum, Aberdeen, to be transferred to Scottish Catholic Museum, Glasgow).

Because the Blairs version of the *Memorial Portrait* is documented as extant and in the possession of the Curle family by September 1618, it is older than the portrait of Mary on copper set into the Curle monument in Antwerp, despite subsequent assertions by local antiquarians (which are discussed below). The official listing of historic monuments in Belgium ascribes the portrait on the monument to Frans Pourbus the Younger (1569–1622).[15] Indeed, it would seem a very reasonable conjecture that the *Memorial Portrait* itself was by Pourbus or his studio. The handling of the face, especially the eyes, and the way in which the white starched ruff is painted would accord well with known portrait work from that studio. The features that set the *Memorial Portrait* apart from the normal output of a Netherlandic portraitist of the late sixteenth century, however, relate to its unique status as a record of witness, both sacred and political: the dense explanatory and commemorative inscriptions, the witnessing figures, the documentary scene of execution in the background. Presumably, the motionless and dominating figure of Mary is intended as a potential model for subsequent sacred images of her, and it can be conjectured that the design of the whole was directed by the Curle family, possibly with some degree of collaboration from their Antwerp neighbour Richard Verstegan. In type, the portrait can also reasonably be identified as a formalised version of a 1576 miniature of Mary Stuart by Nicholas Hilliard (1547–1619), now in the Royal Collection, and with a version in the Victoria and Albert Museum, a derivative of which forms the centrepiece of the Blairs Jewel, which is discussed below.[16] It seems likely that this copied miniature itself was in the possession of the Curles, and was made available to the artist of the *Memorial Portrait* by them. The Royal Collection's item description for Hilliard's miniature notes that 'there are many references to miniatures of Mary Queen of Scots being distributed by the Queen to her scattered sympathisers at this period'.[17] The dating of the Blairs portrait can be narrowed further, if the attribution to Frans Pourbus the Younger is accepted, since both Pourbus and the Curles were in Antwerp from 1590; Pourbus completed his apprenticeship in that city in 1591, and was active in the Spanish Netherlands until his departure for Mantua in 1600. Even if the attribution to Pourbus is questioned, a date range is defined by, on the one hand, the clear use of an engraving in Verstegan's *Theatrum Crudelitatum* (1587) as a basis for the scene of Mary's execution and, on the other, by Hippolytus Curle's 1618 testament.[18] The way in which Verstegan's image has been used raises important questions about memory and representation in the late Renaissance, and, in particular, the degree to which his image may derive from verbal descriptions, and how the weeping gentlewoman in his engraving may represent a symbolic rather than actual presence at the place of execution.[19] Significantly, this figure is absent from the *Memorial*

Portrait, in which the women are shown on the other side of the formalised figure of the queen.

Hippolytus Curle's 1618 testament also donates 1,000 guilders for the erection of a monument to Curle's dead mother and to commemorate his aunt, then still living – although she died in May 1620, before this work, by sculptors Robrecht de Nole (also known as Robert Collyns) and Jan de Nole, was completed.[20] The monument was described at length by a mid-nineteenth-century priest of the church in which it is situated, who thought that its painting was the work of the celebrated Pieter Pourbus (1523–84) and painted in France in the 1550s, despite the fact that it quite clearly shows a woman in her forties.[21] He also quoted this description of it from an unnamed Antwerp antiquarian, presumably of the eighteenth century:

> [A]en de selve pilaer de weleke noch te sien is, alwaer boven oick staet het contre fytsel van de Coninginne Maria Stuarta nae t' leeven.[22]

> [[O]n the same pillar ... is the likeness of Mary Stuart, Queen of Scotland, from the life.]

He also quoted the following comment, preserved in the church register:

> [B]oven staet het portret van Maria Stuart Coniginne van Scotlant op copere plaete originel uijt des selfs cabinet.[23]

> [Above is the portrait of Mary Stuart, Queen of Scotland, on copper, an original from her own cabinet.]

It seems highly unlikely that either of these statements is true. It is much more plausible that the portrait on the Antwerp monument is posthumous, and based on the same source material as the *Memorial Portrait*, as the only iconographic difference between them is the inclusion of an imperial or closed crown in the version on the monument. The monument was almost certainly devised by Hippolytus Curle, possibly following directions from his mother and aunt, and commemorates the whole Curle family as they stood in relation to the martyred queen, whose portrait surmounts the whole composition. The small panel below that portrait gives her styles and titles and the date of her martyrdom, while the main inscription panel presents a succinct history of the family group as defined by loyalty to her and to the Catholic Church, as exiles and as keepers of her memory. The status of both sons as Jesuits is noted: James, the elder, entered the Society of Jesus in Madrid and died there; the closeness of Elizabeth to the queen on the day of her execution is emphasised; and the floor slab near the monument reasserts the status of both Curle women as Mary's waiting gentlewomen.[24]

As briefly noted above, the miniature from which the Curles derived both the Blairs and Antwerp cenotaph memorial portraits of Mary Stuart would eventually serve as the centrepiece of the Blairs Jewel. This oval composite reliquary, made for the circle of Hippolytus Curle and his Jesuit contemporaries in the Low Countries around 1620, takes the form of an elaborate mounting on one side for the miniature of Mary, which is closely framed by an inscription giving the date of her martyrdom. This, in turn, is surrounded by cut-work of flowers incorporating small fragments of relics of women saints and *beati*, who are identified in golden letters on a blue oval border that surrounds the whole. The obverse has the crowned monogram MRA, for Maria Regina Angelorum: Mary Stuart's name-saint and patron. The crown and letters are both of inscribed cut-work, also surrounded by symbolic flowers. This side of the Blairs Jewel, which closely parallels the arrangements of relics at Saint-Omer, includes a sequence ranging from a fragment of the True Cross to a minute relic of St Edmund Campion, martyred in 1581; thus, like the published *Ecclesia Anglicanae Trophea*, it represents a continuous history of suffering for the Church that stretches from antiquity to the Jesuit martyrs and *beati* of the present. The whole is preserved under rock crystal or (more likely) high-quality glass and is framed in gold.

The miniature of Mary Stuart, standing in for her corporeal relics (which the Elizabethan authorities controlled stringently, thus creating the strange circumstances for commemoration which this chapter considers), is set in the context of women saints through the ages, but also firmly associated with the Jesuits, whose 'IHS' badge is placed immediately above it. The relics of women saints associate Mary Stuart with martyrs going back to the persecutions of the Roman Empire, but also with royal saints and a recent *beata* admired throughout Catholic Europe, including Theresa of Avila, beatified in 1614 and soon thereafter adopted as patroness of Spain. The other saints whose relics are associated with the miniature are St Scholastica, St Barbara, St Aldegonde (a French abbess of royal blood), and, significantly, St Margaret of Scotland.[25]

The other side of the Blairs Jewel is an exposition of the continuities of the saints of the Roman Church, but also a bold assertion of the status of Mary Queen of Scots as a contemporary martyr, and, crucially, one associated with the Jesuit mission to England. The crown, which is surmounted by two splinters 'ex ligno S. Crucis', contains relics of St Bernard of Clairvaux, and of St Quirinus and St Victor, both first-millennium martyrs. A relic of another first-millennium martyr, St Florian, is placed amid the letters 'MRA'.[26] All the other relics are of Jesuits, however, either formally beatified or martyrs on the English mission. Among the former are B. Aloysius (notably, the spelling is 'Aloysij', suggesting that the calligrapher of the Blairs Jewel was a Dutch-speaker), B. Stanislas, B. Pater Xavier, and B. Pater Ignatius ('Ignatij', again written with the Dutch 'long i'). The English Jesuits who died on the mission – 'B. Garneti', 'B. Walpoli', and 'B. Campiani M' – are today known as Henry Garnet SJ, St Henry Walpole, and St Edmund Campion. The descriptions of both Ignatius and Francis Xavier as '*beatus*', together with the presence of St Teresa as *beata*, indicate a date range not earlier than 1614, when St Teresa was beatified, nor later than May 1622, when St Ignatius and St Francis Xavier were canonised.

A second, parallel narrative is expressed by the flowers that surround both the miniature of Mary Stuart on one side of the jewel and the crowned monogram on the other, for the Blairs Jewel is one of the most explicit articulations of the sacred paradox that seems to attend all reliquaries which are also, in however modest a sense, works of art. The detritus of human bodies is incorporated into a gold-framed heavenly garden that expresses, emblematically, the blessed condition of those whose physical remains are the focus of devotion. The scraps of their mortal tissue, wisps of hair, and discarded clothes are placed among the ordered flowers of a microcosm of the garden of paradise. The association of martyrdom and flowers goes back to Prudentius's hymn for the feast of the Holy Innocents, *Salvete flores martyrum.*[27] Within the eight-year period during which the Blairs Jewel could have been assembled, the English martyr B. Thomas Maxfield was executed at Tyburn in 1616, an event that was symbolically subverted by members of the Spanish ambassador's entourage, who formed a guard of honour for Maxfield on the way to the scaffold, which had been adorned in the night with garlands of flowers and strewn with herbs.[28] A pink that Maxfield had carried in his hand on that day was still preserved as a relic in the early twentieth century.[29]

In the cut-work of the Blairs Jewel, roses and marguerites surround the miniature, and immediately below the portrait are two symmetrically disposed marigolds. On the reverse side, with the monogram, there are marguerites and marigolds as well as primulas and blue and white irises. Marguerites, the name signifying 'pearl' in Latin, have many associations with virtue as well as with St Margaret, first saint of the Scottish royal house. Roses are associated both with the Blessed Virgin and with martyrdom, and the irises recall the form of the fleur-de-lis of France. It is the marigolds, however, which are arguably the most important of the flowers present. Although it is not necessary to rehearse here Michael Bath's exemplary investigation of the emblematic sources of Mary Stuart's embroideries, it is important to recall that the marigold, with its proverbial capacity to follow the sun faithfully, was an image frequently associated both with Mary's person and with her anagram-motto *Sa virtu m'attire.*[30] She herself associated this phrase with various emblematic images expressive of loyalty and devotion: of the magnet to the magnetic pole, and of the devout eye to the crucifix, as well as of the marigold to the sun.[31] In the specific context of the

Blairs Jewel, this flower therefore memorialises not only the dead queen's loyalty to the Church but the degree to which the women of the Curle family were faithful to their royal mistress in life and death.

To conclude, although this group of objects relating to the Curle family has a clear connection to the Society of Jesus and, more immediately, to the Jesuit-run English College at Saint-Omer and the Scots College at Douai, its narrative whereby Mary Stuart is associated with recent Jesuit martyrs and also placed at the forefront of the martyrs of England relates closely to the intense Catholic propaganda then being written and published in Antwerp. Specifically, this propaganda effort sought to focus European attention on the barbarity with which the reformed nations were enforcing Protestant observance. Campion's death had formed the culmination of the *Trophea*, and Verstegan's publication of an account of it had forced him to flee England for France, and ultimately, Antwerp. It is notable that, by the time he published the *Theatrum Crudelitatum* in 1587, the narrative had changed – that is, the degraded cruelty of England culminated not in Campion's death, but in Mary Stuart's.[32] Sustained in part by the preservation and creation of the relics and memorial objects which have been considered here, this perception remained powerful even into the nineteenth century – so much so that, when the cause for the canonisation of the martyrs of England and Wales was begun in 1874, Mary Stuart's name was placed first among them.[33]

Each object in the whole group of relics and memorials discussed above was intended by its custodians to bear just one meaning and to embody only one narrative. In this context, it is instructive to consider the shifts in meaning driven by changing political circumstances – as most clearly exemplified by the second version of the *Memorial Portrait*, with its altered inscriptions.[34] This was copied in the Low Countries, presumably from the *Memorial Portrait* at Douai, by a lesser hand, also probably Netherlandish. This newer version of the portrait is recorded as forming part of the collection of James II and VII, so there are perhaps two possibilities: that this copied version dates from the time of the civil wars, or else that it was made in Douai under Jesuit auspices for the last Catholic king of Britain.[35]

One minor difference between the two versions is of considerable art-historical interest, despite it not affecting the iconographic meaning of the whole. In the Blairs version, the crucifix in Mary's hand is a fairly conventional representation of a contemporary wooden cross, apparently set in a base of stone engraved with a skull, with an ivory *corpus*, shown as dead, and conventionally draped. In the Royal Collection version, however, the depiction of the same object conforms to a single, strong archetype: Michelangelo's starkly individual Mannerist crucifixion drawing, now in the British Museum, and its various realisations in colour by his colleagues, especially Marcello Venusti.[36] In this highly recognisable image, the still living Christ turns His head upwards, His body curves in pain, and the drapery is scant and asymmetric; His left hand is clenched, while His right is flat against the cross. How this striking and individual representation of the crucifixion came into the orbit of the copyist of this second version would be a study of considerable interest in its own right.

Other key differences between the two painting versions include that the latter does not assign names to the figures of Elizabeth Curle and Jane Kennedy – their witness having faded into the past – and considerably simplifies the scene of the execution, seemingly without reference to Verstegan's engraving. This change of emphasis, and the fact that the copyist no longer entirely understands the costume worn by the queen in the Blairs portrait, suggests a considerable lapse of time between the two portraits. Specifically, the version of the overgarment in the copy has scalloped hanging sleeves, as in baroque theatrical and painted representations of antiquity. The inscriptions, too, are considerably altered, softening the original questioning of Elizabeth Tudor's legitimacy and right to her throne (the inscriptions on the Blairs version deny her the title 'Queen' and stress her personal perfidy), instead blaming the cruelty and religious enmity of the '*senatus*' of England – Parliament. All of this suggests that the Holyroodhouse version is a reinvention, an appropriation, created at some point in the seventeenth century either to elicit sympathy in Catholic Europe for the grandson of Mary Stuart, the defeated Charles I, or to remind her Catholic great-grandson of his martyred ancestor.

Notes

1 SCA, PL/8/24, 'Testament of Hippolytus Curle', an authenticated copy transcribed at Douai on 21 March 1772, now on deposit in the Special Collections Centre, University of Aberdeen.

2 Jos E. Vercruysse SJ, 'A Scottish Jesuit from Antwerp: Hippolytus Curle', *The Innes Review*, 61.2 (2010), pp. 137–49.

3 *Ibid*., p. 138.

4 *Ibid*., p. 139.

5 Richard Verstegan, *Theatrum Crudelitatum Haereticorum Nostri Temporis* (Antwerp: Adrian Hubert, 1587), pp. 84–5.

6 Inventaris, Parochiekerk Sint-Andries, https://inventaris.onroerenderfgoed.be/erfgoedobjecten/6299 (retrieved 27 July 2016).

7 All the documents relating to the ownership and transmission of this relic are preserved in Stonyhurst MS A VI 84.

8 Vercruysse, 'A Scottish Jesuit', p. 139.

9 This is SCA relic no. 40, and is the property of the British Jesuit Province, housed at Stonyhurst College. The Sichem reliquary also includes relics arranged in

careful sequence. See Janet Graffius, 'Relics and Cultures of Commemoration in the English Jesuit College of St Omers in the Spanish Netherlands', in James Kelly and Hannah Thomas (eds), *Jesuit Intellectual and Physical Exchange between England and Mainland Europe, c. 1580–1789: The World Is Our House* (Leiden: Brill, 2019), especially pp. 128–30; Janet Graffius, 'English Catholic Material Culture', in Robert Scully SJ (ed.), *A Companion to Catholicism and Recusancy in Britain and Ireland* (Leiden: Brill, 2021), pp. 549–87.

10 The subject is treated in detail in Janet Graffius's doctoral dissertation, '"*Bullworks against the Furie of Heresie*"'.

11 Janet Arnold, *Queen Elizabeth's Wardrobe Unlock'd* (Leeds: Maney, 1988), pp. 48–9. The further information in this paragraph comes from information and photographs most kindly supplied by the family who own the veil, to whom I am most grateful.

12 This transcript is not from the veil itself, which is now folded and in a glazed case, but from a photograph of an engraving commissioned by Sir John Coxe Hippisley (1746–1835) in 1818. He had been given the veil by Henry Benedict, Cardinal York, who was Mary's great-great-grandson. The Cardinal York may have acquired it at the suppression of the Jesuits in 1773.

13 Vercruysse, 'A Scottish Jesuit', p. 148.

14 *Ibid.*, p. 148.

15 Inventaris, Parochiekerk Sint-Andries.

16 RCIN 420641, www.royalcollection.org.uk/collection/search#/9/collection/420641/mary-queen-of-scots-1542–1587 (retrieved 29 July 2016). The Victoria and Albert Museum version is no. P.24–1975.

17 *Ibid.*

18 Although the painting does not slavishly copy every detail of the engraving's disposition of spectators, the representation of the scaffold and the cloaked figure in the foreground establish this derivation beyond doubt.

19 Patricia Phillippy observes that both Catholic and Protestant writers emphasise that material care of the dead fell to women: 'Sisters of Magdalen: Women's Mourning in Aemilia Lanyer's Salve Rex Judaeorum', *English Literary Renaissance* 31.1 (2001), pp. 78–106. Robert Southwell, *In Marie Magdalen's Funeral Teares* (London: John Wolfe for Gabriel Cawood, 1591), pp. 1–4, emphasises that Magdalen both witnesses Christ's death and has gone to render final services to his corpse when she finds it missing. We might see the gentlewoman depicted here as a Magdalen figure.

20 Vercruysse, 'A Scottish Jesuit', p. 146.

21 Petrus Visschers, *Aenteekening nopens het eergraf van Barbara Moubray en Elizabeth Curle, Staetdamen van de Koningen Maria Stuart in St. Andries kerk te Antwerpen* (Antwerp: Janssens, 1857), p. 14.

22 *Ibid.*, p. 11.

23 *Ibid.*, p. 12.

24 A full text of the Latin inscriptions is provided in Visschers, Aenteekening, pp. 11–13.

25 An area of water damage has partially erased a name, which might be that of St Catherine.
26 The English Jesuits of Saint-Omers had a relic of St Florian which they had obtained from Italy: further evidence that the relics gathered in the Blairs Jewel came from Jesuit sources, almost certainly Saint-Omers and Douai.
27 Aurelius Clemens Prudentius, 'Salve flores martyrum', https://hymnary.org/text/salve_flores_martyrum (retrieved 10 August 2016). This phrase is specifically linked to the English martyrs by the tradition that St Philip Neri would greet the English seminarians in Rome with these words.
28 *Miscellanea III*, ed. John Hungerford Pollen (London: Catholic Record Society, 1906), p. 43.
29 *Ibid.*, p. 58.
30 Michael Bath, *Emblems for a Queen: The Needlework of Mary Queen of Scots* (London: Archetype Publications, 2008).
31 For a detailed consideration of a panel worked by Mary Stuart with the marigold and the anagram-motto, forming part of the Marian hanging at Oxburgh Hall in Norfolk, see Rozsika Parker, *The Subversive Stitch: Embroidery and the Making of the Feminine*, rev. edn (London: I.B. Tauris, 2010), p. 87.
32 This progress is admirably documented in Gerard Kilroy, *Edmund Campion: A Scholarly Life* (London: Routledge, 2015), pp. 360–79.
33 Archivio Segreto Vaticano, Con. Riti. 5087–88: 'Servorum Dei Mariae Stuartae Scotorum Regina, Johanni Parslaeo ... Jacob Leyburn cum aliis ... in Anglia pro Fide interfecti'.
34 Rosalind K. Marshall, *Mary Queen of Scots: 'In My End Is My Beginning'* (Edinburgh: National Museum of Scotland, 2013), pp. 2–3. Another subsequent version is also recorded as having been in a private collection. The catalogue for the 1888/89 *Exhibition of the Royal House of Stuart* at the New Gallery, Regent Street, London, has as its nos. 38 and 39 the Royal Collection version and the Blairs version, and as its no. 40 another copy, with the execution scene further altered, on loan from the Earl of Darnley, pp. 22–3.
35 I am grateful to Dr Deborah Clarke of the Royal Collections, Holyroodhouse, Edinburgh, for this information, and for directing my attention to item no. 94 in Oliver Millar, *The Tudor, Stuart and Early Georgian Pictures in the Collection of Her Majesty the Queen*, 2 vols. (London: Phaidon, 1963), which confirms that the Royal Collection portrait is a copy of the Blairs one. The former was first recorded in the Royal Collection during the reign of James II and VII, but was not one of the pictures that had belonged to Charles II. It was probably in the Princess's Drawing Room, where it was hanging during the reign of Queen Anne.
36 The primary version by Venusti, part of the collection of Campion Hall, Oxford, is on loan to the Ashmolean Museum, Oxford.

9

Viper wine

In December 1623 John Donne (1572–1631) fell seriously ill with relapsing fever. While in its grip, he wrote his *Devotions vpon Emergent Occasions and Seuerall Steps in my Sickness*.[1] It was published in print by 1 February of the following year, and complimentary copies were sent to Prince Charles, Princess Elizabeth, the Duke of Buckingham, and at least one other, unknown recipient, addressed simply as 'My Lord'.[2] Donne was still not fully recovered from his illness by the following February 1625, since he did not preach his usual sermon at court for the beginning of Lent that year, and he is not known to have taken the pulpit again until his Easter Day sermon in St Paul's on 28 March. The *Devotions* are discursive, learned, and full of strange information. One of the odder statements they contain is in Prayer XI: 'Thou, O Lord, who hast imprinted all medicinal virtues which are in all creatures, and hast made even the flesh of vipers to assist in cordials, art able to make this present sickness everlasting health.'[3] This is of particular interest, since a cordial made of vipers played a key part in a *cause célèbre* of the next decade: the death of Venetia Digby.

There were persistent rumours in the London of 1633 that Sir Kenelm Digby (depicted in Figure 9.1) – a much-travelled virtuoso whom no single discipline could long contain – had poisoned his wife, despite his extravagant and public protestations of devotion to her. The underlying reason for these rumours lies in a nexus of unresolved tensions relating not only to the perceived foreignness of Catholicism to England but also to England's relationship with the international manner in all the arts identified as 'baroque'. This vexed relationship produced extraordinary contradictions, evasions, and distortions of focus, of which the *cause celèbre* surrounding the death of Lady Digby is only one example. Whereas the public articulation of John Donne's death – as self-dramatizing and, indeed, bizarre a performance as one could imagine – has somehow been perceived as a belated outpouring of the hyperbolic energies of Elizabethan England, the works in a variety of media with which Kenelm Digby mourned for Venetia are generally contemplated with a measure of disquiet, or even distaste. In an attempt to cope with the baroque

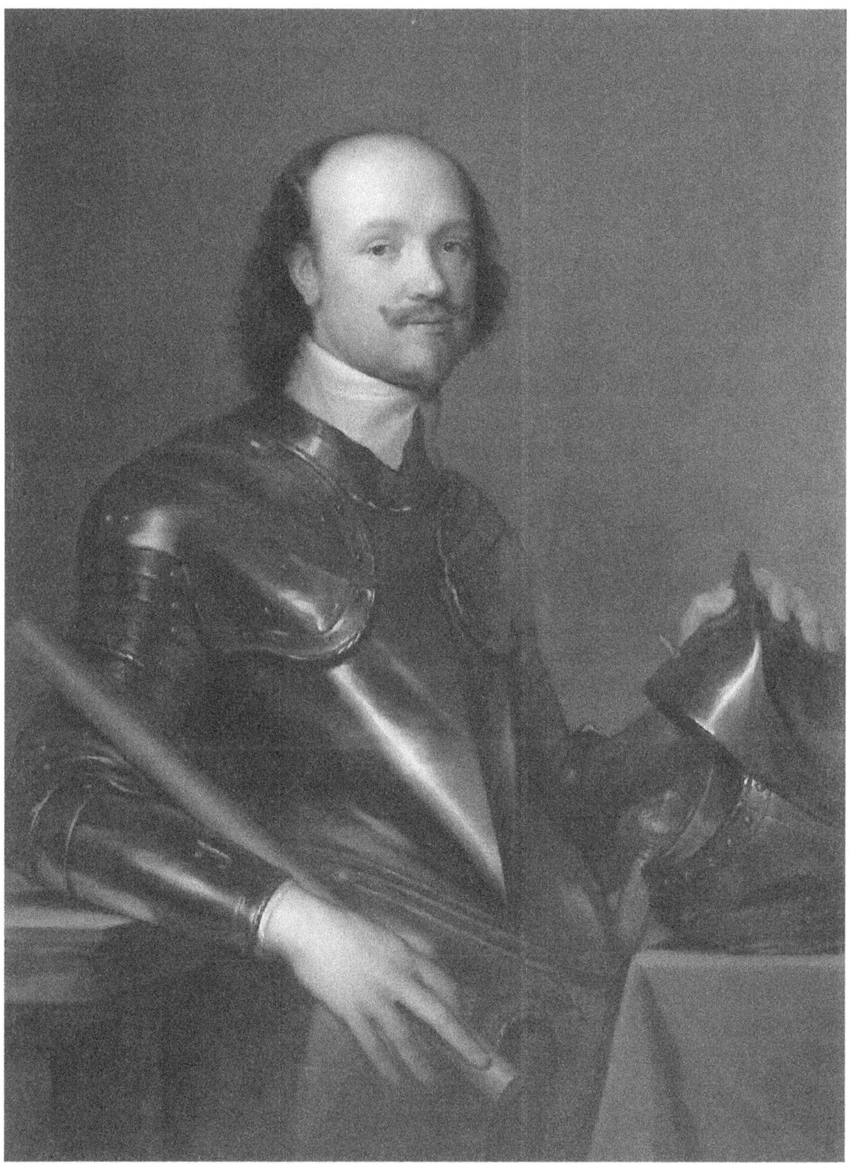

Figure 9.1 Anon. (after Anthony van Dyck), *Sir Kenelm Digby*, 1640, oil on canvas. Whereabouts unknown (private collection).

John Donne, the English critical tradition from Samuel Johnson onwards invented the term 'metaphysical'.[4] Whether consciously or otherwise, this term detached Donne and his contemporaries from any consideration of their work in a European context, in which it would inevitably have attracted the word 'baroque', and left them, instead, suspended in an aesthetic limbo.[5]

Until very recently the baroque has been identified by anglophone critics as extravagant and foreign, an attitude that emerges from that submerged stratum of the English consciousness that regards Catholicism as the dark obverse of Englishness. For early modern Protestant England and its inheritors, the 'other' of fantasy and nightmare is Counter-Reformation Europe, whose paradigmatic style is the baroque.[6] The anti-Catholicism of early modern England is clearly displayed in its response to the recusant Catholic Kenelm Digby, the internationalised baroque Englishman par excellence.[7] Born in 1603, the son of the soon-to-be executed gunpowder plotter Everard Digby, he was Chancellor to Queen Henrietta Maria in her later years until his death in 1665. His patronage of the arts extended to Ben Jonson and Anthony van Dyck, among many others. He was a freelance naval commander, theologian, diplomat, Catholic apologist, and prolific writer on diverse subjects, often scientific.[8] His scientific writings were received with respect on the Continent and translated into Latin, French, German, and Dutch. He undertook an unsuccessful diplomatic mission to Pope Innocent X on behalf of Henrietta Maria, and travelled extensively on the Continent, remaining abroad for much of the period of the Civil Wars, but reconciled himself to the English Commonwealth and returned to Cromwellian England in the 1650s. Typifying the apparent contradictions of seventeenth-century scientific learning, he was both an early member of the Royal Society and published a discourse on the possibility of curing sword wounds by sympathetic magic in 1658.[9]

Around 1625 he married Venetia Stanley, a woman of distinguished ancestry and ambiguous reputation. Her past will perhaps never be wholly recovered from the territory of rumour, but she seems to have been left to the care of servants in her late teens, and to have set up a household for herself in London. She had at least one child by the Earl of Dorset, and probably had other lovers. During her marriage, however, she was strictly faithful to Digby and bore him at least three children. In this period, at least according to Digby's posthumous testimony, she was a most devout Catholic. She died suddenly on 1 May 1633. The rumours that attended her death are the main focus of this chapter, since they are the point in Digby's biography where tropes of early modern English anti-Catholicism can be seen most clearly.

The first near-contemporary witness to Digby's life is Anthony à Wood's Oxford prosopography, the *Athenae Oxonienses*. Wood begins with complimentary generalisations:

> Kenelme Digby, the magazine of all Arts, or as one stiles him The ornament of this Nation [...] For this his Valour, and by his Travels into several Countries, and converse with the *Virtuosi* of most civilised Nations, he became
> *The age's wonder for his noble parts,*
> *Skill'd in six tongues, and learn'd in all the arts.*

But Wood does not maintain this even tone for long:

> His person was handsome and gigantick, and nothing was wanting to make him a compleat Chevalier. He had so graceful elocution and noble address, that had he been dropt out of the clouds in any part of the World, he would have made himself respected; but the Jesuits, who cared not for him, spoke spitefully and said *'twas true, but he must not have stayed there above six weeks.*

After this, the author's hostility becomes unequivocal:

> [A]s he was most exactly accomplish'd with all sorts of Learning, so was he guilty with all of extravagant Vanities. Nay one, a most noted author, does not stick to say that this our eminent *Virtuoso* was *the Pliny of our age for lying.*

Wood goes on to tell a Münchausenesque story of a petrifying vapour that turned a city of Barbary to stone, and to claim that Digby supposedly heard about this via an exiled Catholic contact in the service of a foreign prince in Italy before spreading it in England. Wood goes on to report that Digby went abroad during the Civil War,

> [n]otwithstanding which, he did afterwards return for a time, and, as 'tis said, cringed to *Oliver*, but in what sense, whether in order for the good of the Rom. Catholicks, or for the carrying on of some publick design, I cannot now tell. About the same time, he being Chancellour to *Henrietta Maria* the Queen mother of *England*, she sent him as her Envoy from *France* to the Pope, was at his first coming to *Rome* highly venerated by all people, as being a person not only of a majestick port and carriage, but of extraordinary Parts and Learning. At length growing high, and huffing his Holiness, he was in a manner neglected, and especially for this reason, that having made a collection of money for the afflicted Catholicks in *England*, was found to be no faithful Steward in that matter.[10]

Wood's discourse is full of tropes and patterns that have their origins in distrust not only of Catholicism *per se* but of baroque internationalism. Digby is far too much at home on the Continent. He is the agent of the unpopular Henrietta Maria and is not even a faithful son of the pope, despite being prepared to cringe to Cromwell for the sake of advancing those English Catholics whose money he embezzles.

There is a prevailing sourness about Wood – a disappointed academic who had quarrelled with everyone – that informs many of his lives of his contemporaries. His *Athenae Oxonienses* brought him only trouble.[11]

This trouble also touched the generous-minded John Aubrey, whose notes formed the main basis of Wood's work.

Aubrey's *Brief Lives* are truly represented by their title. They are partly unsorted *collectanea*, partly snatches of haunting and finished writing. Aubrey was extraordinarily, even archaeologically, scrupulous in recording the status of his information. Given how influential Aubrey's account has been on all subsequent writing about the Digbys, it is critically important here to remember the scope and limitations of the *Lives*. They have the authenticity of notes recording direct speech, but, by the same token, they share the limitations of all orally collected material. The memories of Aubrey's informants are vulnerable to retrospective falsification, to prejudices, fears, and rumours. Aubrey is clearly aware of all this. His descriptions of the Digbys probably came to him via the Wyld family, who were his hosts and patrons in his later years, and, although the account of Venetia's appearance has all the weight and emotion of first-hand recollection, it is prudent to be wary of some of the generalisations about the life of her husband, which reflect the hostility felt by Aubrey's informants towards a representative of the court of Henrietta Maria, foreign in language as well as religion. (Kate Bennet's exemplary edition of the *Brief Lives* captures this complex texture perfectly.)

Aubrey's description moves from documentation, the whereabouts of surviving portraits, to first-hand transcribed speech:

> Sir Edmund Wyld had her picture (and you may imagine was very familiar with her) which picture is now at Droitwytch in Worcestershire, at an Inne, where now the Towne keepe their Meetings. Also at Mr. Roses, a jeweller in Henrietta-street in Convent garden is an excellent piece of hers drawne after she was newly dead. She had a most lovely and sweet turn'd face, delicate darke browne haire: she had a perfect healthy constitution; strong; good skin; well-proportiond; enclining to a *Bona Roba*, her face, a short ovall. dark-browne eie-browe: about which much sweetness, as also in the opening of her eie-lidds. The colour of her cheekes was just that of the Damaske-rose, which is neither too hott nor too pale. She was of a good <just> stature, nott very tall.[12]

But then Aubrey moves into either rumour, or the selective inflation of the baroque physicality of the process of her husband's mourning: 'Sir Kenelme had severall pictures of her, by Van dyke etc: He had her hands cast in playster: and her feet: and her face.'[13]

Aubrey's life of Venetia Digby ends in a welter of miscellaneous gossip, and with Aubrey's own recollections of her various memorials, monumental, literary, and pictorial. It is clear that the Digbys, although they had both been dead for some time, stirred the emotions of those who remembered them, as well as those of their biographer. But it was the passing of Venetia's beauty that elicited one of Aubrey's most famous and moving utterance on the gravely limited power of the historian or antiquary to preserve the textures of things from the attrition of time:

> About 1676, or 5, as I was walking through Newgate street, I saw <Dame> Venetia's Bust standing at a Stall at the golden Crosse, a Brasiers shop [...] they melted it downe. How these curiosities would be quite forgott, did not such idle fellowes as I am putt them downe![14]

In his life of Kenelm Digby, Aubrey reflects upon both his own memories and the intensity of his feelings about the recent past. He is much less equivocal than Wood in praising Digby: 'He was of an undaunted courage: yet not apt in the least to give offence, his conversation was both ingeniose and innocent.'[15] When Aubrey comes to the description of Digby's marriage, he is scrupulous in distinguishing fact from rumour; but one may nonetheless suspect that many of his informants had fallen into the tropes of the anti-Catholic Black Legend:

> [M]uch against his Mothers etc: consent He married that celebrated Beautie and Courtezane, Mrs Venetia Stanley, whom Richard Earle of Dorset kept as his Concubine; had children by her: and settled on her an Annuity of 500^{li} per annum <which after Sir Kenelm Digby married was unpayd by the Earle> and for which annuity Sir Kenelm sued the Earl after marriage and recovered it.[16]

This is followed by speech and action, clearly identified as rumour:

> He would say that, a handsome lusty man that was discreet, might make a vertuose wife out of a Brothel-house. Richard Earl of Dorset invited her and her husband once a yeare, when with much desire and passion he beheld her; and only kissed her hand, Sir Kenelme being still by. This Lady carried her selfe blamelessly yet (they say) he was jealous of her.[17]

Then, the crucial sentences:

> [S]he dyed: suddenly, and hard hearted people <woemen> would censure him severely. After her death; to avoyd envy and scandal, he retired in to Gresham-colledge at London [...] he wore there a long mourning cloake, a high crowned hatt, his beard unshorne, look't like a Hermite, as signes of sorrowe for his beloved Wife, to whose memory he erected a sumptuouse monument.[18]

This is amplified in the notes for a life of Venetia:

> She dyd in her bed suddenly. Some suspected that she was poysoned. When her ~~braine~~ <head> was opened, there was found but little braine, which her husband imputed, to her drinking of viper-wine; but spitefull woemen would say, 'twas a viper husband who was jealous of her that she might steale a Leape'.[19]

An indicative final rumour leads us back to the fantasised figure of Digby the sensualist baroque monster, like Sir Epicure Mammon: 'Sir John Hoskyns enformes me, that Sir Kenelme Digby did translate Petronius

Arbiter into English.'[20] This was not the case. Digby's great love among the Latin authors was that perennial English favourite, Horace. But the fantastical, shapeless, and sexually and socially transgressive hotchpotch that is Petronius's *Satyricon* is the sort of thing Digby 'ought' to have translated, to live up to this image of him.[21] Many tropes, many of them essentially anti-Catholic, have influenced the memories and narrations of Digby's informants: the virtuoso as monstrous sensualist, experimenting not with natural philosophy so much as with the refinement of pleasure. This derives from similar sources as the persistent rumours of poisoning, deception, and play-acting: from the Black Legend, and from Jacobean revenge drama, a genre that depicted continental Europe as overrun by corrupt churchmen, who were very often monsters and poisoners as well.[22] Beyond this, the idea of the savant or philosopher who chooses a whore for his wife has some very odd parallels indeed. I would suggest here that the trope has been picked up from the story of Simon Magus finding Holy Wisdom in a brothel in Tyre. This story is recorded by Irenaeus of Lyons in his *Libros Quinque adversus Haereses*, written in the late second century AD:

> Simon [Magus] was a Samaritan, and from him arose a universal heresy: the substance of the sect is this. He took a certain Helen about with him, whom he had bought out of a brothel in Phoenician Tyre, claiming that she was the first conception of his mind and mother of all, through whom she had mentally conceived in the beginning and had created angels and archangels. Her father wished to know this Ennoia, springing from him, and to bring her to an inferior station, and to generate angels and Powers, from which, he said, this world was made. After he had generated them, she was withheld from them through envy [... and] was prisoned in a human body, and throughout the ages transmigrated from one female body to another. She had been that very Helen on whose account the Trojan war was fought ... [M]igrating from body to body, enduring contempt in each one, in the end, she was prostituted in a brothel, and was thus a lost sheep. When he came, so that he might first take her up and liberate her from her chains, he was restored to power among men through her recognition.[23]

This piece of long-lived Gnostic nonsense would seem to haunt the memories and recollections of Digby's marriage, even among his more educated contemporaries.

Let us turn now to the central allegation against Digby: that he poisoned Venetia with a wine or broth of vipers. It seems highly unlikely that he deliberately poisoned the wife to whom he was devoted and would mourn with such baroque intensity. The apparent motive attributed to him is the purest Black Legend: that he would have rather had her dead than even *thinking* of being unfaithful. This is the dark world of Calderón's *El médico de su honra*, which was published four years after Venetia's death. It seems inevitable, given the place Digby occupied in the imaginations of his contemporaries, that he should be accused of the very Catholic – and, indeed, characteristically Italian – crime of poisoning.[24]

Inadvertent poisoning seems a more likely explanation. The pharmaceutical use of animals, or parts of animals, goes back to the beginnings of European medicine: it is part of the *scientific* medicine of antiquity, the Middle Ages, and the Renaissance. Pliny, for example (to whom Digby was compared, not to his credit), noted in his *Historia naturalis* that 'fiunt ex vipera pastilli, qui theriaci vocantur a Graecis' ('they make pastilles from vipers, which are called theriacs by the Greeks').[25] Galen and other ancient medical writers were unanimous as to the beneficial properties of vipers' flesh when eaten.[26] There was a constant risk attending any use of the random pharmacopoeia of the mid-seventeenth century, but in this case it is possible to be more specific. To put the allegation in context, it is worth noting that the formula for the Great Cordial of Sir Walter Raleigh was collected by Digby and printed by his laboratory assistant George Hartman in *The True Preserver of Health* (1689). It included the flesh, hearts, and livers of vipers, along with much else, some of it poisonous.

We can find the culprit, with some certainty, among Hartman's *Choice and Experimented Receipts* (1668), presented as a writing up of Digby's own laboratory notes, in the form of *Bezoardicum Theriacale*. Both elements in this name are terms of art. Bezoar stones of animal origin (calculi from the stomach of a rare goat) were cure-alls, prescribed, for instance, to Charles II during the prolonged medical martyrdom that was his 1685 deathbed. Digby's recipe is thus for an artificial bezoar. The term 'theriac' had, by that time, evolved into a technical medical term for any medicine of animal origin. The theriacal bezoardicum in Hartman's book is prepared thus: take vipers, behead, skin, and gut them; then separate body, tongue, hearts and livers, and fat. Dry out the bodies with the hearts and livers in a slow oven. Once thoroughly dried, powder the lot and mix it with a balsam composed of rosewater, spirits of wine, myrrh, aloe, yellow sander, and attar of roses.

Hartman also gave directions for the administration of the mixture:

> Of this Bezoardique Theriacal Powder you are to give four or five grains for a dose *in some Broth or Wine*, either to be freed of a disease, that hath left great weakness behind it, or else for a preservative against the Infection of the whole nature, or bad air, and to keep ones self in good health, by continuing the same for some days. The Author [i.e. Sir Kenelm] doth commend a *continual* use of this Powder, for the keeping of one in good health.

This brings us to the crucial question of how dangerous this practice really was. The answer would seem to be 'not very', though it was doubtless unpleasant. The heads and skins of the vipers were kept for other uses. The venom, if any survived heating (and most snake poisons are very fugitive), would presumably be in the salivary glands and thus in the head, which is recommended only for external use: '[W]orn near the throat [it] is excellent against the Squinsie.'[27]

So, the evidence vindicates the *Inglese italianato* and unconventional husband from the charge of being an Italianate poisoner. Ironically, Digby's medical praxis, sophisticated and scientific by the standards of his times, was misinterpreted by English gossip according to the prejudices of the unscientific belief – recorded, for example, in the well-known ballad *Lord Randal* – that snakes are venomous through and through.[28]

Ironically, Digby cast the image of the viper, which was so central to the libellous rumours which branded him a poisoner, back at the chorus of calumny and censure that had surrounded Venetia:

> [W]hensoeuer enuy or malice bitt att her with their poisonous tooth, euen their tongues would att the same time confesse that what in her first and vnripe youth they would call an *easinesse* or a fault in her, proceedeth from such a sweetenesse of nature and such a confidence of worth that usually raigneth in noble minds, as it was a question whither they dispraised or commended her more.[29]

Here, we are confronted by yet another irony. At this point in his life, Digby would have appeared, on a rising curve of success at court, to have conformed for a short time to the Church of England. Perhaps the popular estimation of Digby did not believe overmuch in this apostasy. It is more likely that, at the time of Venetia's death, Digby was looking dangerous. Despite his outward conformity, he was still a papist by negative family associations, namely his father's treason, his uncle's involvement in Charles I's ultimately unsuccessful nine-year campaign to marry a Spanish princess, and his unpopular cousin hovering on the fringes of conversion to Rome. Yet there had also been two notable and relatively recent successes: his naval victory over the Venetians and the plundering of antique marbles from the Mediterranean. To hostile eyes, Digby must have seemed a papist with a great deal of power. He had appointments at court, enjoyed the queen's favour and protection, was unrestricted in his movements, and enjoyed a defiantly exotic life, adorned by wealth and success. Thus, I suspect that a confected sense of Digby's foreignness was the crux of his unpopularity, and that all his activities were inevitably construed in the set terms of this public perception of him as an 'Inglese Italianato'.

In conclusion, it is instructive to return to Donne, whose reception, particularly in our own era, has been wholly different from Digby's. They had a good deal more in common than a taste for viper wine. Donne's family, like Digby's, was recusant Catholic. His marriage, like Digby's, arose from romantic passion, and was judged unwise by contemporaries, albeit for other reasons. Both saw naval action as gentlemen adventurers and travelled abroad with embassies. Above all, Donne, like Digby, was the subject of legends. In the case of Digby, however, the structural principle of the stories was of a leopard unable to shed his spots, even by apostasy, whereas, regarding Donne, the common elements were peripety and transformation. He was the promising young man undone by marriage, and the man dramatically transformed from 'Jack Donne' to 'Doctor Donne'; and, underlying both, the man who decisively rejected his family's Catholicism.[30]

Donne, like Digby, was an artist of death: his response to his own mortality was as nuanced, as complex, and as theatrical as Digby's responses to the death of his wife. Both men had an extraordinarily specific perception of the body as meat; their fascinated imaginations pursued the corpse – whether generic or specific – into the grave, and through the intimate processes of corruption.

> Where be all the Atoms of that flesh, which a *Corrasive* hath eat away, or a *Consumption* hath breath'd, and exhal'd away from our arms, and other Limbs? In what wrinkle, in what furrow, in what bowel of the earth, ly all the graines of the ashes of a body burnt a thousand years since? In what corner, in what ventricle of the sea, lies all the jelly of a Body drowned in the *generall flood*? [...] One humour of our dead body produces worms, and those worms suck and exhaust all other humour, and then all dies, and all dries, and molders into dust, and that dust is blowen into the River, & that puddled water tumbled into the sea, and that ebs and flows in infinite revolutions, and still, still, God knows in what *Cabinet* every *seed-Pearle* lies.[31]

> My thoughtes haue bin all this morning running in this endelesse circle, and haue tumbled euery corner of her graue. This day three weekes, late att night, she was buried; and by this time God knows what alteration that faire bodie hath sustained ... [B]y this time peraduenture her louely face, that was the miracle of nature for beauty and sweetnesse, is farre gone towards being turned to earth, and is couered ouer with slime and wormes ... [H]er heart that was the seat of goodnesse, truth and vertue, hath now nothing in it but peraduenture some presumptuous worme feeding on the middle of it.[32]

Donne's *Devotions vpon Emergent Occasions* are extraordinary in many respects, but not least for their formal structure. Wracked with sickness, Donne dramatized himself as an object, referring to his own sweats and suffering from an extraordinary distance. The *Devotions* are articulated by titles: the first onset of sickness; the action of disease on the perceptions of the sufferer; taking to bed; a doctor is called; and so forth. That these are not generic but specific to Donne's personal experience is indicated most clearly by number VIII, 'The King sends his owne Phisician'. Yet the content is almost completely abstract: the arrival of the royal doctor prompts not an account of his diagnosis or advice but a dissertation on the relationship between kings and God. Donne contrived to write nearly 50 pages on his subjective experience of an illness without detailing any of its symptoms. Likewise, Digby treated the death of his wife, and his own experience of mourning, in the manner common to international baroque culture: as simultaneously sensual and emblematic.

Notes

1 John Donne, *Devotions upon Emergent Occasions*, ed. Elizabeth Savage, 2 vols (Salzburg: Institut für Englische Sprache und Literatur, 1975).

2 R. C. Bald, *John Donne: A Life* (Oxford: Clarendon Press, 1970), p. 455, suggests that this was possibly the Earl of Dorset.

3 Donne, *Devotions*, p. 84. Donne was interested in paradox throughout his life, of which this is an obvious example.

4 Samuel Johnson, 'Cowley', in *The Lives of the Most Eminent English Poets*, 4 vols (London: C. Bathhurst *et al.*, 1781), I, pp. 3–102, at pp. 27, 55, 59–60.

5 As Harold B. Segel comments, '[M]ost specialists in late-sixteenth and seventeenth-century English literature continue to favor the originally disparaging and not quite apt term "Metaphysical" for literary developments that are not, of course, exclusively metaphysical in any strict sense and for which most critics on the Continent have long ago accepted the validity of Baroque.' Harold B. Segel, *The Baroque Poem: A Comparative Study* (New York: Dutton, 1974), p. 4.

6 See Peter Davidson, *The Universal Baroque* (Manchester: Manchester University Press, 2007), pp. 25–93.

7 The principal sources for his life are Anthony à Wood's *Athenae Oxonienses: An Exact History of All the Writers and Bishops Who Have Had Their Education in the Most Ancient and Famous University of Oxford*, 2 vols (London: Printed for Tho. Bennet, 1691–92), cols 238–42; and John Aubrey's lives of Kenelm and Venetia Digby, which are, as it were, the research notes made for Wood's larger project: see Aubrey, *Brief Lives*, I, pp. 324–34.

8 He seems to be remembered chiefly, however, for a remarkably precise and scientific cookery book, compiled from his papers after his death: *The Closet of the Eminently Learned Sir Kenelme Digbie Kt. Opened whereby Is Discovered Several Ways for Making of Metheglin, Sider, Cherry-wine, &c.: together with Excellent Directions for Cookery* (London: Printed by E.C. for H. Brome, 1669).

9 Kenelm Digby, *A Late Discourse Made in a Solemne Assembly of Nobles and Learned Men at Montpellier in France … Touching the Cure of Wounds by the Powder of Sympathy*, trans. R. White (London: Printed for R. Lowndes and T. Davies, 1658).

10 Wood, *Athenae Oxonienses*, cols 238–40.

11 In addition to causing a falling out with his chief collaborator, Aubrey, the publication of Wood's work in 1691–92 'aroused the anger of numerous gentlemen', not least Henry Hyde, second Earl of Clarendon, who sued for libel and won. The offending pages were publicly burnt. Graham Parry, 'Wood, Anthony (1632–1695)', *Oxford Dictionary of National Biography* (2008) [https://doi-org.ezproxy-prd.bodleian.ox.ac.uk/10.1093/ref:odnb/29864] (retrieved online 19 February 2008).
12 Aubrey, *Brief Lives*, I, p. 331.
13 *Ibid.*
14 *Ibid.*, p. 333.
15 *Ibid.*, p. 328.
16 *Ibid.*, p. 326; 'courtesan' becomes an unequivocal term over the course of the seventeenth century. The *OED*'s examples include 'Your whore is for euery rascall, but your Curtizan is for your Courtier' (1607) and 'Quality Whore' (*c.* 1700).
17 *Ibid.*, pp. 326–7.
18 *Ibid.*, p. 327.
19 *Ibid.*, p. 332.
20 *Ibid.*, p. 329.
21 An imitation by of Petronius by a Scoto-French Catholic, John Barclay, *Euphormionis Lusinini Satyricon* (Paris: François Huby, 1605), was successful throughout Europe and frequently reprinted.
22 See Shell, *Catholicism, Controversy and the English Literary Imagination*, pp. 23–55.
23 Sancti Irenaei Episcopi Lugdunensis, *Libros Quinque Adversus Haereses*, ed. W. Harvey, 2 vols (Cambridge: Cambridge University Press, 1857), I, pp. 191–2.
24 See R. J. Knecht, *Catherine de' Medici* (London: Longman, 1998), pp. xii–xiii.
25 Pliny, *Historia naturalis*, XXIX, ch. 21, cited in Jarltzberg, 'Serpent Eating', *Notes and Queries*, first series, 6.147 (21 August 1852), p. 177.
26 Viper wine was recommended as a strengthening draught (with an implication that it was sexually invigorating) by Digby's contemporaries Philip Massinger and Francis Quarles. Philip Massinger, *Believe As You List: A Tragedy* (*c.* 1623) [ed. T. Crofton Croker, first printed edition (London: Percy Society, 1849)], Act 4, Scene 1, lines 65–9; Francis Quarles, *The Historie of Samson* (1631), in the *Complete Works in Prose and Verse of Francis Quarles*, ed. Alexander B. Grosart, 3 vols (Edinburgh: Chertsey Worthies Library, 1881), II, p. 149. Beliefs in the strengthening powers of viper wine or broth still had some currency in the Victorian period: see, for instance, 'Viperidae', in Society for the Diffusion of Useful Knowledge, *The Penny Cyclopaedia*, 27 vols (London: Charles Knight and Co., 1835–43), XXVI, pp. 347–54.
27 Digby, *Choice and Experimented Receipts in Physick and Chirurgery […] Translated out of several languages by G.H.* (London: Printed for H. Brome, 1668), pp. 245–9, 250, 253.
28 See *The English and Scottish Popular Ballads*, ed. Francis J. Child, 5 vols (Boston: Houghton Mifflin, 1882–98), I, pp. 151–66.

29 Digby letter to his sons, dated 18 May 1633, quoted in Vittorio Gabrieli, 'A New Digby Letter-Book', *National Library of Wales Journal*, 9.2 (1956), pp. 113–48, at p. 123.

30 The principal source for the life of Donne is the biography by Izaak Walton, *The Life of John Donne, Dr. in Divinity, and Late Dean of Saint Pauls Church London* (London: Printed by J.G. for R. Marriot, 1658). Nevertheless, Donne's high visibility among coterie poets who were university-educated and trained at the Inns of Court, who tended to be great compilers of manuscript miscellanies, has ensured the preservation of stories about him as well as of copies of his poems themselves. See Arthur F. Marotti, *John Donne: Coterie Poet* (Madison, WI: University of Wisconsin Press, 1986).

31 John Donne, 'A Sermon Preached at the Earl of Bridgwaters House in London at the Mariage of His Daughter [...] Novemb. 19, 1627', in Donne, *Fifty Sermons* (London: Printed by Ja. Flesher for M.F., J. Marriot, and R. Royston, 1649), pp. 1–9, at p. 3.

32 Digby letter to his brother, dated 24 May 1633, quoted in Vittorio Gabrieli, 'A New Digby Letter-Book (continued)', *National Library of Wales Journal*, 9.4 (1956), pp. 440–62, at p. 455.

10

The assassin's new castles: frescoes and textiles for the Leslies at Nové Město nad Metují and Ptui

The Aberdeenshire branch of the Leslie family were intensely involved with the material culture of Catholicism, before and after the Reformation. The Leslies of Leslie and the Leslies of Balquhain and Fetternear (subsequently the Counts Leslie in the Holy Roman Empire) played a part in the survival of pre-Reformation objects – most notably the unique print of the *Compassio Beatae Mariae*,[1] now in the National Library of Scotland, and the Fetternear Banner, now in the National Museum of Scotland.[2] Once they had established themselves on the Continent, their fortunes were advanced rapidly by the part which Walter Leslie (1606–67) played in the assassination of Albrecht von Wallenstein at Cheb (Eger) on 25 February 1634; a cycle of painted ceilings survives at their castle of Nové Město nad Metují in the Czech Republic; the collections which they formed at their castle at Ptuj (Oberpettau) in Slovenia survive intact to a remarkable degree to the present day.[3] Little of what James Leslie, second Count Leslie, sent to Scotland in the 1690s to furnish the castle or palace of Fetternear in Aberdeenshire (either sacred or secular) has survived two Jacobite risings, serial lawsuits, and a fire, but one superb set of High Mass vestments survived, which were long at the Blairs Museum, and these are the main focus of this chapter.

The Leslies were one of the most successful families of the Scottish military diaspora, a notable part of that long tradition of foreign service which extends temporally from the Garde Ecossaise in medieval France to General Barclay de Tolly in Russian service in the Napoleonic Wars. Both northern Catholic Leslies and their Protestant kinsmen from the Lowland Rothes branch of the family seem to have prospered in this arena.[4] Five generals of the name of Leslie commanded the armies of four different nations – 'Scotland, Germany, Sweden, and Russia – nearly all at the same time' – in the seventeenth century.[5] As well as Walter Leslie, first Count Leslie, and Count James Leslie in the Habsburg Empire, these included the Protestant Lord Leven, who served in Sweden and then in civil-war Scotland, as well as David Leslie, Lord Newark, of the Rothes family, who commanded in Sweden and England. In addition to this, the family produced 'many

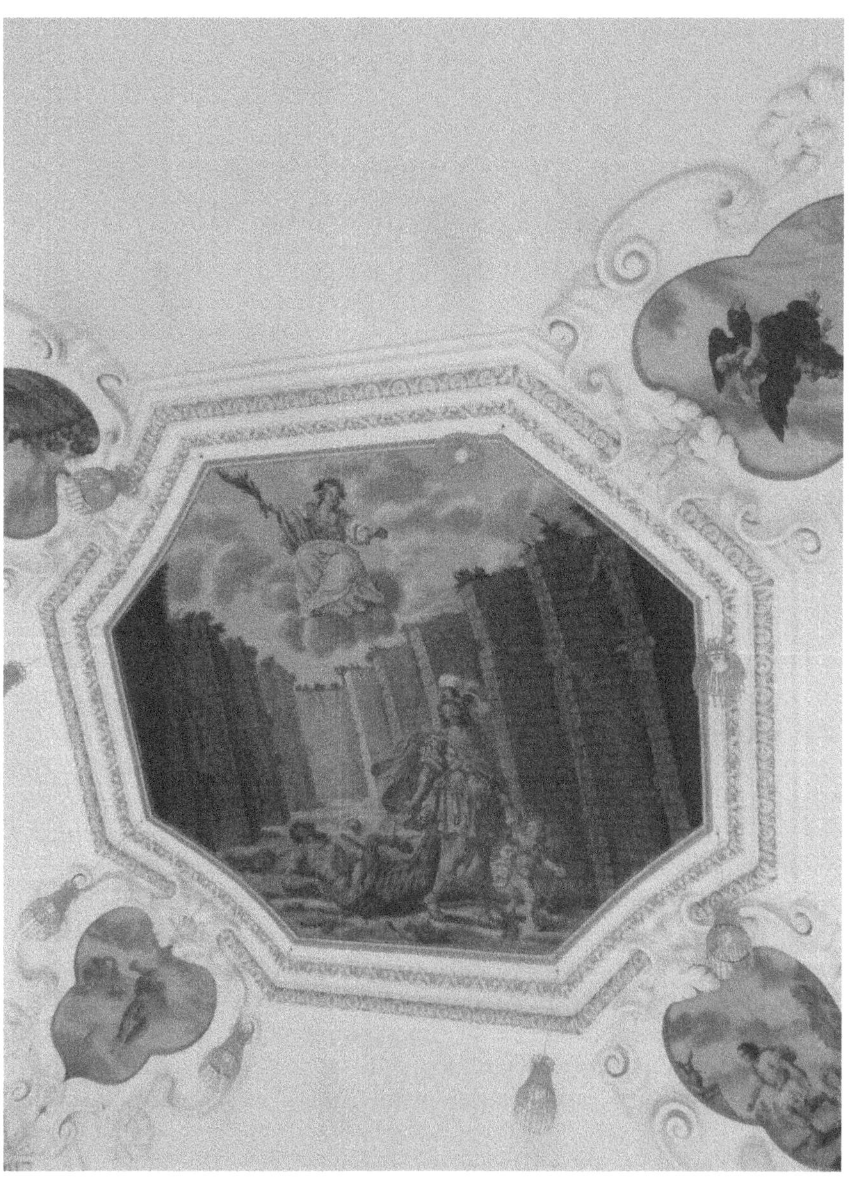

Figure 10.1 Šebestián Václav Harovník (*c.* 1637–83), *Theseus and the Minotaur*, ceiling fresco, *c.* 1650, Castle of Nové Město nad Metují, Czech Republic.

colonels' and lesser officers. Leven led between 4,000 and 5,000 troops as Swedish military governor of Stralsund in Swedish Pomerania, to which post he was appointed in the middle of the unsuccessful 1628 siege of that city by the Imperial general Albrecht von Wallenstein.[6]

It was the assassination of Wallenstein in February 1634 which brought about the dramatic rise of the Balquhain branch of the Leslie family in the person of Walter, later first Count. As the second son of the third marriage of John Leslie of Balquhain to Jean Erskine of Gogar, he had no expectations of inheritance in Scotland, and initially served in the Protestant armies of the Netherlands and either Denmark or Sweden, in a lowly rank. He appears to have either converted or reconverted to Catholicism after his part in the assassination of Wallenstein in 1634, but before his elevation to the rank of *reichsgraf* in 1637.[7] In his early career he seemingly identified as 'Calvinist', although David Worthington's authoritative study describes Walter as being 'an Episcopalian by background'.[8]

In an echo of earlier Leslie alliances with the leading Catholic family of Aberdeenshire, Sergeant (and future Count) Walter Leslie's commanding officer in the War of the Mantuan Succession (1628–1631) and at the subsequent Thirty Years' War battles of Bentheim, Freistadt, and Lutzen was a Colonel John Gordon. Despite their large difference in rank, the two men were close friends, and a commission for Leslie had been procured by the end of 1632. Their joint assassination of Wallenstein in 1634 was lavishly rewarded, but thereafter Walter Leslie's focus seems to have been ceremonial (including an embassy to the Sublime Porte in 1665–66) rather than military: '[H]is subsequent military career was sporadic and frequently disastrous, and absenteeism led to his being deprived of his last regiment by 1642.'[9] Writing in a different venue, however, Worthington qualifies his own statement:

> [N]one of this ended his military influence. In 1650, besides receiving appointment to the rank of Field Marshal, Leslie became warden of the 'Sclavonian marches' and a general on the aforementioned 'Croatian-Slavonian Frontier', while, seven years on from that, he received promotion to the Vice-Presidency of the Imperial War Council.[10]

With this sudden advance of his fortunes in the Empire, Walter Leslie also acquired new influence in Britain; he played a part in obtaining Prince Rupert's release from prison in Linz in 1638 and, apparently at his behest, his elder brother William Leslie became a member of the Privy Chamber of King Charles I in 1642. Count Walter bought Ptuj Castle 'from the Jesuits at auction in Zagreb in 1656'.[11] Childless, he arranged that he would be succeeded in his various possessions by his nephew James Leslie (*c.* 1621–1694), later second Count Leslie, who is best known for his service as General of Artillery at the Battle of Vienna in 1683.

Count James Leslie purchased the castle in Graz now known as the Leslie-Hof in 1684, and furnished it with costly textiles from the Low Countries, most notably a set of verdure hunting tapestries with figures woven from gold and silver threads.[12] By 1692 he was so profoundly associated with the Catholic community in Scotland that he was addressed as 'Domino ac Patrono nostro Gratiosissimo' ('our most gracious lord and patron') by his kinsman William Aloysius Leslie SJ (1641–1704), who described himself and his Jesuit colleagues as 'Patres Societatis Jesu, Missionis Scotiae' in a remarkable baroque history of the family published as the *Laurus Leslaeana*.[13]

This *Laurus* is a work of considerable interest: seldom did a British Catholic family, successfully established on the Continent, set forth their perception of themselves, their position, and their origin with more confidence. It may reasonably be conjectured that the contents of the *Laurus* accord, to a considerable degree, with the version of their own history that would have been put into circulation in central Europe when Walter Leslie was raised to the nobility of the Empire.[14] As well as emphasising the family's Catholicism, especially the connection to John Leslie (1527–96), last Catholic bishop of Ross and apologist for Mary Queen of Scots, it emphasises the military successes of both the Catholic and Protestant branches of the family, claiming that Leslies simultaneously held commands in Scotland, Muscovy, and Germany.[15]

Perhaps the most surprising aspect of the book is that it claims a central European origin for the Leslies, as well as continuous connections with central Europe throughout the Middle Ages. It was (and is) reasonably common for Scottish élite families to attribute their origins to a specific warrior arriving from outside the borders of the Kingdom of Scotland as recently as the 1200s; logically, this suggests that early modern Scots in general – and certainly those of noble rank – would have seen Scotland to some degree as a 'nation of immigrants', and themselves as personally linked to one or more specific other European countries. In the case of the Leslies, there is a suggestion of a very long and perhaps unbroken tradition of military activity in what might be broadly termed the Hungarian or anti-Ottoman interest, offering past parallels for the recent achievements of Count James. The account of origins offered by the *Laurus Leslaeana* is a great deal simpler and more immediate than the extraordinary world history offered in the genealogy of their Aberdeenshire neighbours, the Urquharts of Cromarty (latterly, of Craigston). As set forth in 1652 in the *ΠΑΝΤΟΧΡΟΝΟΧΑΝΟΝ* by Sir Thomas Urquhart, it began with the creation of red earth by God the Father, Son, and Holy Ghost, and finally gets the Urquharts to Scotland 41 generations later via the sister of Hiber (who gave his name to Hibernia) and Scota the daughter of Pharaoh (from whom the Urquharts as well as the Stuarts are descended, the Urquharts in the female line).[16]

The first ancestor claimed for the Leslies is Bartolf (or Berthold or Bartholomaeus) the Hungarian, who is said to have accompanied St Margaret of Scotland from Hungary to England and thence to Scotland. He is claimed to have directly founded the Leslie fortunes by standing in such high regard with King Malcolm that, as well as being knighted and made Keeper of Edinburgh Castle, he was granted lands in those parts of Scotland where branches of the Leslies were to become established: Fife, Angus, the Mearns, Cushnie in Mar, and Leslie in the Garioch.[17] Perhaps because he was writing in exile, the earliest Scottish evidence for the history of the family which William Leslie can produce is a fragment of a ballad:

> Between the Lesse Ley and the Mair
> He slue the Knight and left him there.[18]

He also leaves an honourable central European origin open for the name, by advancing a possible alternative derivation from Ladislaus.[19] The Victorian historian of the family, Colonel Charles Leslie of Balquhain, accepted the Bartolf narrative, including a date of 1067 for his arrival in Scotland and 1121 for his death.[20] He also accepted almost all of the account offered of the Balquhain branch of the family, despite being intensely sceptical of the narrative of the Rothes branch, especially the emphasis on continuous military service abroad. Bartolf's grandson Malcolm was killed on crusade in the twelfth century, and a great-great-grandson, Leonard, 'went to the wars abroad' in the thirteenth.[21] Norman de Leslie was reportedly in the party that conveyed King Robert Bruce's heart to the Holy Land in 1330,[22] and Walter Leslie, fourth son of the sixth laird, 'served in the Imperial army under the emperors Louis IV and Charles IV (1346–1378), with great distinction, against the Saracens ... [and went] to the wars in Germany in 1356'.[23] This same Walter Leslie later served in the army of King Charles V of France, and received an annuity of 200 gold francs for his services against the English at the 1370 Battle of Pontvallain.[24]

Moving towards the time of the Reformation, it becomes possible to trace something of the religious and political position of the Leslies. The generally accepted version is the one set forth by David McRoberts in his classic article on the Fetternear Banner:

> In the wholesale alienation of ecclesiastical property which was such a marked feature of sixteenth-century Scotland, the barony of Fetternear with its castle and pertinents passed from the bishopric of Aberdeen into the possession of the family of Leslie of Balquhain. The Leslies of Balquhain retained possession of the Fetternear lands from that time down to the present century ...

> The Leslies of Balquhain, unlike many other beneficiaries of the sixteenth-century economic revolution, maintained their adherence to the Old Faith, and, under their protection, the lands of Fetternear, lying between Bennachie and the Don, have ever remained a traditionally Catholic district.[25]

This needs to be weighed, however, against the evidence David Worthington has advanced for Walter Leslie having been Protestant in youth. It is a complex undertaking to trace religious confession in this period and in Aberdeenshire society with any precision. George Gordon, Earl of Huntly, took a 13-year lease of the 'barony and shire of Fetternear' from William Gordon, bishop of Aberdeen, in 1549.[26] A little less than 18 months later, however, the same bishop leased the same lands to John, eighth Baron Leslie of Balquhain, for 19 years at approximately the same annual rent as before.[27] It is not easy to reconstruct this sequence of events, but the general implication would seem to be that valuable Church property was being placed in the hands of sympathetic Catholic laymen at a time of heightened tension. John, fifth Baron Leslie of Leslie, was an ally of the Gordons in the Scottish Wars of Religion.[28] William, ninth Baron Leslie of Balquhain,

> afforded great assistance to the Bishop of Aberdeen in protecting the cathedral from the ravages of the Reformers, and ... supported the bishop in his diocese when all other bishops in Scotland were persecuted.

It appears to have been in gratitude for this that the bishop granted William Leslie the barony, palace, fortalice, and tower of Fetternear in 1566.[29] Remarkably, this ownership was confirmed by both King James VI, in 1602, and Pope Clement X, in 1670.[30]

Although members of the family, like many Aberdeenshire gentry Catholics, conformed to the Protestant Church at times of conflict and crisis, or simply to secure employment with the army of a reformed state, there can be little doubt of the religious position that Patrick, Count Leslie (15th Baron of Balquhain), expressed in stone by the time that he took possession of Fetternear in 1690.[31] He seems to have gone out of his way to proclaim not only his foreign title (a count's coronet over the substantial carving of his and his wife's arms above the central door) but also Roman Catholic devotion in lettered panels with 'I.H.S.' and 'M.R.A.' (i.e. Maria Regina Angelorum).[32] It was at this point that those extraordinary hybrid trophies, the Fetternear vestments, would appear to have been sent to Scotland:

> Count Patrick Leslie fitted up the mansion-house of Fetternear in a magnificent manner, and furnished and adorned it with a valuable collection of pictures and objects of art which were sent to him from Germany by his uncle, Count Walter Leslie, by his brother, Count James, and by his son, Count James Ernest. Many of these articles had been taken from the Turks, by Count James

Leslie, during the siege of Vienna in 1683, and in other battles in which he defeated them. Amongst them were pieces of rich silk and gold and silver brocade stuffs, which were made into church vestments, and some of which still remain at Fetternear.[33]

The castle of Nové Město nad Metují is situated on, and externally of a piece with, the sixteenth-century Husovo Square in the Czech town that shares its name. The building of the castle commenced in 1501, but few if any of its numerous early modern renovations were ordered by Wallenstein, who acquired it in the early 1620s when (and because) the previous owners took up arms in the Protestant cause in the Thirty Years' War.[34] The region in which this castle sits is still known as the 'Kladsko Borderlands', presumably in recognition of the fact that the neighbouring county of Kladsko or Glatz, though then also part of the Kingdom of Bohemia, was in rebellion against the Emperor for virtually the whole of that conflict.[35] The remainder of this section provides a detailed description of the surviving baroque decoration applied to the interior of the second floor of Nové Město nad Metují Castle by Wallenstein's assassin, Walter Leslie, who owned it from 1634 until 1667.[36]

On the second floor of the castle, Leslie's heavily Graeco-Roman self-mythologisation unfolds in a sequence of ten rooms painted by the Bohemian Fabián Šebestián Václav Harovník (*c.* 1637–83). The most likely date for this work is after 1652, when Leslie was recorded as undertaking substantial works on the castle. The author of the only study of these paintings to appear to date, Dr Radka Nokkala Miltová, emphasises that they are typical of the work for the (often new) nobility who emerged after the Battle of the White Mountain, that they celebrate dynastic alliances (in Leslie's case with the Dietrichsteins), and that there is evidence of the involvement of a (sadly anonymous) learned iconographer.[37]

The first room has a central ceiling panel, with the four elements pouring their riches into an urn, personifications of Fame and Triumph bearing laurels, trumpets, and the Leslie badge of the three-buckled belt. Four painted emblems framed in plasterwork cartouches adjoin this scene at its four corners. One, featuring bees swarming from a knight's helmet, bears the motto 'EX BELLO PAX' ('Out of war, peace').[38] This can be traced to the *Emblematum Liber* of Andrea Alciato (Ausburg: Heinrich Steyer, 1521), and here may represent the peace that flowed from the death of Wallenstein. Its companion piece, of a storm-stilling halcyon in its nest made up of cornstalks and grapes, bears the legend 'EX PACE UBERTAS' ('Out of peace, abundance'), and is a close copy of a woodcut that appears on page 192 of the Lyon, 1550, edition of Alciato.[39]

The other two emblems in this room are rather more unusual. 'FIDE ET VIDE' ('Believe and see') features a right hand with an eye in the palm emerging from cloud and balancing what appears to be an obelisk. This previously appeared on page 95 of *Selectorum Symbolorum Heroicorum Centuria Gemina* (Frankfurt: Iennis, 1619), clarifying that the balanced object is an obelisk – the moral being a simple one: that faith in God opens the mind to a true vision of the world. The final emblem depicts a building consisting of a very steep four-sided pyramid resting on a cube, with the motto SIC SEMPER and indications of sun and wind, representing good and bad weather.[40] The faithful pyramid or obelisk stands strong regardless of the change of weather. I hesitate to say that these four emblems taken together represent the good effects of a timely assassination, together with the praise of the character of the assassin, but that is roughly the message which is conveyed.

Exiting the room containing the emblems brings us to a further glorification of Leslie's deeds of arms: a Roman triumph forms the centre panel of the ceiling. A reasonably explicit reference to Wallenstein occurs in the form of an empty set of three-quarter cavalry armour, clearly intended to be from the 1620s or 1630s, which is being held aloft at the centre of an otherwise standard scene of a Roman triumph – importantly, one in which all *other* clothing depicted, including armour, is all conventionally ancient.

The next room, the third in the enfilade, establishes a link between Leslie and the ancient Greek hero Theseus. The painting on its ceiling is of a deep pit, the Cretan labyrinth, overshadowed by buttressed stone walls (see Figure 10.1). Theseus, having defeated an almost distressingly centaur-like minotaur that lies bloodied and dead on the labyrinth floor, regards it over his right shoulder with a look of sorrow mingled with disgust as he follows a cupid, holding the guiding thread through the labyrinth, the other end of which is held, in the heavens, by a figure of Victory, crowned with laurels and holding the victor's palm. The application of the fable to Leslie and Wallenstein is audacious, to put it mildly. This image has at its corners four plasterwork cartouches, each containing an image from Ovid: the fall of Icarus, Zeus and Ganymede, Narcissus, and the famed 'golden apples' foot race between Atalanta and Hippomenes/Melanion. Icarus was of course the son of Daedalus, architect of the Minoan Labyrinth, but the context of these four figures is to reflect and admonish. Once the Minotaur is dead, and order and balance have been restored, the thread guides the choice of the right path through the maze, through life. The four subsidiary figures reflect on power, and ambition. Ganymede raised to Olympus, Icarus falling, Narcissus obsessed only with himself, the worldly golden apples that distract the runners in the race. That Count Walter Leslie might wish to see himself as Theseus is perhaps unsurprising, given the hero's status as an effective serial murderer (generally using their own weapons and methods) of men who had made public nuisances of themselves: Sinis, Sciron, Cercyron, Procrustes.

In the next room, presumably a state bedchamber, the ceiling's plasterwork is more elaborate, and eight rather than four cartouches surround the main painting, which is of the five senses, figured as sleeping boys, in the power of Morpheus, the poppy-wielding god of sleep. The cartouches are all emblems, all derived from Jacobus Typotius's *Symbola divina et humana pontificum* (Prague: Sadeler, 1601–03), and all reflect on royal and noble virtues in a Christian context, about worldly power being sustained by the grace of God. The count's coronet is borne up by the patient slow-growing palm tree with the motto CUM TEMPORE *Vias tuas demonstra* ('Lord, show me your ways'); *in fide et justitia fortitudo* ('In faith and righteousness is bravery'); *deorsum nunquam* ('Never downwards' – hand clasped in a handshake strike the flame of fidelity); *secura veritas* ('Steady truth'); *te gubernatore* ('With you as ruler' – crown and sceptre rest on the globe under the protection of the Holy Spirit); *luceat* ('Let it shine'); *nemo sine te* ('Nobody without you').[41]

In this sequence of rooms everything is martial, masculine, and triumphal, with constant references to Walter Leslie's swift and effective rise to power. Perhaps what is astonishing here is the audacity of the iconographer, and his very baroque ability to find a discourse to express and condone a rise to power and honour by violent means. The suite of rooms in the other wing of the castle are most likely to have belonged to the countess, since their ceilings mostly depict the deeds and virtues of muses, goddesses, and heroines – the Muses, the Judgement of Paris, Flora and the nymphs – although there are also scenes from Homer and from the narrative of the Golden Fleece. The order of the same name was bestowed on Walter Leslie in the 1660s, thus suggesting either that these ceiling paintings were executed over a period of time or that the main painting campaign took place in the third quarter of the century. That these ceremonial rooms fall within what is, to a considerable degree, the countess's wing might be explained by the fact that the whole enfilade is an adaptation of a pre-existing building. The Homeric material and the episodes from the narrative of Jason and the Golden Fleece suggest a level of confidence, even maturity. Unexceptional use of generalised antique images of military and heroic success have moved far from the recent, opportunist violence encoded in the disquieting imagery of Theseus and the Minotaur.

Two rooms remain which speak to the status and ambitions of count and countess together. In the first of them, the Great Room, the ceiling appears to reflect widely on the passage of times and seasons: it depicts a figure of Time presenting a golden chariot (presumably that of Helios) to the enthroned figures of Night and Day. Time is surrounded by the seasons; the hours fly above with a wreathed garland. Minor ceiling panels in the same room depict a banquet on Olympus, Bacchantes, Daphne, and Europa.[42]

Last, in the Great Bedroom, various heroic themes are gathered together, with the main panel showing the apotheosis of the houses of Leslie and Dietrichstein, with four subsidiary panels of exemplary heroines of antiquity. To paraphrase Dr Miltová's meticulous description and analysis of the iconography:[43]

> The decoration of the ceiling of the room presents a very public message and shows a composition traditionally referred to as *The Apotheosis of the House of Leslie*, but in fact the putti who tumble diagonally into the composition carry the arms of Leslie impaling Dietrichstein, which they garland with laurel and crown with a Count's coronet, for the title which Leslie had received in 1637. Alliance with the family of Dietrichstein culminated in the marriage of Walter Leslie with the daughter of Prince Maximilian of Dietrichstein, Anna Franziska, on April 23, 1647. This alliance gave Leslie full entry to the Austrian-Czech elite.

The diagonal formed by the cherubs with arms and coronet is balanced by the rainbow diagonal of the winged goddess Iris, who reclines comfortably, her right arm hooked through the rainbow. Her presence here is presumably as the messenger of the Olympian Gods, figuring the aristocracy of the Empire, to which Leslie is now fully admitted.

Dr Miltová observes that an ingenious balance is struck here between the glorification of martial achievement and success and a maintenance of the female dimension of this wing of the enfilade with all female figures as personifications of virtues, based on the classic *Iconologia* of Cesare Ripa, first published in 1603 and often reprinted. On a raised podium, the figure of Aristocracy sits on a golden throne, also ciphering Prudence, whose snake and mirror she bears in her right hand, as she is crowned with double laurel crowns (for the alliance of the two families, presumably) by Honour. On the steps of the throne sits Vigilance with an oil lamp, accompanied by the emblematic watchful crane, with a stone in its claw. At ground level are more personifications of the Virtues: Temperance diluting wine with water in a remarkable floating golden punchbowl, then Fortitude in armour, with lion and column. Behind Fortitudo, Envy (Invidia), traditionally depicted as an ugly old woman with snakes in her hair, is driven from the scene by an Amazon with a firebrand and a cohort of cupids. These female allegories are extended by the pendant scenes to this apotheosis of the conjoined houses of Leslie and Dietrichstein, which depict heroines of classical antiquity – Dido, Lucretia, Sophonisba.

Having established something of the family context, and having surveyed briefly the cycle of decorative paintings commissioned by Walter Leslie after his rise to power, honours, and social elevation, we can now turn to those vestments made of gold and silver brocade, and captured Turkish armoury, which Count James Leslie, his nephew and his heir, sent back to the family estates in Scotland at some point after the 1683 siege of Vienna, at which he commanded the artillery of the Austrian army. Over the years most of the vestments have disappeared or been displenished, but one High Mass set seems to have survived at Fetternear, where the pre-Reformation 'Fetternear banner' (an unfinished sixteenth-century embroidered banner for a confraternity of the Holy Blood, probably that at St Giles's in Edinburgh) was also preserved.

Formerly on display in the Blairs Museum, Aberdeen, was the magnificent composite chasuble known as 'the Fetternear vestment', together with two matching dalmatics, maniples, and stoles (see Figure 10.2). These came to Blairs College, the former Scottish Junior Seminary, as part of a bequest made by the last Leslie laird of Fetternear in 1921, when he left to the diocese of Aberdeen such items as it was looking after at that time. The vestment can be identified in photographs of the opening of the new buildings at Blairs in 1901, so it must have been in the possession of the Church by then, and the Leslie provenance would appear to be established.

These vestments claim to be those sent back by Count James after 1693 which are listed in an inventory as being made from the 'spoil of the Moslem army defeated at Vienna'.[44] A case can most certainly be made for this when the techniques and materials, especially of the chasuble, are examined.[45] The vestments comprise a richly embroidered chasuble in the baroque style, two dalmatics, two stoles, and two maniples, but the most interesting item is the chasuble, which is my main focus. It is of the Roman or Latin shape with a ground of white satin, covered in embroidered flowers worked in polychrome silks and interspersed with padded goldwork. The orphreys are silk-embroidered vine leaves and clusters of grapes embroidered over a background of laid couched silver thread – a pillar orphrey to the front and a cross orphrey to the back. The back orphrey also has the sacred monogram 'IHS' in the form customary on the badge of the Society of Jesus, with a cross surmounting the 'H'. (The Scottish Jesuits in Graz were under the protection of Count James Leslie.) The monogram has heavily padded areas, giving a raised effect. Both orphreys are edged with an embroidered strip of even basket couching in metal threads and silk-work, resembling a braid or heavy ribbon.

The silverwork on the orphreys has been likened to south German work, but there are similar examples on part of a frontal in the Marienkirche in Lübeck and on a chasuble in the cathedral of Frankfurt am Main which bears the arms of the Thurn und Taxis family.[46] There was an Ursuline convent at Neuburg am Donau which was noted for its metal thread-work, but the Ursulines more generally seemed to have been fond of doing such work, and an Ursuline convent was established by Eleanora Gonzaga, the wife of

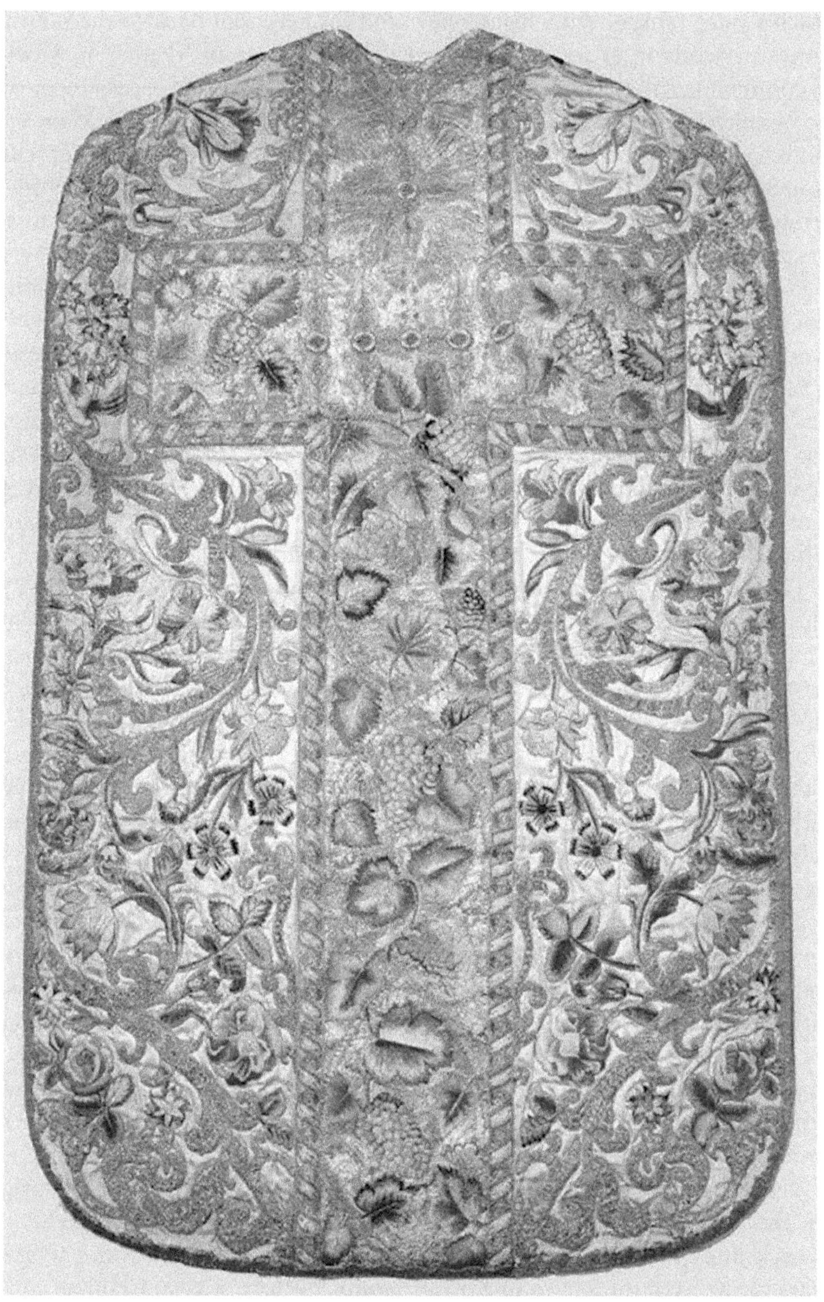

Figure 10.2 The Fetternear chasuble, embroidered silk and gold and silver thread, including elements of reused Turkish goldwork, central Europe, late seventeenth century. Formerly at Fetternear, Aberdeenshire, then in the collection of the Blairs Museum, Aberdeen, to be transferred to Scottish Catholic Museum, Glasgow.

Emperor Ferdinand III, in Vienna in 1663. An outstanding example of their work, the Rosenornat chasuble, can be seen in the Museum Angewandte Kunst in Vienna.[47] It is of gold, silver, and coloured silk embroidery on a ground of laid silverwork. Comparison suggests that perhaps the orphreys were worked in Vienna.[48]

The silk flowers on the chasuble were worked as 'slips' individually onto linen and then laid on the satin ground, being edged up with a fine silver cord. The flowers are obviously European work and represent roses, lilies, tulips, and cornflowers; and the polychrome silks are still stunning in their brilliance. The immediate assumption would be that they were worked in the same convent workshop, but, interestingly, the flowers bear a strong similarity to the Pázmány chasuble in the cathedral of Estergom in Hungary. The seventeenth-century Holy Roman Empire included, of course, a considerable tranche of central Europe beyond the German-speaking countries, and the Leslies owned estates at Ptuj in what is now Slovenia, so a Hungarian origin for some elements of the embroidery seems wholly possible. It seems therefore equally possible that there could have been Sisters of Hungarian origin in whichever convent worked the embroideries.

It is the goldwork on the chasuble that can finally be identified as 'the Turkish or Moslem armoury'. There are Turkish saddles in the Esterházy collection in the Iparművészeti Museum in Budapest, and another in Krakow in Wawel Royal Castle. The elaborate saddles and the caparisons of war-horses were not merely for ornamental purposes; their use was protective, to prevent the mounts being slashed and so debilitated. Heavily embroidered cloths with metalwork in the embroidery allowed for ease of movement, while preventing superficial injury to the horse by deflecting sword blades.[49] All of this explains where the goldwork may have been obtained, but where did it originate and how can it be identified?

There was a fraternity of Turkish goldwork embroiderers, the Cemaat-i Zerduzan, established in the Topkapı Palace in Istanbul. Their work was used to cover saddles, quivers, bow bags, garments, and furnishings.[50] Like the Broderer's Company of sixteenth-century England, theirs was an all-male guild. In the early modern period their main skills were *zerzud*, couching in gold threads; *dival*, known in Europe as *guipure* (and which became popular in the West around the turn of the eighteenth century); and *sama*, a satin stitch worked in gold. As well as working on cloth, the zerduzans also worked on leather, but it is their work on fabric which appears on the Fetternear vestment in the form of scrolling and stylised arabesques.

Elaborate patterns of stitching in gold and silver thread have been worked over areas padded with silk-work. These would have been carefully eased from their original ground and laid as slips onto the chasuble, then edged up with the same fine silver cord as the slips with flowers. The skills of the workers are evident from the variety of their stitch work. Fine passing (wire wrapped round a silk core and thin enough to be used to stitch through fabric) is used in the many ways: counching, stars, cables, coils, figures of eight, herringbones. Gold plate, flat metal with a ribbon effect, is laid in strips over a padded silk ground, tied down with diagonals of fine thread and topped with coils and scrolls of passing, metal-wrapped thread.

It is this final type of gold plate work, which 'added lightness and texture to the embroidery and a touch of brilliance when worked in metal thread and plate' and was one of the highly prized crafts in Ottoman times, which characterises the goldwork as Turkish.[51] The use of plate was not common in European work at the time. That on the chasuble resembles a modern Turkish embroidery called *tel kakma*. The plate would have been hammered to get it to lie smooth and flat.

The Fetternear chasuble goldwork is all made from passing and plate: there is none of the bullion which forms the basis for so much more recent work, with its smooth and rough purls and its check metal wire threads. The artistry of the workers has to be seen to be believed; it is no wonder that their work was so highly prized, and, indeed, that to be a zerduzan was to have achieved the height of one's profession in the Ottoman Empire.

Mention has been made above of a difference between the orphreys on the chasuble and those on the dalmatics. The laid silverwork ground on the chasuble varies in direction, as though to accommodate the leaves, and has no cord edgings. The silverwork on the dalmatic orphreys is much more uniform, and it is interesting to note that the grapes and the leaves on them have been laid on as slips, and edged with the same silver cord, whereas it is impossible to discern whether the silver goes under the leaves and grapes on the chasuble in whole or in part. At times the silk covers a thread or two of the silver, while at others it appears to run alongside it.

The orphreys on the dalmatics are edged with a narrow silver braid, rather than the braid-effect embroidery of the chasuble. The leaves and grapes are the work of different embroiderers, since the treatment of the shading of the coloured silks varies despite a certain uniformity. There are no embroidered flowers on the dalmatics, whose background is of woven floral patterned silk brocade, possibly eighteenth century, which raises the possibility that they are of slightly later date, and that the orphreys may have been sent to Scotland before being mounted. It is known that orphreys were frequently transported separately as strips, rolled up, for ease; but more research into the background fabric is needed. Interestingly, the stoles and maniples are on the same white satin ground as the chasuble, and have flowers as their sole decoration apart from Latin and saltire crosses, braid, and fringe. Some of the flowers are of a higher standard than others, but they are all beautiful and still exquisitely coloured.

In conclusion, a case has been made for the possible provenance of the various elements that make up the Fetternear chasuble and dalmatics, but it can only be conjectural. It is possible – indeed, likely – that Count James Leslie commissioned the central European Ursuline Sisters to make a vestment using embroideries captured from Turkish officers while incorporating their own specialist skills. It may be the sole survivor of several items of the same sort: an implication that could easily be drawn from Colonel Leslie's *Historical Records of the Family of Leslie*,[52] which records dispersals of the rich furnishings of Fetternear throughout the eighteenth century. Between 1715 and 1720, in the wake of the Jacobite rising of 1715, chapel furnishings and vestments were sold by the Hon. Margaret Elphinstone, Protestant widow of Count Patrick Leslie's son George, due to the fact that she 'shared in the bitter anti-Catholic spirit of the times'; and one of the buyers was James Gordon of Cowbairdy, a younger son of Sir James Gordon of Park.[53] In 1762 an officer in the Dutch army named Peter Leslie-Grant sued his distant relative Anthony, Count Leslie, for possession of Fetternear and Balquhain, on the grounds that the latter was 'a Papist and an alien'; the House of Lords found in Leslie-Grant's favour, but he had only lived in the house for six years when, 'much pressed for money', he leased it to a Edinburgh lawyer named Orme.[54]

Many of the records of the family were lost when Fetternear House, the former summer palace of the bishops of Aberdeen, burned to the ground in the 1920s.[55] Happily, the vestment was then already in the possession of the diocese of Aberdeen, or there would be nothing left for our conjecture, wonder, and amazement. How much else was lost cannot now be assessed.

The composite nature of the vestment, Turkish goldwork, and central European embroidery accords very closely with the image that the late seventeenth-century Counts Leslie projected of themselves and their antecedents: as long-time guardians of the eastern frontier of Europe, from whence, according to the baroque history of the family by William Aloysius Leslie SJ, the *Laurus Leslaeana*, they derived their own origin. The vestment is the combination of the spoils of war and the labours of the Ursuline Sisters, among whom there many well have been Hungarians. Although much more of the Leslie inheritance is now preserved in Slovenia and the Czech Republic than in Scotland, the Leslies were instrumental in preserving some of the finest Catholic material objects in Scotland from before and after the Reformation.

All the baroque cultural production discussed in this chapter arose from the single act of successful violence which precipitated a marginal Scottish soldier of fortune into the heart of the central European elite. Not the least remarkable feature of it is the speed with which an iconography (Theseus and the Minotaur) was found to legitimise his violent entry into the nobility, and subsequently their whole history was comprehensively recast, complete with distinguished central European origins, in the ramifying baroque family tree of the *Laurus Leslaeana*.

Notes

1 Stevenson, Beavan, and Davidson, 'The Breviary of Aberdeen', pp. 28–9. The only surviving copy of the early sixteenth-century *Compassio* is now bound in with the first volume of the *Breviarium Aberdonense* formerly in the library of the earls of Strathmore at Glamis Castle, now National Library of Scotland, RB.x.002–003, and bears the early seventeenth-century ownership mark 'Liber Joannis Lesly de eodem' – i.e. John Leslie of Leslie. The Glamis copy of the *Breviarium* belonged in the seventeenth century to Count Walter Leslie's nephew Francis Hay of Delgaty, who accompanied his Turkish embassy in 1665–66: David Worthington, *Scots in Habsburg Service* (Leiden: Brill, 2004), pp. 279–82. It is unknown how or where these copies of the *Breviarium* and the *Compassio* were brought together and eventually bound together.

2 Rev. David McRoberts, 'The Fetternear Banner', *The Innes Review*, 7.2 (1956), pp. 69–88.

3 David Worthington, Eduard Damisch, Igor Weigl and Marieke Ciglenecki, in *The Legacy of the Leslie Family at the Castle of Ptuj*, catalogue of an exhibition held at Narodna Galerija, Ljubljana, 22 January–24 February 2002.

4 A recent overview can be found in Steve Murdoch and Alexia Grosjean, *Alexander Leslie and the Scottish Generals of the Thirty Years' War, 1618–1648* (London: Pickering & Chatto, 2014).

5 Colonel Leslie of Balquhain, *Historical Records of the Family of Leslie from 1067 to 1868–9* (Edinburgh: Edmonston & Douglas, 1869), pp. viii, ix.

6 Leslie, *Historical Records*, p. ix.

7 See David Worthington, 'Leslie, Walter, Count Leslie in the nobility of the Holy Roman Empire (1606–1667)', *Oxford Dictionary of National Biography* (2008) [https://doi-org.ezproxy-prd.bodleian.ox.ac.uk/10.1093/ref:odnb/16501] (retrieved online 12 February 2016).

8 David Worthington, *British and Irish Experiences and Impressions of Central Europe, c.1560–1688* (Farnham: Ashgate, 2012), p. 170. Other members of the Leslie family seem at various times to have converted to both German Lutheranism and Russian Orthodoxy. The religious position of the Balquhain Leslies is considered in more detail below, but there seems every reason to concur with David McRobert's assertion that the family were essentially Roman Catholic – a position to which they, at the least, continually reverted. It would appear that there were Catholic members in every generation from the Reformation onwards; see McRoberts, 'The Fetternear Banner', p. 69.

9 Worthington, 'Leslie, Walter, Count Leslie'.

10 Worthington, *British and Irish Experiences*, p. 111.

11 Worthington, 'Leslie, Walter, Count Leslie'.

12 Marjeta Ciglenecki, 'A Set of Verdure Tapestries in Ptuj Castle', in Jiří Kroupa, Michaela Šeferisová Loudová, and Lubomír Konečný (eds), *Orbis Artium: Jubileu Lubomíra Slavíčka* (Brno: Masarykova univerzita, 2009), pp. 721–35, at p. 724.

13 William Aloysius Leslie SJ, *Laurus Leslaeana explicata, sive clarior enumeratio personarum utriusque sexus cognominis Leslie* (Graz: Haeredes Widmanstadii,

1692). See Thompson Cooper, revised by Brian M. Halloran, 'William Aloysius Leslie (1641–1704)', *Oxford Dictionary of National Biography* (2004) [https://doi-org.ezproxy-prd.bodleian.ox.ac.uk/10.1093/ref:odnb/16481] (retrieved online 12 February 2016).

14 This contrasts with the random and improvised allegories of at least the earlier ceiling paintings at the Castle at Nové Město nad Metují.

15 'Walter SRI Comes de Leslie in Germania, Alexander Comes de Leven in Scotia, tertius Alexander Eques Auratus de Auchintoul in Muscovia', *Laurus Leslaeana*, sig. G2v.

16 Sir Thomas Urquhart, *ΠΑΝΤΟΧΡΟΝΟΧΑΝΟΝ: or a peculiar promptuary of time ... deducing the true pedigree and lineal descent of the most ancient and honourable name of the Urquharts in the house of Cromartie, since the Creation of the World until this present yeer of God, 1652* (London: for Richard Baddeley, 1652); *The Works of Sir Thomas Urquhart*, ed. T. Maitland (Edinburgh: for the Maitland Club, 1834), pp. 155, 159.

17 *Laurus Leslaeana*, sig. A1r.

18 *Ibid.*, sig. A1v.

19 *Ibid.*, sig. A2r.

20 Leslie, *Historical Records*, pp. xxiii, 1–9.

21 *Ibid.*, pp. 10–14.

22 *Ibid.*, p. 39.

23 *Ibid.*, p. 65.

24 *Ibid.*, p. 66. 'Like many of David II's favoured retainers, Walter and Norman Leslie were active crusaders, obtaining numerous safe conducts for expeditions to the Holy Land and to the Baltic crusades. Walter's exploits were commemorated in the Saracen's head crest adorning his coat of arms in the late fourteenth-century "Armorial de Gelres" [*sic*] and may well have provided the inspiration for a now lost vernacular work, "The Tail of Syr Valtir the Bald Leslye". In 1363–5 Walter and Norman, possibly at the instigation of David II, seem to have been involved in the crusade organized by Pierre I of Cyprus which ended in the sack of Alexandria (where Norman Leslie may have been killed).' S. I. Boardman, 'Leslie, Sir Walter, Lord of Ross (d. 1382)', *Oxford Dictionary of National Biography* (2004) [https://doi-org.ezproxy-prd.bodleian.ox.ac.uk/10.1093/ref:odnb/54256] (retrieved online 9 February 2016).

25 McRoberts, 'The Fetternear Banner', p. 69.

26 Leslie, *Historical Records*, p. 112.

27 *Ibid.*, p. 113.

28 *Ibid.*, p. 55.

29 *Ibid.*, pp. 113–14.

30 *Ibid.*, p. 114.

31 *Ibid.*, pp. 103–4; for a consideration of post-Reformation Catholics in the Leslie family, see Alasdair Roberts and Ann Dean, 'The Leslies of Balquhain and the Burial of Bishop Hay', *Recusant History*, 22 (1995), pp. 536–48.

32 Joseph Sharples, David W. Walker, and Matthew Woodworth, *The Buildings of Scotland, Aberdeenshire: South and Aberdeen* (New Haven, CT: Yale University Press, 2015), pp. 490–3. This arrangement may well be a deliberate recollection

of the elaborate, defiantly Catholic, scheme of carving on the courtyard elevation of Huntly Castle. Dated 1602, the latter included the Huntly arms and the royal arms but also the Instruments of the Passion, a representation of the Resurrection, and a figure of St Michael. It was defaced by a Covenanting garrison in 1640: Sharples *et al.*, *Aberdeenshire*, pp. 537–44.

33 Leslie, *Historical Records*, pp. 121–2.

34 'Castle History', www.zameknm.cz/en/castle-history.html (retrieved 23 May 2022).

35 Kladsko became part of Poland only in 1945.

36 The authoritative discussion of these ceilings by Fabián Šebestián Václav Harovník is R. Nokkala Miltová, 'Ex Bello Pax: oslava Waltera Leslieho v malbách na zámku v Novém Městě nad Metují', *Oposcula historiae artium*, 64.1 (2015), pp. 32–49, https://digilib.phil.muni.cz/bitstream/handle/11222.digilib/134408/1_OpusculaHistoriaeArtium_59–2015–1_3.pdf?sequence=1 (retrieved 16 April 2023).

37 *Ibid.*, p. 32.

38 Cf. the Glasgow emblem database, www.emblems.arts.gla.ac.uk/alciato/emblem.php?id=A31a046 (retrieved 16 April 2023).

39 This, in turn, seems to be an elaboration of Alciato's *Emblematum Liber* (Augsburg: Heinrich Steyer, 1531), sig. B1v. Glasgow database: www.emblems.arts.gla.ac.uk/alciato/emblem.php?id=A31b020 (retrieved 16 April 2023). These Latin mottoes were used together as a single phrase on the reverse of a medal struck for Henry IV of France in 1599, for which see Corrado Vivante, 'Henry IV, the Gallic Hercules', *Journal of the Warburg and Courtauld Institutes*, 30 (1967), pp. 176–97, at p. 183.

40 See http://emblematica.grainger.illinois.edu/detail/emblem/E015675 (retrieved 16 April 2023), citing Daniel de la Feuille's polyglot *Devices et Emblemes* (Augsburg: Lorentz Kroniger and heirs of Gottleib Gèobels, 1695), but the use of the obelisk or pyramid as a symbol of perdurance dates back into the sixteenth century.

41 Miltová, 'Ex Bello Pax', p. 49.

42 *Ibid.*, p. 49.

43 *Ibid.*, pp. 55–9.

44 McRoberts, 'The Fetternear Banner', p. 84.

45 I cannot emphasise too strongly that the section on needlework which follows was written with my expert friend and colleague Prue King, then of the Blairs Museum, whose knowledge of historic needlework is encyclopaedic, taking the leading role.

46 Margaret Swain, *The Needlework of Mary, Queen of Scots* (New York: Van Nostrand Reinhold, 1973), p. 52.

47 Pauline Johnstone, *High Fashion in the Church: The Place of Church Vestments in the History of Art from the Ninth to the Nineteenth Century* (Leeds: Maney Publishing, 2002), pl. XIX; Mehmet Ozel (Director General, Fine Arts, Ministry of Culture, Istanbul), www.turkishculture.org/textile-arts/embroidery/turkish-embroidery-598.htm?type=1 (retrieved 29 March 2016).

48 Interestingly, there is a slight difference between the orphreys on the chasuble and those on the dalmatics.

49 There is a magnificent diorama of Gustavus Adolphus in the stables of the Royal Castle in Stockholm which shows the king thus mounted and ready for battle with full accoutrements.

50 Ozel, www.turkishculture.org/textile-arts/embroidery/turkish-embroidery-598.htm?type=1 (retrieved 16 April 2023).

51 Pauline Johnstone, *Turkish Embroidery* (London: Victoria & Albert Museum, 1985), p. 141.

52 Leslie, *Historical Records*, p. 122.

53 *Ibid.*, p. 122.

54 *Ibid.*, pp. 123–4. According to *Burke's Landed Gentry*, 1871 edn, II, p. 785, Leslie-Grant was a grandson of Count Patrick Leslie's second daughter.

55 A few scattered manuscripts from Fetternear are preserved at Stonyhurst College, Clitheroe, Lancashire, whither they were removed in the nineteenth century.

11

A Jesuit reliquary crucifix from Japan[1]

The gilding has worn thin with time and veneration, but the lacquer is dense and solid still. Black and gold. The drops of gilded blood from Christ's hands are patterned like leaves on a twig; the drops from his feet, like fruit on a tree. He has a sharp-pointed golden star for a halo. The gilding has worn away altogether from his head, perhaps because it is the point of highest relief in this weighty, beautiful crucifix, just small enough to be worn as a neck jewel (see Figure 11.1). Or, perhaps, it is because the thorn-crowned head has been most often touched, most often kissed.

The reverse of the cross is a night sky strewn with stars. Black and gold. Angels and noctilucent clouds bear the Virgin up the sky, the marigold – punning emblem of utter fidelity – below her feet, and the dove of the Spirit hovering above her. Her hair falls about her shoulders, her hands are joined on her breast, her eyes are almost closed. Drapery falls in straight folds to her feet; the animation of the baroque is far off, even though this sacred jewel dates from the early seventeenth century. It embodies absolute stillness at the point of confluence between the two traditions that brought it into being: the Europe of the end of the Renaissance and the Japan of the turn of the seventeenth century.

This work occupies two aesthetic worlds simultaneously and is thus typical of a global phenomenon in the early modern arts: the hybridity born of Jesuit respect for the cultures that they encountered in Asia and Ibero-America. And, in a complementary paradox, this object is both a sacred simulacrum and a container for the sacred. The cross is hollow, and the compartments within it were designed to receive small fragments of human remains: bones and hairs of martyrs and saints. In design and conception, this crucifix is in a long European tradition. It is at once a jewel (in the far-reaching Renaissance sense) and a reliquary, both an adornment and a talisman. Apart from the local innovation of the star-halo and the foliate patterning of the drops of blood, the design on the crucifix's face is more or less unchanged from European work of a hundred years earlier. It is, for instance, very like the early sixteenth-century golden crucifix that belonged

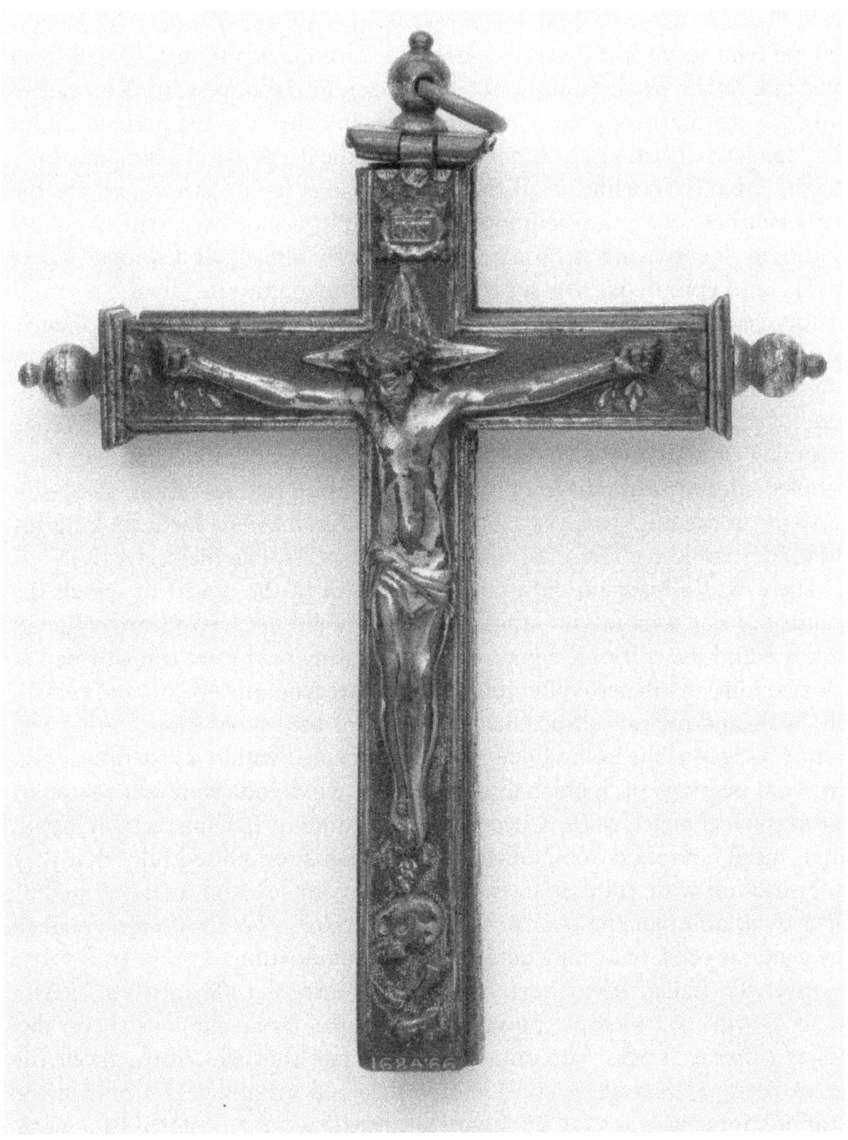

Figure 11.1 Brass and lacquer reliquary crucifix, Japan, Edo period (early seventeenth century). © Victoria and Albert Museum, London.

to St Thomas More, containing a relic of the Apostle Thomas. The latter double relic survived in secret among the Catholic community exiled from England, at the Jesuit College in Saint-Omer, in the same way that we can only assume that this gold and lacquer crucifix survived the persecution of the Japanese Christians, either in exile or in the deepest concealment.

The Japanese crucifix is all the more precious for its rarity, and for the witness it bears to a transient moment of confluence of two great world art traditions, a confluence whose productions were almost all destroyed in the savage and comprehensive suppression of Christianity in Japan – a tragic history recently made visible once more by Martin Scorsese's film *Silence*. But how did such things come into being? How did these tentative moments of accommodation arise? In part, because of an anachronistically open attitude of mind. When other missionaries went forth from Catholic Europe assuming that all world civilisations were essentially barbarians, and their peoples inferior to the bearers of both civilisation and salvation, the Jesuit 'way of proceeding' was very different. The Jesuits went forth looking for those they could recognise as, in significant aspects, like themselves.

There was almost no cultural phenomenon in the world to which the Jesuits did not respond; no language that they did not try to learn. Human sacrifice and the cult of the god of the generating seed were transformed in Mexico into an intense contemplation of the regenerative death and rebirth of Christ and expressed in crucifixes made of the sacred maize pith.[2] The family badges of the noble Inkas were transformed within a generation into armorial bearings of Spanish grandees; Inka wind-gods were reinvented as the musketeer angels of the Cuzco school of painters. In China and in Japan, after initial hesitation and clumsiness, the Jesuits recognised fully that they were dealing with cultures in every way as complex and as developed as their own, and that the only possibility of progress lay in '*il modo soave*', the gentle process of acculturation and accommodation.

After the Italian Alessandro Valignano SJ (1539–1606) arrived in Asia in 1579 with considerable powers to direct the Jesuit missions there, this policy came to govern all contact with a Japan that was, throughout the Jesuit years, in a state of considerable flux and instability. Indeed, in the year of Valignano's arrival, 26 Japanese Christians were executed by a member of the military élite hostile to foreigners and their religions. Japanese society's combination of cultural richness and crisis facilitated the Jesuits' success with individual local leaders, but precluded a settled establishment, apart from a small territory conceded to the foreigners in Nagasaki. An aristocratic warrior society had to be matched with a learned and cultivated mission. 'Magnificenza', expressed in local building styles, appealed to the aesthetic sensibilities of Japanese élites, and the founding of a school of painters and craftsmen became one of the mission's highest priorities.

Valignano's first official act upon arriving in Japan was to intensify the pace and quality of Japanese language learning by all new missionaries. By 1595 he could report that the Jesuits had printed a comprehensive Japanese grammar and dictionary as well as a number of Christian books, all in Japanese. Early in his mission Valignano recognised that the semiotics of Japanese art were often contrary to those of its European counterpart. Specifically, he noted that dark colours were valued, especially purple and black, and that they did not connote death or mourning, as in the West. As Gauvin Bailey narrates in his classic work on Jesuit mission art, the Jesuit art academy in Japan was founded in 1583 and reached full productivity seven years later.[3] Its director was the Jesuit Brother Giovanni Niccoló (1563–1626), who was praised not only for his artistic ability but for his skills and talents in the fields of mathematics, mechanics, and clock making. The academy, despite its prodigious output, was subject to the instabilities of the time and moved often, before finding a home for a decade near the Jesuit Church of the Assumption in Nagasaki. At the expulsion of all missionaries from Japan, in 1614, it was relocated to Macau.

From the beginning, the academy's output was various and wide-ranging. Typography and engraving were practised, and panel and scroll paintings produced, both in oils and in traditional Japanese colours. Exquisite portable shrines of lacquer work and inlay were also constructed to contain sacred pictures in European styles. Metal-founders made casts of sacred images – including, it can be conjectured, the black and gold reliquary crucifix that is the focus of this short chapter. But the academy also produced secular images, many painted by its non-Christian pupils. These included European pastoral scenes, depictions of warfare, and magnificent figures of mounted knights, many of them painted on folding screens. These works served both as high-status gifts for the local aristocracy, who seemed to relish items of *occidenterie* as much as did the Mughal courts of India, and as export wares, some of which found their way, via the famed Manila galleons, to the Spanish territories in Mexico and Peru. These secular works also had a lasting influence on the mainstream of Japanese painting, and, in particular, on the screens made in late sixteenth- and seventeenth-century Kyoto which showed European and other exotic peoples, ships, and buildings.

Sacred works from the Jesuit academy have a very low rate of survival, and those that are extant were probably either taken abroad or kept in the deepest concealment in secretly Christian families, so absolute was the persecution of the Japanese Christians under Tokugawa Ieyasu in the early seventeenth century.

Works of art which have survived times of violence always have a certain power. The little black and gold reliquary crucifix has a particular claim on our attention as a witness to a moment of genuine intercultural understanding which was then swept away. That moment, remembered as 'the Christian century in Japan', survives only in rare objects in European collections: a wonderful gold and inlaid lacquer pyx in the British Museum;[4] and an extraordinary grey-glazed ceramic basin marked with a cross, perhaps a *lavabo* for the ritual washing of a priest's hands, but taking on the appearance of a slop bowl for the tea ceremony, now in the Jesuit collection at Campion Hall, Oxford. Also in the Campion Hall collection, but from a period of even deeper secrecy, there is a little bronze statue of the secret Virgin, the Virgin in the guise of the goddess Kannon: 'Maria-Kannon'. In it, the Christ Child is shrunken, almost to nothing, hardly disturbing the contour of her robe, barely more than a fold of cloth above her enfolding arm.

Notes

1 Victoria and Albert Museum, accession number 168A-1866.
2 For example, there is a sixteenth-century crucifix of the Señor de la Sacristía, made of polychromed corn pith in the Cathedral of Morelia, Michoacán, Mexico. See Elena Fitzpatrick Sifford, https://smarthistory.org/corn-pith-sculptures (retrieved 3 July 2023). Cf. also brief consideration of the background to this phenomenon in the Prologue to this book.
3 Gauvin Bailey, *Art on the Jesuit Missions in Asia and Latin America, 1542–1773* (Toronto: University of Toronto Press, 1999).
4 Museum number 1969,0415.1.

12

The Jesuit garden

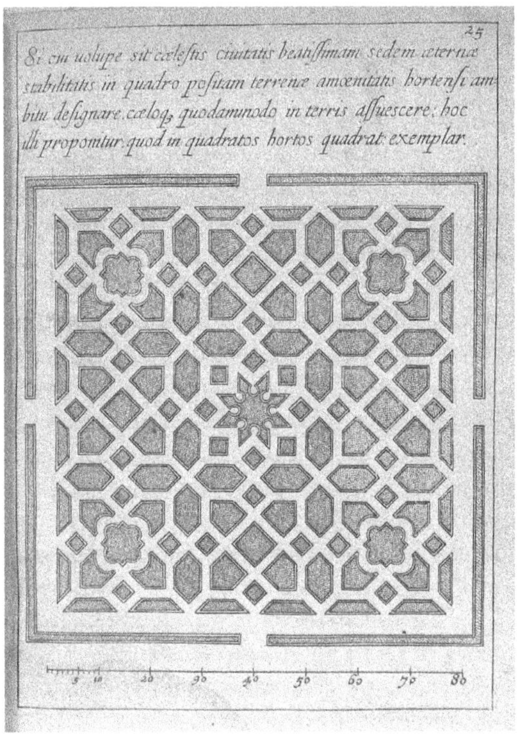

Figure 12.1 Johann Friedrich Greuter, 'Parterre design in imitation of the Heavenly City', copper engraving, from Giovanni Battista Ferrari SJ, *Flora, sive de Florum Cultura*, vol. IV (Rome, 1635).

This chapter traces some plants of the Jesuit garden, using 'plants' in both the archaic sense of footsteps and the modern meaning, of living herbs, trees, and flowers. I am particularly concerned with the idea of the garden, with Jesuit ways of thinking about gardens, and with the ways in which

Jesuit writers of the seventeenth century related an external or veridical garden to a mental or devotional map (see Figure 12.1). In the writings of the Jesuit *savants* of the seventeenth century, the old, accretive tradition of 'an interior garden' acquired a focus and precision that it had rarely attained beforehand.

One important aspect of this phenomenon which I would like to consider is the richness of Jesuit participation in the élite interest in gardens, which was such a notable international feature of the seventeenth century. The kinds of information codified by Giovanni Battista Ferrari SJ, in his suggestions about the meanings of garden layouts – discussed below – are invaluable for decoding a number of surviving late Renaissance gardens as spaces charged with meaning. Likewise, an attentive reading of the Jesuit Louis Richeôme's meditations on the gardens of the Novitiate of Sant'Andrea al Quirinale inevitably acts as a key to seventeenth-century ways of responding to gardens. Richeôme offers an invaluable theoretical and interpretative tool for the understanding of such diverse texts as the *buitengedichten*, the country house and estate poems of the North Netherlandic golden age, and even of such apparently familiar mid-seventeenth-century texts as Andrew Marvell's 'Upon Appleton House'. At the end of the century Réné Rapin SJ drew together the diverse ideas of the garden that had been so important throughout the preceding decades, and Alexander Pope, who revised the English translation of Rapin, created a garden and grotto which are much more closely related to the world of the seventeenth-century Jesuit *savants* and *virtuosi* than is allowed by the conventional historiography of landscape art.[1] Indeed, landscape art itself is arguably a Jesuit invention. Certainly, the letters of the Chinese mission describing the gardens of Emperor Qianlong played no small part in at least the theory of the landscape garden in Europe. Although, inevitably, I discuss the introduction of northern European skills and collected plants into southern Europe through the work of Giovanni Battista Ferrari, I must emphasize that it is not my intention here to trace the whole rich history of Jesuit botany and plant collecting. Rather, I would like to offer a consideration of Jesuit ideas of the garden and of its imaginative, physical, and pedagogical possibilities. Nevertheless, I would like to advance one piece of evidence of how far ahead of their contemporaries Jesuit plant collectors appear to have been, even as early as the 1590s. In his *Voyage en Italie*, Michel de Montaigne reported a visit to the Gesuati of Ferrara, undertaken on 16 or 17 November 1580. Though few, his words seem to describe a rose which must have come from the Far Eastern missions of the Society of Jesus:

> Nous fûmes tout ce jour-là à Ferrare, et y vîmes plusieurs belles églises, jardins et maisons privées, et tout ce qu'on dit être remarquable, entre autres, aux

Jésuates, un pied de rosier qui porte fleur tous les mois de l'an: et lors même s'y en trouva une qui fut donnée à M. de Montaigne.[2]

[We saw all the notable sights of Ferrara, churches, gardens, and palaces; among others, in the house of the Gesuati we saw a rose tree which bears flowers in every month of the year; and one of these was found as a gift for M. de Montaigne.]

If Montaigne's suggestion could be substantiated, this would constitute another botanical triumph for the Society of Jesus: the introduction of the remontant oriental rose a century and a half before the arrival of the 'Banksian' rose at Kew Gardens in London in 1807.

The centrality of gardens to the concerns of early modern Europe hardly needs to be emphasised. It is not surprising to find a rich Jesuit contribution to such a major cultural phenomenon – which was, moreover, clearly well suited to attracting élite interest in Jesuit colleges and could also be seen as having a worthy place in the educational formation of the Christian citizen. In this context, it should be noted that Jesuit poets were active in this sphere. The great Maciej Casimir Sarbiewski wrote a magically compressed ode to the family who patronised Giovanni Battista Ferrari, the Barberini of Rome, who certainly had wonderful gardens, described by Sarbiewski as the green native land – the '*viridem patriam*' – of the golden age of the Barberini, over which their heraldic bees fly at will:

Laboribus quid iuvat volatibus ...
Si Barberino delicata principe
Saecula melle fluunt,
Parata vobis saecula?[3]

[What need to fly with labouring wings ...
If the epoch of the Barberini
Flows with that delicate honey
Which will sweeten your years?]

Sarbiewski also revisited one of the crucial sources of all subsequent writing about gardens, the *Canticum Canticorum*. The most celebrated Jesuit poet of Germany, Jacob Balde, also wrote charmingly of the garden world of his time, addressing an ode to one of the topiary figures in the gardens of Prince Albert of Bavaria, and predicting the reward of this modest guardian of that world:

Te Zephyritidum
Fratrum coronabit quotannis
Et violae linet aura succo.[4]

[Each year, the breeze will crown you, brother of the wind, and bedew you with the sap of violets.]

In another sphere of artistic endeavour, Daniel Seegers SJ (1590–1661), an associate of Rubens, was noted as a painter of flowers and of the *guirlandes* of flowers surrounding sacred images that were popular in the southern Netherlands. His celebrity was such that he drew high praise from the Calvinist statesman and polymath Constantijn Huygens in an elegant Latin ode: 'vivus/ Coram factitio flosculus umbra fuit' ['the painted flower renders the real flower a shadow'].[5] Early modern Jesuits did not merely describe physical gardens, but also made them. The testimony of magnificent engravings of the Jesuit colleges suggests that this is a rich field for future investigation, as is the subject of Jesuits as designers of dials for gardens.[6]

It is with another horticultural practice that I would like to continue: the Collegio Romano's collection formed by the great virtuoso Athanasius Kircher, and, in particular, its splendid set of devices.[7] What interests me here is that Kircher used this set of kaleidoscope-like devices to multiply to infinity the image of a formal garden, producing by the adroit manipulation of light and mirrors a parterre vast beyond even the imaginings of Louis XIV or of the scenography of the Bibbiena family. Not coincidentally, the three locations Kircher proposed for multiplication by his device – the garden, the library, and the palace – were three crucial sites of the élite baroque imagination.

Another, more familiar kind of interior garden is set forth in the Marian garden meditations, the *Partheneia Sacra*, published by the English Jesuit Henry Hawkins in 1633.[8] This is a complex, transitional book. Hawkins makes us aware that he is at ease with a medieval tradition of reading the physical world allegorically. There is, after all, strong precedent for allegorical readings of gardens, reaching as far back in time as the twelfth-century Byzantine-Greek manuscript in the Laurentian library in Florence known as *The Symbolic Garden*, with its simple, one-to-one readings of plants as allegories of virtues set out by Christ, the master of the garden.[9] But Hawkins's readings of objects constitute a delicate balancing act between the traditions of crypto-Ignatian meditation, of *ars memorativa*, of emblematics, and of medieval allegory. Hawkins's mental garden is constructed in an imagined space that alters as the devout reader progresses through the book. Initially Hawkins organises the garden and its contents into small sections, so that readers have before them a ninefold set of meditations, emblems, essays, and expositions of each element. But, at the very end, Hawkins sets the devout soul free to ramble at its own speed in the interior garden, constructed under his direction, as if it were a place now susceptible of infinite deepening, infinite recessions of new meaning – a place capable of containing everything that the devout mind can feel.

The engraved frontispiece of the book suggests the degree to which Hawkins was working from an established tradition. Its enclosed garden with roses and lilies is a constant in a tradition applying the praises of the Song of Songs to the praise of Our Lady; the house of gold and the tower of ivory are from the Litany of Loreto; and the palm and the olive are figures for Holy Wisdom in Ecclesiasticus. It is not hard to discern the essentially Edenic nature of the circular walled garden depicted here. What is fascinating in the *Partheneia Sacra*, however, is the use Hawkins makes of these garden elements. In the epistle, which he addressed to his primary audience, the Parthenian Sodality, he is unequivocal about the complex status of his material. Proceeding from the idea of Christ's appearance as a gardener after the Resurrection, he moves rapidly to the enumeration of ways in which the garden is both Our Lady herself, mystically considered, and also a pattern of the soul of each spectator:

> [Christ] evidently declared his good affection towards the *Garden* of the Soule, which then he came to cheer-up … You, deerest Parthenians, yet greeued and groaning with the burden of your pressures, for his sake who is the curious *Gardener* indeed, that from the beginning planted the same for himself from al Eternitie … [Y]ou heer behold our Sacred Parthenes, who presents herselfe for your delights in Garden-attire … [I]n this coole and rural array, of hearbes and flowers, as if she were clothed with the Sunne, crowned with the Starres and trampling the moone … Nor would I wish you perfunctoriously to view her only, and passe her over with a slender glance of the eye, but to enter into her garden which she is herself, and survey it well.[10]

The symbolic garden is essentially, but subtly, educative: readers are invited to participate so fully in the progressive exposition that, by the end of each section, they are ready to own the closing address, as it were adding their voices and their assent to the words of the author. And, when Hawkins at last comes to describe the garden to be contemplated, a lavish and contemporary layout is evoked rather than the simple *hortus conclusus* pictured on the frontispiece. Indeed, Hawkins himself at one point compares the garden to a 'cabinet of flowerie gems', echoing the *wunderkammer* aspect of the flower garden, expressed by Ferrari in his publication of the same year.[11] 'Cast your eyes,' Hawkins instructs the reader,

> on those goodlie allies, as sowed over with sands of gold, drawne-forth so streight by a line. Those Cros-bowes there (be not affrayd of them) they are but crossbowes made of Bayes; and the Harquebusquiers, wrought in Rosemarie, shoot but flowers and dart forth musk … Behold those daire and beautiful Tulips there, those rich amaranths, cerulian Hiacinths, Pansies, the gemmes of the goodlie IRIS … O what a paradice of flowers is this! What a heaven of muskie starres, or Celestial earth al starred with flowers, empearled with gemmes and precious stones.[12]

Having established that the imaginary garden is baroque both in the way it is apprehended and in its collection of fashionable bulbous plants and florists' flowers, Hawkins proceeds to his discourse, in which he allegorises these elements in a manner poised between tradition and innovation. A fairly brief extract gives an idea of the whole:

> [Here] are faire and goodlie Allies, streight and even, strewed all with sands, that is, a streight, vertuous, and Angelical life, yet strewed with the sands and dust of her proper Humilitie; where are arbours to shadow her from the heats of concupicense; flowerie beds to repose in, with heauenlie contemplations; Mounts to ascend to, with the studie of Perfections.[13]

As the 'Discourse' continues, it becomes clear that we are indeed contemplating a baroque garden on a vast scale, perhaps not unlike the semi-sacred Paradise Garden of Valsanzibio in the Veneto:

> Heer are Pooles for the harmles fry of her innocent thoughts, like fishes heer and there to passe up and downe in the heauenlie element of her mind; heer and there certain labyrinths formed in the hearbs of her endles perfections. Heer lastly are statues of her rare examples to be seen, Obelisks, Pyramids, Triumphal Arches, Aquaducts, Thermes, Pillars of Eternal Memorie, erected to her glorie on contemplation of her Admirable, Angelical, and Divine life.[14]

When we consider the work of Richeôme, particularly that section of his 1611 *La peinture spirituelle* which deals with the gardens of the Jesuit house of Sant'Andrea al Quirinale in Rome, we find some of the same perceptions and readings being applied, but, crucially, to a real, known garden (see Figure 12.2).[15] His meditation upon this garden forms the sixth section of an interpreted walk through various parts of the Jesuit Novitiate. Gauvin Bailey has insightfully analysed the paintings described in the section on the infirmary.[16] Naturally, the kind of interpretation that Richeôme offers is consistently spiritual: there is no visible thing that does not ring forth immediately with the overtones of its spiritual resonance. He is patently aware of all the Renaissance modes of symbolic discourse: he was himself an emblematist, and well aware of the debate on hieroglyphics, and the history of speaking pictures. It is clear, too, that he was aware of the kinds of medieval traditions of interpretation to which Hawkins also had access. All these inheritances, as well as allegorical traditions of reading scripture, combine to give him the reservoir of material with which he interprets the material world.

The garden section of *La peinture spirituelle* offers us a considerable insight into the mind of the seventeenth century. On the simplest level, we are presented with a detailed representation of – and, indeed, a plant list for – an actual Jesuit garden of the beginning of that century. If we trust that Richeôme's list of flowers and trees is specific rather than general – and the layout of his text as a walk through this specific garden strongly suggests as

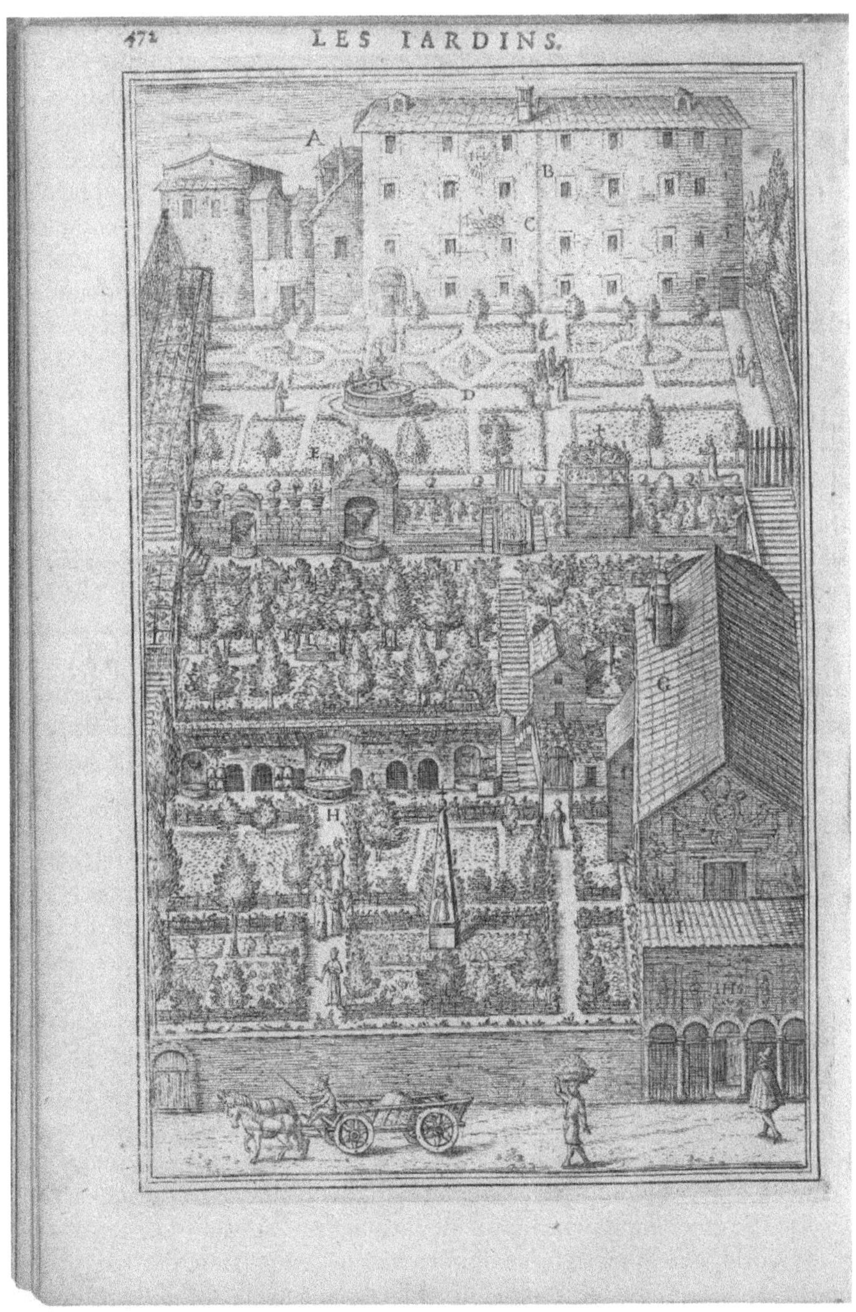

Figure 12.2 Illustration of 'Les Jardins' from Louis Richeôme, *La peinture spirituelle, ou, l'art d'admirer aimer et louer Dieu et toutes ses œuvres, et tirer de toutes profits salutere* (Lyon: Pierre Rigaud, 1611).

much – then we have a record of an extremely rich planting, almost comparable to the published plant lists of much more celebrated institutions, such as the botanic gardens of Padua or Leiden. We also have a representation, in this terraced and productive garden, of something very like the apparently unique survivor of the same moment in the history of the Italian garden, the Giardini Buonaccorsi near Macerata, which I consider in some detail below.

As well as providing fascinating documentation of one garden, complete with sundials and a symbolic obelisk already contributing an extra layer of meaning to its layout, Richeôme's text offers clear insight into a process of mental training in 'right' perception of the world. No object observed in the garden is allowed to pass without being at once supplied with a spiritual reading, an interpretation concerned with the virtuosity and mercy of the Creator as well as with the perceptions and spiritual growth of the observer. This flow of interpretation is itself virtuosic: in the whole course of Richeôme's spiritual perambulation of the garden, there are hardly any strained interpretations.

It is not necessary here to follow the complete course of his progression, from the garden gate at the top to the pyramid or obelisk in the lowest terrace. Nonetheless, it is useful to give some indication of the nature of the complex process of education, in the literal sense of training of the mind to produce a particular set of responses, which Richeôme sets forth for the walk through the gardens. The essential conjunction of physical and spiritual is offered early – unsurprisingly, with a pun on fruits as the results of a process of maturation – by means of an immediate contrast between the fugacity of the earthly and the eternity of the heavenly: '[E]t vous donnant interieurement l'adresse de cueillir non seulement les fruits temporels, mais encore les fruicts spirituels d'incorruption.' As in the Giardini Buonaccorsi, the central position of the fountain on the upper terrace at once evokes the earthly paradise, Eden. This symbolic perception is common in the recorded layouts of many early modern botanic gardens, in accordance with the idea of the sacrality of such gardens as divinely sanctioned reassemblages of the flora of the earthly paradise, scattered at the fall.

Richeôme's response to the florists' flowers of the upper garden is simply one of humble contemplation of the inexhaustible riches of divine creation: '[N]e sentez vous pas vostre ame rauie a l'admiration, & amour du Createur, qui les a produictes?' The superb Jesuit sundials of the upper garden, on the other hand, which provide readings of the hour in various parts of the world, offer an intriguing opportunity to contemplate the light orbiting the globe as an image of the universality and endless wakefulness of the Universal Church: '[F]acon qui se garde encor en l'eglise Romaine, & partoute la Chrestienité, [d]és festes & iours mysterieux.' The fountains of the lower garden, by contrast, are read as symbols of the humility and usefulness of water. This is followed by a reading of the 'arbre triste' of Goa (presumably sent back to Rome by the established Jesuit mission there) as a symbol of the true Christian in penitence, in that it casts its night-borne flowers at the moment the sun rises, and so represents the triumph of penitence in the religious soul. This kind of allegorisation of newly introduced trees can be linked forward to an emblem book of the later seventeenth century, *Ashrea, or The Grove of Beatitude* (London, 1665), possibly a Jesuit product, which offers a highly ingenious set of readings of exotic trees, overlaid with a contemplation of the limbs of Christ on the cross. Finally, Richeôme dwells upon the pyramid or obelisk in the lower gardens, which is supplied with *imprese*. (One of these on the eastern face, incidentally, is identical to that on the tomb of John Donne, the English poet from a Catholic family: the eastern face with the figure of Christ and the sun and the words 'His name is Orient', albeit in French rather than Latin.)

If Richeôme's description of the garden is indeed accurate as an itemisation of an extensive Jesuit flower collection, it is easy to see how the culture of the Roman houses would have fostered the work of the last Jesuit writer to be surveyed here: Giovanni Battista Ferrari, who published his central work in 1633, the same year as Hawkins's *Partheneia Sacra*.[17] Ferrari was born in Siena in the early 1580s, entered the Society of Jesus at Rome in 1602, and was professed in May 1621. He had studied at the Collegio Romano from 1606 to 1611, and taught Hebrew there from 1618 until some time in the 1620s, when he changed his career path completely to become gardener, designer, and horticultural consultant to the Barberini family, shortly after Maffeo Barberini became Urban VIII – a position he retained until he retired on the ground of ill health in 1647.[18] His *De Florum Cultura*, a treatise on the flower garden, was published under the patronage of Cardinal Francesco Barberini. Beautifully produced, it includes designs engraved after Pietro da Cortona and Guido Reni.[19] In 1646 Ferrari published an equally lavish and encyclopaedic work on the history, cultivation, and uses of citrus fruits: *Hesperides, sive De malorum aureum cultura*. After his retirement he returned to his native city, where, after the publication of his virtuoso's jottings in *Collocutiones* in 1652, he died in February 1655.[20]

Ferrari's garden writing is encyclopaedic in the best sense: a summary of what is known. His *Hesperides* of 1646 begins by recording all ancient records of the golden apples of the Hesperides, and all representations of them in surviving classical art. From there, it proceeds to a treatise on the types and cultivars of citrus trees, with beautifully detailed notes on their culture and magnificent plates of orangeries; and a dissertation on why the citrus has been identified with the biblical apple of Adam. A question that would bear further investigation is the degree to which the iconography and layout of this work coincides with that of the Villa d'Este at Tivoli, outside Rome. The educative function of the book is confirmed by its exhaustive concluding section on the uses of citrus fruits, which includes what looks like an early recipe for lemon marmalade.

Ferrari's *De Florum Cultura* of 1633 is a remarkable work. It covers all matters to do with the layout of a garden, including the symbolic force of different ground-plans. It details the florists' flowers of the seventeenth century, including the recently introduced bulbous plants. It concludes with a section – of the highest interest for what it records – on the uses of flowers, including the subtle baroque tricks that can be played with their scents and colours. In addition to the recording of marmalade, we must credit the Society of Jesus with being the first to record the green carnation.[21] The book has magnificent engraved plates, including an allegorical representation of Flora turning idle gardeners into slugs. In addition to these allegorical illustrations, there are numerous ones of flowers and of garden tools. The whole feeling of the book is one of a new aspect of civil life being grafted into Italian society from the flower-mad northern Netherlands. In Ferrari's work, the garden is seen very much as a living *wunderkammer*, an outdoor extension of the global scope of the *Musaeum Kircherianum*. There may also be found in Ferrari's work, I suspect, a reluctance to allow primacy in horticulture, horticultural collecting, or horticultural innovation to pass into Protestant hands.

Like the *Hesperides*, *De Florum Cultura* ends with a lengthy section on the uses of flowers. Here, the sense of a real transplantation of a culture is palpable, in the numerous and fascinating plates detailing the arrangement of flowers, their transportation, and ingenious vases which display them in such a way as to form a wreathed column, or so that the badge of the Society can be picked out in the heads of one's best tulips. As well as these baroque 'subtleties', Ferrari records a strange ephemeral work of Bernini's: the coat of arms of the Barberini formed in flowers, with its bees realistically formed out of wax and stuck with flower heads of broom and African marigolds to simulate their stripes.[22] The effect must have been comparable only to the flower sculptures which today accompany the better class of gangland funerals in the East End of London. But it is to Ferrari's itemisation of symbolic garden plans that I would now like to turn.

When the English poet Andrew Marvell wrote of 'Paradise's only map', the image in his mind may have been a specific one, for in *De Florum Cultura* there are five plans that assign specific meanings to what might otherwise be taken for purely abstract patterns. These patterns for intricate garden cut-works of geometric flower beds and paths offer a revelation about the workings of the baroque imagination. Many garden parterres all over Europe that hitherto have been thought of as purely decorative may yet prove to be bearers of meaning as much as any statue or inscription. As so often, a little-studied treatise (though one certainly known in seventeenth-century Britain, as John Evelyn's surviving annotated copy testifies) provides a 'key to the garden' by recording information about ways of thinking and feeling which were once all but universal yet which are now forgotten. I provide four examples. The first is a description of a square plan of four quarters:

> Si cui volupte sit caelestis civitatis beatissimam sedem aeternae stabilitas in quadro positam terrenae amoenitatis hortensi ambito designare, caeloque quodammodo in terris assuescere: hoc illi proponitur, quod in quadratos hortos quadrat, exemplar. (p. 25)

> [If it might be a pleasure to someone to design within the bounds of a garden the blessed seat of the Holy City in its eternal stability, laid out in four quarters of celestial beauty, and to acclimatise something heavenly on the earth, this is proposed here, since the diagram divides the garden into patterns of fours.]

The second is this interpretation of a circular garden:

> Si mundi ornatissimam rotunditatem hortensis ornatus rotunda imagine lubet aemulari, vel aetati florum novum orbem condere: orbiculatum habes rudimentum quadrata in area lineatum; cuius continenti muro circumseptae superuacaneis quatuor in angulis tum hortensis supellectilis cellas, tum congruentia floribus aviaria poteris excitare: ut florea in silva silvestres Orphei ne desint. Cavebis tamen, ne munimentum circa extructum vel altitudine nimia, vel minimo intervallo areolas incommode opacet. Quare caute excitandum. Et latiore ambulacro distinendum erit [*sic*]. (p. 29)

> [If you wish to imitate the rotundity of the world with a round image in a garden, or in a flowering (or flourishing) age to found a new world, here you have a little world outlined within a square, of which, inside the surrounding wall, you have four little chambers, in which you may place aviaries to complement the flowers, so that as in a flowery wood there is no lack of woodland Orpheuses. Be careful, however, that the surrounding defences are not built too tall or that there is so little space between them that they overshadow the garden beds: they should be raised circumspectly, and the encircling path should be broad.]

The third explicates an oval scheme:

> Si circense spectaculum non olim procurrentium equorum fugitiva, sed assidue vernantium florum stataria voluptate exhibere mavis: en tibi ovati circuitus commodum circum honestissimae Florae novus Aedilis aperio, iisdemque cellis extruendis opportunos simillimos angulos propono. (p. 33)

[If you wish to set forth the spectacle of a circus, not, as once, with the flight of swiftly running horses but with the fixed delight of blooming flowers, here I open to you a new structure for flowers of elegant roundness, oval in form, and I set down external structures of the same form in the equivalent corners.]

The fourth and final example represents a labyrinth:

Si velis denique florae curae quam facilem aditum, tam difficilem exitum hortensi representare simulacro: tuos hortos in labyrinthi arcolae vel caeterarum instar humiles subsidere, ut oculi tantum implicatis flexibus irretiantur: vel as quatuor circiter palmoslateritia structura excitari, ut pedes quoque inter flores errabundi iucundissume impediantur. (p. 37)

[If you would like to represent in an image the easy entrance to the growing of flowers but the difficult exit [from such a beguiling study], entwine your garden into a labyrinth, the image of which is set forth here. The 'hedges' of the labyrinth may be sunk down or represented by low-set plants, so that the eye can take in the whole design at one glance; or alternatively the beds can be raised about four palms' width above the earth, so that feet wandering among the flowers may be delayed in the most pleasant way.]

These plans serve to identify the ancient botanic garden at Padua as a microcosm of the world, and the botanic garden at Leiden as a combination of the Celestial City plan with an evocation of the Garden of Eden and its central fountain. At the same time, however, they offer a rich set of possible readings for that most ambitious of late Renaissance gardens, the Hortus Palatinus at Heidelberg, laid out by the savant Salomon de Caus for the illuminatus Elector Palatine and his bride, Elizabeth Stuart. This garden, described in lavish contemporary engravings, brings us neatly full circle as the most probable source for many elements in Marvell's poem 'The Garden', including his famous 'flowering Zodiac'.

By an extraordinary series of coincidences, a flower garden laid out according to one of Ferrari's plans survives in Italy to this day. The Giardini Buonaccorsi are famous for their extraordinary statuary and for their preservation of a layout dating generally from the early eighteenth century (see Figure 12.3). Yet they also preserve, on their uppermost terrace between the villa itself and its chapel, a mid-seventeenth-century *giardino segreto*, not only laid out from Ferrari's plans but maintained in accordance with his precepts. Lower terraces extend this original layout into a superb eighteenth-century flower garden, very much within the aesthetic defined by Ferrari and Rapin.

The source is unequivocal: the Conte Buonaccorsi's copy of the 1637 Italian reprint of *De Florum Cultura* survives in the section of the Biblioteca Nazionale di Napoli kept at Macerata.[23] This layout, with its statues and little obelisks and stone-edged geometrical beds, gives the fullest sense possible of the ambitions and pleasures of the baroque flower garden that Ferrari sought to transplant from the Low Countries to Italy. The upper terrace is laid out from the first of Ferrari's plans: evoking both the Celestial City and the Garden of Eden, insofar as the central part of Ferrari's plate 25 is repeated four times, symmetrically around a central fountain that evokes the unfallen garden with its central fountain, whence flowed the four rivers of Paradise; while the whole, in its symmetries of fours, corresponds to Ferrari's apprehension of what Thomas Browne called 'the mystical Mathematicks of the City of heaven'.[24]

The visitor to the Giardini Buonaccorsi is privileged to experience an aspect of baroque thought and aesthetics which survives nowhere else: deserted but not abandoned, and, indeed, kept in wonderful order by its local custodians. Flora's bouquet and crown still spray water at the unsuspecting visitor, and, in the grotto at the bottom of the slopes, skeletal automata of Turk and Pierrot still stand in their eighteenth-century rags. But the most remarkable survival of all is the *giardino segreto*, an ephemeral flower garden laid out on one of the symbolic plans of Ferrari's treatise, now three and a half centuries old.

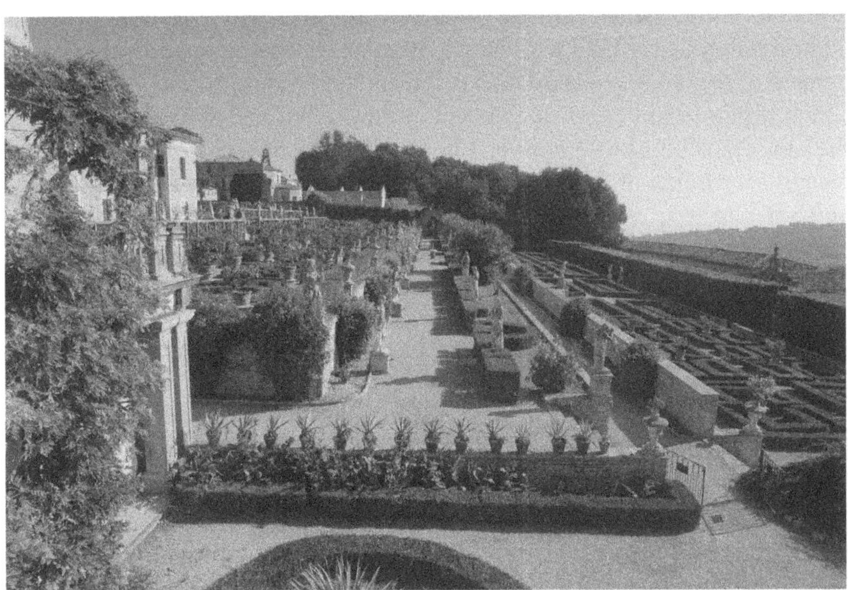

Figure 12.3 Gardens of the Villa Buonaccorsi, Marche, Italy, laid out for the Counts Buonaccorsi from the 1630s.

The Jesuit writer on gardens who was best known in the eighteenth century was the French Jesuit Réné Rapin (1621–87), whose didactic Latin poem *Hortorum libri quatuor*, published in Paris in 1665, was translated successfully into English heroic verse by James Gardiner and (according to tradition) polished for its third edition by no less a poet than Alexander Pope.[25] It is slightly less well known that much of Rapin's first book clearly derives from *De Florum Cultura*, certainly in the lists of flowers cited; and, indeed, its aesthetics are clearly fixed in the flower garden of the seventeenth century. Even the frontispiece, which seems to have travelled across various editions and translations of Rapin (it faces page 1 of the English translation), is very clearly derived from Ferrari's plate of a rectangular flower garden layout, even if Rapin's own instructions tend to point instead to a box-edged arrangement with *plat-bandes*, perhaps rather like the restored garden of Het Loo at Appledoorn in the Netherlands.

It is not, I hope, a perverse ending to this survey to focus on a celebrated, if vanished, English garden, and to speculate for a moment on its Catholicity and on the Jesuit horticultural and scientific atmosphere that shaped it. I refer – with an element of paradox – to the famous garden at Twickenham, near London, of the poet and aesthetic theorist Alexander Pope, reviser of Gardiner's translation of Rapin. As well as being Georgian England's most celebrated poet, Pope was, as we have seen in Chapter 4, one of its most visible Catholic laymen. I use the word 'paradox' because Pope is generally credited with having been at least a godfather to the development of the landscape garden in eighteenth-century England, a movement which began in imitation of classical antiquity but ended in simulation of the random sublimity of nature. I have thus also traced a trajectory away from the encoding of meaning in a place, and towards a condition in which only the aesthetic impact was deemed to be of significance. The eighteenth century began with the construction of Pope's grotto, but it ended in the demolition of 'columns erected only to receive quotations'.[26] Yet, even in the naturalistic landscape movement, we may discern Jesuit influence. A constant point of reference for early theorists of the landscape garden was the Chinese garden, accounts of which inevitably derive from the Jesuit missions there. The classic text in this regard is a letter from the Jesuit Jean-Denis Attiret, published in Paris in 1749, which described the Yuan Ming Yuan of the Qianlong emperor, emphasising the extent to which everything – trees, rocks, and water – was meant to appear natural, however much thought had gone into its positioning.[27] Even so, I would contend that Pope's practices as a deviser of gardens were infinitely closer to the Renaissance and baroque tradition than they were to the 'natural' landscapes, which were, arguably, as much the outcome of his innovations as of the letters from the Pekin mission. His garden functioned as a place for contemplation of the passage of time and of the succession of generations, focused as it was on a long, hedged green space, closed at one end by an obelisk, inscribed in Latin, to the memory of the poet's mother, a gentlewoman of recusant ancestry.

Pope's celebrated grotto is a place as much retrospective as prospective in its meaning and arrangement. In this context, it is essential to remember that it was remodelled in the last few years of Pope's life as an imitation, however mannered, of the natural arrangement of rocks and minerals within a cave. The earlier, pre-naturalistic state of that grotto, as it was for most of Pope's lifetime, bore a clearer relation to the world of the seventeenth-century virtuoso. Originally, spars, shells, fossils, and precious minerals were displayed as in a virtuoso's cabinet, albeit one masquerading as an enchanted cave in a late baroque romance. We are not far from the world of the Collegio Romano, and Kircher's wonderful and prodigious stones. As we saw in Chapter 4, its inset mirrors for catching reflections and lens set into the door, which transformed the grotto itself into a camera obscura, owed much to the moment in scientific and aesthetic history embodied by Kircher's *Ars magna lucis et umbrae* (1646) and *Mundus subterraneus* (1665).

I have concluded with Pope's garden to demonstrate that those aspects of the seventeenth-century Jesuit interest in gardens which I have been considering had distinct echoes as late as the Augustan age. The questions of place, meaning, and meditation that occupied Richeôme and Hawkins were no less long-lived than the elements of symbolism and virtuoso collecting that distinguished the works of Ferrari. As so often in seventeenth-century cultural history, the members of the Society of Jesus were not only early participants in a cultural movement but also attentive codifiers and describers of the often fugitive essentials of early modern intellectual and aesthetic experience.

Notes

1 Although Mavis Batey's *Alexander Pope: The Poet and the Landscape* (London: Barn Elms, 1999) offers wonderful illustrations, it typifies an overwhelming reluctance to read Pope's gardens as closely modelled on seventeenth-century precedents, as also a general refusal to give due consideration to his Catholicism.

2 Michel de Montaigne, *Journal de Voyage en Italie*, ed. Paul Faure (Paris: Gilbert Jeune, 1948), p. 89.

3 *Jesuit Latin Poets of the 17th and 18th Centuries: An Anthology of Neo-Latin Poetry*, ed. James M. Martz, John P. Murphy, and Jozef Ijsewijn (Wauconda, IL: Bolchazy-Carducci, 1989), pp. 30–1, 20–3.

4 *Jesuit Latin Poets*, pp. 116–19.

5 *A Selection of the Poems of Sir Constantijn Huygens (1596–1687)*, ed. Peter Davidson and Adriaan van der Weel (Amsterdam: Amsterdam University Press, 1996), p. 128.

6 See especially Ludwig Schwab, 'Das Jesuitenkollegium des 16. und 17. Jahrhunderts der Oberdeutchen Ordensprovinz' (PhD dissertation, Technical University Darmstadt, 2001); for at least one fascinating instance of a Jesuit as diallist – and, possibly, mediator between Charles II and his illegitimate son – see Coffin, *The English Garden: Meditation and Memorial*, pp. 15–16.

7 [Athanasius Kircher], *Collegii Rom: Sac: Jesu Musaeum* (Amsterdam: Janssonio-Waesbergiana, 1678), pp. 35–7.

8 Hawkins, *Partheneia Sacra.*

9 Margaret H. Thomson (ed. and trans.), *The Symbolic Garden: Reflections Drawn from a Garden of Virtues* (North York, ON: Captus Press, 1989).

10 Hawkins, 'The Epistle to the Parthenian Sodalitie', *Partheneia Sacra*, sigs A1r–2r.

11 Hawkins, *Partheneia Sacra*, p. 6.

12 *Ibid.*, pp. 8–9.

13 *Ibid.*, p. 11.

14 *Ibid.*, p. 13.

15 Louis Richeôme, *La peinture spirituelle* (Lyon: Pierre Rigaud, 1611). 'Le sixieme livre … des Iardins', from which I quote in the text, describes the gardens.

16 Bailey, *Between Renaissance and Baroque*, pp. 74–106.

17 Giovanni Battista Ferrari, *De Florum Cultura Libri VI* (Rome: Stephanus Paulinus, 1633). Quotations in the text are from this edition.

18 David Freedberg, *The Eye of the Lynx: Galileo, His Friends, and the Beginnings of Modern Natural History* (Chicago: University of Chicago Press, 2002), p. 38.

19 Cortona was also in receipt of Barberini patronage, notably his commission for the heroic fresco *The Triumph of Divine Providence* (with particular reference to the care of Divine Providence for the Barberini family) in the Palazzo Barberini, Rome.

20 The *Collocutiones* include a very early commentary on a match of ur-football: see David Freedberg, 'Cassiano on the Jewish Races', in Jennifer Montagu, Henrietta McBurney, and Joseph Connors (eds), *Cassiano dal Pozzo's Paper Museum II* (Ivrea: Olivetti, 1992), pp. 41–56, at pp. 51–2.

21 Ferrari, *De Florum Cultura*, pp. 458–9.

22 *Ibid.*, p. 426.

23 By the great kindness of Dr Gabriele Cingolani of the University of Macerata, who arranged my access to the gardens, I am able also to report that this copy was definitely in the possession of the Buonaccorsi family by the time the top terrace of the garden was laid out. Unfortunately, it is not annotated.

24 Thomas Browne, *The Garden of Cyrus or the Quincuncial Lozenge* (London, 1658), p. 73.

25 René Rapin, *Rapin of Gardens, A Latin Poem, English'd by Mr Gardiner, the Third Edition, Revised and finish'd* (London: Bernard Lintot, 1728). Book 1, the section that describes the garden proper, occupies pages 1 to 63.

26 Thomas Whatley, *Observations on Modern Gardening* (London: T. Payne, 1770), quoted in Coffin, *The English Garden*, p. 222. Coffin's beautifully nuanced discussion of the fading of signification from the English garden is highly relevant in this context.

27 Quoted in Maggie Keswick, *The Chinese Garden: History, Art and Architecture* (London: Academy Editions, 1978), pp. 9–11.

Part III

Designs of the imagination

13

The dream of Raphael

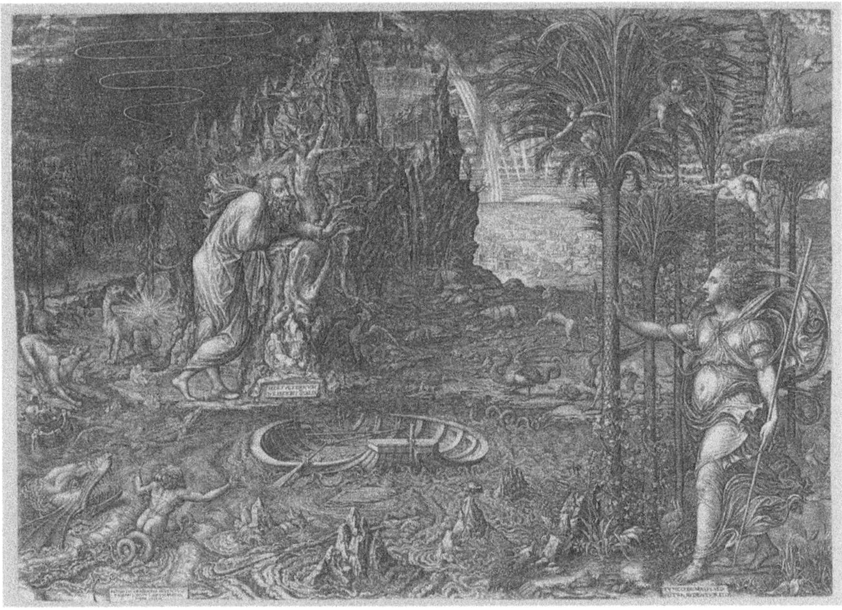

Figure 13.1 Giorgio Ghisi, after Raphael, *Allegory of Life* (sometimes called *The Dream of Raphael*), 1561, engraving.

This chapter discusses two sixteenth-century engravings – one from the beginning of the century, one from the 1560s – that depict scenes from dreams, or, at least, scenes which are dream-like. The two prints now share a title, *The Dream of Raphael*, which perhaps gives a false, or chimeric, impression of a shared debt to a work that no longer survives – if, indeed, it ever existed. One was executed by one of Raphael's assistants, Marcantonio Raimondi (*c.* 1480–1534), and the other by a Mantuan artist at the court of Catherine de Medici, Giorgio Ghisi (1520–82). The latter, a beguiling night-piece which has attracted radically differing interpretations, is my main focus here (see Figure 13.1).

The title often used informally to identify the work by Ghisi, *The Dream of Raphael*, takes its cue from a mysterious inscription found on the second state of the engraving, which asserts that the conception of the work had been Raphael's: 'RAPHAELIS URBINATIS INVENTUM'. The print is sometimes referred to by the more general title *Allegory of Life*, whereas Raimondi's has intermittently borne the title *The Dream of Raphael*.[1]

These two original and haunting etchings by Ghisi and Raimondi seem at first analysis to derive from the same source, and to exhibit a certain similarity. Both are nocturnal scenes; both have water as their central motif (a Lethean lake in Raimondi's work, and a turbulent river in Ghisi's); and both feature unnatural lighting that produces a sense of threat and fear. On the other hand, a more careful analysis reveals that the differences between the two are more marked than their similarities. Raimondi's image is one of nightmare and anguish, whereas Ghisi's – despite its nocturnal tonality – represents the moment of awakening after the nightmare, and of the return of hope at the first light of day.

I would like to propose a new interpretation of the iconography of Ghisi's engraving, proceeding from the fact that in the year shown on the image, 1561, Ghisi was working for his patron Catherine de Medici, queen mother to King Charles IX of France. This engraving can be linked to other images commissioned by Catherine, in an extensive programme of using the visual arts as a public expression of her position – a strategy she had pursued since the death of her husband, King Henri II, in 1559. There was no clear consensus on how to interpret this dream image even among contemporary observers, in or out of France; and it was read, as we will see, sometimes as Circe and Ulysses and sometimes as the Temptation of St Anthony. Raphael's 'original' dream, meanwhile, seems not only to be irretrievably lost but also to have never been mentioned by any contemporary writer; nor has it ever been included in any catalogue of Raphael's works produced to date, even in those concerned with works that are lost or of doubtful attribution. (The little panel of the *Dream of a Knight*, now in the National Gallery in London, with the sleeping warrior placed in a daylit landscape between personifications of Virtue and Pleasure, is a different order of dream entirely.) The title *Il Sogno di Raffaele* itself seems to have been ascribed to Ghisi's engraving, or to a painted copy of it, because of the above-mentioned inscription in its second version; but, subsequently, this title would acquire a life of its own, being applied to an increasing number of nocturnal-themed works featuring monsters, sometimes retrospectively. After discussing both works, and the prior interpretations advanced for Ghisi's, I set forth my reading of that image as an allegory of the French political situation in the years 1560 and 1561.

Raimondi's much earlier *The Dream of Raphael* (*c.* 1508–09) is announced directly to the viewer as a dreamlike work (see Figure 13.2).[2]

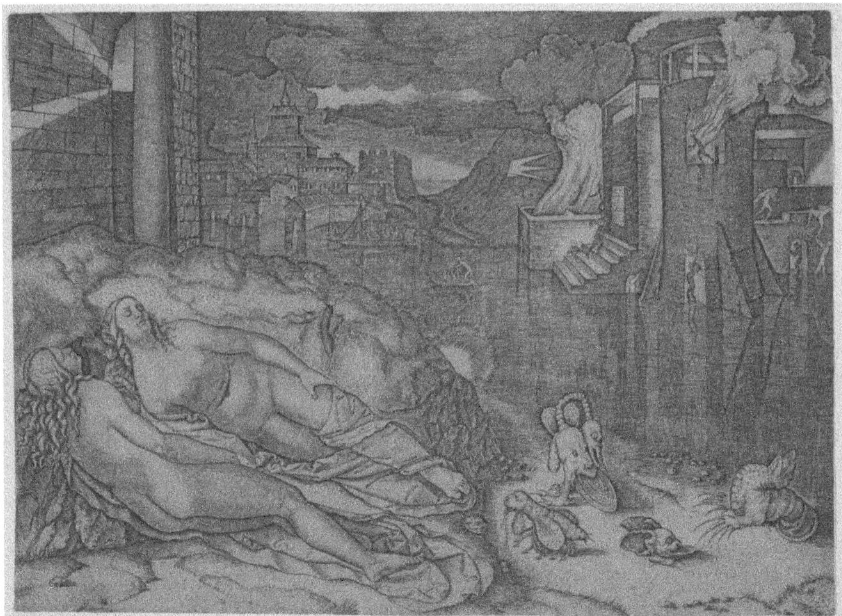

Figure 13.2 Marcantonio Raimondi, *Raphael's Dream*, *c.* 1508/09, engraving.

Its most striking element is the foreground, in which two naked women lie asleep on the banks of a dark lake that occupies much of the engraving; at their feet are four monstrous creatures. In the background, across the water, is a burning riverside town with a fortress, under a moonlit sky. Near it, there are naked figures among the rocks, and a naked ferryman carries five figures across the water.

It is difficult to connect this image with Renaissance interpretations of the classical world. Nor does it seem to be connected with any of Raphael's works, except insofar as the poses of the naked women refer to his drawings of ancient sarcophagi, which would certainly have been known to Raimondi as Raphael's assistant.[3] The town in flames inevitably recalls Aeneas's account of the sack of Troy in the second book of Virgil's *Aeneid* – especially because, among the small figures of fugitives in Raimondi's engraving, at least one carries another on its shoulders, recalling how Aeneas bore his father Anchises away from the city to safety. Likewise, the indistinct depiction of one or more figures being tortured on a wheel recalls (again, in general rather than specific terms) the punishment of the wicked in the Virgilian Hades.[4]

This image shares the vagueness of a dream. It is possible to identify the serene and rather beautiful figures of the sleeping women as dreaming, unaware of the horrors that surround them.[5] The engraving's lack of a precise *topos*, of any element that focuses attention, and of any explanatory key, either moral or referential, mark it as typically oneiric, and perhaps even as the representation of an actual dream. This renders at least plausible the hypothesis that it is meant to be a dream of Raphael's. Of the two engravings, this seems more likely to represent an authentic dream.

The 1544 painting called *The Night* or *The Dream* by Raphael's pupil Battista Dossi (1490–1548) derives its background of a burning city seen across a dark lake fairly directly from Raimondi's engraving, but in itself offers only an uncomplicated representation of night and dream.[6] In the foreground, under a full moon, Morpheus shakes poppy over a sleeping woman, placed between nightfall and dawn (represented by an owl and a cockerel), who is surrounded by grotesque, bird-like, dream creatures, not unlike the four monstrous animals in Raimondi's image. Dossi's iconography is as scrutable as Raimondi's is elusive.

In contrast to Raimondi's, Ghisi's engraving immediately provides us with three images that can easily be read according to the iconographic conventions of the Renaissance. The first to strike the observer's eye is the boat without a rudder, drifting towards cliffs in the foreground, rendered in magnificent detail. The second, dominating the space beyond the boat, is a bearded figure, who leans forward from a dark place framed by rocks and a dead tree. And the third, in the foreground, is a crowned female figure that advances holding a javelin, and touches the straight trunk of a palm tree, which reaches up to a more brightly illuminated area where cherubs hover among its fronds. The rudderless boat on treacherous waters was a highly recognisable contemporary representation of a state in danger. The figure of the man leaning out of an inhospitable landscape evokes the Renaissance perception of 'melancholy' as sterile contemplation or mental separation from the life of the world. Finally, the crowned female figure, while not carrying a precise meaning in itself, is clearly meant to convey decisiveness, and the palm she touches connotes victory and triumph in adversity.[7]

Read from left to right, the image takes us from the deepest darkness towards the relatively intense light of the distant background, which in turn falls on the female figure and the cherubs surrounding her in the foreground on the right. In the sky there are six stars, the moon covered by clouds, and a comet with a prominent white trail, about to strike the Earth behind the central male figure. There is a mysterious detail in the sky at the source of the comet, unnoticed hitherto, to which I return later. An inscription in the left foreground, rather than offering explanations, creates further mysteries: 'RAPHAELIS URBINATIS INVENTUM. PHILLIPUS DATUS ANIMI GRATIA FIERI IUSSIT' (literally, 'Raphael of Urbino invented it. Philippus Datus commissioned it for the good of his soul').[8]

The centre of the image is dominated by the male figure, whose left hand extends forward. Around him are creatures associated with evil and death: crows, snakes, a toad. The rock behind him is cut at the top, and a structure that could be a classical amphitheatre can be discerned in it. At its foot, on a marble slab, is the inscription 'SEDET AETERNUMQUE SEDEBIT INFOELIX' ('Unfortunate he sits and evermore will sit'). The water around the base of the rock is full of monsters: a mermaid, a sea snake, a skeleton. Inside the elegant shell-shaped boat adrift near the rock is another slab, this time bearing Ghisi's signature: 'GIORGUS / GHISI / MA[N]T / F.1.5.6.1.' To the right of the rock and behind the water there is an ambiguous area, dark throughout and inhabited by animals. In the distance beyond this, represented on a lower level – as if the viewer is looking from a mountaintop towards a plain – there is a peaceful inhabited landscape illuminated by the rays of the rising sun, with a rainbow rising from its horizon.

The right foreground is like a paradise garden. The palm tree extends from the bottom to the very top of the engraving; from its branches one cherub shoots an arrow in the direction of the male figure, while another carries palms of victory. To the right, another putto flies towards him bearing a palm. This whole area is dominated by the crowned female figure, who places her hand on the tree trunk as if she wants to identify with it. At its feet is the inscription 'TU NE CEDE MALIS SED CONTRA AUDENTIOR ITO' ('Do not yield to evils but more bravely strive against them').

The trees which surround this female figure have strong positive connotations. A very extensive literature treats the palm itself as a symbol of patience, victory, and survival in adversity. The olive, cedar, and cypress, meanwhile, are connected with the female personification of Sacred Wisdom in Ecclesiastes 24.[9] The ivy and vine which wrap the trunks of the two palm trees denote, as in the Bible, marriage and fidelity.

Given the important positions of the inscriptions in the engraving, it is clear that they are meant to communicate much of its meaning. Two come from the sixth book of the *Aeneid*, which, more than any other text in the Renaissance, was used as a source of dream content. The inscription at the foot of the male figure is taken from *Aeneid* VI, l. 617, and that at the foot of the female figure, from the Sybil's speech, *Aeneid* VI, l. 95. In both cases, the Virgilian context appears particularly relevant. The former verse describes the place where traitors, adulterers, and the greedy are punished and the latter is the Sybil's exhortation to Aeneas. The secrecy – or, according to some, the dream logic – surrounding Aeneas's passage through the world of the dead is very marked; the Sibyl's insistence that Aeneas try not to discover what misfortunes or punishments afflict the damned (ll. 614–15) makes the inherent horror of the scenes of eternal punishment even more disconcerting. In the verse which immediately follows the words in Ghisi's engraving, however, the soul of Phlegyas gives an indication of the origin of the crimes for which they are punished:

> [S]edet aeternumque sedebit
> infelix Theseus, Phlegyasque miserrimus omnis
> admonet et magna testatur voce per umbras:
> 'discite iustitiam moniti et non temnere divos.'[10]

> [Hapless Theseus sits and evermore shall sit, and Phlegyas, most unblest, gives warning to all and with loud voice bears witness amid the gloom: 'Be warned; learn ye to be just and not to slight the gods!']

Immediately after this the Sibyl provides some further information on the nature of the crimes committed:

> [V]endidit hic auro patriam dominumque potentem
> imposuit; fixit leges pretio atque refixit.[11]

> [This one sold his country for gold, and fastened on her a tyrant lord; he made and unmade laws for a bribe.]

At the end of her prophecy the Sibyl had declared that, although the fate of Aeneas would be unhappy, his people would eventually be glorious:

> [T]u cede malis, sed contra audentior ito,
> qua tua te Fortuna sinet.[12]

> [Yield not to ills, but go forth all the bolder to face them as far as your destiny will allow!]

Ghisi's female figure, with her hunting javelin, is especially similar to Mantuan representations of Diana and her nymphs, which would certainly have been known to him. As we shall see, the combination of visual and verbal echoes to Diana and Virgil's Sybil respond creatively to the iconography and preoccupations of the French court.

Ghisi's image has received various different interpretations. A painted version of it demonstrates in a very interesting way how the meaning of the whole can be altered by subtle changes of iconographic details. Created in 1595 by Jan Breughel the Elder (1568–1625), in collaboration with Hendrik van Balen or, more likely, Hans Rottenhammer,[13] this painting radically simplifies Ghisi's work, transforming it definitively into a depiction of Circe and Ulysses. Every element of the original composition with any political connotation has been removed. This is accomplished in part by means of a literal transcription of the earlier composition's two figures, and the addition of typical baroque cupids who carry an arch rather than palm branches. Even the boat has become a purely pictorial element; indeed, it is fair to say that the image has been transformed from a symbolic object into a simple narrative.

The Virgilian Hades and the enchanted island of Circe were both important as dreamlike places in the late Renaissance. Another such site was the desert where the ascetic St Anthony was subjected to temptation; and, in the eighteenth century, Ghisi's engraving was interpreted as depicting precisely that place and event, as the late Gioconda Albricci's research on the meanings and context of *The Dream of Raphael* revealed.[14] Albricci found references to an image, entitled 'The Temptation of St Anthony', in the 1786 and 1787 editions of Bianconi's Guide to Milan, as part of a description of the treasure stored in the place identified by Boorsch and colleagues with what is now called the 'crypt of San Carlo'.[15]

> É degno d'osservazione il belliffimo Quadretto in asse, che si è creduto mal' a proposito per lungo tempo rappresentare la tentazione di S. Antonio nel deserto inciso in Rame della stessa grandezza da Giorgio Ghisi Mantovano, nel qual rame, benchè vi fi legga Raphaelis Urbinatis Inventum, pure alcuni dubitano, che non fia di lui Invenzione. I Francefi chiamano questa rara stampa, il sogno, e gl' Italiani la Saetta di Raffaelle.[16]

> [The beautiful painting on the axis is worthy of observation, which was believed erroneously for a long time to represent the temptation of St Anthony in the desert, engraved in copper to the same size by Giorgio Ghisi of Mantua, on which plate, although there is written 'Raphaelis Urbinatis Inventum', some doubt that it was not his [Raphael's] invention. The French call this rare print 'The Dream [of Raphael], and the Italians 'The Lightning-flash of Raphael'.]

There is no trace today of such a painting. Perhaps there was confusion: the suggestion is that a painting, identical to Ghisi's engraved image, perhaps by implication its original, once hung in the crypt of San Carlo. Possibly the ascribed subject was a simple misreading of the solitary male figure in a deserted place with rock formations, which recall those in numerous Renaissance depictions of hermits and ascetics. The animals and female figure alike could, in such a view, be read as demons that torment or tempt the saint. 'Raphael's Lightning' could simply refer to the looping, swashing train of the comet at the left of the engraving. This comet half conceals a mystery: the looping flash of light from the star falling to earth has as its point of origin a bearded head almost entirely hidden by the darkness of the sky around it.

Without deviating too much from the work of modern scholars who have read Ghisi's print in an essentially optimistic key, I would like to argue for one possible geographically and chronologically specific interpretation. I propose that the engraving can be seen as a complex representation of the state of the French monarchy, commissioned by Catherine de Medici from one of her trusted Italian court artists during the months following the death of her son, King François II.[17] In this light, the female figure represents

Catherine – or, at any rate, her influence and politics: this identification is supported by several secondary details of the composition which are closely related to the iconography surrounding Charles IX's subsequent entry into Paris, Like the ship, the palm tree was frequently utilised as a representation of the state in late Renaissance Europe. Nevertheless, the Virgilian motto in combination with the emblematic and allegorical meaning of the palm tree provides the main key for my interpretation. It is essential at this point to bear in mind how important implied contexts attached to particular words and images can be when used in sententious and emblematic ways. In this case, words used specifically to prophesy the survival of the royal house are associated with a figure that bears a strong resemblance to the legendary mother of Aeneas and of the Roman people, the goddess Venus, as described near the opening of Virgil's poem:

> [N]amque umeris de more habilem suspenderat arcum
> venatrix dederatque comam diffundere ventis,
> nuda genu nodoque sinus collecta fluentis.[18]

> [From her shoulders in huntress fashion she had slung the ready bow and had given her hair to the winds to scatter; her knee bare, and her flowing robes gathered in a knot.]

Compositionally, the palm, which represents both rebirth and survival, is closely linked both with the female figure and with the inscription below it. Elsewhere in the emblematic culture of the Renaissance, the phrase 'tu ne cede malis' is associated with a tree that signifies the survival and duration of a family. Accompanied by a depiction of women sowing seeds under a fruit tree, it appears on the emblematic ceiling of the castle of Dampierre-sur-Boutonne.[19] It also appears on one of the two medals made by Leone Leoni for the Gonzaga family in 1551: that of the father bears the motto, while that of the daughter depicts her as the goddess Diana, with a pose and clothing very similar to the female figure in Ghisi's engraving.[20]

Depictions of trees were widely used in Renaissance and early modern Europe to represent the survival or reassertion of a royal family. Such a use of the palm emblem gives weight to the interpretation I would like to put forward: that Ghisi's enigmatic image refers to the state of the French monarchy in 1560. In that year the young François II, eldest son of Henri II and Catherine, had died during a period of profound religious and political crisis, marked by the rise of the Guise faction at court and the intensification of tensions between Protestants and Catholics throughout France.

The crown passed to François's brother, Charles IX, but, because he was still a minor, the queen mother took over the reins of power in his stead. As regent, Catherine became patron of numerous Italian artists and artisans who were working in France in those years. Various aspects of Ghisi's engraving reflect the visual language through which Catherine presented herself and her children to the public. It is by no means inconceivable that Ghisi's *Dream of Raphael* should offer Venus in the first book of the *Aeneid* as a direct parallel for the French regent: the *mater nutrix* of a royal dynasty destined to endure, and to overcome seemingly insurmountable present difficulties.

It is striking how many details and symbols contained in the image can be related to the Medici context, to Catherine's public image, and to the precarious position of the Valois dynasty in 1560/61. The Medici had already made use of the Virgilian image of the golden bough to publicly express the continuance of their family's authority and prominence and its ability to provide suitable heirs, such as with the motto 'UNO AVULSO NON DEFICIT ALTER' ('When one is torn away, another succeeds') intertwined with laurels in the portrait of Lorenzo de Medici by Pontormo. Catherine had adopted the rainbow as a symbol of her roles as both bringer of peace and patroness, like the classical Juno, of her children's weddings; and a rainbow is in evidence in the centre of Ghisi's engraving. The weapon – arguably a lightning bolt – held by the figure of Venus with the tip pointing downwards could be another expression of the peaceful role preferred by Catherine. In 1561, the year the engraving was completed, Catherine organised the Colloquium of Poissy, during which she unsuccessfully tried to reconcile Catholic and Protestant France.

The possibility that the female figure represents Catherine as the mother-Venus of the first book of the *Aeneid* has further consequences. In the same book, Virgil describes Venus in another guise:

> [A]mbrosiaeque comae divinum vertex odorem
> spiravere; pedes vestis defluxit ad imos,
> et vera incessu patuit dea.[21]

> [From her head her ambrosial tresses breathed celestial fragrance; down to her feet fell her raiment, and in her step she was revealed a very goddess.]

Here Venus reveals her true identity, which had been hidden at first behind the appearance of a nymph of Diana. The resonances of this image become clear when we consider that, in typical portraits, Catherine wears solemn black widow's robes (as, for instance, in the Valois tapestries). Another important element in the Virgilian revelation narrative is the sudden flow of the divine clothing towards the feet, for, in Ghisi's engraving, the female figure wears markedly swirling, flowing garments as she advances. This aspect of Venus, as the mother of the royal dynasty, leads us rather precisely to a new way of looking at Ghisi's engraving: the presentation of a handmaid of Diana who turns out to be Venus would have had a particular, precise and relevant resonance in the France of 1560.

The visual language used by Henri II's lover, Diane de Poitiers, was fittingly centred on the image of herself as the goddess of the moon. Other surviving works of art commissioned by Catherine emphasised that she surpassed Diane de Poitiers in importance upon Henri's death. This is particularly apparent in a series of tapestry designs that glorify Catherine by identifying her with the classical widow Artemisia (widow of Mausolus): Artemisia takes the place of Artemis.[22] The same series of drawings also offers us a possible interpretation of the architectural structure that stands behind the male figure in Ghisi's engraving. It resembles two edifices in the Artemisia drawings: the mausoleum and the cut-out amphitheatre in which Catherine-Artemisia oversees her son's education as a horseman.[23]

Moreover, this scene in the Artemisia series evokes the jousting arena where Henri II lost his life in 1559. In Ghisi's engraving, the cherubs who shoot arrows in the direction of the male figure, and carry the palms of victory, could give further substance to my hypothesis, if we identify the male 'hermit' figure with the deceased Henri II, regretting the removal of his government from the country. The water flows from the amphitheatre – that is, from the arena where Henri died – such that the water on which the ship of state is drifting represents the confusion caused by his death.

The French cockerel next to the male figure, and the lilies – symbol of both France and Florence – placed at the foot of the Catherine-Venus, could likewise be imbued with a parallel meaning. Rather than embody a static evocation of mourning, Catherine-Venus strides forward authoritatively, reminding us of her fecundity and highlighting the hopes that crowd around Aeneas-Charles IX. Indeed, Charles was explicitly identified with Aeneas at other occasions; for instance, his mythical Trojan ancestry was emphasised in the iconography of his entry into Paris in 1571.[24]

The conventional allegory of the ship of state also occupied a prominent position on the arch erected at the Pont Notre-Dame for Charles's entry. It should likewise be noted that the crescent, which appears in the night sky of Ghisi's engraving, was a symbol of Henri II. In this context, the six stars and the comet can also be interpreted symbolically. In 1561 Henri and Catherine still had six children living, and so the comet can be seen as the representation of the recently deceased François II. Catherine, ever attentive to the details of astrology, would certainly have been aware of the comet sighted in the year of François's death.[25] I would suggest that the ball of light, with its looping trail to the left of the central male figure, is partially a representation of the comet as understood in the sixteenth century: literally, a star falling towards the Earth. This trail of light is presumably the reason why the print is sometimes called 'Raphael's flash of lightning'. But Catherine also recounted a vision, in which a flash of light predicted her husband's death. I would submit that a half-concealed detail in the engraving is crucial to an understanding of its meaning: at the point of the origin of the trail of light there is a head, so delicately engraved as to be almost invisible in the dark sky. It is the head of a bearded man, bearing a considerable likeness to the 1559 portrait of Henri II by Clouet, of which multiple copies survive, at Versailles, in Florence, and at the Palace of Holyroodhouse in Edinburgh. The head appears to be emerging from a cloud slightly brighter than the surrounding sky. Its presence, if the identification with Henri can be sustained as I think it can, is a half-hidden indication that the print does indeed treat, however obliquely, of the state of France in the early 1560s.

The tracing of the multiple meanings of this exceptionally complex image is still unfinished, and is likely to remain unfinished. but, on balance, reading Ghisi's engraving as a reflection of the French political situation of 1560/61 seems at least plausible, and the discovered, lurking detail of the possible portrait of Henri II hidden in the night sky adds considerable weight to this conjecture (see Figure 13.3). To what extent, then, can we see a connection between Ghisi's and Raimondi's images? It is conceivable that the only connection is the sharing of a dubious and attributed title between Ghisi and Raimondi. The latter work seems to be precisely what the former is not: the representation of an actual dream in which memories of omens and the disasters of classical antiquity (drawn in particular from the Virgilian Hades and the account of the destruction of Troy in *Aeneid* II) combine with zoomorphic monsters, typical of Flemish painting, to express disorientation and trauma without ever becoming completely lucid or legible. Raimondi's engraving recalls Virgil's account of Hades in the sixth book of the *Aeneid* not only in its depiction of the more negative aspects of an imagined afterlife but also in its evocation of a similar underground and dreamlike experience. Virgil, it should be noted, imagines his epic hero placed under the protection of unnamed divinities, of the master of silence, of the shadows and souls of the dead, and beyond the portals of sleep.[26] This represents a possible starting point for further investigation of many other Renaissance nocturnal

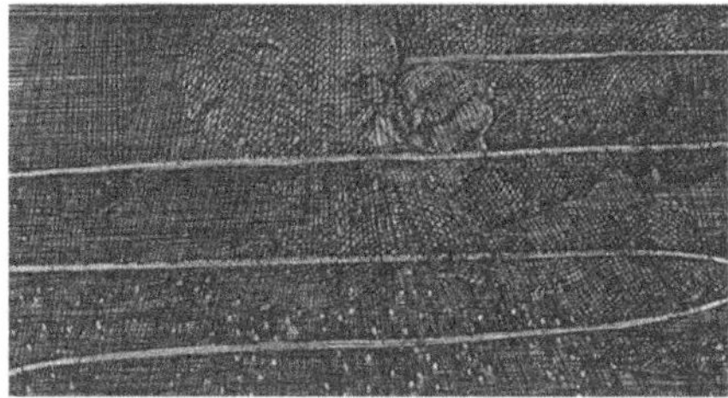

Figure 13.3 Giorgio Ghisi, after Raphael, *Allegory of Life* (sometimes called *The Dream of Raphael*), 1561, engraving, detail.

pieces that might also be read as dream images, or memories of the Virgilian Hades rendered with a dreamlike sense of urgency and discontinuity.

To conclude, it can also be said that Ghisi's image belongs to the world of dreams only insofar as it necessarily refers to Virgil's Hades. This aspect of the engraving would surely have struck any educated individual of the sixteenth century who contemplated it, given the connotative meaning of the male figure – perhaps the only authentic point of contact between this work and Raphael – standing next to the murky water, and the inscription that fleetingly identifies him with Virgil's Theseus. Yet the other, more optimistic quotation from the *Aeneid* shifts the focus of the engraving towards the female figure, who, as we have seen, may possibly represent Queen Catherine de Medici herself in the guise of the benevolent Venus of the *Aeneid*'s first book, protector of her dynasty. This identification withdraws the engraving from the world of dreams and all but rules out the possibility that it was derived from an alleged original executed by Raphael.

Of course, any reading of such a prodigiously complex image must remain provisional. Nevertheless, an interim conclusion can be drawn from the fact that Raimondi's 'underground' vision is palpably more dreamlike than Ghisi's, especially since the former refers to places that lie beyond the portals of sleep, whereas Ghisi most likely represents the moment of *awakening* from a dream, or, rather, a hope of awakening from a moment in history that had taken on the aspect of a nightmare.

Notes

1 A reference to this engraving can be found in Adam Bartsch, *Le Peintre Graveur* (Leipzig: J. A. Barth, 1867), XIV, p. 274, catalogue no. 359. Bartsch was aware that he was using a name for this work that some other authorities had not used, and never mentioned any verifiable connection between it and Raphael's work.

2 The copy I have studied most carefully is in the British Museum, Department of Prints and Drawings, Bartsch no. B.XIV.274.359.

3 Raimondi was born in Bologna in 1480 and went to Rome in 1510, where he became Raphael's servant and assistant. Vasari wrote of his genius for engraving. During the sack of Rome in 1527 Raimondi lost everything, after which he returned to Bologna, dying there around 1534.

4 *Aeneid* VI, l. 595 and following. All quotations and translations from the *Aeneid* are taken from Virgil, *Eclogues, Georgics, Aeneid*, trans. H. Rushton Fairclough, rev. G. P. Goold (Cambridge, MA: Harvard University Press, 1916). Notably, these verses recall the description of the eternal stasis of the unhappy Theseus (VI, ll. 617–18), which, as we shall see, provide the inscription found at the foot of the central male figure in the Ghisi engraving.

5 This may evoke the idea that the virtuous sleep unscathed amidst dangers, but I have yet to find a Renaissance image that treats this theme in the same or similar terms.
6 Staatliche Kunstsammlungen Dresden, Gemäldegalerie Alte Meister, Gal.-Nr.131. The image was made as part of a series of *Times of Day* painted for Duke Ercole II d'Este, for his new apartments in the Palazzo di Corte in Ferrara.
7 For the use of this emblematic image in Renaissance Europe, see Peter Davidson, *The Vocal Forest: A Study of the Context of Three Low Countries Printers' Devices of the Seventeenth Century* (Leiden: Academic Press Leiden, 1996).
8 As translated in Suzanne Boorsch, Michal Lewis, and R. E. Lewis, *The Engravings of Giorgio Ghisi* (New York: Metropolitan Museum of Art, 1985), p. 114. 'Animi gratia' could also be translated as 'from a grateful soul', however, or, in a more colloquial tone, 'with gratitude'. Exhaustive research by Gioconda Albricci and Boorsch *et al.* centres on the attempt to discover a Dati who had a plausible connection with Ghisi or with his patrons.
9 'I grew tall like a cedar in Lebanon and like a cypress on the heights of Hermon. I grew as tall as the palm of Engeddi, like roses in Jericho. Like a beautiful olive tree in the field and like the plane tree near the water I grew tall': Ecclesiastes 24:17–19.
10 Virgil, *Aeneid* VI, ll. 617–20.
11 *Ibid.*, 621–2.
12 *Ibid.*, 95–6.
13 This oil painting is signed and dated 1595. Breughel's collaborator is identified as Hans Rottenhammer in Klaus Ertz, *Jan Breughel der Ältere (1568–1625): Die Gemälde mit kritischem Oevrekatalog* (Cologne: DuMont Buchverlag, 1980), pp. 114, 559, catalogue no. 15. The Sotheby's cataloguist identified the collaborator as Hendrik van Balen, however, in the catalogues dated 25 June 1969, p. 50, and 12 December 1979, n. 21. These references were kindly supplied to me by the Hon. J. A. Stourton *olim* of Sotheby Parke-Bernet.
14 Gioconda Albricci, '*Il sogno di Raffaello* di Giorgio Ghisi', in *Arte Christiana*, 71 (1983), pp. 215–22; C. Bianconi, *Guida per Milano coretta* (Milan: stamperia Sirtori, 1786) [republished under the title *Nuova Guida di Milano per gli amanti delle Belle Arti* (Milan: stamperia Sirtori, 1787)], p. 48 in both editions.
15 Boorsch *et al.*, *Engravings of Giorgio Ghisi*, p. 117.
16 Bianconi, *Guida*, p. 48.
17 Useful information on Ghisi's movements around the time he made this engraving can be found in Paolo Bellini, *L'Opera Incisa di Giorgio Ghisi* (Bassano del Grappa: Tassotti, 1998), pp. 20–5. In 1551 we find Ghisi in the list of members of the Guild of St Luke in Antwerp, and in 1554 he is almost certainly among the Italians working in Fontainebleau. Three years later he may have returned to Mantua; but he was again working in France by 1559, when his engraving of the Three Fates was published with French royal privilege. In 1560 his *Allegory of the Destinies of Human Life* was published, also with royal privilege. It is probable that he worked in France without interruption following the 1561 publication of his engravings after Primaticcio's paintings in the Ulysses Gallery

at Fontainebleau; and, from a letter Ghisi wrote from Paris, dated 15 December 1561, we can be fairly certain that he was in Paris throughout that year.

18 Virgil, *Aeneid* I, ll. 318–20.

19 Boorsch et al., *Engravings of Giorgio Ghisi*, p. 115.

20 *Ibid.*

21 Virgil, *Aeneid* I, ll. 403–5.

22 Sheila Ffolliot, 'Catherine de Medicis as Artemisia: Figuring the Powerful Widow', in Margaret Ferguson, Maureen Quilligan, and Nancy Vickers (eds), *Rewriting the Renaissance: The Discourses of Sexual Difference in Early Modern Europe* (Chicago: University of Chicago Press, 1986), pp. 227–41.

23 This similarity is particularly striking, as illustrated in figure 14 of Jean Ehrmann, *Antoine Caron, peintre à la Cour des Valois* (Geneva: Droz-Giard, 1935). For a full and pertinent discussion of the Artemisia series of drawings, see Ulrika von Haumeder, *Antoine Caron: Studien zu seiner 'Histoire D'Arthemise'* (Heidelberg: Staufen, 1976), which includes a facsimile of BNF MS Fr. 306, *Histoire de la Reine Arthemise*, by Nicolas Houel, dedicated to Catherine.

24 *La ioyeuse Entrée de Charles IX Roy de France en Paris, 1572*, facsimile with introduction by Frances A. Yates (New York: Johnson Reprint Corp, 1976), p. 16.

25 See R. J. Knecht, *Catherine de' Medici* (London: Longman, 1998), pp. 222–3. For Catherine's interest in alchemy and astrology, see also the corroborating evidence provided by F. M. Grangée in 'La Medaille de Catherine de Medicis', a lecture of 11 November 1912, a copy of which pamphlet is held in the Warburg Institute Library, London, f.b.b.50. The comet is mentioned in Noah Webster, *A brief history of epidemic and pestilential diseases; with the principal phenomena of the physical world, which precede and accompany them, and observations deduced from the facts stated*, 2 vols (Hartford: Hudson & Goodwin, 1799), I, p. 157: 'In 1560 a comet, and a dearth of corn in England.'

26 See especially Virgil, *Aeneid* VI, ll. 264–7 and 893–9 – passages that emphasise darkness and dreams as key images of the protagonist's experience in Hades.

14

Alexander Seton, his house, his library, his world

The consideration of material culture remains a fruitful element in the study of the lives and mentalities of the Catholics of early modern Britain (see Figure 14.1). It is axiomatic that the Catholic community acted as preservers of the past, carrying relics, textiles, and the other elements which made up the tissue of the memory of their community 'beyond the seas under colore of safe custodie', but they were also active in commissioning new objects of memory from the artists and craftsmen of baroque Europe to take their places alongside salvaged objects, such as the cope at Saint-Omer from the chapel of Henry VII, and found emblems, such as the statue of the Virgin vandalised by the Earl of Essex's expedition to Cadiz, subsequently venerated at Valladolid.[1] By the later sixteenth century British Catholics were existing within a new, Tridentine order, so that the objects which furnished their lives, libraries, and altars reflect continually, and inevitably, a process of adaptation and negotiation of identity through the fabrication, collection, and arrangement of the tangible world.

There is much scope for further investigation in these questions of material preservation and reinvention, and the probability remains that the Reformation constituted in itself a major stimulus (perhaps *the* major stimulus) to the collection of the material past of Britain and, subsequently, to the beginnings of archaeology in the British Isles. It is of particular interest to look at material culture in the context of Scotland, in that it is still widely believed that almost nothing survived Presbyterian iconoclasm, and that the post-Reformation climate would have been so hostile to any attempts at Catholic revival that nothing would have been created by or for the Catholic community. This was demonstrably not the case, particularly in the northern counties of Aberdeen, Banff, and Moray. One indication of the mentality of the Catholic community there is given by the pattern of post-Reformation preservation of Scotland's first printed book, the ambitious *Breviarium Aberdonense*.

After the Reformation, two of the five surviving copies were in the possession of Catholic gentry in Aberdeenshire: the 'Strathmore' copy (now

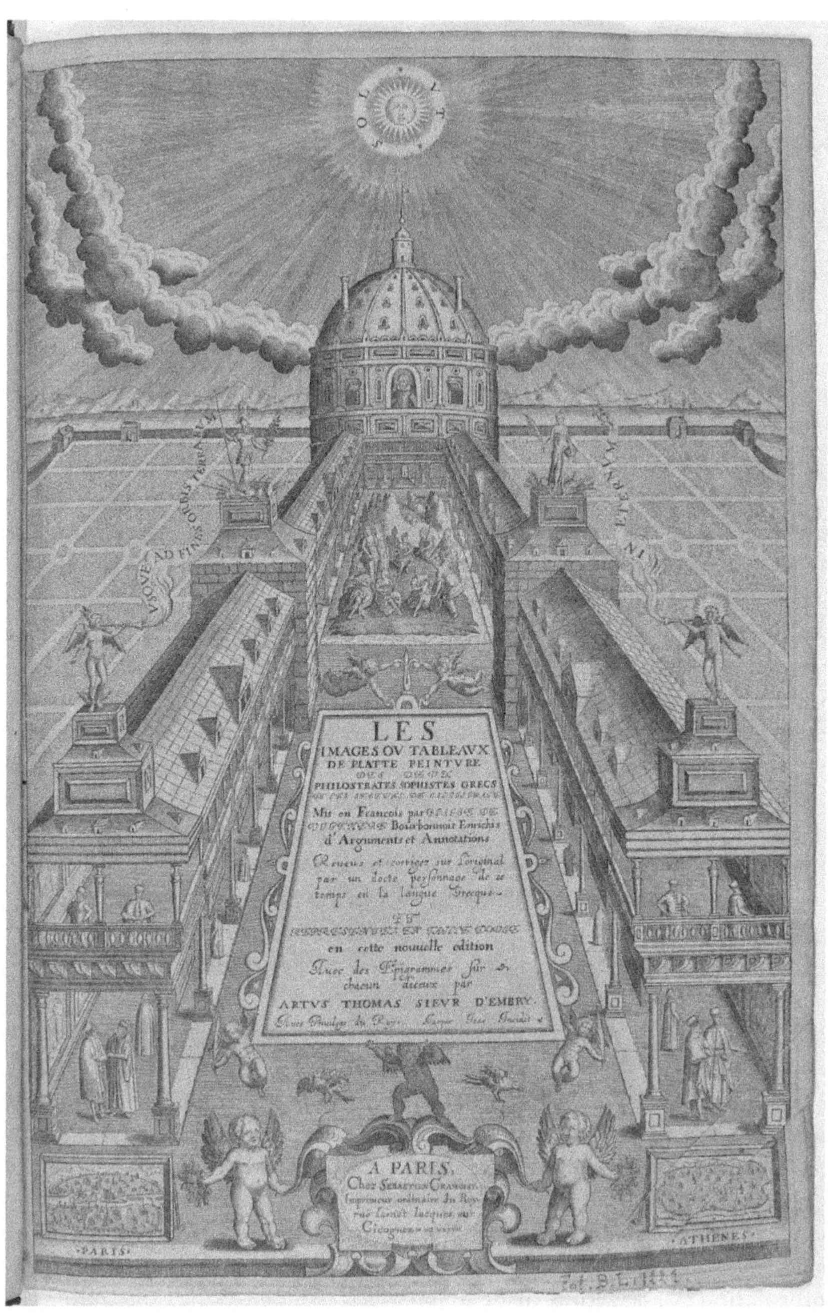

Figure 14.1 Jasper Isac, engraved frontispiece for Blaise de Vigenère, *Les Images ou Tableaux de platte peinture des deux Philostrates sophistes grecs* (Paris: Sebastien Cramoisy, 1637).

National Library of Scotland) belonged to Francis Hay of Delgaty (fl. 1676); the 'Ker' copy (also in NLS) belonged to a George Arbuthnot. The *Compassio Beatae Mariae* pamphlet, now bound with the Strathmore copy, belonged to John Leslie of Leslie. Copies now lost belonged to the Scots College in Paris and the controversialist Thomas Dempster of Muiresk in Bologna.[2] Although the interest of Dempster can be assumed to be primarily rooted in the study of history as a weapon of religious controversy, and the use later made of the Paris copy by the Abbé Thomas Innes was historical and scholarly, the value of a pre-Tridentine prayer book, which had not been a particular success within Scotland at the time of its publication, to Catholic laymen in Aberdeenshire in the seventeenth century poses worthwhile questions. The breviary cannot have been of contemporary devotional use, so its preservation necessarily implies a degree of awareness of the present and the past states of Scottish Catholicism, or even simply a desire to maintain the commemorations of local saints contained in the text. Consciousness of a community and its history, as recorded by the *Breviarium*, must have constituted an element of personal identity.

Within a few miles of Muiresk and the castle of the Hays at Delgaty is Fyvie Castle, owned and extensively remodelled from 1596 by Alexander Seton, Lord Fyvie, later first Earl of Dunfermline (1555–1622). Seton was a preserver of the past: he is now known to have owned and preserved one of the manuscripts of the *Scotichronicon* from Scone Abbey in Perthshire, the *Liber Sconensis* or 'Black Book of Scone'.[3] He may also have acted as preserver, possibly even at one point repairer, of the abbey of Pluscarden in Morayshire, whose revenues had been bestowed on him as a christening gift by his godmother, Mary Queen of Scots. His work at Fyvie has to a considerable degree been overlaid by later building campaigns, but his works at Pinkie House in East Lothian survive, with the iconographically rich ceiling of the magnificent long gallery intact.[4]

Seton is in every respect a figure worthy of study, a 'Church papist' of continental education, who contrived to hold high government office in Scotland during the violence of the Calvinist Reformation and even to act as guardian of the infant Charles I, ending his career as Earl of Dunfermline and Lord Chancellor of Scotland.[5] Our knowledge of him is considerably deepened by the recent discovery of a document which sheds considerable new light on his education, his mentality, and his world. This is a partial library list, found among the papers of the earls of Crawford and Balcarres on deposit in the National Library of Scotland: 'Inventair of som of the Earill of Dunfermline his buiks in Pinkie, 1625'.[6] It would appear to be in the hand of David Lindsay (1587–1642), created Lord Lindsay of Balcarres in 1633, who married Seton's daughter Sophia in 1612, and who may possibly have received his education in Seton's household. This document would appear to be a listing of books in a private or semi-private book room: it seems to be a shelf-by-shelf listing, in that the books are grouped more or less by order of size. There are such notable absences – for instance, there are only five copies of the Greek and Latin classics – that it can be assumed that there was another library elsewhere in the house. It also seems possible that the presence of explicitly Catholic works of religious controversy might argue that these books were kept in a space at least to some degree private.

In addition to some surprises and illuminations, such as the presence of a copy of Palladio's *Quatro Libri*, this list offers a real insight into an individual, a circle, and the mind of that circle. It might, without exaggeration, be claimed as a crucial document in the history of the later Renaissance in Scotland. It also offers evidence of the transmission of key texts and ideas from the international world of the Counter-Reformation baroque. Here is concrete evidence for the aspiration, at least among the élite of Scotland at the turn of the seventeenth century, to live in a way which participated in the international civilisation of Europe. Here also is a document which enables us to attain a considerable degree of certainty about the sometimes elusive nature of Catholic culture under penalty.

Seton's biography explains much about his cosmopolitan and comprehensive library. Archibald Symson, minister of Dalkieth, wrote in his *Hieroglyphica Animalium*, which is dedicated to Seton's son Charles, a sequence of elegiac verses on the death of the Chancellor, 'Musarum Lachrymae de obitu Cancellarii'.[7] Dalkeith is in East Lothian at no great distance from Seton's Pinkie House at Musselburgh, and there are suggestion of a patronage relationship in the verses, all of which would tend to suggest that Symson may have known about Seton's career in some detail. Extraordinary as the *curriculum vitae*, which Symson outlines, might appear for the Chancellor of Scotland in the years between the Reformation and the Covenant, the years which included the conversion of Queen Anne in the late 1590s and the martyrdom of St John Ogilvie in 1615,[8] his statements should be accorded a degree of credence:

> Scotia prima dedit lucem:
> dat Gallia semen Grammatices:
> docuit juraque Patavium
> Romaque rhetoricem, ubi notus Tullius ille
> Noscere scripta patrum, sic Salamanca dedit.
> Scotia prima dedit cui lumina, et ultima ademit;
> Haec fuit ipsa Parens, ipsa Noverca fuit.[9]

> [Scotland first gave him the light, France, the rudiments of grammar, Padua taught him the laws, and Rome, rhetoric, where [lived] that well-known Tullius, to know the words of the fathers, thus Salamanca taught him. Scotia

first gave him the light, and took it away at the last; she was thus both his parent and his stepmother.]

Given the political and religious position of Seton's father, as described by a hostile witness, it is unsurprising that he chose to educate a promising younger son in élite universities and colleges on the Continent:

> George Seton; an auncient baron, and of reasonable lyuinge, which lyeth all in Lothian, within 6 or 7 miles of Edenburgh. His power is not greate, nor his frendis or followers many. He hath ben alwayes Frenche in affection, and is in harte a Papiste, thoughe he dare not aduowe it. Of a nature busye and curyous; of more speche than iudgement; a principall instrument [of the] Sc. Quene and a harbourer of Jesuitis, and fugitiues of a countrye, and enemye to a peace.[10]

It seems unproblematic that Seton should have received his first education in France, but his Roman education needs an element of explanation. The *Oxford Dictionary of National Biography* confirms that '[i]n 1571, when he was about fifteen, he became a student at the Jesuit-run German College in Rome'.[11] This fact coexists with persistent assertions that he was a student of the Jesuit Collegio Romano, which has given rise to speculation that he might have studied for the priesthood.[12] The facts are less complex. The Collegium Germanicum functioned as a school for the sons of the nobility of many countries in Europe, and it was perhaps because of the status of the pupils that a student of the college had the privilege of making an oration to the Pope annually, Seton among them:

> He declaimed, not being 16 years of age, ane learned oration of his own composing, *De Ascensione Domini*, on that festival day publickly before the Pope, Gregory the 13th, the cardinall, and other prelats present, in the pope's chapel in the Vatican, with great applause.[13]

The older pupils had the opportunity of studying philosophy at the Collegio Romano, without being students for the priesthood themselves. Seton clearly stayed in Rome for long enough to undertake this senior study, probably until about 1576. From Italy he went to France, where he studied law. It is also perfectly possible that he spent some time in Padua: short periods of study at a celebrated college were very much a part of the early modern academic life. Symson's statement that Seton studied theology at Salamanca seems to be unique, however, although the sometimes inaccurate account in the continuation of Richard Maitland's *The History of the House of Seytoun to 1559* does assert that Sir John Seton of Barnes was in Spain and at the court of Philip II there, where he was awarded a golden key – perplexingly, like the one worn at Alexander Seton's wrist in the portrait of him by Marcus Gheeraerts now in the Scottish National Portrait Gallery.[14] According to his kinsman Alexander Seton Viscount Kingston (*d.* 1691), the results of the Chancellor's education were that he became 'a great humanist in prose and poesie, Greek and Latine; well versed in the mathematics and great skill in architecture and herauldrie'.[15] At last, the discovery of the library list enables some estimate to be made of this learning and cultivation, and it would seem that his consistent application of the examples of high Renaissance design and ideas of civility to his own environments indeed validates this estimate of him. His inscription on his house and garden at Pinkie is well known: in a polity in which the possession of a fortified house was perhaps the prime signifier of gentry status, he makes a point that his is an unfortified 'villa suburbana' dedicated to the Horatian virtues of friendship and temperate hospitality.[16]

In February 1588 Seton's religious position was forced to a crisis when the king named him an ordinary lord of session; his colleagues were understandably suspicious about his religious views, given his personal and family background, and insisted that he commit himself to the established Church by taking communion and making its confession of faith.[17] He did so, and for the rest of his life apparently conformed, although he continually maintained contact with proscribed Catholics, especially Jesuits. His success as a civil servant in a time when able government ministers were crucial to the survival and governance of the Scottish kingdom seems in practice to have bought him a very considerable latitude to practise – and, indeed, promote – his religion in private, albeit at no great distance from the capital. To two Scottish Jesuits who visited him clandestinely in 1605 Seton professed his loyalty to the ancient faith, but explained that the time for an attempt to restore it had not yet come. 'He is now all-powerful in Scotland, but he will attempt nothing until he sees a solid foundation of hope,' they concluded. 'Meanwhile he takes his portion in this life, though at the risk of that which is eternal.'[18] The origin of this opinion summarised by Forbes-Leith would seem to be a letter dated 30 September 1605 from William Crichton SJ to the superior general of the Society of Jesus, Claudio Acquaviva in Rome, in which he expresses his conclusion that, although Seton is a 'Church papist', he fosters Catholicism at home in the context of a wholly Catholic family: 'For the present several times he went with the others to confession and communion, with his mother, brother, sister and nephews who are more resolute Catholics.'[19]

Seton's religious status is also brought into a letter expressing Jesuit wishful thinking about the conversion of James VI:

> Alexander Seton was created Chancellor of the Realm of Scotland, by command of the King, he [Seton] being an alumnus of the College [re]founded by Gregory 13 of happy memory. He studied Philosophy and Theology in the Seminarium Romanum, but to a considerable extent, and to his own great harm, pretends to agree to the religion of the Heretics, however the King in truth knows him to be a Catholic.[20]

Perhaps it is only now, in possession of an indication of the contents of Seton's private library, that it is possible to know the extent to which he remained Catholic in private. As a 'Church papist' (if the phrase is wholly applicable to Scotland) he contrived to elude serious public trouble on account of his religion, perhaps with the exceptions of his early indiscretion in 1583 in corresponding with the Collegio Romano using a Jesuit courier, and the more serious religious riot in Edinburgh, mostly directed at him, in 1597. Perhaps it is worth remembering that those who governed Scotland throughout the reign of James VI were in many cases pragmatically suspicious of the extreme forms of Calvinism, simply because they rendered governance so problematic.[21] The retrospective Victorian narrative of a united Calvinist nation is far from the truth, especially in the north-eastern counties of Scotland, where Seton held the castle and lands of Fyvie as well as the former priory of Pluscarden. In Aberdeenshire and Moray mutual toleration between an Episcopalian majority and an influential Catholic minority seems to have coexisted with widespread suspicion of the more extreme manifestations of Presbyterianism. At Fyvie, there is some archaeological evidence for a building standing in Seton's time which may well have been a Catholic chapel.[22] Certainly, post-Reformation oratories survive to this day at the neighbouring castles of Towie Barclay and Delgaty, and the neighbouring gentry families of Dempster of Muiresk and Conn of Auchry both produced notable Catholic writers and apologists in the early modern period.

Even at Pinkie House at Musselburgh, near Edinburgh, which Seton remodelled extensively, the style of architecture is to a notable extent that of the contemporary Continent. The remarkable painted gallery there is a learned room, most certainly an evocation or recreation of classical antiquity, but, in its series of emblem paintings and related inscriptions, it is also redolent of contemporary Jesuit cultures of emblemata and the *affixiones*. Indeed, the ranks of emblems on the unified theme of the wise conduct of a life recall the visual culture of festal days in a Jesuit college.[23] Certainly, the gallery's emblems and inscriptions convey a message of stoicism, self-control, and wariness as well as praising the merits of friendship, hospitality, and retirement. It also seems wholly possible that Seton fostered an explicitly Counter-Reformation educational culture there, whereas on his lands in Moray he seems to have gone to some lengths to preserve his control over what remained of the priory of Pluscarden. All of Seton's known activities, cultural and religious, can to some degree be related to the books listed as being in his private library, so the remainder of this chapter looks first at the composition of the library as recorded and then at some key works in it, considering their relation to Seton's house and world.

First, it must be emphasised that this list cannot encompass all the books which can be conjectured to have been in Seton's possession: not only are the

Greek and Latin classics almost entirely absent, with only three ancient Latin works and two Greek (as well as, possibly, the *Corpus Poetarum* – a title widely used, and therefore hard to identify with a specific book), but there are also several works which can be identified as having been used in the composition of the gallery ceiling but which are not in the book list. Even so, the document is rich in its implications. Perhaps the first thing to strike a historian of the book in Scotland is the ease with which Seton would appear to have obtained continental editions. Many of the books which he owned can be identified with works published mostly in northern Europe in the 1580s and 1590s. There are continental printings from the first two decades of the seventeenth century, and there seems to be a small group of early seventeenth-century London printings. If Seton did indeed own the whole of the *Annales Ecclesiastici*, which appeared at Rome volume by volume from 1588 to 1607, beginning eight years after Seton's own return to Scotland, then he must have obtained it directly from the Continent, perhaps through those Jesuit contacts which he apparently maintained despite his outward religious conformity. It is, in any case, of some significance that he owned such a current and distinguished contribution to the debate on contemporary religious confessions and ecclesiastical history. Compared to the library of Seton's friend and fellow 'Octavian' in the governance of Scotland, John Lindsay (Lord Menmuir as a law lord), in so far as ongoing research has been able to reconstruct it largely from copies now at Balcarres House, Seton would appear to have had greater funds to lay out on recent editions, many of them expensive illustrated folios, than his friend, and he seems also to have had access to continental books far beyond that afforded by the comparatively modest book trade of Scotland in his time. A number of his noble Scottish contemporaries sent to Paris for their books, as he may also have done.[24]

The first reflection prompted by this list of some 85 volumes is that Seton owned a remarkable number of illustrated books concerned with art and architecture. His copy of Palladio is certainly the first recorded in Scotland, but it appears among ten works on related subjects, including 'Architectura de Marchii folio', 'Architectura di Sebastiano Serlio folio', and 'Leçons de perspective positive folio' – altogether an exceptional number. Seton's interest in current debates and controversies between religious confessions, particularly those drawing on ecclesiastical and secular history, is not only attested by his ownership of Baronius and eight volumes of works by Greek Fathers of the Church (his holdings of Latin fathers are considerably more modest at four volumes) but is also evinced by the fact that he owned ten works of pro-Catholic controversy and apologetics, including the profoundly Counter-Reformation St Robert Bellarmine. His ownership of the works of St Thomas More may have been prompted by an interest in More both as a martyr and as a humanist. There is a group of six works on clocks, chronography, and the reckoning of time – an interest unsurprising in a modernising statesman who also had mathematical and technical interests, attested by three and four books respectively. These interests were evidently known to contemporary Scottish scientists, since Seton was the dedicatee of John Napier's celebrated book on logarithms, *Rhabdologia* (1617). Another mathematician, Robert Pont (father of the famous cartographer Timothy Pont), dedicated *A Newe Treatise of the Right Reckoning of Year and Ages of the World* (1599) to him, describing him as foremost of the 'rare Mecenases of this Land'.[25]

Overall, we can observe that he owned an exceptional number of books in Greek and in French. The influence of Seton's continental education is everywhere apparent, and the library list indicates a man and a circle of exceptional cultivation – perhaps the single household in Scotland most in tune with the later continental Renaissance and the emerging baroque of the Counter-Reformation.

One use of Seton's library may have been for the purpose of education: there are several indications that there was sustained educational activity within his household, and that the instruction offered was distinctly Catholic. There is reason to think that the son of Seton's colleague Lord Menmuir, David Lindsay, later Lord Balcarres and husband of Seton's daughter Sophia, may have received his education with Seton. His mother, Marion Guthrie, requested, in her final letter to her husband, that her brother-in-law Lord Edzell, along with Edzell and Menmuir's nephew by marriage, Alexander Seton, be asked to extend their protection to the Balcarres children.[26]

A notebook of 1603 belonging to the young David Lindsay survives in the Crawford papers in the National Library of Scotland.[27] In the last months of that year, at the age of 16, Lindsay was engaged in serious and intensive study of the Latin classics. The notebook records a thorough study of each text, excerpting vocabulary and 'sententiae' – interesting, pithy phrases which might in future ornament a speech or an essay. When he finished with a work, he noted the date in Latin form, which shows that he was reading with some intensity: in September he read Terence, Sallust, the third book of Cicero's *De Officiis*, Plautus's *Miles Gloriosus*, Tibullus, Catullus, Cicero on Sallust, Juvenal, Cicero's *Ad Familiares*, and Propertius. On the one hand, this demonstrates he was already well able to comprehend long and complex works of Latin literature. On the other, unless he was an exceptional 16-year-old, it also strongly suggests that he was reading under direction; the dates suggest as much, as does the assiduity with which the notebook is maintained.

One specific indication that the studies represented by David Lindsay's 1603 notebook may have taken place at Pinkie is an unusual inclusion.

Along with the standard authors, Lindsay was reading Cassander on rhetoric, by which he presumably means *Tabulæ præceptionum dialecticarum, quæ quam breuissimè & planissimè artis methodum complectuntur*, printed by Wechel in Paris in 1548. George Cassander (1513–1566) was an eirenist who attempted to reconcile the Catholic and Protestant Churches. He did so from genuine knowledge of the theologies of both, thus constituting himself precisely the kind of writer to interest Seton, whose private library is heavily inclined to questions of religious controversy.

There is certainly clear evidence for educational activity late in the sixteenth century: in 1593 Lord Seton's children were being tutored by Steine Ballantyne, a Catholic who had been forbidden to teach in schools on account of his religion.[28] Balcarres was both intimate with the family, choosing Seton's daughter Sophia as his wife, and evidently knew Seton's library at Pinkie House well, since it was he who drew up the list of books at Pinkie which is the focus of this chapter.

Thomas Seget or Segetius (1569–1627), a wandering scholar and distinguished Latin poet who came from Seton in East Lothian, was also associated with Seton's household. Seget was in the Lothians, making a living as a schoolmaster in the 1590s: in the summer of 1594 Alexander Seton ignored the presbytery of Haddington's warning against employing Seget (a Catholic, probably a convert) to compose a funeral oration on one of his brothers.[29] A few months after this defiance of the Kirk, Seget was in Antwerp, and never again returned to Scotland.[30] Thereafter he travelled widely, wrote admired verse, and met many of the leading scholars of his day. The astronomer Johannes Kepler (1571–1630) records Seget and himself looking for the moons of Jupiter together in the autumn of 1610 and confirming Galileo's epoch-making discovery of satellites which did not go round the Earth.[31] There is no evidence that Seget stayed in touch with Alexander Seton, although it is worth noting that Seton owned the complete works of Justus Lipsius, Seget's friend and patron in the years immediately after he first left Scotland. Nevertheless, Seget did meet both a William Seton, possibly Alexander's brother, and David Lindsay of Balcarres's Catholic uncle, Walter Lindsay, in Louvain in 1597.[32]

Seton's ownership of Baronius and his interest in ecclesiastical history, demonstrated by the library list, both serve to focus attention on his relationship with the one ecclesiastical building (if we except the probable chapel at Fyvie Castle in Aberdeenshire) which was, to a considerable extent, under his control: Pluscarden Priory, near Elgin in Moray. Seton's relationship with Pluscarden lasted throughout his life and offers at least one possible piece of evidence for a limited survival of monasticism in Scotland, as well as a striking instance of the degree to which the Catholic magnates of the north-eastern counties could, with discretion, continue to practise and advance their religion.

Seton was given the title and office of prior of Pluscarden as a baptismal gift by his godmother, Mary Queen of Scots in 1556, and, after the Reformation, he continued to hold the temporalities of Pluscarden, controlling the lands and revenues of a monastic house which had (at least in theory) been dissolved. Between 1571 and 1580, when Seton was absent on the Continent, he was deprived of Pluscarden for his failure to conform to the established Protestant Church in 1577. He recovered the temporalities of the abbey in 1581, however, with the fall of the regent, James Douglas, fourth Earl of Morton. In 1587 an exception was made in Seton's favour (he had just played a considerable part in implementing James VI's legislative programme) when all other Church lands came into the possession of the Crown.[33] He received the lands of Pluscarden as a barony later in the same year, thus obtaining a considerable degree of autonomy and control over monastery buildings and lands on the edges of the area where there was most support for the survival of Catholicism.[34]

The reticence of the dissident areas in the northern counties complicates any certainty about the state of Pluscarden under Seton's protection, but there are possibilities that some form of monastic life continued there after the Reformation, although considerable caution is required when advancing this theory as anything more than a conjecture.[35] Certainly, Stephen Holmes's 'Sixteenth-Century Pluscarden Priory and Its World' reminds us that Pluscarden was unusual 'in that none of the monks were known to have served the new Kirk and Dom Thomas Ross ... certainly remained loyal to the old Kirk', to the extent of annotating his Bible as though preparing to compose a work of religious controversy, distinctly hostile to Protestantism.[36] It seems that Dom Thomas was the only monk left at Pluscarden by 1587, but the records of the kirk session of Elgin note that 'the monk of Pluscarden' baptised children in April and May 1599.[37]

Although Pluscarden was subjected to iconoclastic vandalism at the Reformation, the presence there of a tabernacle or aumbry which looks as though it is made up of two distinct pieces which do not quite match raises the possibility of a repair sponsored by Seton in the shadowy period of the 1580s or 1590s, as part of some kind of continuance as suggested by the activities of Dom Thomas Ross.[38] Given the degree to which the Catholics of the north managed both to practise their religion and to cover their tracks, such a repair remains within the realm of the possible.

This chapter finds a conclusion in the next generation, with another composite tabernacle in a secluded chapel. During Seton's lifetime David Lindsay, later first Lord Balcarres, married Seton's daughter Sophia, in 1612. There survives at Balcarres, near the house, a free-standing chapel, which bears a datestone for 1635 and the initials of David Lord Balcarres and Sophia Lady Balcarres.[39] This also contains what appears to be a composite aumbry or tabernacle, one of two niches, 'two late-gothic aumbries set in the eastern ends of the side walls. They are similar in character but the southern one has a garland issuing from a cartouche carved on either jamb.'[40] Although it is course possible that the late Gothic niche was united at some subsequent date with the stylistically mid-seventeenth-century garlands which flank it, if it was part of the original scheme of 1635, as seems probable, it is, as the *Buildings of Scotland* entry for Balcarres phrases it, 'a surprising feature for a protestant chapel of this date'.[41] It certainly bears the appearance of a tabernacle, and the strong possibility exists that Seton's daughter was responsible for building one of the very first free-standing post-Reformation Catholic churches in Britain – an honour usually awarded to the Weld chapel at Lulworth in Dorset, a century and more later.

Notes

1 The quotation is of the words of Helena Wyntour, designer and maker of ecclesiastical textiles; George Gray SJ to Joseph Simons SJ, 17 November 1668, ABSI, Mount Street, London, MS A.I.22.1; Cardinal Guido Bentivoglio to Cardinal Borghese from Saint-Omer, 18 October, 1609, 'I wore a cope which once belonged to Henry VIII [*sic*] and which is preserved here as a rich and rare memorial': Henry Foley (ed.), *The Records of the English Province of the Society of Jesus* (London: Burns and Oates, 1883), p. 1153. On the Madonna Vulnerata and commissioned works in the chapels of the English Colleges at Rome and Valladolid, see chapters 6 and 7.

2 For a census of all surviving copies of the *Breviarium*, see Stevenson, Beavan, and Davidson, 'The Breviary of Aberdeen'.

3 The *Liber Sconensis* would seem to have been a manuscript of Walter Bower's *Scotichronicon*, most probably that identified in a manuscript list of the Abbé Thomas Innes, Edinburgh University Library, MS Laing iii, 513, vol. 3, ff. 57–69, as in the possession of 'D. Robt Sybbald', and possibly to be identified with the 'Brechin' MS of the *Scotichronicon*, now Scottish Record Office, MS GD 45/26/48. See Bower, *Scotichronicon*, IX, pp. 188–9.

4 On Seton's work at Fyvie, see Shannon Marguerite Fraser, '"To Receive Guests with Kindness": Symbols of Hospitality, Nobility and Diplomacy in Alexander Seton's Designed Landscape at Fyvie Castle', *Architectural Heritage*, 26.1 (2015), pp. 121–40. On the ceiling at Pinkie House, see Bath, *Renaissance Decorative Painting in Scotland*, pp. 79–103, and 'Philostratus Comes to Scotland: A New Source for the Pictures at Pinkie', *Journal of the Northern Renaissance*, 5 (2013), www.northernrenaissance.org/philostratus-comes-to-scotland-a-new-source-for-the-pictures-at-pinkie (retrieved 17 January 2015).

5 Maurice Lee, 'Seton, Alexander, First Earl of Dunfermline (1556–1622)', *Oxford Dictionary of National Biography* (2015), https://doi-org.ezproxy-prd.bodleian.ox.ac.uk/10.1093/ref:odnb/25113 (retrieved online 12 August 2023).

6 National Library of Scotland, Crawford and Balcarres Papers, Acc. 9769/14/2/2. All quotations from the papers are by kind permission of the Earl of Crawford and Balcarres.
7 Archibald Symson, *Hieroglyphica animalium terrestrium, volatilium, natatilium, reptilium, insectorum, vegetivorum, metallorum, lapidum: &c: Quae in scripturis Sacris inveniuntur & plurimorum aliorum, cum eorum interpretationibus, ob theologiae studiosos* (Edinburgh: Thomas Finlason, 1624).
8 Thomas McCoog SJ and Peter Davidson, 'Father Robert's Convert: the Private Catholicism of Anne of Denmark', *Times Literary Supplement* (24 November 2000), pp. 16–17.
9 Symson, *Hieroglyphica animalium*, sig. ¶ 2.
10 '*Present State of the Nobility of Scotland*, 1583', in *Bannatyne Miscellany* I (Edinburgh: for the Ballantyne Club, 1827), p. 69.
11 Lee, 'Seton, Alexander'.
12 This confusion may even lie behind the puzzling entry in one of the lists of men on the Scottish Mission in ARSI, MS Anglia 42: Alexander Seton, 'si sit sacerdos'.
13 Richard Maitland, *The History of the House of Seytoun to 1559, with the continuation by Alex. Viscount Kinston to 1687* (Glasgow: Maitland Club, 1829), p. 63.
14 *Ibid.*, pp. 61–2.
15 *Ibid.*, p. 63.
16 Inscription reproduced and discussed in Bath, 'Philostratus Comes to Scotland'.
17 Lee, 'Seton, Alexander'.
18 William Forbes-Leith SJ, *Narratives of Scottish Catholics under Mary Stuart and James VI* (Edinburgh: William Paterson, 1885), p. 187.
19 'Interim aliquoties in omno venit ad confessionem et communionem catholicum cum matre, fratre sorore ac nepotibus qui sunt catholici constantiores': William Crichton to General Acquaviva, 30 September 1605, ARSI, Rome, MS Anglia 42, f. 197.
20 'Regni Scotiae cancellarium qui pro Regis officio fungitur creavit Alexandrum Setonium, piae memoriae Gregorii 13 alumnum. Hic in Seminario Romano studuit Philosophise et Theologiae et quamvis suo magnomalo simulavit cum Haereticis consentire, Rex tamen probe scit eum esse Catholicum': ARSI, Rome, MS Anglia 42, f. 261.
21 Seton's friend and associate, John Lindsay of Balcarres, Lord Menmuir (1552–1598), Secretary of State, is recorded as having owned a now lost copy of the Jesuit James Tyrie's *The Refutation of ane Answer made be Schir John Knox to ane letter be James Tyrie* (Paris, 1573), and, certainly, his own attempts to foster Protestant episcopacy elicited the continual hostility of the Presbyterians.
22 See Fraser, ' "To Receive Guests with Kindness" ', p. 131.
23 For Jesuit festal *affixiones*, see Porteman, *Emblematic Exhibitions (Affixiones)*.
24 Jane Stevenson, 'Centres and Peripheries: Early Modern British Writers in a European Context', *The Library: The Transactions of the Bibliographical Society*, Seventh Series, 21.2 (2020), pp. 157–91, at pp. 162–5.

25 Robert Pont, *A Newe Treatise of the Right Reckoning of Yeares, and Ages of the World, and Mens Liues, and of the Estate of the Last Decaying Age Thereof* (Edinburgh: Robert Waldegraue, 1599), sig. A2.
26 His first wife was Lilias Drummond, daughter of Menmuir and Edzell's sister Elizabeth Lindsay and Patrick, third Lord Drummond. She died in 1601.
27 NLS, MS Acc 9769 14/8/2.
28 Keith Brown, *Noble Society in Scotland* (Edinburgh: Edinburgh University Press, 2003), p. 183.
29 Brown, *Noble Society*, p. 264. Seget appears to have matriculated at the University of Leiden in 1589; after intensive humanist study under Justus Lipsius, he returned to Edinburgh in 1595. Szabolcs Ö. Barlay, 'Thomas Seget's (from Edinborough) Middle European Connections in Reflection of Cod. Vat. Lat. 9385', *Magyar Könyvzsemle*, 97 (1981), pp. 204–20, at p. 208.
30 Seget's *album amicorum*, Biblioteca Apostolica Vaticana, Vat. Lat. 9385, yields information about his peregrinations and distinguished contacts in the late 1590s; further information about Seget can be found in Tom McInally, *The Sixth Scottish University: The Scots Colleges Abroad, 1575–1799* (Leiden: Brill, 2012), pp. 91–4.
31 Edward Rosen, 'Thomas Seget of Seton', *The Scottish Historical Review* 28 (1947), pp. 91–5.
32 In 1596 Spanish sources speak of Lindsay as in Spain, negotiating with the government under the pseudonym of Don Balthasar. He must then have gone to Italy. While abroad he composed his *Relación del estado del reyno de Escocia, en lo tocante a nuestra religion catolica*, which was printed in Madrid in 1594.
33 Lee, 'Seton, Alexander'.
34 A 'barony' in this context is, approximately, a landholding with certain rights of exercising justice.
35 I am much indebted to Dr Stephen Holmes for his published work on this subject, and for his advocacy of caution.
36 Stephen Holmes, 'Sixteenth-Century Pluscarden Priory and Its World', *The Innes Review*, 58.1 (2007), pp. 35–71, at p. 62. Holmes here cites Mark Dilworth, *Scottish Monasteries in the Late Middle Ages* (Edinburgh: Edinburgh University Press, 1995), p. 79. Thomas Ross's annotated Bible survives at Aberdeen University Library, BCL A648.
37 Holmes, 'Sixteenth-Century Pluscarden', p. 70.
38 I am most grateful to Dr Holmes, Dr David Walker *filius*, and Professor Richard Fawcett for their kind advice on this matter. It seems clear that the present state of the tabernacle is the result of a repair but that the date of that repair must remain an open question, in that there is no visual record of the state of the church at Pluscarden before the late eighteenth century.
39 Royal Commission on the Ancient and Historical Monuments and Constructions of Scotland, *Eleventh Report with Inventory of Monuments and Constructions in the Counties of Fife Kinross and Clackmannan* (Edinburgh: HMSO, 1933), no. 311, pp. 163–4.
40 *Ibid.*, p. 164.
41 John Gifford, *The Buildings of Scotland: Fife* (London: Penguin, 1988), p. 83.

15

Paper gardens

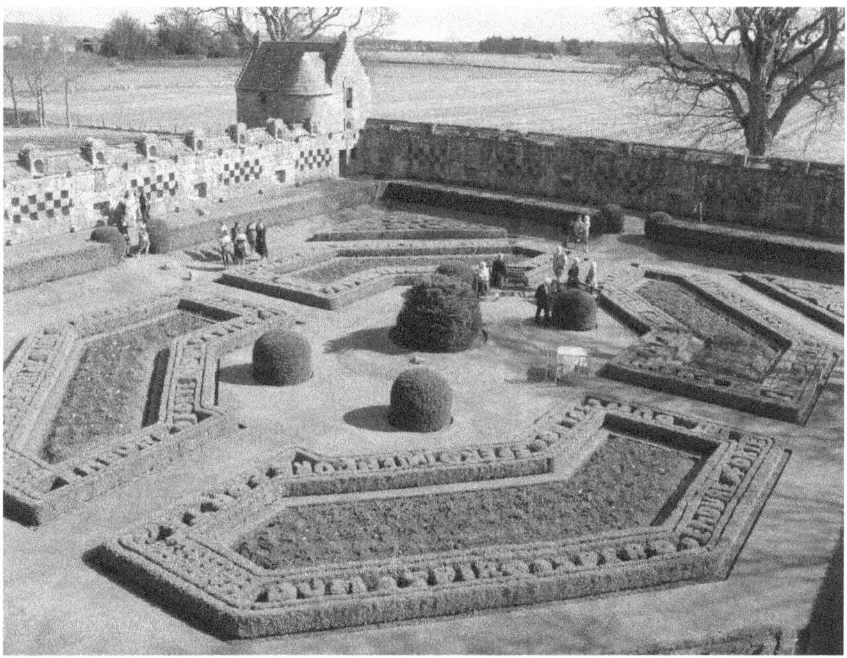

Figure 15.1 The early seventeenth-century walled garden at Edzell Castle in Angus, Scotland, laid out for Sir David Lindsay, Lord Edzell (*c.* 1551–1610).

Scottish links to the Continent in the Renaissance and early modern periods were complex and far-reaching: close cultural relations with France – court culture, publication, education – lasted for centuries before dwindling after the disastrous reign of Mary Queen of Scots. After the Reformation, Scotland turned increasingly to the United Provinces of the Netherlands, developing an increasingly close cultural and education relation particularly with the Dutch universities of Leiden and Utrecht. In this chapter a series of

Scottish gardens are investigated. First, we look at the Scoto-French garden at Edzell in Angus, laid out for Sir David Lindsay (Lord Edzell, as a Scottish law lord) in the very early seventeenth century (see Figure 15.1). Then there is the fictitious garden of the protagonist of Scott's novel *The Antiquary*, and the late seventeenth- and early eighteenth-century garden writings of Sir George Mackenzie of Rosehaugh, of his gardener John Reid, and the writings of the Leiden graduate, and likely model for Scott's antiquary, Sir John Clerk of Penicuik.

The French influence on Scottish élite gardening of the end of the sixteenth century, and the very beginning of the seventeenth, is exemplified by the partially surviving layouts at Edzell Castle in Angus, for Sir David Lindsay, Lord Edzell. Study of the early libraries belonging to the Lindsay family[1] adds to our knowledge of one probable source for the garden which Lord Edzell laid out there in the first decade of the seventeenth century. Some knowledge of the relevant works in his library, together with an antiquarian (or chorographical) description of the Edzell gardens as they were in maturity, offer some clues about the nature of the whole layout, of which the celebrated walled pleasance which survives today formed only a comparatively small, if important, part. These sources, together with what survives of Lord Edzell's correspondence, suggest a prudent mode of interpreting what Marilyn Brown has called the 'elaborate intellectual framework' of the walled garden,[2] further developing the lines of investigation set forth in a 2004 article on the garden by the present Earl of Crawford and Balcarres.[3]

It would be hard to better the summary of the surviving garden at Edzell offered by Marilyn Brown's book,[4] with its comprehensive account of the whole layout as Lord Edzell's creation, her survey of his activities as grower and planter of trees, his exchanges of seeds and saplings with other noblemen, and his horticultural correspondence with his brother, Lord Menmuir. She gives an admirably clear account of the three sequences of carved panels in the walled garden: planetary deities, liberal arts, and cardinal virtues. She also notes, importantly, that 'the walled garden was part of a larger scheme for the policies of Edzell Castle', and cites the late seventeenth-century description by Mr Ouchterlonie, minister of Guynde,[5] as evidence for this the last state of the garden before its sale and decline. Presumably this decline accounts for the estate's minimal appearance as 'Slatefoord', with only a faint indication of crossing avenues, in the Great Military Survey of Scotland, made under the direction of General Roy in the aftermath of the Jacobite rising of 1745.[6]

Brown also cites the loan of books between the brothers, which offers us these further clues as to the nature of the whole layout:

> David Lindsay also sent Lord Menmuir a copy of a work by the Roman writer Columella and *La Maison Rustique*, presumably the book by Charles Estienne and Jean Liebault, published in Paris in 1578.[7]

Neither of these copies, 'whilk will serve for my idleness in Balcarres', as Lord Menmuir wrote, seems to have survived the troubles which beset the Lindsay libraries later in the seventeenth century, but it is clear that these two treatises on the cultivation of land and husbandry were valued as guides for the family's intense improving projects in the later sixteenth century.

It is not possible to reconstruct which of the editions of the book by the Roman writer on agriculture, Lucius Junius Moderatus Columella's *De Re Rustica*, might have passed between the brothers. There were Paris editions of 1533 and 1556, a Lyons edition of 1548, and a Heidelberg edition of 1595. There were also numerous editions of the highly popular *Agriculture et Maison Rustique*. Charles Estienne (1504–64), a physician and polymath from a family of humanist printers, published *Praedium Rusticum* at Paris in 1554, which was republished posthumously in French translation as *Agriculture et Maison Rustique*, most probably in 1567, with a celebrated augmented edition in 1586. In this form it became one of the most successful books of horticulture and estate management of the later Renaissance, and was frequently reprinted. We know that it formed part of the library at Edzell because of the loan cited above, but it is not possible to conjecture precisely in which edition.

Records of the state of the policies at Edzell as improved by Lord Edzell are, unfortunately, extremely sparse. Sadly, the drawn proposal for the construction of a walled 'City of Edzell', among the Crawford papers in the National Library of Scotland,[8] does no more than indicate a schematic plantation of trees near the castle: there is no more precise indication of that larger layout which can be conjectured from descriptions and from the assumption that at least the broad guidelines of *La Maison Rustique* influenced the design.

If we explore the theory that the layout at Edzell beyond the surviving walled garden might plausibly have followed the directions of *La Maison Rustique* (and there is certainly enough level or levelled ground around the castle and garden for this to be wholly possible), the only witness to these extended policies in their brief maturity is Mr Ouchterlonie, the minister of Guynde in Angus, writing, according to Lord Lindsay, in the very early eighteenth century:[9]

> Edzell, says an Angusshire gentleman, reporting the statistics of his county to Sir Robert Sibbald, at the beginning of the last century, 'lies close to the hills, betweixt the water called the Wast-water and the water of North esk, which, joining together, make as it were a demi-island therof. It is an extraordinar warm and ear place, so the fruits will be ready there a fortnight sooner than in any place of the shire, and hath a greater increase of bear and other grain than can be expected elsewhere.
>
> The Castle or Place of Edzell is an excellent dwelling, a great house, delicate garden, with walls sumptuously built of hewn stone, polished, with pictures and coats of arms in the walls with a fine summer house, with a house for a

> bath on the South corner therof, far exceeding any new work of their times – excellent kitchen garden and orchard, with diverse kinds of most excellent fruits and most delicate ...
>
> It has an excellent outer court, so large and level that of old, when they used that sport, they used to play at the football there, and there are still four great growing trees, which were the dools [goalposts] ...

Lord Lindsay also mentions 'avenues of most stately beech' which approached the castle until the early eighteenth century; these are perhaps the features no more than sketched on Roy's map.

All of this would be congruent with a layout along the lines of those proposed in *La Maison Rustique*, which recommends a private flower garden for the master of the house, with fragrant plants planted within a formally patterned parterre, that this enclosure should be hedged or walled, and that it should be divided by handsome walks or alleys from extensive kitchen gardens and orchards.[10] This would be an entirely possible overall scheme for Edzell, and would at least raise some concrete possibilities for the planting and layout of the walled garden itself.

Sir David Lindsay of Edzell wrote from Edinburgh in 1588 that 'the sound of chirping birds' brought to mind the northern mountains, 'albeit presentlie environit with thair quhyte winter robbes, yit befoir I visie thame sall be deckit with thair grene fragrant May garmentis'.[11] This sounds very like a concentrated recollection of the opening of chapter XLVII of book II of *La Maison Rustique*,[12] which describes the pleasures of having the parterre or private flower garden under the windows of the house – as at Edzell – with the music of birds joining with the scent of herbs and flowers: 'La ioyeuse Musique d'une infinité d'oizillons, qui sans cesse iour et nuict degoisent leur natif et naturel ramage sure les hayes et arbres du parterre.' The layout of the pleasance at Edzell is also congruent with that suggested in *La Maison Rustique*, although the Scottish requirement for garden walls and the decision to adorn them has taken the place of covered walks of trained trees surrounding the garden; even so, the summer house and former bath-house at Edzell serve the purposes of Estienne's corner cabinets of verdure 'comme petites chapelles et oratoires'.[13]

Estienne's chapter XLIX ('La forme de disposer les herbes par compartimens de diverses façons')[14] offers a very reasonable suggestion as to how the area within the walled garden may originally have been laid out: an overall pattern formed of low hedges of lavender or rosemary (Estienne suggests that box, 'with its unpleasant smell', is a last resort for inclement sites) fills the whole of the enclosed space, and within it the beds are filled with sweet-smelling flowers. Indeed, scent would seem to be the defining factor of the private flower garden as envisaged in *La Maison Rustique*, and we are reminded that Lord Edzell's English employee, Henry Lok, wrote on 29 May 1592 that 'I sent yow of late some sorts of seeds, most of flowers, I hope they will growe',[15] which suggests that some scheme of this sort was in fact being tried as early as the 1590s. It is also emphasised by Estienne that access to this scented parterre should be restricted,[16] and that it is a place which chiefly belongs to the master of the house,[17] as opposed to the more practical gardens 'potagers' of medicinal herbs, vegetables, and the orchards which lie beyond its enclosure.[18]

Bearing in mind this identification of the private garden, the pleasance, with the master of the house, another beneficial aspect of a comprehensive re-examination of the early Lindsay family libraries in this context is to place in proportion persistent 'urban myths' that David Lindsay of Edzell was unusually interested in Hermetic philosophy, following an extensive continental education, and that the relief panels in the walled garden accordingly follow some esoteric programme.[19] In fact, Lord Edzell's foreign experience consisted only of a short period in Paris and a few months of auditing lectures at Cambridge;[20] his education otherwise was restricted to Scotland. Although it is absolutely the case that his nephew, Lord Balcarres, had an intense interest in Hermetic and Rosicrucian texts, copying, disseminating, and translating them, this was in the next generation. Indeed, Lord Edzell ceased to take an active interest in his estates in the last two years of his life, overshadowed as they were by family catastrophe, and the diminishing quality of the work on the cardinal virtues panels in the walled garden seems to indicate this general slackening and decline. Thus, if Lord Edzell ceased to take an active and creative part in the making of the garden around 1608, this is distinctly too early for even the earliest Rosicrucian texts to have reached him from the Continent.[21]

It is extremely difficult to deduce a character of Lord Edzell from his surviving books: it is hard to feel that any sort of indicative sample survives, but there is nothing to contradict the view that, compared to his brother, he was intellectually cautious, although he was clearly committed to the modernisation of his estates and of the kind of life which he lived on them, bringing his own experience into line with that of the élite of northern Europe. In the context of this, it is worth remembering that the greater part of the content of *La Maison Rustique* is devoted to the improvement of the kitchen garden and the orchard, and therefore to the provision of a better range of material to the kitchen and table – something which Lord Edzell would appear to have valued.[22]

Although the exploitation of the mineral potential of the Angus estates and the employment of continental mining experts was clearly of importance to Lord Edzell, these enterprises were very much undertaken in partnership with his brother, Lord Menmuir, and they seem to have been strictly practical.[23] Inferences that his interests extended to alchemy are not supported by what has survived of his library and correspondence. The Earl of Crawford's study of the gardens, however, sets forth the connections frequently made in the late Renaissance between the chief metals and the planetary deities – which provides a solid context for their presence within the microcosmic scheme at Edzell, although we could further observe that Lord Edzell also owned what is now known as the 'Inchbrake Medical Manuscript', which contains an astrological calendar and a work on the zodiac, a treatise on auspicious days for bloodletting, as well as a treatise by an unknown author: *Expositio Effectuum Planetarum*.[24] None of this is exceptional; it might be said to be a summary of standard Renaissance beliefs about the planets, but it provides a general background for the bas-reliefs in the Edzell garden as part of a scheme with a straightforward focus on what we might call 'man the microcosm, formed by natal influences (as expressed by the planets), education, and the practise of virtue' – a scheme wholly congruent with contemporary ideas about the individual and the individual's place in the world.

Insofar as a reading suggests itself for the sequences of bas-reliefs on the garden walls, it is the kind of microcosm which might be expected of a Renaissance garden: the human individual is a little universe, and that individual is made up of innate influences, education, and the cultivation of virtues. Each sequence at Edzell is progressive: the planets in their ancient order, progress through the educational curriculum and, finally, the theological virtues lead to the quotidian virtues to be manifested in the life of a Renaissance individual – Fortitude, Prudence, Temperance. Of course, such an easily memorable scheme, with its logical sequences, would have lent itself to use in the widespread early modern art of memory, essentially a scheme for complex memorisation based on the visualisation of real or imaginary space and the physical arrangement of mnemonic objects therein. But it is not especially arcane; more a scheme based in the solid basis of the humanistic learning of the time.[25]

So, as something of a microcosmic, idealised self-portrait of the master of the house, the pleasance at Edzell could be compared to the neo-Stoic painted gallery executed for the Lindsays' friend and connection Alexander Seton, first Earl of Dunfermline at Pinkie House,[26] a self-portrait which is also a place of contemplation. The other point of comparison would be with the sadly rearranged, and disarranged, sequence of carved panels at Craigston Castle Aberdeenshire, which also includes the virtues, as well as Scottish monarchs and the Nine Worthies – quite possibly the jumbled remains of a mnemotechnic scheme.[27] All of this combines to suggest that Edzell Castle and its estate, as it survives and as it was, offered and offers yet another testimony to the Lindsay family's early and thorough reception of the humanistic learning of their day – learning which came to them through those works which constituted the early Lindsay libraries.

Sir Walter Scott's knowledge of early modern Scotland seems ever more remarkable as present-day historians' investigations catch up with his casual encyclopaedism. Even in the obscure and thinly documented area of early modern relations between Scotland and the Netherlands in the sphere of the garden, he had some knowledge on which to draw. Indeed, his entire novel *The Antiquary*, first published in 1816 and reissued in revised form in 1829, is an incidental monument to the long intellectual connection between the Kingdom of Scotland and the universities of the United Provinces of the Netherlands, especially Leiden.

The novel's titular hero, Jonathan Oldbuck – descendant of a fictional German printer of *incunabula* – draws his information from Netherlandic savants, corresponds with, and is visited by, the Rev. Dr Heavysterne, of Utrecht, and can fairly be said to owe his intellectual world to the long Scoto-Dutch academic connection.[28] Oldbuck's focus on the (largely illusory) *Romanitas* of the Scottish past, as opposed to its veridical Celtic and northern European elements, is very much of a piece with the ideas that the Scottish jurist and virtuoso Sir John Clerk developed while studying at Leiden at the dawn of the eighteenth century. It is typical of the depth of Scott's knowledge that he should quietly furnish his Georgian protagonist with a suitable Scoto-Dutch garden, derived from the otherwise almost untraced tradition that is the subject of the present chapter:

> It was surrounded by tall clipped hedges of yew and holly, some of which still exhibited the skill of the *topiarian* artist, and presented curious arm-chairs, towers, and the figures of Saint George and the dragon. The taste of Mr Oldbuck did not disturb these monuments of an art now unknown, and he was the less tempted so to do, as it must necessarily have broken the heart of the old gardener.[29]

Thus, the garden of Oldbuck, a laird in late middle age, and the training of his even older gardener take the fictional estate of Monkbarns securely back to the era of the great Scoto-Dutch academic connection of the earlier eighteenth century: the epoch of the early archaeologist Spanhemius and of the medical connections initiated by the international group of medical students known as 'Boerhaave's men'. It is also mentioned, later in the novel, that Oldbuck is at least potentially a customer for 'fresh flower-roots from Holland'.[30]

Evidence of this hortulan interchange is admittedly sparse. Here, I propose a brief investigation of the unique Scottish seventeenth century country house poem *Caelia's Country-House and Closet*, a poem by Sir George Mackenzie of Rosehaugh which relates closely to the Netherlandic tradition of country house poetry, particularly as exemplified by Constantijn Huygens's *Hofwijk*. Demonstrating the seventeenth-century movement to Dutch influence, I briefly consider the strongly Dutch character of the garden practice set forth in the first Scottish treatise on gardening, *The Scots Gard'ner*, by Mackenzie's head gardener, John Reid, and in *Celia's Country House and Closet*, which was published in 1683. I then discuss one fragmentary, but extremely interesting, piece of evidence for symbolic or emblematic garden layouts in southern Scotland; and conclude with a brief look at the garden aesthetic of one of Scott's models for his antiquary: the distinguished Leiden alumnus Sir John Clerk of Penicuik (1676–1755).

At this point it is necessary to stress that these Dutch and Scottish garden layouts are the inheritors of a tradition of applied emblematics, and, particularly, of a tradition of using a real place or person as the *pictura* to which the poet supplies the motto or interpretation. This tradition was delineated by Karel Porteman in his fine *Emblematic Exhibitions at the Brussels Jesuit College (1630–1685)*, in which he identifies the Jesuit Louis Richeôme as an emblematic and spiritual interpreter of things seen daily.[31] To be more precise, it was Richeôme who defined the subsidiary tradition of emblematics whereby an emblematic reading may be made of an actual person or thing. Thus a person – for example, a sick student in the Jesuits' House of Studies – or a stand of trees, or the waters of a castle's moat receives a motto or moralised discussion, the function of which closely parallels the threefold exposition of the emblem. Recent work, particularly Michael Bath's considered exposition of the *architecture parlante* of Alexander Seton's *villa suburbana* at Pinkie House in East Lothian, remodelled at the very beginning of the seventeenth century, stresses that the formal emblem-images of the painted gallery are only one of the ways in which the heavily inscribed house functions as a complex act of communication with an informed visitor. The crypto-Eucharistic inscription on the courtyard fountain – which itself serves as the *pictura* of the quasi-emblematic exposition – is equally part of the stoic, 'Church papist' self-portrait that the whole complex of building, painting, and inscription offers.[32]

In this context, we should also remember that the overall design of Huygens's *Hofwijk* is a self-portrait in a different mode, insofar as the entire estate is anthropomorphic, with the castle itself standing for the head; and, as we progress around the 'body' over the course of the poem, we are invited to meditate on the applications of the different trees we encounter. Thus, Seton can be located within the same, essentially emblematic tradition as Huygens's great poem, and, indeed, Andrew Marvell's celebrated 'Upon Appleton House to my Lord Fairfax', with its clear formal inheritances from Dutch *Buitengedichten* – country house and garden poems.[33]

Two examples clearly illustrate Huygens's continual moralisations and emblematisations of real places within his garden. First, when the moralised tour of the estate has reached as far as the moat around the house, and pauses there to make the conventional emblematic reflection on shadows in the water and fugacity, Huygens turns the moment into a baroque conceit of time passed worthily and unworthily – that is, in the garden or in the pursuit of riches:

> Ghij meent een' dobb'le kans te nutten, en ick ook;
> Ick teer op schaduwen, en ghij verteert in roock. (ll. 2715–16)[34]
> [I thrive on shadows doubled by my waters, while you live
> On smoke. My shadows last; your smoke dissolves away.]

Huygens meditates upon a real place in a way that clearly parallels the emblem tradition again later in the poem:

> Die schettern't mij toe, terwijl sij dusend quicken
> In heen en wederbaen om Hofwijk henen stricken,
> En tuijgen bijden draed van 'tslingerende stael
> Hoe oneenparigh is het menschelick gemael,
> Hoe vele naer en witt door vele wegen trachten,
> En elck door andere. (ll. 2745–50)[35]
> [The skates cry out reply and tie a thousand knots
> And bows, skating around the pond about the house.
> And witness by their wavering thread of cutting steel
> How random are the whirling courses of our life;
> How crooked are the roads by which we reach our goal,
> Each by a different road.]

This is a beautifully complex, developing nexus of visual image and verbal and moralising expansion upon it. The scraped traces of the skates on the ice are compared to the complex maze of providence which is the path through individual existence. But, like the most successful emblems, the image goes further: the slipperiness of the ice – one's sense of not being wholly in control – deepens the sense of human limitations and of the uncertainties of the path that one can steer through life. The temporary nature of the skating pond and its susceptibility to thawing at the approach of warmer weather adds a further emblematic element to the image: that the ice itself is the world through which the skater makes a way, a world which – despite its manifest solidity – owes its continued existence only to the providence that, for the time being, maintains the winter temperatures.

There are many more examples of Huygens's moralisations and emblematisations of real and visible places within his orchard and garden, but let us return to Scotland, and to Sir George Mackenzie of Rosehaugh's *Caelia's Country-House and Closet*, conjecturally dated to the years 1666/67. This important document has been overlooked until comparatively recently. This is an early work by Mackenzie (1636–91), scholar, poet, jurist, and landowner.[36] Founder of the Advocates' Library, the germ of what is today the National Library of Scotland, and an enlightened lawyer who almost succeeded in ending witch persecutions in Scotland, Mackenzie has been unjustly traduced by Calvinist mythology as 'the bloody Mackenzie'. He was almost exceptional, as a Scot of his generation and class, *not* to have been educated in Leiden or Utrecht at least briefly. Instead, he attended the universities of St Andrews, Aberdeen, and Bourges, and in doing so absorbed a good deal of contemporary horticultural and (in the terms of his day) 'polite' culture. This is evidenced by his publication of a Barclayan romance, *Aretina*, in 1660,[37] and by his friendship with the magnates Lord and Lady Carnegie, whose house forms the subject of *Caelia's Country-House and Closet*. Lord Carnegie had travelled extensively in France and Italy, and his wife was a daughter of the great Duke of Hamilton. Later in life Mackenzie employed the above-mentioned John Reid as his head gardener, and, on the evidence of Reid's treatise, the garden and gardening at Mackenzie's East Lothian house in the early 1680s were unequivocally Dutch in style. Nevertheless, Mackenzie's political and religious leanings did not render him *persona grata* with the patron of the great parterres at Het Loo when the latter ascended the throne of Great Britain in 1688. Mackenzie resigned his high legal appointments and spent the rest of his life in retirement at Oxford.

Although Mackenzie's own continental education was limited to France, that of most of his friends and colleagues was Dutch; and, as such, we should not be at all surprised that Netherlandic ideas and, quite possibly, Netherlandic garden poems would have been current in his thinking. His country house poem – arguably, the *only* surviving Scottish country house poem – was published, in 1709, in the second volume of a fascinating miscellany of Scottish poetry from all periods: *Watson's Choice Collection*.[38] It was reprinted in 1715, and then as part of Mackenzie's collected works in 1716–22. All these printed texts are, of course, posthumous. A particularly attractive manuscript version, possibly dating from Mackenzie's lifetime, survives as NLS Advocates 500 LC 636, however. It identifies the garden and private room described in the poem under pastoral names as belonging to the real Palace of Leuchars in Fife, and the Caelia of the title as Lady Carnegie. It is known that Mackenzie himself circulated this poem, which is written in Standard English, in literary circles in England soon after its composition, sending a copy to the laureate, Sir William Davenant, under cover of a letter to John Evelyn.

Although one excellent Dutch-language study is available, the influence of the Dutch country house poem or *buitengedicht* on other European literatures has rarely been traced.[39] This is particularly to be regretted, as scholarly inattention to the Netherlandic model of associational, moralised, and sometimes emblematised estate walks has allowed the confusingly general term 'country house poem' to come into widespread use in English. This, in turn, has had the unfortunate effect of grouping together patronage poems such as Ben Jonson's 'To Penshurst' with such moralised estate tours as Marvell's 'Upon Appleton House'. Adriaan van der Weel and I have argued elsewhere not only that the commonalities in the imagery in Huygens's and Marvell's respective poems are too extensive to be attributed to coincidence but that many of these shared images are widely regarded by English critics as the most strikingly 'Marvellian'.[40] If we accept the importance of this kind of Dutch estate walk poem, however, and observe its relation to French models such as St Amant's *La Maison de Sylvie*, we have a useful precedent with which to add nuance to the study of the so-called country house poem in Britain, and, in particular, to this unique Scottish example.

Mackenzie's poem follows the style established by the *Buitengedicht* in the earlier part of the seventeenth century. He first gives a general description of the layout of the gardens at Leuchars Palace, and then touches in turn on the palace itself, the surrounding woods, and the statue of Lady Carnegie's father the Duke of Hamilton, before proceeding to a more detailed consideration of the flower garden, including its structures in artificial rock-work. Following a transitional passage of conventional praise for country life, Mackenzie provides a very detailed consideration of Lady Carnegie's closet, although it remains unclear whether this is a private room within the palace or a free-standing garden structure. The pictures within it include religious scenes, contemporary and antique landscapes, and portraits of figures from classical antiquity and the recent past, with King Charles I and Scottish royalist general the Marquis of Montrose prominent among the latter. There is also a Dutch church interior, which sounds very like the work of Pieter Jansz. Saenredam (1597–1665). Mackenzie then considers (and moralises at some length upon) the clock on Lady Carnegie's table, before moving on to a consideration of her collection of natural curiosities, containing shells, ambers, and corals, and concluding with a feature unique in British poems of this type: a rapid itemisation of the books in Caelia's closet. This leads to a final, highly complimentary, consideration of her character.

It is possible that there is some element of idealisation in this description – as, indeed, in Huygens's *Hofwijk*, which constantly reminds us that we are walking around a recently planted estate, but being invited to consider it in its maturity. It is equally possible, however, that much of Mackenzie's poem was simply a factual account of a fashionable Scottish country house in the middle of the seventeenth century. Certainly, there is nothing intrinsically implausible in the idea that a noblewoman could have had a cabinet containing fine pictures and natural curiosities. There is a portrait by Jamesone from the earlier part of the century, now at Duff House in Banff, of a noblewoman in just such a setting.[41] Equally, Mackenzie's opening description could well be a realistic one, of an actual garden scene in the style of the Netherlands:

> Long Rows of Orange-trees upon each side,
> The wond'ring eye to that great Palace guide:
> Betwixt which rows, most pleasant ponds they see,
> Which with the avenue in length agree.
> The pleasure garden is described as being in much the same style.
> Here Labyrinths so please that we may doubt
> If Art or Pleasure hinder getting out,
> A Fountain-Nymph darts water up on high
> And from the centre doth the garden spy,
> Which does with Eden in all things agree,
> Save that its mistress will not tempted be.[42]

Although it must be owned that some of the general points of the poem are clearly derived from *La Maison de Sylvie* or from Thomas Stanley's translation of it as *Sylvia's Park*, just as the descriptions of the paintings are – however remotely – derived from Giambattista Marino's *Galleria* (1620), the movement and scheme of the poem are much closer to Netherlandic originals.

When Mackenzie's poem is considered in parallel with Huygens's *Hofwijk*, one must acknowledge that there are important differences to be observed. The chief among these is that Huygens is very much the proprietor showing a guest around his own estate. Mackenzie, on the other hand, is a client – albeit one of gentry status – describing the house and garden of his magnate patron from a respectful distance, carefully complimentary about everything he sees. Among the many resemblances between the two poems, the most striking is how they are organised: in the form of a walk around the estate, with moralisations and digressions prompted by what is seen along the way. Another strong commonality is the sense they give of progressing through the grounds in a particular sequence: from the outer wooded portions to the garden by the house, and thence to the house itself and its contents. Quietly, unostentatiously, both poems share an assumption that the house and garden cannot but compose a picture of their owner. This is perhaps seen most clearly in Mackenzie's description of Caelia's closet as her accurate location in the moral world, with the globe inlaid in the floor below her and the heavenly light of the chandelier above. In Huygens, as already noted, the estate itself is anthropomorphic, with the house at the head of a layout in the shape of the human body; so, in a nicely complicated way, the estate is a portrait of its owner doubly. Both poems assume that the house and garden compose a microcosm of the world as it ought to be, furnished both with natural necessities and artificial or intellectual delights.

The two poems' detailed descriptions of their focal estates' respective collections of books are a feature found nowhere else. In Huygens, lines 2805 to 2813 describe the books that are at the disposal of his imaginary guest: first agricultural texts, and then 'town books' in Latin, Greek, Spanish, English, and Italian, as well as Dutch.[43] Mackenzie, on the other hand, ascribes to Lady Carnegie a fashionable taste – even including one, slightly outdated, curiosity – that is resolutely vernacular. The passage is worth quoting, not only for its rarity but as a fitting conclusion to this brief survey of Mackenzie's poem:

> But Dryden's works did turn from them my Eyes:
> Whose lofty lines I do above them prize:
> Cowley by him, whose works are ever new,
> Denham whose lines are sweet, whose sense is true;
> Waller the just, whose least corrected line
> The best may own, and I could wish it mine:
> Here toiling Jonson, easy Fletcher lie,
> And Donne into whose mysteries few pry.[44]

Mackenzie's own garden practice obviously followed Dutch precedents, if we are to believe the evidence set forth in the first Scottish garden treatise, which John Reid composed between 1680 and 1683 at Mackenzie's garden at Shank, South Esk.[45] Much of it is taken up with routine matters of surveying, layout, and the levelling of grounds. (Reid had a charming theory that laying out straight avenues can be accomplished with candle lanterns on a still night.) It also devotes much attention to the kitchen garden, again arguing an awareness of the comparatively new fashion for the élite consumption of salads and vegetables, which indeed might have derived in part from Reid's employer's contacts with John Evelyn, but which were just as likely to have been influenced by the Netherlandic consumption of vegetables – a habit introduced into Scotland by the steady stream of new lawyers and doctors returning home from the universities of the United Provinces.

The Dutch orientation of Reid's manual becomes absolutely clear when we examine those parts of it which deal with the overall layout of a garden. Indeed, his general precepts recall, however distantly, Huygens's microcosmic garden at Hofwijk:

> As the Sun is the Centre of this World: as the heart of the man is the centre of the man; as the nose is the centre of the face … Just so with the House-courts, Avenues, Gardens, Orchards etc.[46]

Reid's views as to what constitutes a garden were all essentially Netherlandic. He assumed, for instance, that geometrical ponds or canals were essential to a garden's completeness, and that the south side of the house should have 'the pleasure or Flower-Garden called the *Parterre*'.[47] Reid's instructions for the layout of this pleasure garden, moreover, were wholly in the Dutch taste.

Stylistically unequivocal, they insisted upon the importance of surrounding hedges, recommending holly – another indication of the accuracy of Scott's imaginary Scoto-Dutch garden – and a strictly symmetrical layout, modular to the house itself. Reid also recommended the kind of surrounding terrace walk that ornaments Het Loo to this day, and claimed that Netherlandic herringbone was the only way to lay a brick path. He felt it to be equally clear that a house front should only be approached through a symmetrical grass-plat, modular to the house, with broad brick or gravel paths, edged with a double band of dwarf box, and flowers planted in strict symmetry within this *plat-bande*. The only point on which he differed from the Dutch garden custom of the seventeenth century was in his objection to covered *berceaux* of trained trees, which he termed 'close walkes'.[48]

A particularly appealing aspect of Reid's treatise is its insistence that its set of prescriptions can be applied to gardens of almost all scales, from the grandest to the comparatively modest. In the 1680s the kind of Dutch garden Reid advocated could have been found in England as well as in Scotland. In that context, it is particularly to be noted that English taste, partly led by Alexander Pope and Joseph Addison, revolted against the purely Dutch elements in garden design as early as the second decade of the eighteenth century.[49] Scotland, on the other hand, seems to have remained very much more faithful to the Dutch symmetries. Scott's fictive estate of Monkbarns was by no means an isolated anachronism; and, indeed, the more modest kind of Scoto-Dutch layout can be glimpsed in fragments even today, in settings otherwise wholly altered. The walled garden at Candacraig, Aberdeenshire, for example, retains its lead statue of Mercury spouting water into a central stone basin and symmetrically placed gate piers, fine shallow steps, and regular cross-walks.

Another point of connection between the garden practice of Scotland and of the Netherlands can be found in the survival, to this day, of sundials from the seventeenth and eighteenth centuries. These are often of the greatest complexity, usually free-standing stone pillars with multiple dials, although quite a few are attached to the faces of buildings. In their great nineteenth-century survey of early modern Scottish building, David MacGibbon and Thomas Ross detailed no fewer than 200 of these objects then surviving.[50] The Netherlandic connection here was strong; dialling was a Low Countries speciality, so much so that, when King Charles II wanted to set up elaborate multiple sundials in the Privy Garden at Whitehall, he sent for an elderly English Jesuit of Liège, Fr Francis Line, who devised a set incorporating different systems of time measurement as adopted by different nations. These dials were notoriously destroyed by the Earl of Rochester in a drunken rage, a fact that was reported in a letter to Edinburgh by George Scott in 1676, suggesting again that an interest in sundials may have been a particular preoccupation of the designers and owners of Scoto-Netherlandic gardens.[51]

A fascinating trace or shadow of a seventeenth-century garden layout in southern Scotland can be found in the romance *Cloria and Narcissus* by Sir Percy Herbert, one of the Catholic Herberts of Powis Castle, a place noted for its remarkable terraced garden.[52] This is a royalist work, set in a thinly disguised Britain after the Civil War. It is an outstanding example of what the seventeenth century called a 'concealed history', or what we might call a *roman à clef*. In it, a composite figure of the first and second Earls of Nithsdale is concealed under the name of Augusinius. The year is 1651, between the Battles of Dunbar and Worcester, and the future Charles II is in the midst of his unsuccessful attempt to invade England from Scotland, when the romance's hero – led through the woods by a wildman who utters prophecies in verse – is brought to Augusinius's castle: possibly a fictionalised version of Caerlaverock with its Ovidian carvings. But it is the description of the grounds that is of interest to our present investigations.

Herbert describes a clearing in a sloping wood, and a low mound in it encircled with a wall of flint, embellished by crude carvings. At one end of the mound is a banqueting house covered in scallop-shaped blue slates. In the middle is an oratory containing altars and images of the gods (presumably the romance's version of a discreet chapel of the Catholic Maxwells). The third building within the enclosure is a two-storey grotto, the lower level occupied by a stream, the upper by a library furnished with maps and globes. There is no particular reason to believe that Herbert was describing a wholly imaginary site. And, if his description is in fact of a real place, then here we find an example of an associational, even emblematic, garden of a distinctly continental type in mid-seventeenth-century Scotland, with a grotto-*cum*-study strongly reminiscent of Thomas Bushell's imitation of continental prototypes at Enstone in Oxfordshire, erected in the 1640s.[53]

In conclusion, I return to John Clerk, and suggest that much more awaits discovery in this field. As we have seen, Clerk of Penicuik, friend of Herman Boerhaave and distinguished early eighteenth-century graduate of Leiden, was one of the models for the title character in Scott's *Antiquary*. But Clerk's achievements as a patron of architecture, as a composer, and as a jurist should not lead us to forget that he was also an idiosyncratic garden theorist, anticipating in some respects the landscape developments of the later eighteenth century, especially in his emphasis on the importance of landscape settings and 'borrowed views' for the villas which he and his friends and imitators built in the countryside around Edinburgh, very much in the Dutch classical style.

In John Clerk of Penicuik's little Georgic verse treatise *The Country Seat*, the garden layouts which he advocated were in the purest Dutch taste, as seen today in the gardens of Het Loo, or in the restored Great Fountain Garden at Hampton Court from the William and Mary era. Indeed, the only kind of surrounding for a country house that struck Clerk as acceptable was a parterre of the kind advocated by Reid some 50 years earlier. Clerk's reference to the fringing of the mantle would certainly suggest that he envisaged parterres, edged with *plat-bandes* with specimen flowers planted symmetrically between two low hedges of clipped box:

Around the Fabrick spread the wide Parterre
Like to a verdant mantle edged with gold
Or an embroydered carpet all perfumd
With Indian Sweets, here with a mystick mein
Let Nature in the pride of blooming flowers
Triumphant sit, and all the Gardiners Toils
Direct with matchless grace, here let her show
How wild and shapeless fields may be adorned
With easy Labour and without constraint.[54]

This is hardly the view of a proto-Brownian; rather, it is *exactly* what one would expect from a man whose taste had been formed in continental Europe at the turn of the eighteenth century and who continued all his life to correspond with his student friend, the celebrated medical innovator Herman Boerhaave, as much about the latter's plantations at Poelgeest as about medicine and politics.[55] If the lines just quoted evoke the grander layouts of Het Loo, or of the magnates' country houses and formal gardens along the river Vecht which were engraved by Daniel Stoopendaal,[56] then the general aesthetic of the seventeenth-century Dutch garden – at any scale – is expressed by Clerk's summary of the essence of a garden:

Stretch out the lines of every Avenue
With spreading Trees in many stately Rowes;
Display the Parterres and the Shady Walks
The sloping greens, the Ponds and water-works.[57]

And in these lines, we have come full circle to Clerk's fictional incarnation as Scott's antiquary: with 'flower-roots from Holland' in his parterre, and walks and topiary trees surrounding and defining the old-fashioned Netherlandic garden of Monkbarns.

Notes

1 Kelsey Jackson Williams, Jane Stevenson, and Williams Zachs, *A History and Catalogue of the Lindsay Library, 1570–1792* (Leiden: Brill, 2022).

2 Marilyn Brown, *Scotland's Lost Gardens* (Edinburgh: RCHMS, 2012), p. 143.

3 The Earl of Crawford and Balcarres, 'The Garden of Edzell' (Edinburgh: publications of the Clan Lindsay Society, 2004), I, pp. 9–56. This work offers a comprehensive overview, and also details and reproduces the sources for the three sequences of bas-reliefs in engravings by Georg Pencz for the planetary deities (this identification was first made by Douglas Simpson in the 1930s; it may still require a little nuancing as to the addition of a *mandorla* or *vesica* around each figure, for which see below); in engravings by Johannes Sadeleir after Maarten de Vos for the liberal arts; and in engravings by Crispijn de Passe the elder, also after Maarten de Vos, for the virtues (these identifications made by Anthony Wells-Cole in 1997).

4 *Ibid.*, pp. 143–50.

5 *Ibid.*, p. 149.

6 See http://maps/nls/uk/geo/roy (retrieved 25 May 2013).

7 Brown, *Scotland's Lost Gardens*, p. 144, citing Lord Lindsay, *Lives of the Lindsays*, 2 vols (London: John Murray, 1849), I, pp. 345–6.

8 NLS, ACC 9769/4/1/97.

9 Lindsay, *Lives of the Lindsays*, I, pp. 349–50.

10 The very popularity of *La Maison Rustique*, and the repeated editions, make it a complex work to cite; I have tried therefore to cite by book and chapter number and subtitle, which remain relatively constant, although the edition which I have had to hand is a later one: that published at Rouen by Maury in 1658.

11 Brown, *Scotland's Lost Gardens*, p. 209.

12 *La Maison Rustique*, edn cit., p. 222.

13 *Ibid.*

14 *Ibid.*, p. '242' (pagination out of sequence).

15 NLS, ACC 9769/4/3/3.

16 *La Maison Rustique*, p. 269.

17 One of the beguiling puzzles of the early Lindsay libraries is the copy of Garcia de Orta, *Aromatum, et simplicium aliquot medicamentorum apud Indos nascentium historia* (Antwerp: Plantin, 1593) (current shelfmark D1), which contains MS plant lists. The book belonged to Lord Edzell's brother Lord Menmuir, but the lists are not in his hand.

18 The last section of *La Maison Rustique* is concerned with hunting, especially wolf hunting. Edzell hunted wolves on his estates; a friend wrote to him in 1588 that he looked forward to being in Angus in the spring to hunt at 'Willie wolfis taill': Keith Brown, *Noble Power in Scotland from the Reformation to the Revolution* (Edinburgh: Edinburgh University Press, 2011) p. 213, citing *Registrum de Panmure*, i.p.xxxv, NRA(S) 237/F/475–8.

19 As in Adam McLean, 'A Rosicrucian/Alchemical Mystery Centre in Scotland', *The Hermetic Journal*, 4.11 (1979), pp. 11–13.

20 Jackson Williams, Stevenson, and Zachs, *A History and Catalogue*, pp. 10–13.

21 *Fama Fraternitatis*, the manifesto of the Rosicrucians, seems first to have been written in German, circulated in manuscript from *c.* 1610, and it was first printed (in Kassel, Germany) in 1614. An English translation was published by Thomas Vaughan in 1652.

22 The two-volume typescript by the 28th Earl of Crawford and Balcarres, entitled *Bibliotheca Lindesiana*, kept at Balcarres House, Fife, itemises references to the generous table at Edzell served by a professional English cook, who also worked as a skilled gardener there. I, pp. 29–32.
23 Brown, *Scotland's Lost Gardens*, p. 61.
24 Now Glasgow University Library, MS Hunter 414. This contains 27 medical treatises, among them a few which certainly relate to the perceived effects of the planets on human health, an *Expositio Effectuum Planetarum* by an unknown author, and an anonymous work on the zodiac, *De XII Signis*. It also contains a treatise, *De Mensium Virtutibus,* which may be the work attributed to 'Alexander physicus' called, in full, *Tractatulus de virtutibus et proprietatibus mensium per circumum anni*, found also in the monastic library of Sankt Florian in Austria (Codex San-Florianensis XI.187).
25 Adam McLean's suggestion ('A Rosicrucian/Alchemical Mystery Centre in Scotland') of the misleadingly named *Mantegna Tarot* as part of the background to the selection of subjects for the bas-reliefs is an interesting and valuable one. This sequence of cards, unconnected with Mantegna and almost certainly not a tarot, produced in Ferrara in the third quarter of the fifteenth century, would appear to be some kind of educational game for élite children, offering a humanistic model of the cosmos. Included in the sequences are the planets, the arts, and the virtues (although not in the same sequence as at Edzell), and the striking representation of the elephant-tusk throne of Jupiter may have influenced Edzell's or his sculptors' decision to place each of Benz's figures of the planets in a *mandorla* or *vesica*. Although a set of the *Mantegna Tarot* entered the *Bibliotheca Lindesiana* in the early twentieth century, there is no evidence for its presence in the sixteenth.
26 Cf. Michael Bath, 'Ben Jonson, William Fowler and the Pinkie Ceiling', *Architectural Heritage*, 18 (2007), pp. 73–86.
27 I am more than grateful to David Walker (*filius*) for what was then an early view of the typescript of his 'Buildings of Scotland' volume for Banff, Buchan, and Formartine, published as David W. Walker and Matthew Woodworth, *The Buildings of Scotland: Aberdeenshire, North and Moray* (New Haven, CT: Yale University Press, 2015).
28 Scott describes the antiquary's study with its vast Dutch cabinet, and a learned professor of Utrecht accidentally sitting on some caltrops retrieved from the site of the Battle of Bannockburn during his visit, in the revised version of the novel, printed in the *Magnum Opus Waverley*, Walter Scott, *Waverley Novels*, V, *The Antiquary* (Edinburgh: Cadell & Company, 1829), pp. 33–4.
29 Scott, *The Antiquary*, pp. 28–9.
30 As well as smuggled genever: *ibid*., p. 217.
31 Porteman, *Emblematic Exhibitions (Affixiones)*, pp. 18–21. See Chapter 12 for a detailed consideration of Richeôme.
32 Bath, *Renaissance Decorative Painting in Scotland*, pp. 79–103.
33 Many Marvellian scholars hold that 'Upon Appleton House' dates from the very early 1650s, at which time Marvell was with the Fairfax family at Nun

Appleton in Yorkshire. But, in fact, there is no evidence that it could not have been composed in part *after* Marvell had read the 1653 edition of *Hofwijk*, or possibly a manuscript copy deriving from Huygens's 1651 fair copy. Certainly, 'Upon Appleton House' expresses trauma and grief at recent events in Britain (as Huygens also looks back on the trauma of episodes of the wars in the Low Countries) and there are substantial parallel runs of imagery, as well as close formal resemblances. It has been assumed that, since Marvell accepted the position of tutor to Cromwell's ward in 1653, he had by that year reconciled himself to the new regime. But such an assumption does not logically preclude the composition of the last elements of the poem in the same year.

34 *Poems of Sir Constantijn Huygens*, pp. 152–3.

35 *Ibid.*, pp. 154–5.

36 Clare Jackson, 'Mackenzie, Sir George, of Rosehaugh (1636/1638–1691)', *Oxford Dictionary of National Biography* (2007), https://doi-org.ezproxy-prd.bodleian.ox.ac.uk/10.1093/ref:odnb/17579 (retrieved online 6 April 2023).

37 *Aretina, or, The Serious Romance* (Edinburgh: Robert Broun, 1660).

38 The only modern notice of it is in Alastair Fowler's anthology *The Country House Poem* (Edinburgh: Edinburgh University Press, 1994), in which an extract and a brief discussion can be found on pp. 343–53.

39 Willemien B. de Vries, *Wandeling en verhandeling: de ontwikkeling van het Nederlandse hofdicht in de zeventiende eeuw (1613–1710)* (Hilversum: Verloren, 1998).

40 *Poems of Sir Constantijn Huygens*, pp. 208–14.

41 I refer to George Jamesone's 1630s portrait of Anne Erskine, Countess of Rothes. See Stephen Lloyd, *Catalogue of the Paintings and Sculpture at Duff House* (Edinburgh: National Galleries of Scotland, 1999), p. 35.

42 George Mackenzie, *Caelia's Country-House and Closet*, in *A Choice Collection of Comic and Serious Scots Poems both Ancient and Modern, by Several Hands*, part II (Edinburgh: James Watson, 1709), pp. 73–6.

43 *Poems of Sir Constantijn Huygens*, pp. 156–9, ll. 2805–13.

44 Mackenzie, *Caelia's Country-House and Closet*, p. 92. Donne is an unusual taste for a Scotswoman; by contrast, William Drummond of Hawthornden expressed his unhappiness at the abstruseness of Donne and his school. *The Works of William Drummond, of Hawthornden* (Edinburgh: James Watson, 1711), p. 143.

45 John Reid, *The Scots Gard'ner* (Edinburgh: David Lindsay, 1683).

46 *Ibid.*, p. 2.

47 *Ibid.*, p. 3.

48 *Ibid.*, p. 31. The owner of a Scottish garden would seldom have required protection from the sun.

49 See John Dixon Hunt and Peter Willis, *The Genius of the Place: The English Landscape Garden, 1620–1820* (London: Elek, 1975), pp. 204–7.

50 David MacGibbon and Thomas Ross, *The Castellated and Domestic Architecture of Scotland*, 5 vols (Edinburgh: David Douglas, 1892), V, pp. 358–513.

51 Coffin, *The English Garden: Meditation and Memorial*, pp. 16–17.

52 I am indebted for this, and much other exotic information, to I. W. McLellan, Esq., the publication of whose study of the 'Concealed Histories' or *romances à clef* of the mid-seventeenth century would transform our understanding of the period. Herbert's romance is titled in full *Cloria and Narcissus: A Delightfull and New Romance* (London: Anthony Williamson, 1653–54).

53 Aubrey, *Brief Lives*, I, pp. 312–14. See Prologue above.

54 National Records of Scotland, the Clerk Papers, GD 18, substantially transcribed in Hunt and Willis, *The Genius of the Place*, pp. 198–9.

55 These letters are all among the Clerk of Penicuik deposit in the National Records of Scotland in Edinburgh, NRS GD 18. They abundantly deserve study and translation out of their original Latin.

56 Daniel Stoopendaal, *De Zegepraalende Vecht* (1719).

57 *The Genius of the Place*, pp. 198–9.

16

Imaginary baroque cities: the Chearnley circle and the Earl of Mar

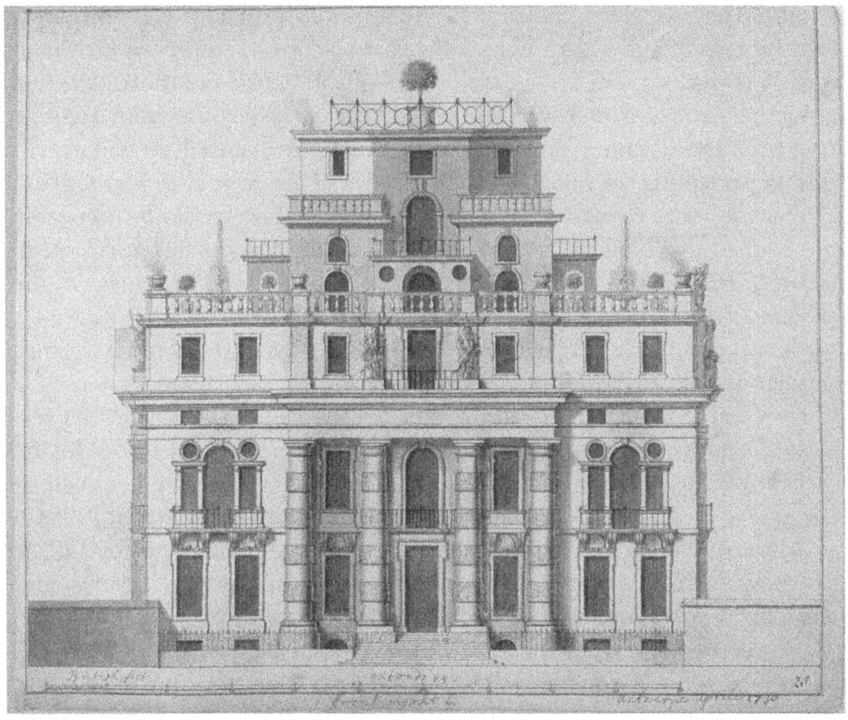

Figure 16.1 John Erskine, Earl of Mar, *House L, Elevation F*, drawing with wash and some colour, dated Antwerp, April 1720.

The spatial imagination of the baroque world was dominated by the reconstructed grandeurs of the past and by visions of their development into the grandeurs of the future. Here, I consider two extraordinary sets of unexecuted architectural drawings, dating from the first half of the eighteenth century, both of which made full use of the baroque, not merely stylistically but as an international symbolic discourse. These two examples are also political imaginings of future spaces, shaped by the political and religious conflicts which imposed upon the citizens of baroque-era Ireland, Scotland, and England a bewildering choice between two opposed authorities, amounting almost to two separate realities.

The first of these two sequences of imaginary architecture consists of three albums,[1] drawn in continental exile by the Scottish Jacobite magnate John Erskine, sixth Earl of Mar (1675–1732), in the years after the failed 1715 rising for the Catholic king-in-exile James Francis Edward Stuart against the Protestant king-in-possession, George of Hanover (see Figure 16.1). The second, now at Birr Castle, County Offaly, Ireland, was drawn by Samuel Chearnley (1718–47) in collaboration with his cousin Sir Laurence Parsons, third baronet (1709–56), both of whom were members of the Protestant and Whig circle of the Parsons family, squires of Birr (then called Parsonstown).[2] The Chearnley–Parsons designs were mostly created during the anxious winter of 1745/46, the year of the second major Jacobite rising for James Francis Edward Stuart, this time against King George II. Thus, in presenting the imagined future spaces of gardens, towns, cities, and palaces, the two sequences make highly charged statements on opposing sides of the same long political conflict. Victor and vanquished alike speak the same architectural and symbolic language: the universal language of the baroque.

When the Catholic King James II of Great Britain and Ireland went into continental exile in 1688, the alternative realities that had clamoured for the assent of Ireland and Britain during the civil wars of the middle of the seventeenth century returned with greater force. To borrow Jelena Todorović's excellent phrase, there were two systems of authority: one in power, one in exile; one in the light, one 'in the shadow'.[3] The successive courts of William and Mary, William, Anne, and the Georges claimed, from a position of de facto possession, the loyalty of their subjects in Britain and Ireland, and their official publications described the exiled Stuart royal line as 'pretenders'. The courts of James II and his son James Francis Edward (or James VIII and III) claimed the same loyalty, but from a position of dispossession and exile, and issued official publications describing the monarchs reigning in London as 'usurpers': not queens and kings but 'the Princess of Denmark' or 'the Elector of Hanover'. As time passed, these two opposed realities produced not only their own respective sovereigns, princes, princesses, courts, and courtiers but almost led to two opposing Protestant ecclesiastical hierarchies; separate systems of aristocratic titles; and even two mutually hostile, red-coated armies. Only against that background can our two sequences of imaginary architecture be properly understood.

Baroque 'paper architecture' – the era's imagined cities, towns, and estates – was and remains a fascinating and complex phenomenon. Where it takes the form of an imagined architecture projected onto an actual site, it inhabits a genuinely problematic region that is simultaneously real and fantasised. This is best understood in relation to two other baroque combinations of real and imagined space: the paper museum and the garden. The former was a dedicated space for study and imagination, filled with representations of distant objects and places. Beginning with the Villa of Hadrian in ancient times, gardens have been filled with structures evoking or alluding to a plurality of pasts and distant places.[4]

One of the major British architectural enterprises of the baroque era was the extraordinary paper museum assembled by the English Catholic virtuoso John Talman (1677–1726).[5] Like all such enterprises, its sheer scope is obscured retrospectively by the scattering of its components.

Speculative or imaginary architecture, like all paper places, inevitably has the melancholy and haunting quality of what might have been, of the path not taken. Both of this chapter's examples also carry a disquieting sense of personal obsession, and, specifically, of the fantasy of compensation. The baroque era was characterised by alternative possibilities, alternative histories, some real and some imagined. Those in the light and those in the shadow both asserted irreconcilable claims on the dignity and power of the past to shape fictive splendours for the future. In its creation of paper places of refuge and consolation, imaginary architecture is one of the most fascinating imagined spaces of the baroque: the ultimate *locus consolationis* of the fallen magnate, the member of the élite in adversity or under threat.

The Earl of Mar and the Chearnley–Parsons circle at Birr offer contrasting examples of the universal use of pattern books in the baroque world, although their first-hand experiences of architecture were very different. Mar had lived at the centre of things, both at the court of Queen Anne and at the exiled court of James III, and had been instructed in architecture in his youth by Alexander Edward (1651–1708), a member of a Scottish family of Episcopalian clergymen and minor architects. Mar had visited, and fallen in love with, Louis XIV's hunting palace at Marly, built between 1679 and 1686 to designs by the architect Jules Hardouin-Mansart and the painter Charles Le Brun.[6] The plan of the royal pavilion there haunts Mar's imaginary palaces, with their domed salons rising from the centre of square blocks. Mar wrote to James III soon after his visit, noting how he had been inspired by its architecture, and remarking on his hope that 'the time will yet come when some of these thoughts may be put in practice'.[7] Le Brun's grand theatricality, which at Marly took the form of *trompe l'oeil* painted façades, lived on as a proposed frescoed pediment in Mar's scheme of additions to Alloa Tower, the Scottish estate to which he was unlikely ever to return. A variant of the same element was also incorporated into Mar's royal palace for the London-to-be of James III. This constitutes an extraordinary double imagining of future space, whereby Mar's country house records his achievements as the architect of a Jacobite London.

In contrast to Mar, who had seen the baroque idioms of the English and French courts at first hand and made a palpably Scottish synthesis of them, the Chearnley–Parsons circle obtained a notable proportion of their extraordinary range of architectural ideas from pattern books.[8] The main visual reference that the two sequences of architecture shared was the published work of James Gibbs.[9] There was a more direct and thoroughly remarkable source for the Irish fantastical architecture, however, in the ephemeral decorations painted by William van der Hagen (*fl.* 1722–45) for the 1731 state ball at Dublin Castle.[10]

Both sets of plans were the products of adversity. Mar was on the losing side of the 1715 rising, though not from a hardcore Jacobite background: his relatively impoverished father had acquiesced in the earlier Williamite revolution. The Parsons and Chearnley families, on the other hand, were part of Ireland's minority English Protestant and pro-Hanoverian community, but in the winter of 1745/46, when most of their architectural designs were created, another Jacobite rebellion was reaching its high-water mark. Whether or not the military action spread across the Irish Sea – and there was no particular reason, at the time, to assume that it would not – things might have gone very hard with them indeed under a restored, Catholic King James or his viceroy.

Mar's extraordinary repertory of imaginary or projected architecture was drawn in various places of continental exile after he had contributed notably, by his military incompetence, to the failure of the 1715 rising. Although he wished – or even expected – to be allowed to return to Britain at some stage, he never did so. At Urbino, Paris, Antwerp, and Aix-la-Chapelle he began to draw his vast plans for the estates to which he would never be restored, and to plan the rebuilding of London for his king who would never rule there. He accepted a Hanoverian pension in 1721, James III disowned him in 1724, and he died – mistrusted as a double agent at the Hanoverian and Stuart courts alike – in 1732.

Margaret Stewart's excellent dissertation, now published as a book, on Mar's plans has emphasised that he was a conscious and learned architect, yet capable of importing his early direct experience of vernacular castle architecture into even his most sophisticated plans, as one element in a baroque stylistic blend of international and local.[11] In 1717 at Urbino, Mar remarked that he would 'die of the spleen ... were it not for building castles in the air of several kinds'.[12] His architecture relates to an incoherent, but heartfelt, set of political positions that he adopted and elaborated between 1715 and 1732. These included a repudiation of the 1707 Union of Scotland with England, espousal of the Jacobite cause, and a belief that

Scotland had taken a disastrous wrong turn in religion and politics from which it needed to withdraw, re-forming as an autonomous, Episcopalian state which respected Highland as well as Lowland traditions. He formalised this further in an unprecedented idea, amounting almost to a constitution, for a loose Celtic federation of Scotland and Ireland in alliance with England and France. These ideas are reflected in Mar's architecture, and especially in his last work: the house which he would have built for himself at Alloa, near Stirling, had he been able to return there – and had he been able to afford to demolish the existing tower-house and build afresh. In its expressive hybrid baroque style, the new Alloa would have become a kind of epitome of the Scotland of Mar's aspirations.[13]

Mar's detailed plans are mostly for the rebuilding of the palace quarter of London, however, as he would have liked to have seen it done in the imagined, unimaginable day when the capital would welcome James Francis Edward Stuart as James III. Made in his long continental exile at Avignon, Lucca, Pistoia, Geneva, Bourbon, Paris, and Antwerp, his ambitious designs' general style was emphatic baroque, essentially French in idiom, but with a frequent Scottish undercurrent. The nearest cognate for these Scottish references among pre-existing buildings was Kinross House, which the Stuart loyalist Sir William Bruce (*c.* 1630–1710) had begun for himself, with its axis focused on the island castle in Loch Leven where Mary Stuart had been imprisoned, and passing through a great space on the *piano nobile* that was left unfinished but presumably intended as a *Kaisersaal*.[14] This Scottish layout planted a seed in Mar's mind that was later watered by his experience of the royal palaces, especially Marly, which he had seen in France.

Mar's first version of an imaginary London palace for the great courtiers of the restored King James included a grand *corps de logis*, quadrants, and wings, and would have occupied a site in Piccadilly. He also drew a developed version of a similar ground plan, but more French in treatment and with a section revealing a lavishly modelled interior.[15]

The royal palace design itself is of predictable grandeur: a dream extension, in a hybrid baroque idiom, of the same loyalty to the Stuarts' absolute monarchy which Bruce had expressed at Kinross. These plans were developed between 1721 and 1729, and all are variations on the same theme: notably vertical blocks of square plan, each rising in the centre to an octagonal tower or to a dome.[16] Terry Friedman has observed that this was a plan type that obsessed Mar from this point onwards, and featured in his redesigns for houses as diverse as Wilton, Longleat, and Drumlanrig.

According to Mar's 1726 memorandum on his redesign of London, the location of the palace in his mind had moved to the upper end of St James's Park, at the hub of a great radial system of canals and avenues.[17] All of London as it then existed was to have been subsumed into a single overwhelming geometry, focused on the house and the person of the monarch. A straight canal was to run down to the Thames, so that the king could embark from his palace directly onto his barge, and continue on its far bank. Courtiers' houses were to be built on this axis on the far side of the river. There were also to be courtiers' palaces to the east and west of the king's great house, both in Piccadilly and in Kensington; an avenue was to stretch north from the palace to the heights of Hampstead; and, presumably after much demolition, a 'Great Avenue' lined with buildings was to lead straight from the palace to the Royal Exchange in the City.

The more modest of Mar's two schemes for Alloa, a remodelling rather than a rebuilding, retains the ancient tower-house, while adding an inscription – probably making a virtue of necessity – asserting that the retention of the old structure was an act of ancestral piety.[18] But he also proposed the addition of two five-bay façades, of differing degrees of elaboration, to the middles of the house's two flanks. The seriousness with which he believed that this scheme would be realised is suggested by a raised flap on the drawing, showing an alternative, much simpler treatment of these central pavilions. As a termination to the view from Alloa, Mar also proposed an extraordinary baroque recasing of the sixteenth-century palace block at Stirling Castle, with oversized finials in the shape of thistles.

Mar's alternative, the complete rebuilding of Alloa, was designed relatively late in his career, in 1730, when he was in exile in Antwerp. There is every possibility that this splendidly strange house, with four façades of different orders, existed in Mar's mind in more than one imagined space; that is, it would make one kind of symbolic sense as a complete rebuilding of Alloa, but another if placed in the King's Paddock at Kensington. Much as the *auteur* theory of the cinema suggests that each director has in mind just one vastly compelling but unexecutable film, so with Mar's compulsive imagining and reimagining of just one vast house, which was at times his own at Alloa, and at others the royal pavilion at Marly or a palace for King James. As he said himself, 'If this designe would not be likt for Kensington, It wou'd serve extreamly well for Alloa if there was a new house to be built where the old house is.'[19] The 1730 Alloa design is Mar's most accomplished baroque work, and also his strangest. It is a rectangular structure, with a portico in the centre of each nine-bay façade, and porticoes also in the shorter, seven-bay sides. The two longer fronts, which face east and west, have their two centre bays recessed. There is an attic storey in the French style; and, above this, a flat roof with a roof garden, including trees and fountains, the leads painted in imitation of parterres, surrounding the inevitable central belvedere, a square rising into an octagon, with another tree surmounting the whole composition. This treatment of roof level is remarkable: a real baroque development of the *meraviglia*, the characteristic ambition to astonish using a fluid variety of materials. This scheme is also remarkable for a fantastical use of hydraulics, with water being drawn up through the body of the house to the fountains and lead tanks on the roofs.

The positioning of the imaginary house is significant: either at the heart of the radiating avenues to the west of London, or at Alloa, situated on a fertile plain at the centre of the Lowlands, but in view of both the sharp rising of Ben Cleugh and the uplands to the north, and the evocative monument of Stirling Castle on its great rock to the west. Conceivably, Mar intended his imaginary palace to be a microcosm of his nation, as well as a built autobiography.

On the 'front markt D' there is a fictive drapery of stone over the recessed portico, held up by the beasts of the Erskine arms – eagle, lion, griffin – and bearing a wreath, which descends towards the master of the house in a fantastical vindication of the rightness of his disastrous political career.[20] The other long side, 'front markt E', is public or political, with 'hieroglyphics' between the metopes of the frieze, weapons of war, and many thistles, with indistinct figures above, though one of them seems to be meant for Justice.[21] The south façade ('front markt F') facing across the gardens and parterres and down to the fertile plain of the river Forth is Corinthian, with female figures possibly meant for Ceres and Astraea, a cornucopia, and an attic-level terrace with another fountain.[22] The last elevation ('front markt G') is the sternest, its massive columns featuring banded rustication and, at cornice level, two giant statues of Highlanders.[23] These figures acknowledge both Mar's debt to those who had risen for him in the 1715 Jacobite rebellion and his vision that their future role in Scotland's history would involve 'relieving our country' from the Union. Mar seems to have been drawing an analogy between the most robust and 'primitive' of all the orders, the rusticated blocked Tuscan Doric, and the nature of Highland life. This façade looks north towards Ben Cleugh and into the hills and the north beyond.[24]

Mar's designs for his lost estates at Alloa also included a complete recasting of the church there, with grand lofts like opera boxes for his own family and for his local Erskine kinsfolk. The most spectacular element of this scheme was to have been the formation of a great top-lit void within the walls of the old church building, where, behind and above Mar's loft and the burial place, was to stand a black marble obelisk commemorating the various branches of the Erskine family. Gilded reliefs on the obelisk would have combined the international and the local: Roman trophies of armour and Highland broadswords. Crowning the obelisk would have been, according to Mar's annotation, a heart 'of white marble with a flame comeing out of it of guilt brass'.[25] The flaming heart represented the ardour and devotion of the followers of the Stuarts, an iconography to which Mar clung even after his falling out with his shadow king and acceptance of a Hanoverian pension.[26]

We now turn to the remarkable set of Anglo-Irish architectural projects from Birr (known as Parsonstown by those then in power in Ireland), which demonstrate the degree to which the baroque arts can flourish at an extraordinarily sophisticated level in places far remote from what are commonly conceived of as 'cultural centres' (see Figure 16.2). The social group out of which these projects emerged was a small one, comprising minor aristocracy, gentry, and clergy – élite Protestants of English and Welsh descent, living in the Midlands of Ireland. Stylistically, the drawings made by Samuel Chearnley in collaboration with, and under the patronage of, his cousin Sir Laurence Parsons are wide-ranging, fantastical, and brilliant. As William Laffan remarks in his introduction to the facsimile publication of the album,

> Chearnley's designs are multi-sourced and sometimes wilfully eccentric in their combination of different architectural modes, demonstrating, in addition to the prevailing Palladian idiom, the clear influence of the European Baroque, even at times that of sixteenth-century Italian Mannerism.[27]

Samuel Chearnley, when the sequence of drawings was begun, was designing in a climate of gloom: there was little chance that the Parsons family would ever have enough money to realise the obelisks and casinos of his

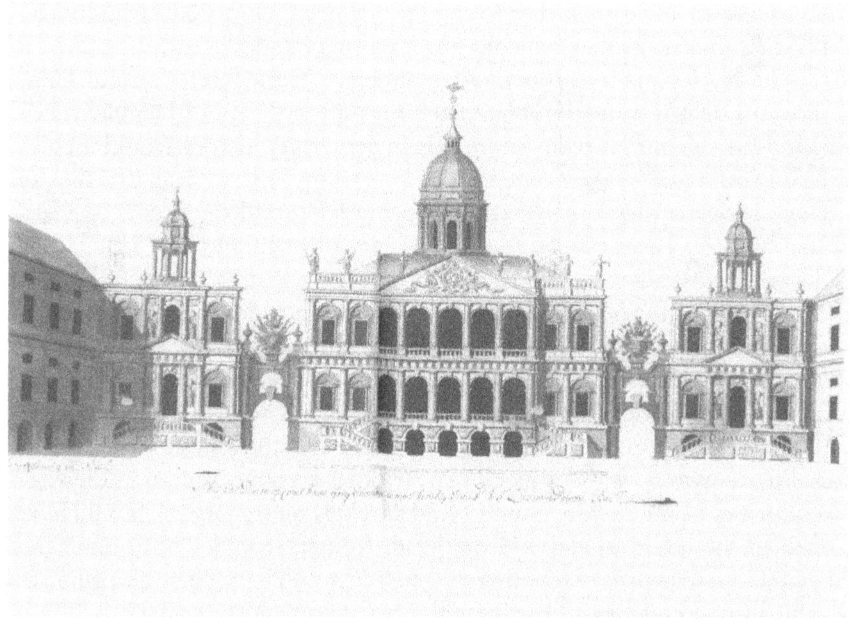

Figure 16.2 Samuel Chearnley, *New Design for a Court House of My Invention*, 1746, pen and wash, Birr Castle, Co. Offaly, Ireland. Birr Scientific & Heritage Foundation, Co. Offaly, Ireland.

fantasy in the demesne of Birr Castle, not to mention that their whole world was under threat from Jacobites, foreign and domestic.[28] Even by the time the later drawings were being made, however much the fortunes of the Irish Ascendancy might have improved with the Jacobite threat finally banished, it is doubtful whether they would have been able completely to rebuild the town of Birr. But, if they had somehow managed to leave its skyline bristling with trophies of arms and statues on Solomonic columns, the town in its 'fantastical grandiosity' – as Toby Barnard has put it – would be, by now, one of the wonders of Europe.[29]

The collection of drawings is baroque in its sheer scope and ambition, but also in its use of games and paradoxes with materials. Its designs for columns use the full baroque repertory of trophies of arms and Solomonic twisting and vine wreathing. Although the chief influence is Palladian, there are elements of French as well as Roman baroque, and elements of sheer fantasy beyond the likely result of exposure to the work of van der Hagen, a scene painter and deviser of capriccio landscapes active in the Ireland of the middle of the eighteenth century. The drawing sequence's ebullient magnificence raises interesting questions about the provenance of the architectural ideas that it incorporates and develops. Christine Casey has argued that Chearnley's sources would have included not only Gibbs but also Daniel Marot.[30] It is the fabulous combinations and use of over-scale elements, however, that lead us beyond these sources towards the wholly fictitious magnificence of van der Hagen's scene paintings and ephemeral festal decoration. Dr Barbara Paca has also emphasised that Chearnley's 'overwhelming sense of theatre is enlivened by the abundance of statues that populate his vignettes'.[31]

The designs in the Chearnley album were almost certainly intended to be more than escapist fantasies during a politically anxious winter for a remote élite circle. Indeed, the sequence of drawings constitutes in itself something of a counterpoint or response to the events of the 1745/46 Jacobite rising. This title page, citing the 'Ruins, Grottoes, Surprizes, Cascades, Fountains, Bridges, Obelisks and Pyramids, Columns, Terminations for Vistows, Temples, Triumphal Arches, [and] Monuments' that one will find within, is dated 24 October 1745. By that time the forces commanded by Charles Edward Stuart – Prince of Wales in the alternative British universe ruled by James III – had got as far as Edinburgh, having defeated the Hanoverian forces at nearby Prestonpans on 21 September. In a year of potential disasters for his community, Chearnley's dated series begins with a sequence of six designs for ruins, the first, oddly, appearing to be at the end of a long drive from a country house gate, thus taking the place of the house itself. This may well have been a sophisticated and rueful joke about the contemporary political situation. Soon there emerges a reasonably close relation between the sequence of drawings in the Chearnley–Parsons album and the arrival in the Midlands of Ireland of campaign news from Britain.

Reckoning that it would take seven to nine days for news of any importance to pass from London to Dublin and probably not more than two more from Dublin to Birr, the sequence comes into focus in one respect. Until at least a week after the Jacobite army began to retreat northwards from Derby on 6 December 1745, only bad news would have reached Birr. November and December dates have been given to all the fantastical garden buildings, both the escapist ones and the tomb-like pyramids and grottoes.

The wonderful pyramidal 'Grottoe' in plate 8 of Chearnley's *Miscelanea*, with its tunnel leading through to a haunting glimpse of water falling in the distance, seems particularly elegiac, and particularly responsive to the military anxieties of the Ascendancy. As Paca has noted, 'The pyramid has long been known to represent a burial site for people of military accomplishment.'[32]

By February 1746, however, Charles Edward's army was in retreat, between Glasgow and Inverness, and the Chearnley album shows a much more optimistic design for a grand garden pavilion: a 'Temple or Cassina' in Gibbsian style with, significantly, a coronet in the entablature over the carved oval for the owner's coat of arms – perhaps indicating that the Parsons circle, none of whom rated heraldic coronets in the here and now, were already hoping for much better times in Ireland. The drawings dated to March 1746 begin to include a number of designs for triumphal arches, and there can be no mistaking that they were, at least in part, a response to the news of further Jacobite retreats and, eventually, the annihilation of the Jacobite forces at the Battle of Culloden on 16 April. The iconography of these triumphal arches, with a mounted, laurel-crowned figure of Cumberland surmounting all, makes the artist's political viewpoint wholly clear. One of them even includes an indication of paintings or bas-reliefs in a broken entablature showing a specifically Hanoverian victory: the recent cavalry charge at Dettingen that had driven the opposing forces into a river, paralleling an iconic historical moment for the Protestants of Ireland – the Siege of Derry.

After this, the album takes a local and hopeful turn. One or two of the drawings toward the end were annotated to show how they could be accomplished with brick and stucco, without going to the expense of cut stone, with the capitals of columns counterfeited from slates or flagstones set on edge. In addition, rather than the garden and estate fantasies for which the Anglo-Irish community were unrivalled, the later projected designs are for farmhouses and townhouses, and, indeed, other elements of a planned town, culminating in a grand town square with trophies of arms: a Birr of dreams, conceived at a moment of considerable optimism in the history of the English in Ireland.

The last dated design is from May 1746, when the sequence may have been interrupted by Chearnley's final illness.[33] Despite his many projects, only one structure by Chearnley is known to have been built. This is the column in the Mall at Birr, erected originally to commemorate the Hanoverian victory at Culloden (thus confirming a partly political reading of his sequence of paper architecture) with a statue of Cumberland in an apposite material: lead.[34]

Fantasy and extravagance are a marked characteristic of Anglo-Irish design, and Irish garden architecture in particular is of unparalleled strangeness. It is worth posing the question of whether this visual *sprezzatura* is, to some degree, born of defiance. The ruling English elite in Ireland were, to continue our earlier metaphor, acutely aware of the shadows that surrounded them. Had the Jacobite enterprise of 1745/46 succeeded, the Catholic Irish, at home and in exile, might well have rallied to displace the Ascendancy in Ireland. In this context, it is hardly surprising that so much of the fantastical energy of the Anglo-Irish went into garden buildings and landscape gardens of superb invention.[35] It could be argued that the vistas through their estates terminate in buildings of ingenuity and beauty, such as Chearnley's plates for 'Termination[s] of a Vistow', partially because of a strong disinclination to look beyond the boundary wall.

Ireland was theoretically shired, and a full Protestant hierarchy was in place for the ancient Irish episcopal sees (to which, in exile, James VIII and III still asserted the right of the presentation of Catholic bishops). In fact, this ordering of Irish society was itself mostly fantasy: the sheriffs were prone to assassination, and many of the higher Protestant clergy felt safer in England than in their isolated Irish palaces. Thus, the gardens and the garden buildings, at which the English and Irish Protestants in Ireland so excelled, are located somewhere between real architecture and architecture that constructs a place wholly in the imagination. This paradoxical region is not real in any simple sense: partly theatrical, partly a representation of an imagined reality, it is a strange Arcadia of denial.

The more that this whole construct is considered, the more Anglo-Ireland comes to seem one of the most extraordinary *imagined* spaces of baroque Europe, a fantasy space of order and control imposed upon an intractable reality. In 1731 the Dutch-Irish stage and decorative painter van der Hagen, then the Chearnley brothers' teacher, expressed these tensions and complexities in a haunting set of temporary painted decorations for a ball given by the Lord Lieutenant of Ireland, Lionel Sackville, first Duke of Dorset. As briefly noted above, the architectural and emotional language of these architectural panels was clearly a most powerful influence on Chearnley's imagined visual world.[36] They are also a remarkable imagined baroque city in their own right, however.

This temporary world created in Dublin Castle was an evocation of an imaginary city, with grand façades, arches and domes seen between great curving pedestals, all crowned by busts. The sculptural elements in the compositions are omnipresent, powerful, and disquieting: Paca has noted the expressions of madness and melancholia in the faces of the feigned sculptures, a world of temporary grandeurs shot through with distraction and despair, splendours framed by suffering and disquiet. It is an imagined space of great power projected into a real space at the centre of political power, a further 'imagined baroque city' as complex as those of the Chearnley circle and the Earl of Mar.

Notes

1 National Records of Scotland (hereafter NRS), RHP 13256–13258. I am grateful to John Bruce of the NRS for much kind and patient help with this chapter. After I had first published a version of this chapter, Margaret Stewart published a revised and expanded version of her earlier dissertation as *The Architectural, Landscape and Constitutional Plans of the Earl of Mar 1700–32* (Dublin: Four Courts Press, 2016). Although I am delighted that this work is now widely available, its appearance does not substantially change the ideas advanced in this chapter.

2 This album of drawings has been published in facsimile, with essays by Toby Barnard, Christine Casey and Peter Harbison, and an introduction by the editor: *Samuel Chearnley: Miscelanea Structura Curiosa*, ed. William Laffan (Tralee: Churchill House Press, 2005). An excellent analysis of the album was also published ten years earlier: Barbara Paca, '"Miscelanea Structura Curiosa": The Cross-Currencies of Vitruvius Hibernicus', *Journal of Garden History*, 16.4 (1996), pp. 244–53. This chapter owes a great debt of gratitude to Dr Paca's generous advice and deep knowledge.

3 Jelena Todorović, 'Spectacles in the Shadow: The Festive Greeting to Mojsej Putnik as a Semi-Official Propagation of Orthodox Power in the Habsburg Empire', in Bepler and Davidson (eds), *The Triumphs of the Defeated*, pp. 55–61.

4 For a full exposition, see William Macdonald and John A. Pinto, *Hadrian's Villa and Its Legacy* (New Haven, CT: Yale University Press, 1995).

5 See Chapter 5 above.

6 Robert W. Berger, 'On the Origins of Marly', *Zeitschrift für Kunstgeschichte*, 56.4 (1993), pp. 534–44.

7 Terry Friedman, 'A Palace Worth the Grandeur of a King: Lord Mar's designs for the Old Pretender, 1718–30', *Architectural History*, 29 (1986), pp. 102–33, at p. 106, quoting Historical Manuscripts Commission, *Calendar of Stuart Papers Belonging to His Majesty the King* (London: HMSO, 1910), IV, p. 123.

8 Christine Casey has traced their sources, from Gibbs to Marot, and William Laffan has remarked on the idiosyncratic Irishness of their use of them, in *Samuel Chearnley*, pp. 35–45, at pp. 9–34.

9 James Gibbs, *A Book of Architecture* (London: no publisher, 1728). Mar also corresponded with Gibbs in 1716/17; see Friedman, 'A Palace Worth the Grandeur', p. 103.

10 I am deeply indebted to Dr Barbara Paca for her generosity in sharing this idea and for her kind permission to study van der Hagen's surviving panels, now in her collection in New York.

11 Margaret Cook Hay Stewart, 'Lord Mar's Plans, 1700–32' (M.Litt. dissertation, University of Glasgow, 1988). This excellent dissertation suggests that this design, the final working out of Mar's favourite plan, was conceived as a complete rebuilding of Alloa rather than a final version of the London palace, and that its iconography would be more resonant on this particular Scottish site.

12 *Stuart Papers*, 5.367, quoted in Christoph V. Ehrenstein, 'Erskine, John, styled twenty-second or sixth earl of Mar and Jacobite duke of Mar (bap. 1675, d. 1732)', *Oxford Dictionary of National Biography* (2015), https://doi-org.ezproxy-prd.bodleian.ox.ac.uk/10.1093/ref:odnb/8868 (retrieved online 8 April 2023).

13 Stuart Erskine (ed.), 'The Earl of Mar's Legacie to Scotland and to his son, Lord Erskine', *Publications of the Scottish History Society*, 26 (1896), pp. 141–243. The drawings, which can be interpreted as a square villa with four elevations of different orders, are NAS, RHP 13256/21 and /23–25. The designs for remodelling and extending the existing tower-house are in NAS, RHP 13258/12–14.

14 For Kinross House, see John Gifford, *The Buildings of Scotland: Perth and Kinross* (New Haven, CT: Yale University Press, 2007), pp. 483–94.

15 NRS RHP 13256/22, 83, 86, discussed at length in Friedman, 'A Palace Worth the Grandeur', pp. 104–5.

16 The development of these plans is discussed in detail in Friedman, 'A Palace Worth the Grandeur', pp. 105–8; for the tower, see NRS, RHP 13256/8; for the dome, see NFS, RHP 13256/9. See also William Adam's posthumously published version of Mar's design in *Vitruvius Scoticus* (Edinburgh: A & C Black, 1812), pl. 110. William Adam's own Duff House, Banff, with its extraordinary verticality and corner towers, perhaps comes closest to Mar's fantasy architecture of any building actually carried out.

17 All information in this and the following paragraph comes from Mar's own 'Description of the Designe for a New Royall Palace for the King of Great Britain at London 1726' (Westminster City Libraries, MS 728.82), transcribed in Friedman, 'A Palace Worth the Grandeur', pp. 110–17.

18 '*Sic domus veterum coluit monumenta parentum*' ['Thus he has preserved an old house as the monument of his forebears'].

19 Written on the 1721 plan for the King's House, NRS, RHP 13256/2, quoted by Friedman, 'A Palace Worth the Grandeur', p. 107. Friedman accepts this as a variant of a London plan, but Stewart argues for its particularly Scottish iconography.

20 NRS, RHP 13256/21; the supporters of the Erskine arms are two griffins gules, winged, beaked and armed. This would seem to reinforce that this was primarily envisaged as a design for Alloa.

21 NRS, RHP 13256/23.
22 NRS, RHP 13256/24.
23 NRS, RHP 13256/25.
24 The original drawing is NRS, RHP 13256/23.
25 NRS, RHP 13258/38.
26 The flaming heart is a shorthand for ecstatic religious devotion for many baroque writers – see Mario Praz, 'The Flaming Heart: Richard Crashaw and the Baroque', in *The Flaming Heart: Essays on Crashaw, Machiavelli, and Other Studies in the Relations between Italian and English Literature from Chaucer to T. S. Eliot* (New York: Doubleday, 1958), pp. 204–63 – and was easily transferable to political enthusiasm. The drawing for the Erskine monument is NRS RHP 13258/39. Its design and its ideas seem to relate strongly to an ephemeral obelisk that was erected at the Scots College in Paris in celebration of the birth of Prince James Francis Edward Stuart, and published in a brief pamphlet as Duc de Rothsay, 'Relation du feu d'artifice et des illuminations qui ont eté faites au College des Escosois de Paris le 8 Juillet 1688, jour de S. Marguérite, reine et patronne d'Ecosse' (Paris, 1688). 'Feu d'artifice tiré le 8 juillet 1688 au Collége des Ecossais de Paris à l'occasion de la naissance du Prince de Galles, fils de Jacques II [estampe]', https://gallica.bnf.fr/ark:/12148/btv1b84066267.item (retrieved 4 July 2023).
27 *Samuel Chearnley*, p. 16.
28 The red-coated Irish Brigade in Louis XV's service, Jacobite at least in origin, had famously put the British Guards to flight at the Battle of Fontenoy on 11 May 1745; and, worse, it was the allied loser of that very battle, Prince William Augustus, Duke of Cumberland, who was now tasked with leading the resistance to the Jacobites on the British mainland.
29 *Samuel Chearnley*, p. 49.
30 Casey, in *Samuel Chearnley*, pp. 35–45.
31 Paca, '"Miscelanea Structura Curiosa"', p. 246.
32 *Ibid.*, p. 249, which also points out, at p. 247, the Hellfire Club associations of Chearnley's *Amphitheatre in Ruin* with the figure of a monk (who has a ridiculous grin plastered across his face) on a pedestal in the middle of a decaying pagan structure. This may have been part of a sardonic dialogue with the Temples of the British Worthies and of Modern Virtue at Stowe, exhibiting a mutual agility in political and social satire. I would also venture that, in an anti-Jacobite context, the ruined amphitheatre surmounted by grotesque heads might well be a negative reference to Roman antiquity, Roman institutions, and Roman superstition.
33 This is the conjecture of the editors of the facsimile. Paca reminds us that Chearnley died in 1747, and that the circumstances of his death are unexplained: Paca, '"Miscelanea Structura Curiosa"', p. 244.
34 The statue was removed in 1915 after protests from Scottish soldiers stationed nearby.

35 An excellent indication of the scope of this achievement can be found in James Howley, *The Follies and Garden Buildings of Ireland* (New Haven, CT: Yale University Press, 1993).

36 Chearnley, *Miscelanea Structura Curiosa*, pl. 64. The 'Elevation of a House in the Theatrical Style' is also extremely close to the manner of van der Hagen's imaginary buildings.

17

Artificial islands: i.m. Peter Scupham

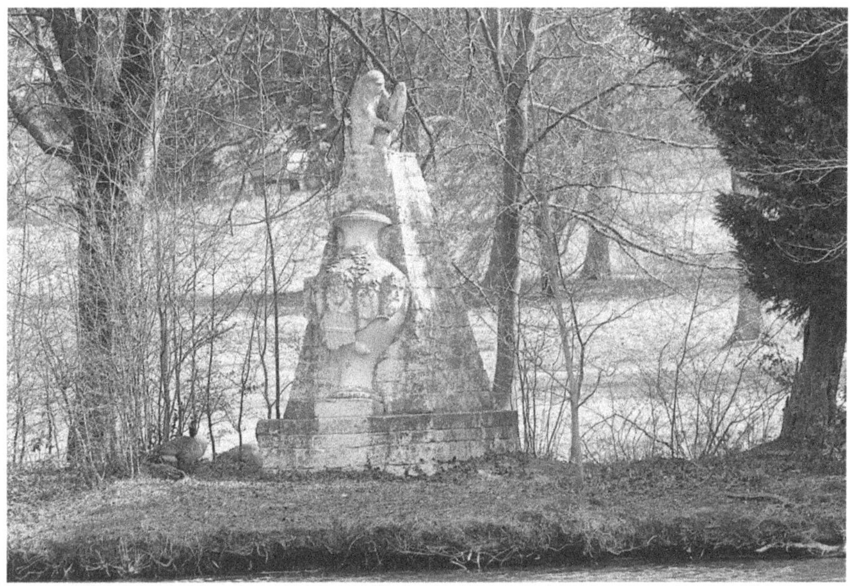

Figure 17.1 William Kent, monument to William Congreve, *c.* 1737, in the grounds at Stowe, Buckinghamshire.

I first saw the Congreve monument, on its island in the lake at Stowe, on an autumn morning 45 years ago. I was with my friend Alan Powers, and we were looking at this eighteenth-century designed landscape in the way that we saw everything then: through the lens of the painters of the middle of the twentieth century. We moved through the glades, rides, and prospects of Stowe as though we were moving through a lithograph by John Piper, or a grisaille drawing by Rex Whistler. It was all around us: urns in weeping groves, a wash of umber on the October trees, columns and arches on the skyline. When the Palladian bridge came into view at the bottom of the shelving valley, I thought, quite simply, that I had never seen anything more beautiful (see Figure 17.1).

This was in the days before the National Trust came to Stowe: a visit to what were then simply the grounds of a working school had to be booked in advance and for a precise time. Alan had parked his little car on the gravel, the ends of the great colonnade disappearing into the mist from which loomed an equestrian statue on a high plinth. There was a brass bell pull; a brusque but not unfriendly bursar sold us two copies of Laurence Whistler's pamphlet guide book, escorted us through one or two stupendous public rooms, and then turned us loose to explore the gardens for ourselves. I do not think that there was any sort of admission fee.

I remember the grounds, at that point, as gently run down; the townscape even of the later 1970s still contained occasional bombsites, so dilapidation was less noticeable then than now. The lower branches of the great trees swept the lawns, the undergrowth was tall and rusty with autumn, there were reeds and silt at the margins of the lakes. There was a little broken stonework scattered in the long grass. We saw nobody for two hours or so, although lights burned in classrooms in the great house and we could hear music from the Queen's Temple. There were goalposts and white lines on the deserted playing fields of the great lawn.

We walked slowly over acres of damp grass, up as far as the Gothic Temple, down as far as the Boycott Pavilions, making our way eventually to the grassy slopes around the Temple of Ancient Virtue. We crossed the narrow water called the Styx ('If we have crossed the Styx, then where are we now?') and made our way past the British Worthies and down through the Fields of Elysium to the shores of the lake. Mist moved on the surface of the great water in the bottom of the valley.

We almost missed the Congreve monument on its island: it is not large and, then, it was almost hidden by overgrown shrubbery. It is a truncated stone pyramid, with a slightly awkward half-urn carved with theatrical masks applied to one of its sloping sides.[1] (Some accounts suggest that a figure of Congreve may have leaned on the opposite face of the pyramid, but there seems to be no surviving representation of such a figure.[2] The physical presence of a likeness of the dead would yet further intensify the atmosphere of the little island.) The very awkwardness of the juxtaposition is typical of William Kent's rough, overscaled, expressive English baroque. There was a little, half-visible figure perched on top of the pyramid. Alan read the guidebook description of the comic dramatist being commemorated by the figure of a monkey holding a mirror. We gazed at the island through the cloudy air ('I can't see the mirror; it must be broken now'), and I think that we were both near to tears. Two undergraduates in tweed coats standing on an autumn morning on the shore of an artificial lake, moved by a complex of emotions only some of which were clear to us. Most obvious was simple awareness of the onward movement of time in the contemplation of this broken memorial to past fashion and dead wit, but, behind that, we were both moved by the very fact of its being the memorial of a minor master, one who achieved a fugitive perfection in a lesser art. I remember that, from Stowe to Oxford, we spoke mostly of Laurence Whistler's brother, the artist killed in the Second World War.

William Congreve was one of the bitter masters whose mature work came early: he wrote nothing for the stage after he was 30, his dramatic career having ended in 1700.[3] His extraordinary awareness of time wasted in a life, and of the undignified power which time has over an individual, was all precocious. Congreve's plays are suave comedies of manners, but they have a powerful undertow of disquiet: comedy shot through with expressions of regret, hints of violence, sudden impassioned longings for escape to anywhere but elegant London – even 'to the other world'. In his later comedies the stakes are extraordinarily high: if the structures of pretence built up by the characters fail, they do not stand to lose only status or reputation; they stand to lose selfhood, subsistence, even life itself.

The owner of Stowe himself chose the lines carved on his friend's monument. Lord Cobham's inscriptions are sophisticated, wise, and alien to us: the first acts as a motto to the representation of the monkey and mirror:

Vitae imitatio Consuetudinis speculum Comoedia

[Comedy is the imitation of life and the mirror of fashion].

The second is an inscription about their friendship, and about the inability of any monument or inscription to serve as an adequate memorial of such 'elegance, polished manners, wit, and piercing intelligence' as Congreve's ('*ingenio acri, faceto, expolito, moribusque urbanis*'). These are all qualities which die with the individual, or, more accurately, die a piecemeal death in recollection as that person's friends die one by one. Cobham's memorial on its island (the island, originally a peninsula, was the stroke of genius) has a clear-eyed awareness of the individual circumscribed by mortality and time, contemplated with no vestige of sentimentality.

In all its immensity and complexity, the designed landscape at Stowe, with its numerous monuments and buildings, is remarkably coherent. Feeling and intellect alike are directed to the contemplation of the passage of time and the commemoration of the dead. The whole landscape and all it contains constitute an eloquent consideration of the attrition of time, the passing of the greatness of the ancients; a sense of modern *translatio imperii* balanced by an awareness of the tightrope walked by the great ones of Georgian Britain (successfully for the moment) between Puritan revolution, on the one hand, and Jacobite invasion, on the other. The only respite in such a place is in the Temple of Friendship or in the Fane of Pastoral Poetry, just as friendship and literature offers the only respites in the magnate's life.

The landscape garden was certainly the only art form that Britain exported to the rest of the world, one which was, in its day, universally admired and esteemed.[4] Indeed, the 'English garden' is so widely imitated (the Congreve island – or peninsula – was imitated too) that it takes more than a moment to realise that, at the very meridian of their triumphs, the great ones of Britain invented an art form that reflected on time, mutability, and the possibility of defeat. The changes of season alone shadow these artificial paradises: frost or fog, rain and fallen leaves, are emblems enough of the presence of death in these Arcadias. The moment of Victory is given over to the contemplation of deep time and the limits of the human.

In the light of all this, it seems the more urgent to return to the question of why this monument doubles its poetic and emotional power by being on an island, originally on a peninsula or quasi-island, but still surrounded by water on three sides, and seen across an expanse of water. The monument itself already carries multiple significations, even apart from the inscriptions: the pyramid for lasting fame, the urn for mortality, the monkey for the acute, difficult imitation of 'things exactly as they are'. All of this would be infinitely lessened in significance if it had been placed merely at the end of a grass walk, or in a clearing among trees, however beautiful. This monument to the lost master of the present moment depends on its surrounding water, on the sense that another element intervenes to keep us at a distance from the grass in front of the pyramid, to keep us from reading the inscriptions. That is, unless, originally, we went round by the narrow land passage to the island, which seems to have been cut off and the monument isolated in the nineteenth century. It also creates a whole field of fruitful speculation, viewed from a distance, about what the sculpture at the apex may signify. Most of all, it gives the monument a removedness, it makes of the little lake island a modest otherworld, a place consecrated to secret contemplation, a place where time and the air move differently from on the bank. And reflection of the monument in the water of the lake potentially multiplies (and dissolves) these mourning otherworlds.

Yet, for a Whig magnate, such a place can be anything but a locus of prayer for the dead; his religion forbids it. Things are perhaps otherwise with the monument to his mother in Pope's garden, the rented, contingent garden of a Catholic constrained by the penal laws. At Stowe the Congreve island can be only a place of remembering and regret. The water, the narrow spit of land originally joining it to the shore, ensures that it is not even easy of access. This use of water is reminiscent of Antoine Watteau, of the water in his *Départ du Cythère* which seems in the painting's two versions to be a medium flowing between the ideal and the real, the world of illusions and lonely reality.

This use of water is shared with another, minute, designed landscape – nothing more than two intensely maintained river islands at Great Amwell in Hertfordshire: the willow-shaded appearance of the islands as they are is now is Regency, but the monuments on the islands (an urn and a long inscription) in fact commemorate the New River which was completed in the early seventeenth century, by the projector Sir Hugh Mydleton, to carry fresh water to London.[5] These New River monuments are different – their patron is a corporation; they commemorate and moralise a feat of engineering – but they do confirm the idea that artificial islands are of their nature uncanny, too intensely discontinuous with the world of the *terra firma* to be anything other than disquieting. On these little islands at Great Amwell the urn and an inscription on the willow-shaded lawns of two very small islands are barely separated from the bank, and with a clearly visible bridge. But the designed island works even on this tiny scale. Standing on the bank, looking at the green shadow and the two pale stones under the willows, there is a feeling of recession in time. There is also the feeling of removedness: the irrational sense that the air on the little islands might be different in its quality from the air on the riverbank, that it may not be of the same century as the air of the towpath. The appearance of a figure on the islands, even though they would be only feet away, might prove disquieting, as if they were removed from the ordinary world and the present time onto the stage of a theatre located elsewhere and in the past.

Water can become the image of distance and death. At Schloss Tiefurt, which was laid out for the widowed Duchess of Weimar, Anna Amalia (1739–1807), the river Ilm runs swift and shallow in a loop which encloses the park. Some distance from the Schloss, three curved steps lead down to the shaded water. A wooded slope rises on the other bank, and a pale stone monument, like a classical altar in form, is visible on the far side. It commemorates the duchess's son Prince Ferdinand Constantin, who died in 1793, estranged from his family, and from the brilliant court of Weimar. Its brief German text could hardly be simpler: 'Amalie, mourning for her second and last son Constantin, who died young.' The white monument amidst the shadowy leaves, so far from the house, is an image of distance already, but no bridge is visible from this part of the park, so it is removed yet further by the swift flow of the river over its pebbled bed. The steps to the water make the distance yet greater. Perhaps they were never intended to do any more than lead to a viewpoint from which the monument can be seen, but steps to water imply a boat – a boat across to the monument to the unreconciled son. But the river is far too shallow for any boat so the lost son recedes further, across impassible water, across the Styx.

The presence of water in the park of Tiefurt complicates and deepens everything. Anna Amalia was one of the most cultivated patrons of her day, herself a musician and composer of considerable achievement. Goethe was a frequent guest here, the confidant, the maker of parks and gardens along the little river Ilm. Nothing here is the product of chance; the only random element in the scene is the row of stones which someone (children? visitors?) has laid in the river, like a little causeway leading across to Prince Constantin's monument. It will carry nobody across, and the next autumn's storms will roll it away.

Nowhere in a landscape garden such as Stowe is a simple space either: every designed landscape is full of emotional and intellectual tripwires. A place intensely allusive to other places is also a representation of places which do not exist in the geography of the real – places which embody memories, ideas, moods, and aspirations. Movement through the designed landscape is therefore, inevitably, a movement within an evolving landscape of thought and memory.[6]

Unless we assume that the peninsular site at Stowe reserved the monument for Lord Cobham's contemplation alone, we must assume that there were occasions when a group of his friends made their way to the island and that small parties took place in the shadow of the monument. But what mood does the island or peninsula impose on such festivities? Inevitably, in the mid-eighteenth century, these must have been festivals shadowed by recollections of friendship. They must have at some point been led by the monument to conversations about those things which very mature people who retain no illusions can bear as pastime when they are already overwhelmingly aware of the passage of time. Did Congreve's comedies perhaps fill the place for that generation which Mozart's operas would later occupy for those of later generations equally clear-sighted about time and its passing, but too stoical to renounce all earthly pleasure?

When Lord Cobham himself died, the meaning of the monument changed: it became a memorial for a circle of survivors. When the last person who could remember Congreve was dead, the island changed its meaning again, becoming a memorial, already a little distanced, to a generation of friends. When that generation started to fade from memory, the island and monument become, first, a monument to the follies and diversions of the past and, finally, a kind of secular *memento mori* for those with the inclination to read it as such.

The philosopher Jean-Jacques Rousseau visited Stowe in the 1750s, and, indeed, his own recollection of the Congreve monument may have played a part in the decision to bury him on an artificial island – L'Île des Peupliers – in the landscape garden at Ermenonville, on which estate he was staying as a guest when he died in 1778.[7] He was buried by night (torches reflected in the water with the summer night still bright above) on the island on 4 July

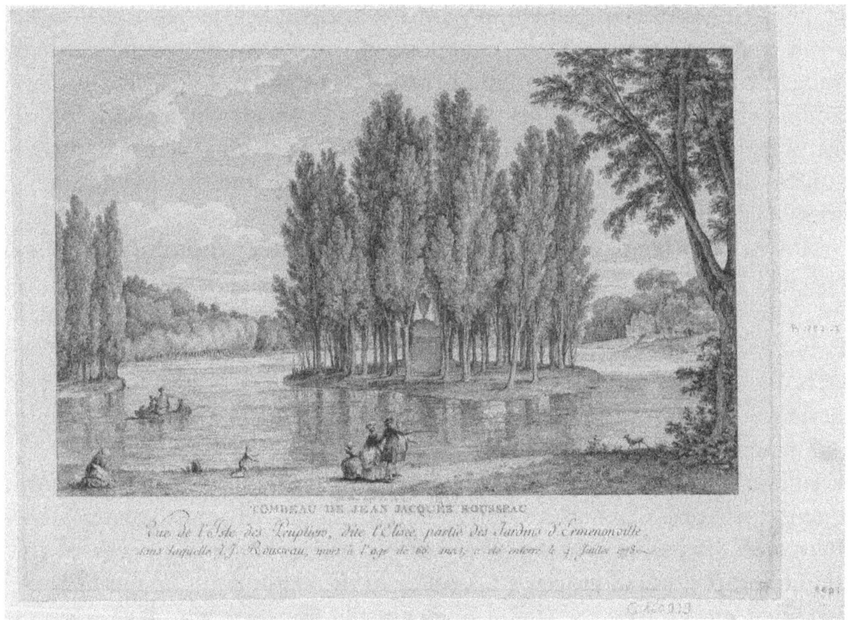

Figure 17.2 Jean-Michel Moreau the younger, *Tombeau de Jean Jacques Rousseau Vue de l'Isle des Peupliers, dite l'Elisée* [*sic*], *partie des Jardins d'Ermenonville, dans laquelle J. J. Rousseau, mort à l'age de 66 ans, a été enterré le 4. Juillet 1778*, 1778, etching and engraving.

that year. Later his body was removed to the Pantheon, one self-reflexive theatrical gesture following another (see Figure 17.2).[8]

Both these island monuments are about the anticipated death of the patron as the goal and completion of the years of reflection initiated by the death of the patron's distinguished friend, to whom the island sepulchre is dedicated. Perhaps, paradoxically, it is rather easier to accept the commemoration of Congreve than of Rousseau in these circumstances.

The Poplar Island at the 'Garden-Kingdom' of Wörlitz (laid out for Duke Leopold III of Anhalt-Dessau in the early 1770s) is simply an imitation of Ermenonville, its tomb a cenotaph.[9] It is a picture beautifully composed, but the most haunting thing about it is its remote position at one corner of the great park, secluded, cut off from the central water, the palace, the little *Residenzstadt*. This Rousseau cenotaph is, on the one hand, highly decorative; on the other, a piece of safe liberal allusion, as well as a most haunting ornament of a distant region of the great liberal garden.

Ian Hamilton Finlay's twentieth-century landscape garden in the Pentland Hills, Little Sparta, is, in part, a reflection on garden history, on classicism and neoclassicism.[10] It is almost inevitable that it should incorporate echoes of Stowe and citations of Ermenonville.[11] Finlay pays his tribute to both in a sheltered hillside area with the still water of a little lake under trees. This area is guarded by an inscribed obelisk, a homage to Claude Lorrain's inspiration of the eighteenth century designed landscape. Claude's most admired effect, in his landscape painting, is one of otherworldly repose, an effect which is known to historians of aesthetics as *il riposo di Claudio*. This phrase itself is the inscription on the obelisk.

Inevitably, this area too has a minute island-peninsula with what at first appears to be another Rousseau cenotaph (which would be wholly in accord with the French neoclassicism of the garden), but the inscription on the table tomb commemorates, rather, the career of a wooden boat (another of Finlay's obsessions): a drifter with the lovely name *Silver Cloud*. So, the minute island becomes a ship, the *Silver Cloud*, and yet, as a visual citation, it inevitably brings Rousseau to mind. As a ship, it returns the memory to the Tiber Island, the river island which the Romans partly clad with a marble prow, one of the first designed elements in any natural landscape. Like all Finlay's allusive constructions, it is adroit and thoughtful – but perhaps almost too much is going on in too small a compass, and all the allusions are pulling in different directions. We cannot quite take it in, as we can take in the complex simplicity of Lord Cobham's statement that his friend is dead, and that – for all his own grandeur, which can flood valleys and raise islands in the waters – he will die too; and that he accepts completely that this is so.

All these artificial islands in designed landscapes lead, in recollection, to the two versions of Watteau's painting variously titled *The Pilgrimage to Cytherea* and *The Embarkation for Cytherea*. This shows a group of men and women, in slightly anachronistic fancy dress as if for a ducal masquerade, leaving an autumnal glade where they have garlanded a statue of Venus and moving towards a waiting gilded barge. One woman pauses on the turn of the path to look back with a regard of comprehensive and mature renunciation. The other shores of the waters, on which the golden boat is waiting, are ambiguous in both the two versions of the composition.[12]

This painting shares precisely with the Congreve island at Stowe a sense of sophisticated regret and awareness of the passing of human pleasure. Michael Baxendall once stated memorably that 'it is not necessary to be a fluffy painter to be a rococo painter'.[13] For all the feathery handling of trees and distances, Watteau's painting is not escapist but unflinchingly realist, the same way that the Congreve monument is unflinchingly realistic about human life and human expectations. The meanings of Watteau's painting are, of course, disputed, but it seems clear (whether or not the moment depicted is a stage on a lover's pilgrimage, or a moment of sombre realisation and departure) that the progress of the figures carries an unequivocal significance. Reading from right to left, they enact a process of turning away from escapism and distraction and heading towards the golden barge, which sails (in the Berlin version) into thick mist on the surface of the lake, or (in the Paris version) into a cold mountain landscape where the waterways fade among the snowy slopes.

The question remains why this effect of intense sadness should attach so much to artificial islands when, for example, the summerhouses and pavilions on the natural islands and outcrops of the Stockholm archipelago, retain, even on an overcast day, an atmosphere of innocent festivity, of temperate leisure.

Or perhaps these artificial islands appear so sad only to the eyes of my own generation, eyes still schooled by the British painters of the 1920s and 1930s, for whom the great designed landscapes in Britain, then mostly seen in a state of romantic dilapidation, were an intense focus of sophisticated regret, a constant metaphor for their own world of 'the between time' and all that menaced it. That is, I think, how Alan Powers and I saw it on that October morning in the 1970s: Stowe seen through the lens of Stowe as depicted by John Piper and Rex Whistler (a juxtaposition which seemed far less of a disjunction half a century ago than perhaps it does now). In the art books owned by my parents, Whistler was more simply canonical – a fine artist and a good soldier – than he was later, in a climate of retrospective visual fundamentalism. It is worth remembering that, to visually aware people who had lived through the last years between the wars, those years had embraced a *plurality* of artistic styles. It was only later that these were divided, in art-historical retrospect, into modernist high art, on the one hand, and 'kitsch and pastiche', on the other. When I went to England for the first time to university (having lived exclusively in Scotland and on the Continent until then) I anticipated an England as Whistler had drawn England, and, on that autumn day at Stowe, that England was suddenly about me, and I was moving through the mossy rides and umbered trees of his drawings, and all the columns, mists, and obelisks seemed to be mourning for those artists lost in the war.

Now that the National Trust has cleared the island at Stowe, and repaired the monument, its details can be seen at last. Once more the monkey holds the mirror up to humanity, and we can see at last that the knop at the top of the mirror frame is a human mask, its face sombre with sadness and regret. The regret is twice removed: it is a carving of a carving, distanced by time and the waters of the lake. So mannered, so appalling the regret. So stoical, so fully adult the acceptance of one's own death, and of the deaths of friends. It epitomises the aching sadness of a sophisticated place of memory that has outlived its day, an emblem whose meanings are in the process of being forgotten (my own generation is the last in Britain that will speak even a pidgin version of Lord Cobham's symbolic language).

It is a thing that is ravishing, permanent, transitory, and (unvisited, now, across the misty water) immeasurably powerful, infinitely sorrowful.

Notes

1 N. Pevsner, E. Williamson & G. K. Brandwood, *Buckinghamshire* (New Haven, CT: Yale University Press, 2003), p. 682.

2 See https://heritageportal.buckinghamshire.gov.uk/Monument/MBC11245 (retrieved 15 August 2023). This source also suggests that the island was remade in the nineteenth century.

3 C. Ferdinand and D. McKenzie, 'Congreve, William (1670–1729), Playwright and Poet', *Oxford Dictionary of National Biography* (retrieved online 8 May 2023).

4 David Watkin, *The English Vision: The Picturesque in Architecture, Landscape and Garden Design* (London: John Murray, 1982), pp. 161–80.

5 Nikolaus Pevsner, *Hertfordshire* (London: Penguin, 1953), pp. 98–9.

6 This might cease to be true of Lancelot Browne's most formulaic works, drained, as they are, of meaning, emotion, and autobiography and attempting only to produce an undemanding aesthetic satisfaction.

7 Watkin, *The English Vision*, pp. 162–3. See, further, Peter Willis, *Rousseau, Stowe and le Jardin anglais: Speculations on Visual Sources for Le Nouvelle Héloise* (Banbury: for the Voltaire Foundation, 1972).

8 Thomas Weiss, *Infinitely Beautiful: The Dessau-Wōrlitz Garden Realm* (London: Frances Lincoln, 2007).

9 The Duke of Anhalt-Dessau also had the strangest island paradise in any landscape garden of Europe. The *Stein* was an Italian Grand Tour compressed into one rocky island, with a clifftop villa and an artificial volcano. The volcano was operated by means of hidden fireplaces to produce smoke, and a cistern for the manufacture of steam at its summit. These could be augmented with fireworks to simulate an eruption on special occasions. Weiss, *Infinitely Beautiful*, pp. 149–52.

10 Jessie Sheeler and Andrew Lawson. *Little Sparta: The Garden of Ian Hamilton Finlay* (London: Frances Lincoln, 2003).

11 Michel Baridon, 'Nature and the Politics of Hope: Ermenonville and Little Sparta', *Word & Image*, 21.4 (2005), pp. 288–93.

12 1717 version in Paris, 1721 in Berlin.

13 M. Baxandall, *Shadows and Enlightenment* (New Haven, CT: Yale University Press. 1995), p. 34.

Afterword

It is a chastening exercise to look back on a book such as this, which embodies, as poetry collections would style it, *new and selected works*. The genesis of this book was a series of conversations which took place after I moved to Oxford in 2015, which convinced me that much of what I had published on the Continent had passed the anglophone reader by entirely, and also convinced me that there was a call for a book about the shadows and exiles of the early modern world, as well as a set of further reflections on that baroque world's mysterious reticulations and connections.

What has resulted is, almost by accident, nearly the book about early modern Scotland, and the Scots cultural diaspora, which I never thought I could write, as perhaps a majority of chapters are about Scottish internationalism, Scottish travellers, Scottish exiles, and – in one case – a very successful Scottish hitman. I am aware that somewhere behind the chapter on 'Paper gardens' there is a lost project to trace the profound cultural connections of Scotland and the Netherlands in the seventeenth and eighteenth centuries – a vital enterprise which I resign to others. I am aware also that behind the chapter on 'Gentileschi and the ancestors' lies another lost project to anatomise the court cultures of Charles I and Henrietta Maria; if nothing else, the chapter here emphasises that Charles I was a Scot by formation, and cultural heir of such Scottish cosmopolitans as the first Earl of Dunfermline.

This book draws together thoughts from two decades, many of which are inevitably thoughts about exiles and the defeated, about the penumbra of near-invisible merchants and intermediaries (so many of them Roman Catholics of British origin) who brought ideas, tastes, wines, and objects (never forgetting that staple of Grand Tour cargoes, the Parmesan cheese) to fortress Britain. For decades I have been haunted by Auden's lines, which have become almost a private academic motto: *the vanquished powers were glad/ to be invisible and free*. The history of the cosmopolitan Scots is a different story again. But there are further reticulations, patterns of connection to be traced, in the Habsburg territories worldwide and in the global networks of the Society of Jesus, which form much of the subject of this book. The 'Prologue', a toccata rather than a conventional introduction, attempts to give some impressionistic account of this endless, self-renewing web of connections and hybridities.

It is my hope that this sequence of histories of exceptions and 'shadow communities' serves to cast light on the majorities and the mainstreams. And there are a few chapters simply on major continental artefacts or phenomena which seem to me internationally important tokens or examples of their times: *The Dream of Raphael*, Jesuit gardens. In short, I hope I have to some degree complied with the delightfully phrased challenge which Seamus Perry issued soon after my arrival in Oxford: 'Peter, you know so many strange and wonderful things, and all too soon you will die; *write them down*.'

Earlier versions of some of these essays have appeared in *British Catholic History*, *Studies in the Literary Imagination*, Glasgow Emblem studies, *Wolfenbütteler Forschungen*, the Wolfenbütteler 'Arbeiten zur Barockforschung' series, *V&A Magazine*, Gabriele Cingolani and Marco Riccini (eds), *Sogno e racconto: archetipi e funzioni* (Florence, 2003), O'Malley, Bailey, Harris and Kennedy (eds), *The Jesuits: Cultures, Sciences, and the Arts, 1540–1773* (Toronto, 2006), *Recusant History*, and Paul Scott (ed.), *Collaboration and Interdisciplinarity in the Republic of Letters: Essays in Honour of Richard G. Maber* (Manchester: Manchester University Press, 2010).

Select bibliography

Manuscripts

Vatican City: Archivio Segreto Vaticano, Con. Riti. 5087–88
Biblioteca Apostolica Vaticana, MS Vat. Lat. 9385
Rome: Venerable English College, MS Farnese Funeral Book; MS Liber 1422
Archivium Romanum Societatis Jesu (ARSI): MSS Anglia 10, 11, 24a, 41, 42
Madrid: Biblioteca Nacional de España, MS 6001; MS 2492
London: British Jesuit Archives: MS Anglia V
The National Archives: Will of James Gibbs, probate 16 August 1754, PROB 11/810/277
British Library: MS Cotton Caligula D. I
Lambeth Palace Library: MS 655
Stonyhurst College, Lancashire: MS A V 40; MS Anglia V 27; MS A VI 84
Edinburgh: National Records of Scotland: GD 18; RHP 13256–13258; GD 45/26/48
National Library of Scotland: MS Inv Dep 184B; MS 10339; MS ACC 9769/4/1/97; Hawthornden MS 2064
Edinburgh University Library: MS Laing iii, 513
Glasgow: Glasgow University Library, MS Hunter 414
Aberdeen: Aberdeen University Library, MS 2538; MS 630; BCL A648; SCA, PL/8/24

Printed works

Abad, Diego José, SJ, *De deo deoque homine* (Casena: apud haeredes Blasinios, 1693)

Anon, *The entertainment of the high and mighty monarch Charles King of Great Britaine, France, and Ireland, into his auncient and royall city of Edinburgh, the fifteenth of Iune, 1633* (Edinburgh: John Wreittoun, 1633)

Aubrey, John, *Brief Lives*, ed. Kate Bennett, 2 vols (Oxford: Oxford University Press, 2015)

Bailey, Gauvin Alexander, *Art on the Jesuit Missions in Asia and Latin America, 1542–1773* (Toronto: University of Toronto Press, 1999)

Bailey, Gauvin Alexander, *Between Renaissance and Baroque: Jesuit Art in Rome 1565–1610* (Toronto: Toronto University Press, 2003)

Bath, Michael, *Renaissance Decorative Painting in Scotland* (Edinburgh: National Museums of Scotland Publishing, 2003)

Bath, Michael, 'Embroidered Emblems: Mary Stuart's Bed of State', *Emblematica*, 15 (2007), pp. 5–32

Bath, Michael, *Emblems for a Queen: The Needlework of Mary Queen of Scots* (London: Archetype Publications, 2008)

Boece, Hector, *Gentis Scotorum Historia* (Paris: Jodocus Badius, 1526)

Boorsch, Suzanne, Michal Lewis, and R. E. Lewis, *The Engravings of Giorgio Ghisi* (New York: Metropolitan Museum of Art, 1985)

Bray, Xavier, *The Sacred Made Real* (London: Yale University Press for the National Gallery, 2009)

Broun, Dauvit, *The Irish Identity of the Kingdom of the Scots* (Ipswich: Boydell Press, 1999)

Brown, Marilyn, *Scotland's Lost Gardens* (Edinburgh: RCHMS, 2012)

Brückmann, Patricia, 'Virgins Visited by Angel Powers: *The Rape of the Lock*, Platonic Love, Sylphs and Some Mystics', in G. S. Rousseau and Pat Rogers (eds), *The Enduring Legacy: Alexander Pope Tercentenary Essays* (Cambridge: Cambridge University Press, 1988), pp. 3–20

Bonifaccio, Giovanni, *L'arte de' cenni: con la quale formandosi fauella visibile, si tratta della muta eloquenza, che non e' altro che vn facondo silentio: diuisa in due parti* (Vicenza: Francesco Grossi, 1616)

Bor, D. Z., *František Antonín hrabě Špork: významný mecenáš barokní kultury v Čechách* (Prague: Trigon, 1999)

Byres, James, *Hypogæi, or Sepulchral Caverns of Tarquinia, the Antient Capital of Etruria*, ed. Frank Howard (London: P. & D. Colnaghi, T. Cadell, 1842)

Circignano, Niccolò, *Ecclesiae Anglicanae Trophaea ... Passiones, Romae in Collegio Anglico per N. Circinianum Depictae* (Rome: Bartolomeo Grassi, 1584)

Coffin, David, *The English Garden: Meditation and Memorial* (Princeton, NJ: Princeton University Press, 1994)

Corthell, Ronald, Frances E. Dolan, Christopher Highley, and Arthur F. Marotti (eds), *Catholic Culture in Early Modern England* (Notre Dame, IN: University of Notre Dame Press, 2007)

Dillon, Anne, *The Construction of Martyrdom in the English Catholic Community 1535–1603* (Aldershot: Ashgate, 2002)

Eclesal, Thomas, *Relacion de un Sacerdote Ingles, Escrita a Flandres ... en la qual de la cuenta de la venida de su Magestad a Valladolid, y al Collegio de los Ingeses ... Traduiza ... por Tomas Eclesal Cavallero Ingles* (Madrid: Pedro Madrigal, 1592)

Evelyn, John, *The Memoirs of John Evelyn Esq. F.R.S.*, ed. William Bray, 5 vols (London: Henry Colburn, 1827)

Fabri, Ria, and Piet Lombaerde, *The Jesuit Church of Antwerp* (Corpus Rubenianum XXII, 3) (London: Harvey Miller, 2018)

Ferrari, Giovanni Battista, *De Florum Cultura Libri VI* (Rome: Stephanus Paulinus, 1633)

Fleming, John, *Robert Adam and His Circle in Edinburgh and Rome* (London: John Murray, 1962)

Friedman, Terry, 'A Palace Worth the Grandeur of a King: Lord Mar's Designs for the Old Pretender, 1718–30', *Architectural History*, 29 (1986), pp. 102–33

Gabriner, Paul, 'The Papist's House, the Papist's Horse: Alexander Pope and the Removal from Binfield', in C. C. Barfoot and Theo d'Haen (eds), *Centennial Hauntings: Pope, Byron and Eliot in the Year 88* (Amsterdam: Rodopi, 1990), pp. 13–63

Garcilán, Alonso Ramos, *Historia del Celebre Sanctuario de Nuestra Senora de Copacapana* (Lima: Geronymo de Contreras, 1621)
Gayton, Edmund, *Epulae Oxonienses* (Oxford: no publisher, 1636)
Grimaldi, Floriano, *La Historia della Chiesa di Santa Maria di Loreto* (Loreto: Cassa di Risparmio di Loreto, 1993)
Hawkins, Henry, SJ, *Partheneia Sacra, or, The Mysterious and Delicious Garden of the Sacred Parthenes, Set Forth and Enriched with Pious Devices and Emblemes* (Rouen: Jean Coustourier, 1633)
Hugo, Hermann, SJ, *Pia desideria emblematis, elegiis & affectibus SS. Patrvm illustrat* (Antwerp: Boetius a Boelswart, 1624)
Huygens, Constantine, *A Selection of the Poems of Sir Constantijn Huygens (1596–1687)*, ed. Peter Davidson and Adriaan van der Weel (Amsterdam: Amsterdam University Press, 1996)
Kircher, Athanasius, *Oedipus Aegyptaicus*, 3 vols (Rome: Mascardi, 1652–54)
Koudounaris, Paul, *Heavenly Bodies: Cult Treasures and Spectacular Saints from the Catacombs* (London: Thames & Hudson, 2013)
Laffan, William (ed.), *Samuel Chearnley: Miscelanea Structura Curiosa* (Tralee: Churchill House Press, 2005)
Lang, Franciscus, SJ, *Dissertatio di Acione Scenica cum figuris eandam explicantibus* (Munich: Riedin, 1727)
Leslie, Charles Joseph, *Historical Records of the Family of Leslie from 1067 to 1868–9* (Edinburgh: Edmonston & Douglas, 1869)
Leslie, William Aloysius, SJ, *Laurus Leslaeana explicata, sive clarior enumeratio personarum utriusque sexus cognominis Leslie* (Graz: Haeredes Widmanstadii, 1692)
Mack, Maynard, *The Life of Alexander Pope* (New Haven, CT: Yale University Press, 1985)
Mack, Maynard, *The Garden and the City: Retirement and Politics in the Later Poetry of Pope, 1731–1743* (Toronto: University of Toronto Press, 1969)
Major, John, *Historia Majoris Britannae tam Angliae quam Scotiae* (Paris: Judocus Badius, 1521)
McInally, Tom, *The Sixth Scottish University: The Scots Colleges Abroad, 1575–1799* (Leiden: Brill, 2012)
McRoberts, David, 'The Fetternear Banner', *The Innes Review*, 7.2 (1956), pp. 69–88
Marcaida, José Ramón, 'Rubens and the Bird of Paradise: Painting Natural Knowledge in the Early Seventeenth Century', *Renaissance Studies*, 28:1 (2014), pp. 112–27
Martin, John Rupert, *The Decorations for the Pompa Introitus Ferdinandi* (Corpus Rubenianum XVI) (London: Phaidon, 1972)
Paca, Barbara, '"Miscelanea Structura Curiosa": The Cross-Currencies of Vitruvius Hibernicus', *Journal of Garden History*, 16.4 (1996), pp. 244–53
Philip, James, *The Grameid: an heroic poem descriptive of the campaign of Viscount Dundee in 1689 and other pieces*, ed. Alexander Murdoch (Edinburgh: Scottish History Society, 1888)
Piggott, Stuart, *Ruins in a Landscape: Essays in Antiquarianism* (Edinburgh: Edinburgh University Press, 1976)
Porteman, Karel, *Emblematic Exhibitions (Affixiones) at the Brussels Jesuit College (1630–1685): A Study of the Commemorative Manuscripts (Royal Library, Brussels)* (Turnhout: Brepols, 1996)
Rapin, René, *Rapin of Gardens, A Latin Poem, English'd by Mr Gardiner, the Third Edition, Revised and finish'd* (London: Bernard Lintot, 1728)

Reid, John, *The Scots Gard'ner* (Edinburgh: David Lindsay, 1683)
Richeôme, Louis, *La peinture spirituelle* (Lyon: Pierre Rigaud, 1611)
Sánchez, Javier Burrieza, *Una Isla de Inglaterra en Castilla: Exposición* (Palencia: V. Merino, 2000)
Scully, Robert, SJ (ed.), *A Companion to Catholicism and Recusancy in Britain and Ireland* (Leiden: Brill, 2021)
Shell, Alison, *Catholicism, Controversy, and the English Literary Imagination, 1558–1660* (Cambridge: Cambridge University Press, 1999)
Stephens, Thomas, SJ, *Kristapurāna*, ed. and trans. Nelson Falcao SDB (Bangaluru: Kristu Jyoti Publications, 2012)
Stevenson, Jane, Iain Beavan, and Peter Davidson, 'The Breviary of Aberdeen', *Journal of the Edinburgh Bibliographical Society*, 6 (2011), pp. 11–41
Todorović, Jelena, *The Concept of Fluidity in the Baroque Age* (Newcastle upon Tyne: Cambridge Scholars Publishing, 2023)
Vercruysse, Jos E., SJ, 'A Scottish Jesuit from Antwerp: Hippolytus Curle', *The Innes Review*, 61.2 (2010), pp. 137–49
Verstegan, Richard, *Theatrum Crudelitatum Haereticorum Nostri Temporis* (Antwerp: Adrian Hubert, 1587)
Verstegan, Richard, *The Restitution of Decayed Intelligence* (Antwerp: Robert Bruney, 1605)
Visschers, Petrus, *Aenteekening nopens het eergraf van Barbara Moubray en Elizabeth Curle, Staetdamen van de Koningen Maria Stuart in St. Andries kerk te Antwerpen* (Antwerp: Janssens, 1857)
Warnke, Martin, *Rubens, Leben und Werke* (Cologne: DuMont, 2011)
Weston-Lewis, Aidan, 'Orazio Gentileschi's Two Versions of *The Finding of Moses* Reassessed', *Apollo*, 145 (1 June 1997), pp. 27–34
Williams, Michael, *St. Alban's College Valladolid: Four Centuries of English Catholic Presence in Spain* (London: Hurst, 1986)
Williams, Michael, 'Paintings of Early British Kings and Queens at Syon Abbey, Lisbon', *Birgittiana: Rivista Internazionale di Studi Brigidiani*, 1 (1996), pp. 123–34
Wood, Anthony à, *Athenae Oxonienses: An Exact History of All the Writers and Bishops Who Have Had Their Education in the Most Ancient and Famous University of Oxford*, 2 vols (London: Printed for Tho. Bennet, 1691–92)
Worthington, David, *Scots in Habsburg Service* (Leiden: Brill, 2004)

Index

EU authorised representative for GPSR:
Easy Access System Europe, Mustamäe tee 50,
10621 Tallinn, Estonia
gpsr.requests@easproject.com

www.ingramcontent.com/pod-product-compliance
Ingram Content Group UK Ltd.
Pitfield, Milton Keynes, MK11 3LW, UK
UKHW022308141225
466068UK00007B/67

* 9 7 8 1 5 2 6 1 9 5 5 4 8 *